SOCIAL CARE
OF THE ELDERLY

Marjorie H. Cantor is Professor and Brookdale Distinguished Scholar of the Graduate School of Social Service of Fordham University and Scholar in Residence of the Lighthouse International. A past President of the Gerontological Society of America, she is a nationally and internationally recognized leader in the field of aging. As co-founder and Director of Research and Evaluation of the New York City Department for the Aging, she was the principal investigator of the landmark 1970 cross-ethnic study, "The Elderly in the Inner City of New York," as well as nine other large-scale studies during her 30 years in the field of aging. In addition to teaching and research, from 1978 to 1993 she was the Associate Director of the University's Third Age Center. Most recently she served as co-principal investigator [with Dr. Barry Gurland] of "Growing Older in New York City in the 1990's," a replication of the earlier study of New York's elderly.

The author of more than 75 publications and presentations, she is the recipient of numerous awards, including "The Certificate of Appreciation from the City of New York for Outstanding Service to the City and its Elderly", the Donald L. Kent Award given annually by the Gerontological Society of America to a member who exemplifies the highest standards of professional leadership through teaching, service, and interpretation of gerontology to the larger society, the Walter M. Beatty Jr. Award for Distinguished Service to Aging, and election to the Hunter College Hall of Fame.

Professor Cantor has served as a consultant to numerous federal, state, and local agencies and boards, was a Senior Fellow of the Brookdale Foundation, a participant in both the 1980 and 1995 White House Conference on Aging, and The International Forum on Aging hosted by the Chinese government in Beijing. She currently serves on the Board of the Council of Senior Centers and Services of New York, the R. S. V. P. International, and is the Program Chairman of the U.S. Committee for the U.N. International Year of the Older Person.

Her research areas of expertise include the elderly in the urban setting, the role of families and other informal supports in caring for the elderly, the interface between informal and formal systems, and the effects of ethnicity and culture on the lifestyles of older people. She is a graduate of Hunter College and Teachers' College, Columbia University.

Mark Brennan completed his B. A. in psychology at the University of Wisconsin-Milwaukee in 1987, and received his Ph.D. in Applied Developmental Psychology from Fordham University in 1995. His dissertation was entitled, "The Context of Integrity Development in Late Adulthood," which examined personal development among older adults according to the psycho-social theory of Erik Erikson. While completing his doctoral studies on a Brookdale fellowship at Fordham's Third Age Center, Dr. Brennan served as a Co-Principal Investigator on a major survey of quality of life among older New Yorkers, "Growing Older in New York City in the 1990s" (Marjorie H. Cantor & Barry Gurland, M.D.—P.I.s).

Dr. Brennan joined the Lighthouse in 1996 after working as Senior Research Associate at the New York City Department for the Aging. Work at the Lighthouse has included secondary analyses of The Lighthouse National Survey on Vision Loss and Aging, examining coping and adaptation to age-related vision loss through qualitative analysis, and an examination of the roles of religiousness and spirituality in adaptation to vision impairment among middle-aged and older adults. His research interests also include the personal development in adulthood in response to life events, the provision of informal and formal social supports, and minority aging issues.

Dr. Brennan has been a fellow of the Hunter-Brookdale Center on Aging of New York since 1993, and has an appointment as Adjunct Assistant Professor at Fordham University's Graduate School of Social Service, where he is an instructor for Social Work Practice in Research. He also is a member of the Executive Board of the State Society on Aging of New York as Co-Chair of the Social Policy and 1999 Program Committees.

SOCIAL CARE OF THE ELDERLY

The Effects of Ethnicity, Class and Culture

Marjorie H. Cantor
Professor and Brookdale Distinguished Scholar

Mark Brennan, PhD

HV
1471
.N48
C37
2000
Wrt

 **Springer Publishing Company**

Copyright © 2000 by Springer Publishing Company, Inc.

Springer Publishing Company, Inc.
536 Broadway
New York, NY 10012-3955

Cover design by James Scotto-Lavino
Acquisitions Editor: Helvi Gold
Production Editor: Jeanne Libby

00 01 02 03 04 / 5 4 3 2 1

Library of Congress Cataloging-in-Publication Data

Cantor, Marjorie H.
    Social care of the elderly : the effects of ethnicity, class, and culture / Marjorie H. Cantor and Mark Brennan.
        p.   cm.
    Includes bibliographical references and index.
    ISBN 0-8261-1263-3 (hc.)
    1. Aged—Services for—New York (State)—New York. 2. Social work with the aged—New York (State)—New York. 3. Minorities—Services for—New York (State)—New York. 4. Social work with minorities—New York (State)—New York.   I. Brennan, Mark (Mark G.) II. Title.
HV1471.N48C37   1999
362.6—dc21   99-38047
                                                                                      CIP

Printed in the United States of America

To the many elderly who shared their lives and
thoughts with us over the years

Contents

Foreword   xi
Acknowledgments   xvii

PART I The Theory of Social Care

1 Social Care Among the Elderly: An Introduction   3
2 Social Care in the United States   13
3 Preferences on the Part of the Elderly for Assistance   47

PART II The Practice of Social Care: Three Case Studies of Older New Yorkers

4 Introduction to the Case Studies   61
5 Growing Older and Jewish in
   New York City in the 1990s   65
6 The Older Latinos of New York City in the 1990s   135
7 Growing Older and African American in
   New York City in the 1990s   201

PART III The Future of Social Care: Implications for Policy and Practice

8 The Elderly and the Informal Social Care System
   of the Twenty-first Century   257
9 The Future of Formal Community-Based Social Care   285

References   305

Appendix A: 321
   Study Methodologies of "The Elderly in
   the Inner City of New York" and "Growing
   Older in New York City in the 1990s"

Index   325

ix

Foreword

Beginning more than three decades ago, two researchers, Professor Marjorie Cantor, now a Distinguished Scholar on the faculty of the Graduate School of Social Service of Fordham University and then the Research Director at the New York City Department for the Aging, and Eugene Litwak, then at Cornell University, and now a Professor at the Columbia University School of Public Health, began publishing works in which they focused their attention on the service needs of the growing number of functionally dependent older people in our society. There are important, although for the purposes of this book, not consequential, differences in the theoretical approaches of Litwak and Cantor, but the common ground on which their work is built consists of their shared interest in the roles that families and other primary groups, on the one hand, the professionals and agencies which constitute the formal system of care, on the other hand, play in the lives of elderly Americans. Both agree that the provision of the care frail older people need requires a partnership between the formal and informal systems, and both are sensitive to the obstacles in the path of collaboration between the two systems.

Social Care of the Elderly: The Effects of Ethnicity, Class and Culture by Cantor and her colleague Mark Brennan is a welcome addition to the literature in this important area of work, and builds on both Cantor's and Litwak's theories and the empirical studies which have illuminated our understanding of the requirements of effective service provision. In their introduction, Cantor and Brennan identify what they call two major themes in gerontological research with respect to the role of social care in the lives of the elderly:

1   . . . (efforts) . . . to understand how the social care system operates . . . (and) . . . to ascertain the relative importance of . . . (the informal system) . . . and formal community-based services . . .

2.   An attempt to elucidate and understand the importance of

race, ethnicity, culture, and social class in the patterning of the social care provided to elderly.[1]

And they write:

". . . (Our) . . . goal . . . is to achieve a synthesis between these two themes by examining both the social support system of older people, and how race, ethnicity, and culture affect the provision of social care . . ."[2]

Two studies of older people in New York provide the basis for *Social Care*: First there was *The Elderly in the Inner City of New York* which was done in the 1970s, and more recently and more central to *Social Care* was *Growing Older in New York City in the 1990s*, a study which, in part, was a replication of the work of the 1970s. A careful read of Part I of *Social Care* is essential if the reader is to understand the theory base of this important book, including the differences among models and theories; the ways in which the complementary roles of informal systems and "mediating and formal systems" change as a function of the health status of older people; and the critical importance of the preferences of older people as they seek the help they need.

In Part II of the book, three groups are chosen to illustrate the ways in which ethnicity, class and culture affect the roles of the formal and informal systems, the reliance of older people on both systems, and the connections between the two systems. The reasons for the choice of African American and Latinos are clear and obvious, Cantor and Brennan tell us. Because these constitute the two largest groups among minority elderly in the United States as a whole, and because of the dramatic increase in the number and proportion of members of ethnic minorities in the 65+ cohort now and in the decades ahead, study of African Americans and Latinos makes this volume particularly valuable in urban communities across the nation.

In addition, both share a common history of discrimination, and also adherence to powerful norms governing the role of families in the lives of older people, and the responsibilities which are seen as singularly familial. Despite these commonalities, there are important differences between the African Americans and Latinos, and attention to these differences adds to our understanding of *Social Care*. The increase in the number of educated, middle class people in the African

---

1. p. 5.
2. Ibid.

American community in New York City and elsewhere provides the opportunity to tease out the differential effects of ethnicity and class on the provision of care. In contrast, the Latino population includes large numbers of relatively recent immigrants, and thus study of them permits analysis of the impact of acculturation on the traditional extended families of their homelands. In addition, the Latino population in New York, as in other urban areas of the United States, numbers people from many nations in the Caribbean and Central and South America, so that there is attention to *intra-group*, as well as inter-group differences, a very important element in our understanding of African American and Asian American elderly, as well as Latino elderly.

The choice of Jewish elderly as the third group attended by Cantor and Brennan rests in part on the fact that they and the members of their descendant generations comprise a numerically important group among White residents of metropolitan New York and in other urban areas in the United States. But more important is the status of Jewish communities as integral participants in the mainstream of American life, and at the same time there is the strength of the group identity among many Jewish Americans, and the strength also of *both* the family and the formal system of communal services which is so central an element in Jewish communities in the United States. Cantor and Brennan write of ". . . the heightened sense of the appropriateness of community intervention and the strong ties to family . . ." in Jewish communities, and it is this reliance on both family and formal system which makes the Jewish elderly so interesting a group to study. Moreover, Jewish communities in the United States are often at "the cutting edge" of emerging trends, and study of these communities can illumine our understanding of the complementary roles of family and formal systems in the future.

We will leave to readers of *Social Care* the exciting prospect of mining the richness of the data Cantor and Brennan present. It is clear that they provide powerful evidence of:

1. The importance for frail older people of having available to them care provided by *both* family and agencies and professionals in the formal systems;
2. The reality that ethnicity, class and culture continue to powerfully affect the roles of the two systems, the preferences of older people in the tasks assigned to each, and the avail-

ability of family members to participate in the care of frail elders;

3. The *absolute* requirement that professionals and other staff of the agencies and institutions which comprise the formal system respect and understand the intra- and inter-group differences, which so powerfully affect items like the ways in which older people and their families connect to the formal system, what they want from the system, how they perceive and relate to staff, *inter alia*.

This is an important book, and one which should be carefully read by service providers in community agencies and in long-term care facilities, by public officials at the federal level and in the area agencies on aging and in the legislative branches at all three levels of government, and by academics, including faculty of schools of nursing, social work, medicine, and health professions, and including also professors in departments of public policy, urban planning, psychology and sociology, etc. Its usefulness extends far beyond the boundaries of metropolitan New York, and its lessons can inform public policy, service organization and delivery, and professional practice in Asian American, American Indian, and other ethnic communities in the United States. This because it turns out that there are differences among ethnic groups in such items as values, norms, family structure and composition, service preferences, and that these differences make a difference in how services should be designed, located, and staffed in various communities.

In the final section of this valuable book, Cantor and Brennan turn from their analysis of their empirical data to consideration of the future, and we believe that a reading of this section is an essential exercise for all of us who think seriously about older people now and in the new millennium. They place emphasis on the tragic reality of the absence in the United States of a coherent and comprehensive long-term care policy and system, and on the price which older people and their families pay for this failure of public policy in the United States. And they remind us also of the particularly disadvantaged position of older women in all of the ethnic communities in the United States. The final section which Cantor and Brennan have written is, in a real sense, a call for action, for all of us in the field and for public officials and "opinion makers" to respond to the need for "Social Care" now and in the new millennium.

We commend Cantor and Brennan's work to the attention of all who are committed to the provision of services and care for older people in all of the ethnic and religious and cultural communities in our nation.

Rose Dobrof, D.S.W.
Brookdale Professor of Gerontology
Hunter College

James R. Dumpson, Ph.D.
Chairman of Policy Center in Aging
New York Community Trust

May 1999

Acknowledgments

Many people contributed to making possible the study "Growing Older In New York In The 1990's" and this book, an outgrowth of that study. First and foremost was the vision of the New York Center on Policy on Aging of the New York Community Trust and its Chair, James R. Dumpson, Ph.D., and Vice Chair, Rose Dobrof, DSW, of the need for such a study and its importance as a planning, policy, and practice resource for New York City. Because of their belief in the importance of such a study, Drs. Dumpson and Dobrof enlisted a group of foundations and organizations to provide support for the study and we are exceptionally grateful to the following funding sources who helped make "Growing Older In New York in the 1990's" possible:

The New York Community Trust
John A. Hartford Foundation
The Commonwealth Fund
Altman Foundation
Florence V. Burden Foundation
United Hospital Fund
Morgan Guaranty Trust Co.
Fan Fox & Leslie R. Samuels Foundation, Inc.
Anonymous Foundation

Additional funding for the in-depth study of the Jewish elderly was generously received from the United Jewish Appeal-Federation of Jewish Philanthropies of New York, Inc. We wish to thank Federation and Robert Wolf and Bethamie Horwitz, for their support and continued interest in our work.

"Growing Older in New in the 1990's" was a collaborative effort of Fordham and Columbia Universities with principal investigators from each institution: Dr. Barry Gurland of Columbia and Professor

Marjorie H. Cantor of Fordham and their co-investigators Drs. Cathy Berkman and Mark Brennan. Louis Harris Associates, Inc. conducted the field work for the study and it was a pleasure to work with them and with Humphry Taylor, President, and Robert Leitman, Vice-President.

Although the study originated while Professor Cantor was associated with the Third Age Center of Fordham, the major data analysis and the writing of this book took place at the Graduate School of Social Service. Special thanks is therefore given to Dr. Mary Ann Quarenta, Dean of the School, for her steadfast support of the project and her encouragement and guidance both with the study and the writing of this book. Other colleagues, both at Fordham and The Lighthouse International, have been most helpful and always available to discuss the findings and the implications for the field of aging. We particularly wish to thank Msg. Charles Fahey, Director of the Third Age Center, Drs. Irene Guitheil and Lloyd Rogler of Fordham, and Drs. Amy Horowitz and Joann Reinhardt of The Lighthouse International. We also wish to express our appreciation to the Brookdale Foundation for its support of the Brookdale Doctoral Training Program, Marjorie Cantor, Director, and to the graduate students in that program who so capably assisted with many aspects of the study, including Drs. Eileen Chichin, Susan Rosendahl, and Louise Schmidt. Special note must also be made of the technical assistance received from John O'Brian of the Computer Center of Fordham University.

Especially we wish to express our appreciation to Helvi Gold, our editor at Springer, for her many suggestions regarding the book, which helped move the manuscript to completion.

And last but not least, Marjorie Cantor wishes to thank her husband of 54 years, Aaron M. Cantor, for his steadfast support and encouragement in all her work. Without his help there would be no book. She wishes also to express her appreciation for the support and pleasure expressed by her children and their spouses, Richard Cantor and Andrea Lilienthal, Nancy Cantor and Steve Brechin, and her grandchildren, Andrew, Eliza, Maddy and Archie, in the writing of this book.

Mark Brennan would like to especially thank his partner, Michael Ing, for his understanding, patience, and support in putting this book together. He would also like to thank his parents, Gloria and Larry, his sisters, Clare, Margaret and Geri, and all other family and friends who have been supportive and given encouragement in this endeavor.

PART I
The Theory of Social Care

1

Social Care Among the Elderly: An Introduction

The creation of the aging network under the aegis of the Older Americans Act and the resultant spread of community-based services has suggested the need for a careful examination of the ways older people receive the assistance they require. The needs of older people range from help needed during times of crisis, such as an acute medical episode, to those circumstances of worsening health and increasing frailty most common in the later stages of life. Who provides this needed assistance to the elderly? Traditionally, care for older people has been the province of family members, especially spouses and children. But the growing number of formal providers who serve the needs of the elderly raises the question: to what extent are families involved in caregiving of their older members, and under what circumstances and in what manner is such informal support provided? This issue is particularly germane in light of the demographic changes that are altering the societal landscape, including the growth of the nuclear family, the growing geographic dispersion of children in response to employment and career opportunities, and the increasing racial and ethnic diversity of the American population.

The role of community services has always been considered residual, but with the increasing numbers of older people, changing family structures, and the increased technical skill often needed to care for frail and disabled elderly, the role of community services has increased in importance. But despite the increased and often critical role of formal service providers to older people, to many the informal and formal elements of the social care system have remained separate, with only scant attention paid to the importance of linkages between informal and formal providers of care. Additionally, early geronto-logical studies tended to view older people as homogenous, failing to recognize the diversity of America's older population with respect to race, ethnicity, culture and class. Gradually, there has been a growing recognition of the great diversity that exists among older people in the United States today, with consequent differences in the availability of resources, life experience, family structure and cultural values and norms associated with different racial and ethnic groups. These differences, as well as the similarities between these groups, are important in understanding fully what it means to grow older in America today.

Over the past decades, there has been a body of research that has examined the potential abandonment of the elderly on the part of younger family members with a concomitant interest in how the social care needs of older people are met. Beginning in the 1970s, a number of landmark studies on the local, national and international level documented the role of kin, friends and neighbors in the informal support of older persons, as well as the importance of help received from community-based providers. These studies have belied the myth of families abandoning their aging members and instead have reported that the majority of older adults have rich informal support networks, with high levels of interaction and reciprocal exchanges of assistance between them and their families, friends and neighbors. Furthermore, formal service providers have been found to play an increasingly crucial role in cases where informal supports are either insufficient or unavailable to meet the social care needs of older adults.

The major thesis of this book, as has been the case for much of our past efforts, is the maintenance of a positive quality of life for older people as a valuable goal from both the individual and societal perspectives. Many components are involved in insuring a positive quality of life, and these include: (a) adequate income and health care; (b) suitable housing and environmental conditions (including personal safety and adequate transportation); and (c) the existence of meaningful and emotionally satisfying personal relationships. Most often, discussions of quality of life revolve around the ability of older people to remain independent in the community, but these factors are important for institutionalized elderly as well (Dobrof & Litwak, 1977). But as people grow older and often face worsening health and growing frailty, their need for assistance to maintain independence becomes increasingly a factor of a sufficiency of social supports. This assistance may range from the minimal level typical of everyday familial

exchanges to the highly extended and technical care most often provided by formal service providers. The particular informal or formal
element of the older person's social support system that is activated
at any time is a function of a combination of factors, including the
degree of assistance needed, the availability of both formal and informal elements, and the preferences of the older person and his or her
family.

The social care system with its variety of both informal and formal support is broad-based, ranging from the intimacy of spousal relationships, extending to children, siblings and other family members,
friends and neighbors, and to the growing constellation of formal
providers of services to older adults, from home health care agencies
to community senior centers. In any such complex system, there are
many potential interactions between the various elements of the social
care system. In a culturally homogenous society like Japan, interactions among such wide-ranging social support elements are guided
by a singularity of norms and values. However, the United States represents, at the other extreme, a plurality of cultural norms and values.
As a nation of immigrants that becomes more racially and ethnically
diverse every day, social care in the United States has the potential for
dissonance between the cultural values and norms of elderly people
and their families and the myriad other elements involved in the provision of assistance. Because adequate social care is essential for many
older adults to remain independent in the community and to maintain positive quality of life, understanding the contextual influences
of race, ethnicity, and culture in the operation of the American social
care system is imperative.

GERONTOLOGICAL RESEARCH ON
SOCIAL CARE OF THE ELDERLY

During the last 20 years, there have been two major themes in gerontological research with respect to the role of social care in the lives of
older persons.

1. An attempt to understand how the social care system operates
    to provide the assistance needed by these older adults to main-
    tain their quality of life. Included in such research is the
    attempt to ascertain the relative importance of family, friends,
    neighbors, and formal community-based services as well as

the impact of providing continual care, especially in the case of frail and disabled elderly.

2. An attempt to elucidate and understand the importance of race, ethnicity, culture and social class in the patterning of the social care provided to older people.

The goal of this book is to achieve a synthesis between these two themes by examining both the social support system of older people and how race, ethnicity and culture affect the provision of social care within this system. The basis for this examination are two landmark studies of older New Yorkers. The first, conducted in the 1970, is The Elderly in the Inner City of New York, and the second is Growing Older in New York City in the 1990s, a replication of the study conducted 20 years earlier. What is particularly unique is the opportunity to examine changes that have occurred over two decades in the characteristics of the social care networks of New York's elderly during a sharp increase in the availability of formal community- based services in the same time frame.

THE 1970 AND 1990 STUDIES OF OLDER NEW YORKERS: SAMPLE AND METHODOLOGY[1]

Before beginning our exploration of the social care systems of older New Yorkers presented in the following case studies of Jewish, Latino, and Black older adults, some contextual information is in order to provide a framework for understanding the data and their implications.

THE ELDERLY IN THE INNER CITY OF NEW YORK: 1970

In 1970, the then recently created New York City Department for the Aging undertook a study of a random sample of adults aged 60 and older living in the 26 poverty areas in the five boroughs comprising New York City to document the lifestyles and quality of life of these elderly. A major goal of this study "The Elderly in The Inner city of New York" (Marjorie Cantor, Principle Investigator) was to examine the operation and effectiveness of both informal and formal social supports in providing assistance to a representative sample of White,

---

1. Details on methodolgy of the two studies may be found in Appendix A at the end of this volume.

African Americans, and Latino elders (n = 1552) who resided in the community, using in-person 1.5 hour interviews. Among the most influential findings from this study was that the informal social networks of older people were not only extremely vigorous, but also the preferred source of assistance and best suited to resolve the conflict between society's norms of independence and the increasing frailty and poorer health that can often accompany growing older. Data from this study were the basis for the Social Care Model and the Hierarchical Compensatory Theory of Social Supports that is discussed in the following chapter.

THE SAMPLE: THE ELDERLY IN THE
INNER CITY OF NEW YORK: 1970

The sample for the original study was nearly equally divided between Whites (49%) and minorities (51%), with African Americans accounting for the greatest proportion of minority participants (37%), and Latino, mainly Puerto Rican, respondents comprising the remaining 13%. Thus, the sample was underrepresentative in terms of Whites 60 and older who accounted for 90% of the older population of the city in 1970. White elderly in the sample were more than twice as likely (37%) to be over the age of 75, as compared with approximately 17% of both Latinos and African Americans. Three-fifths of the sample were female, however, this proportion rose to 65% of African Americans older New Yorkers, while among Whites, a smaller proportion (55%) were female. Slightly more than one-half (53%) of the 1970 sample were born on the US mainland.

Not surprisingly, given the sample frame of poverty, and innercity neighborhoods, the majority of the 1970 study sample were in lower socioeconomic categories; three-quarters were in the lowest strata and Hollingshead's Index of Socioeconomic Status (SES) (1957) based on education and occupation, with two-thirds reporting skilled or unskilled occupations, 60% having educations of 8th grade or less, and two-thirds reporting median annual incomes of $2371. Latino and African American participants were more likely to have lower educational and occupational levels than their White peers. Ninety-one percent (91%) of the sample were heads-of-households, and 39% reported living alone. One third of New Yorkers aged 60 and older were currently married (34%), and 42% were widowed.

GROWING OLDER IN NEW YORK CITY IN THE 1990s

In the years following 1970, both the increase in the number and proportion of older persons as well as changes in access to health care and
the explosive growth of formal community-based agencies for the
elderly in response to passage of the Older Americans Act, made current information on the older population imperative for policy makers, program planners and others engaged in providing services to
these individuals. In recognition of this need, in 1990 the New York
Center for Policy on Aging of the New York Community Trust sponsored a large-scale study, Growing Older in New York City in the
1990s: A Study of Changing Lifestyles, Quality of Life and Quality of
Care. This research was supported by a consortium of foundations
under the leadership of the Center for Policy on Aging (James R.
Dumpson, Ph.D., Chair).

In addition to "The Elderly in the Inner City of New York", 1970
witnessed another major study of the burgeoning older population,
"The US-UK Cross National Geriatric Community Study (1978)",
Barry Gurland, Principal Investigator. Because both studies had collected broad-based data about the needs and lifestyles of older people living in an urban environment, major sections of the two previous
studies were used to design the 1990 survey. Thus, an important feature of "Growing Older in New York City" was its ability to replicate
data collected 20 years earlier for the purpose of comparison, as well
as the opportunity to gather up-to-date information on the current
cohort of older people in New York City. Under the direction of Dr.
Dumpson, The Brookdale Research Institute of the Third Age Center
of Fordham University (Marjorie H. Cantor, P.I. and Mark Brennan,
Co-P.I.) and the Stroud Program on Science Quality of Life Center of
Geriatrics of Columbia University (Barry Gurland, P.I. and Cathy
Berkman, Co-P.I.) were commissioned to undertake the project. The
Fordham team was primarily responsible for demographic, environ-
mental, and social support information, while the Columbia team was
primarily engaged in analyzing physical and mental health data.

Data were collected by Louis Harris and Associates Inc. using a
sample frame of New Yorkers aged 65 and older drawn from the
Health Care Financing Administration's list of Medicare enrollees in
the five boroughs, using a multistage clustering procedure with a
response rate of 60%. Minority elderly and the very old were oversampled to insure sufficient numbers for subgroup analyses, with a
resultant statistical sample of 1570. Data were then weighted in accor-

dance with US Bureau of the Census 1990 population figures to insure that the sample was representative of the 65 and older population in New York City (weighted n = 1577).

THE SAMPLE: GROWING OLDER IN NEW YORK CITY IN THE 1990s

The majority in the 1990 sample were White[2] (76%), 15% were Black, and 9% were of Hispanic origin[3]. Respondents had an average age of 74 years, and two in five were 75 years-of-age or older. Women accounted for 61% of the sample. Forty-two percent of the sample were currently married, and nearly the same proportion were widowed (38%). More than two-thirds of the sample (70%) were born on the US mainland, and 90% reported speaking English at home (except among Latinos, with only one-quarter speaking any English at home).

While some older New Yorkers reported annual incomes in six figures, by far the vast majority of respondents reported incomes significantly lower; nearly one-third reported 1989 incomes of $10,000 or less, while another one-third reported moderate retirement incomes in the $10,000 to $25,000 range. Median annual income for the total sample was approximately $14,000. Thus, one in five older New Yorkers were at or below poverty, and 22% were living in near poverty (101% to 150% of poverty income). In terms of other socioeconomic indicators, over one-quarter reported 8th grade educations or less, and over one-half had worked at skilled or unskilled occupations. Ninety-four percent of respondents were heads-of-households, only 5% reported living with family or friends. Nearly two in five older New Yorkers reported that they lived alone, with 42% living with a spouse, and 19% reporting that they lived in the households of others. The discrepancy between the proportion of respondents living in the households of others (5%) and those reporting living with family or friends (19%) is likely the result of the number of separate apartments in multifamily homes throughout New York City, which are often provided to aging parents so they may be in close proximity to children.

---

2. Less than 3% of the total sample were Asian (1.5%), Native American or Other race/ethnicity, and were included with Whites for purpose of analysis.

3. Throughout this text, the terms African American and Black are both used to describe persons of African origin, including both native-born and West-Indian individuals. Hispanic and Latino are used to describe persons with Spanish language and cultural backgrounds.

COMPARISON OF THE 1970 AND 1990 SAMPLES OF
OLDER NEW YORKERS.

To better understand the context of the social care patterns of Jewish,
Latino, and Black older persons in the following chapters, two important distinctions are worth noting in the overall characteristics of the
1970 Elderly in the Inner City of New York and the Growing Older in
New York City in the 1990s samples. The 1970 sample was comprised
of New Yorkers 60 years and older, but in 1990, to utilize the Medicare
sample frame, adults 65 and older were interviewed. Additionally,
while both samples included all five boroughs of New York City, the
1970 study was mainly targeted at those elderly living in the 25
poverty areas of the City, whereas the 1990 study included a probability sample of all neighborhoods. Thus, the 1970 study was
overrepresentative of minority and younger older persons and underrepresentative of higher income White elderly in comparison to the
1990 data, which was weighted according to population parameters
and representative of the entire 65 and older population in New York
City. However, despite these differences, as discussed below, there is
marked similarity on a variety of indicators between respondents in
1970 and those in 1990.

Both studies share several important characteristics. Both used
large, representative samples of older New Yorkers with sufficient
members of the major ethnic and racial subgroups to make meaningful comparisons. Both sampled older New Yorkers from many different parts of the City; from inner city neighborhoods in the five
boroughs in the 1970 study and from a citywide probability sample of
Medicare enrollees in the 1990 study. While a large focus of these two
studies was the elderly population of New York City as a whole, of
equal importance was the emphasis on the similarities and differences
between Black, Latino, and White older New Yorkers. In the 1990
study, particular attention was paid to conducting both between-group
and within-group analyses to have a better understanding of the relative importance of race, ethnicity, and class in the provision of social
care to the elderly.

Clearly, the experience of growing older in New York is *sui generis*
in some respects, but we believe that it offers a glimpse of the future
as our society becomes even more multicultural and growing numbers of older people are concentrated in urban areas and the suburbs
that surround them. In terms of racial and ethnic diversity, the proportion of minority older people in New York City today reflects what

is projected for the United States as a whole in the year 2050, when 20% of those 65 and older will be non-White and 16% will be of Latino ancestry (US Census Bureau, 1995). As of 1990 in New York City, 27% of the population 65 years and older were non-White; 15% were Black; 9% were Latino; with Asian and other racial groups accounting for the remaining 3% (Hanreider, 1992a, 1992b). Thus, the elderly population of New York City in the 1990s closely resembles the projections of the increasing diversity of older Americans in the twenty-first Century and, in many respects, can be considered prototypical of the older population when the need for elder social care will far outstrip our present experience.

In the succeeding chapters we will address the following questions:

1. What is the nature of social care as found in one of the largest concentrations of elderly in the United States (ie, New York City), and how have the patterns and dynamics of such care changed in the past two decades? What are the implications of these findings for other urban elderly and older people in general?
2. To what extent do race, ethnicity, and culture play a role in the social care of older adults, and how do these factors affect the relative importance of the informal and formal support elements in maintaining an optimal quality of life for them?
3. What are the social care needs of older people from a systems perspective in which the relative roles of informal and formal support elements are seen as complimentary, dependent on the particular circumstances of an older person's need for assistance, the preferences of the older person and his or her family for particular helping partners, and the availability of both formal and informal providers of assistance?

Finally, we will relate these themes to the aging of America, the projections regarding the changing nature of the elderly population in the coming decades, and the public attitudes about the relative responsibility of individuals and society in providing assistance to persons in need. Wherever possible, the research presented here will be tied to other empirical work, but the main focus of our research is the three major ethnic subgroups of Jewish, Latino, and African-American older New Yorkers.

In the following chapters, the theoretical foundations for the study of social care will be reviewed, including a discussion of the major theories in the gerontological literature. A comparison of empirical findings in the preferred sources of social care among older New Yorkers in 1970 and 1990 follows. We will then provide an in-depth examination of the social care systems within the three major racial and ethnic subgroups of New York City's older population in 1990, namely, Jewish, who comprise the largest ethnic subgroup of older Whites, African Americans, and Latinos. After reviewing the similarities and differences between these groups of older New Yorkers, we will consider what the future holds for social care of older Americans in light of current findings and anticipated trends. We will then conclude with implications for gerontologists, program planners, and policy makers about what constitutes a successful provision of social care for both current and future cohorts of older Americans.

2

Social Care in the United States

PART I: DEFINITIONS AND THEORIES

Introduction

In the seventeenth century, the English poet John Donne perceptively noted that no man is an island unto himself and that when the bell tolls for one it tolls for all. Acceptance of this concept of mutual interdependence has varied from society to society depending on its particular history, stage of economic development, and cultural norms. However, a central theme of most cultures has been the balance between the dependence and independence needs of individuals and society. When the pioneers set out to tame the American frontier, out of necessity there was an emphasis on the ability of the individual to survive and prosper with a minimum of assistance from those around. The frontier period of the United States has long since passed, but this ethos of independence and self-sufficiency continues to dominate our culture.

Reliance on others, particularly in the form of governmental assistance, is still considered by many to be a sign of moral weakness, even in the most dire situations. And people are too often judged by how well they can manage on their own with a minimum of assistance. Although the United States may have carried this theme of independence to its extreme, this general notion of self-sufficiency as a sign of maturity and ego integrity is shared by most Western European countries and is gradually permeating the rest of the world with the spread of Western culture and its notions of capitalism and democracy.

However, from the life-cycle perspective, there are two significant stages in which society is more accepting of dependency needs:
at the beginning and end of life. It is considered appropriate for
infants and children to be nurtured by parents and other adults as
they are socialized into the culture. Again, as persons grow older and
their needs for assistance increase, concomitant with increasing frailty,
society looks with greater tolerance on their needs for support both
from the informal and formal social care system. Dependency in these
contexts is normal and not pathological, "a state of being not a state
of mind in which to be old as to be young is to be dependent"
(Blenkner ,1969).

But in the case of old age, as the balance shifts from independence
to dependency, the potential for normative conflicts increases. Thus,
an older person is often caught in a dilemma between adherence to
deeply rooted cultural norms of self-sufficiency and independence so
characteristic of adulthood, and on the other hand, concrete needs for
assistance as health, physical strength, and mobility (and often economic resources decline with age) (Cantor, 1977).

Some insight into how this value dilemma is mitigated and the
potential conflict dealt with by older people comes from an examination of the modern kinship structure in the United States, as well as
the relationship between informal support networks and formal organizations. Industrialization in America and elsewhere has been accompanied by an evolution in kinship structures. There has been a move
away from the traditional extended family to a more modified family
structure characterized by a coalition of separately housed, semiau-
tonomous family units who function in a state of partial dependency,
and who share with formal organizations the function of family. This
has been characterized by Rosenmayr (1977) as "intimacy at a distance." Thus, although a majority of families may live in separate
households, they still maintain close contacts and provide extensive
reciprocal support (Litwak, 1965; Shanas et al., 1968; Sussman &
Burchinall, 1962; Towsend, 1969). As a result, in the United States, as
well as in most other industrialized countries, particularly since World
War II, a shift has occurred in the nature of family and societal roles
regarding elderly members. Today the federal government provides
the floor of basic services for older people in such crucial areas as
income maintenance, health, housing, and transportation. But the family has by no means been usurped by formal organizations with
respect to meeting the more idiosyncratic support needs of the individual. And nowhere is the role of family, friends, and neighbors more

crucial than in the provision of social care (Cantor, 1975a; 1975b; Cantor & Little, 1985).

THE RESOLUTION OF VALUE CONFLICTS REGARDING DEPENDENCY

How do older people attempt to deal with the value conflict between the contrasting norms of independence and dependency as they often face growing needs for assistance? Most important is the notion, supported by three decades of gerontological and family research, that older people perceive the informal network of kin and significant others as the most appropriate source of social support in the vast majority of situations (Adams, 1980; Connelly, 1980; DuKippo, 1980; Gurian & Cantor, 1978; Shanas et al., 1968; Sussman, 1976; Towsend, 1963, 1968; Valle & Mendoza, 1978). Family and other informal network members are seen by older people as natural extensions of themselves, and reciprocal helping patterns, often rooted in earlier phases of the life cycle, are activated in times of crisis. Such a preference is consistent with minimum psychological threat to ego systems based on norms of self-sufficiency and self-reliance (Cantor & Little, 1985).

Not only are kin and significant others so perceived, but it is to the informal system that most older people turn first and most frequently in times of need (Cantor, 1975a; 1975b; 1980; Cantor & Little, 1985; Horowitz & Dobrof, 1982; Shanas, 1979a; 1979b). The primacy of the family and other informal supports in assisting older people does not, however, minimize the important role played by formal social services. Some elderly people do not have kin or other informal networks elements. Others have networks that, because of geography or conflicting obligations, cannot be considered functional with respect to caregiving. For other older people, kin do not have the requisite skills or knowledge to perform the needed assistance. For them, the formal service provider often serves as surrogate family. Furthermore, the many studies involving stress and strain among informal caregivers underscore the crucial role of formal community services in assisting caregivers in maintaining their elderly clients in the community (Cantor, 1989). In such situations the community serves as backup and respite, making it possible for families to continue to keep their elderly members out of institutions.

Litwak (1965) in his theory of shared functions and balanced coordination has postulated that the dependency needs of older people are best met if there is a proper balance between formal services and informal supports, with each performing the task for which they are most suited (Litwak & Meyer, 1966). Ideally, an older person should be able to access the element most appropriate to the particular time and function (Litwak, 1965; 1978; Sussman, 1965). Thus, the social care system of the elderly person is best viewed as an amalgam of kin, friends and neighbors, and formal social services, each having distinct roles and differing relative importance at various stages in the dependency continuum of old age (Cantor & Little, 1985). Such a system involves a pattern of continuous ties and interchanges of assistance from a variety of sources that play a significant role in maintaining psychological, social, and physical integrity over time (Cantor, 1981a).

DEFINITIONS OF SOCIAL CARE

What is social care and how is it conceptualized? We define the concept of *social care* broadly to include the myriad of informal and formal activities as well as personal support services, which taken as a whole, support the efforts of elderly persons to maintain the greatest degree of personal independence and self-sufficiency.

What does social care as defined encompass? Three decades of research and practice have shown that the conditions of the elderly that require support are usually ongoing and call for sustained assistance. Although purely medical or health-related services are sometimes involved, in the main, the supports required are of a social nature (Brody & Brody, 1981). Thus social care can be seen as addressing three main kinds of needs: first, opportunities for socialization, self-affirmation, and self-actualization; second, assistance with everyday tasks of living necessary for independent functioning; and third, help with personal assistance during times of illness or other crisis (Cantor, 1975b; 1991). The social supports provided can be of an instrumental nature, involving tangible, direct assistance or material aid, offering informational help or advice, or be of an affective nature involving emotional support and sustenance (Kahn & Antonucci, 1980; Lopata, 1975; Tolsdorf, 1976). Fundamental to the concept of social care is that such assistance serves to augment individual competency and mastery of the environment rather than fostering dependency. What is particularly problematic in the case of elderly persons is the degree to which they can care for themselves without assistance. When and under what circumstances do they require assistance from others? And how can they most appropriately access the needed assistance from others.

Although the term social care is sometimes used synonymously with formal social services, it is actually a broader concept encompassing both informal and formal social support activities, which, in fact, exist side by side. In this book, the term social care will be used to delineate the broad spectrum of helping, access, socialization, and self-actualization activities, as well as both formal and informal social services that assist older people to maintain themselves in the community and successfully negotiate the challenges of later life.

THEORETICAL FORMULATIONS OF SOCIAL CARE

Perhaps one of the best ways to fully understand the intricacies involved in providing social care to older people is through the use of a macro-level systems model. This model, developed by Cantor in the course of the study, "The Elderly in the Inner City of New York", while recognizing the separate support components (i.e., family, community, social agencies, and government), emphasizes the dynamic and interactive nature of the social care system, both from individual and societal perspectives. Furthermore, because the system of social care involves both informal and formal components, any attempt to understand the operation of the system requires an examination of individual and societal forces and their interactive effects (Cantor, 1975a; 1975b; 1979b; 1980; 1989; 1991; Cantor & Little, 1985).

As depicted in Figure 2.1, the social support system is conceptualized as a series of concentric circles, each containing a different type of support element or subsystem (Cantor 1978; 1980). The older person is at the core of this model, interacting with a series of subsystems, each of which is represented by a separate circle. These subsystems usually operate independently, but at times intersect, illustrating the concept of an interactive, broadbased social support network. The sources of support radiate outward from the older person according to the degree of social distance; from nearest to farthest corresponding to the degree of organization of the element, from informal to formal. Older people interact with the people or institutions represented by each of these circles at varying times according to their particular needs.

At the most distant reaches of this system of social care, represented by the outermost circle and farthest in social distance from the older person, are the political entities such as federal, state and local legislatures, which are responsible for determining social policy and entitlements for older individuals. Such policy formulations have a

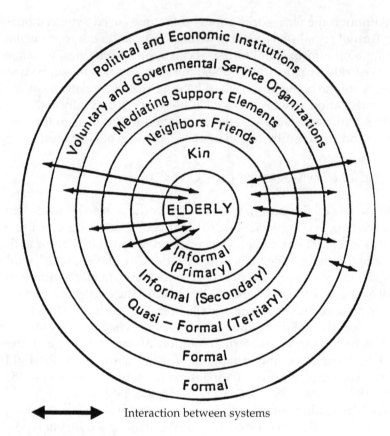

◄──────► Interaction between systems

FIGURE 2.1 The Social Care System of the Elderly:
A Model (Cantor, 1977).

Source: Cantor, Marjorie 1977. Neighbors and Friends: An Overlooked Resource
in the Informal Support System. Paper, 30th Annual Meeting Gerontological
Society, San Francisco, California.

significant impact on the overall well-being of elderly people but are
particularly germane to income maintenance, health care services, the
availability of adequate housing, transportation infrastructure, and
public safety. Somewhat closer to older people in terms of social distance are the governmental and voluntary agencies which execute
these economic and social policies. These bodies provide the actual
services mandated under laws, such as the Social Security and Older
Americans Acts, or those dictated by community need. Thus, organi-

zations in these outer two rings are clearly part of the formal support system. In line with the characteristics of bureaucratic organizations they attempt to function instrumentally and objectively according to an ideology of efficiency and rationality, and to provide services uniformly to large aggregates of the population (Litwak, 1985; Litwak & Meyer, 1966).

Still closer to the older person, and standing between formal organizations and kin and significant others, are the nonservice and the quasiformal organizations and their representatives. Often called mediating structures, they include religious organizations; ethnic, cultural, or social groups; neighborhood and block associations; as well as individuals who informally assist older people such as mail carriers, building superintendents, shop keepers, and even bartenders. Such groups and individuals often serve as links between the elderly person and the broader community and provide direct assistance, particularly at times of crisis (Berger & Neuhaus, 1977). These network elements are labeled as tertiary in the Social Care Model because they resemble the informal network but arise from, and are related to, formal social structures.

Finally, closest to the older person and most directly involved in their day-to-day lives are the individuals who comprise the two innermost circles: the informal social support system of kin, friends and neighbors. It is precisely these significant others who interact most frequently with the older people, who are turned to first when both instrumental and emotional support is needed, and who comprise the broad base of the social support system both in the United States and throughout the world (Antonucci, 1990; Brody, 1966; 1978; 1981; 1985; Cantor, 1975a; 1989; 1992; Cantor & Little, 1985; Harevan, 1978; Jackson, 1980; Shanas, 1967, 1979a; 1979b; Shanas et al., 1968). Caregivers in the informal support system are distinguished from formal service providers in several important ways. Most significantly, many are blood-relations of the individual, or are chosen personally by the older person on the basis of intimacy and personal involvement. Second, usually the assistance provided is not highly technical, for example, simple housekeeping, bathing, or feeding in contrast to specialized medical procedures. However, with increasingly shorter hospital stays, family members may find themselves called on to perform medically oriented tasks that were previously in the domain of nurses or highly trained home health aides.

In addition, informal supports are tailored to the relatively more unpredictable and idiosyncratic needs of individuals and can often respond more quickly to an emergency with greater flexibility with respect to time commitment and task specification. Perhaps most importantly, such assistance rests on a system of mutual reciprocity (Cantor & Hirschorn, 1989; Horowitz & Shindelman, 1982). In the case of kin, such reciprocity stretches over the life cycle. With friends and neighbors, the time frame may be shorter, but reciprocity is still the underlying component of supportive interactions between the elderly person and nonrelated significant others. And finally, the role of informal supports in providing emotional support is often as crucial and equally important as instrumental forms of assistance.

Although older people may receive help from family or tertiary groups, they often provide as much help to other generations in the kinship system, friends, and neighbors as they receive in return, demonstrating the reciprocity of informal social care. Only in the case of extreme frailty does the flow of assistance tend to be asymmetrical, flowing from the younger to the older generation. Yet even in the most difficult caregiving situations involving severely impaired elderly persons, caregivers report important psychological benefits in being able to assist a loved one. And increasingly, older people themselves are a significant force on the political scene, influencing legislation involving younger generations as well as their own, and receiving important psychological benefits from participating in the political process (Brennan, 1995). Thus the interdependence of generations across the life cycle is crucial to the operations of the proposed Social Care Model. This interdependence is represented in the model by the lines that cross subsystems and the bidirectional arrows cutting across the concentric circles (see Figure 2.1).

We have attempted to illustrate the nature of the social care system of the elderly by emphasizing how each element is interrelated and how older people and their significant others operate interactively within this system to provide required social care. Still another way of illustrating the holistic nature of the social care system is from the perspective of the services provided. Only formal organizations by definition provide institutional care. Yet studies of caregiving and service provision report that many of the services provided by nursing homes are also provided by families to their elderly members in the community (Gurland, Dean, Gurland, & Cook, 1978; U.S. Comptroller General, 1977; U.S. General Accounting Office, 1977).

This tendency to overlap is illustrated in Table 2.1, where the major tasks performed by the informal, mediating and formal systems are related to varying levels of functional impairment. These levels range from the well elderly capable of independent functioning except in times of emergency, to the moderately impaired elderly with greater needs for assistance but still relatively independent, to the frailest of the older population who require the most time-consuming and involved services. Need for services in terms of both type and amount is not necessarily age related and is influenced by preferences for assistance and the nature of the disability. However, most research suggests that, in general, there is an age gradient, with the greatest need for direct hands-on assistance occurring mainly among the very old, those who are 85 years old or more. It should be noted that the services shown in Table 2.1 are cumulative, and it is assumed that any services shown in the preceding level will continue to be available if appropriate. Thus, only the additional services required as competency declines are illustrated.

Starting first with the largest group, those with no or minimal needs (estimated at 60% of the current older cohort), the assistance required mainly involves opportunities for socialization, self-actualization, intimacy, and information. When direct instrumental assistance is needed in times of illness or other crisis, it is usually short term. Here kin, friends and neighbors play the most crucial role by providing what Brody (1966) aptly described as "the garden variety" of assistance, which family members and friends provide each other over the adult years of the life cycle. Thus, in the first informal column, we find assistance in the form of visiting, giving advice, escort or transportation help, and assistance in the home or when illness is of a limited nature. But as shown under the Mediating and Formal System heading, many similar services involve the formal subsystem as well.

As greater limitations of physical function and mobility occur, usually stemming from chronic illnesses such as arthritis, vision impairment and heart disease, older people may require more help, especially with the more basic activities of daily living like shopping, difficult household tasks such as heavy lifting, and, in some instances, meal preparation (see Table 2.1). But opportunities for socialization, meaningful roles, as well as information and advice continue, and the amount of assistance may become even more critical. Again, as can be seen in Table 2.1, both the informal and formal systems provide similar and overlapping services to meet these needs.

Finally, when frailty is greatest, the fluidity between the various elements in the social care system is particularly noteworthy. One might correctly assume that the formal sector would take on greater importance in the care of the frail, less functionally able elderly. Such

TABLE 2.1 Major Tasks Performed by Informal, Mediating and Formal Systems According to Level of Functional Impairment of Elderly

Level of Competency		Informal System	Mediating and Formal Systems
Low	Frail Impaired 10%	Co-residence Total Money Management Assistance in home—extensive, light heavy housekeeping, meals, shopping, etc. Personal Care—washing, bathing, super-vision of medical regimes, etc.	Institutional Care Protective Service Case management, counseling—older person and/or families, self-help groups Respite Service—Day Hospital, Day Care, Special Set-aside Beds Homemaker Service Home health Aids, Visiting Nurses Meals on Wheels
	Moderately Impaired 30%	System negotiation Help with financial management Accompanying to medical appointments Assistance in home—more frequent, wider array of tasks, *i.e.,* shopping, occasional mealr preparation, light housekeeping	Linkage to Services, counseling older person Escort, Transportation Friendly Visiting Congregate Housing Chore Service—limited in time and amount
High	Well-elderly 60% of Population	Assistance when ill—short-term Assistance in home—short-term Escort, transportation Advice Gifts, money Visiting, providing affective support	Reduced Fare Programs on Public Transportation Information and Referral Assistance with Entitlements, Cultural and Spiritual Enrichment Programs Socialization, recreation opportunities i.e., Senior Center, nutrition, parks
			Provider of Service

Note: The services shown are cumulative and it is assumed that any services shown in the levels below will continue to be available if a shift is evident in terms of adult day care and institutional services. Additionally, the availability of formal community services is particularly critical in the case of older people with insufficient social networks to meet their needs, for example, those without children nearby or those requiring highly specialized, medically oriented assistance. But, in fact, the vast majority of frail elderly are cared for by family, sometimes with supplemental help from formal providers (Shanas, 1979b). The extensive research on informal caregiving undertaken in the United States in the 1980s and 1990s suggests that family members and significant others perform similar tasks as paid homemakers, home health aides, and case managers (see Table 2.1). Thus, throughout later life the types of services utilized and the source of assistance are, in any given situation, a function of several factors, including the level of frailty, the needs of the individual, the preferences on the part of both the older person and the family regarding the appropriate source of assistance, the effects of these preceding factors on the total family system, and the availability of appropriate services in the formal sector (Cantor 1989; 1994).

To recapitulate, the Social Care Model of the elderly proposed here has five major properties:

1. Social care consists of a constellation of separate elements that serve as sources of social support.
2. Social support elements form a continuum based on the degree of social distance from the older person, for example, kin being closest to the older person and government bodies being farthest away.
3. There is a parallel continuum involving the degree of bureaucracy of the support element, from loose informal structures to highly organized formal service providers and governmental bodies.
4. Exchanges and interdependencies occur among these elements, with interactions flowing in several directions and between elements found at different degrees of social distance from the older person.
5. Several elements may provide the same or similar services either concurrently or *in seriatim.*

Furthermore, this model of social care has attributes that make it equally applicable to elderly and younger populations across the life span. With its notion of concentric circles the Social Care Model emphasizes the relatedness of the informal and formal components, which must both be part of a responsive social care system. The model further underscores the fluidity and overlap of the components of social care, making clear that individual elements and the boundaries between them are affected by a host of factors, including the characteristics of the aging cohort, health and health care systems, economic and social trends, and the important role played by ethnicity, culture, and class in determining the patterning of social care for specific groups of the elderly population, as will be illustrated in this book. Perhaps most importantly, the Social Care Model, with its placement of the older person at the center and informal support elements in closest proximity, clearly illustrates that changes in the status of older people and the availability of informal care are crucial to what will occur with respect to the other, more distant support elements and to social care in the industrialized world, and in time, the developing world as well (Cantor, 1991).

MICRO LEVEL THEORETICAL FORMULATIONS OF SOCIAL CARE

In the previous section, we examined the construct of social care from the macro or societal level as it presently operates in the United States with the Social Care Model. Equally important to a conceptual understanding of social care is to approach the provision of assistance to older people at the micro or individual level. These more micro level theories are informative in terms of comprehending how older people interact with those in close proximity, as well as the mechanisms governing how particular support elements are selected in the variety of situations involving need for assistance. This understanding is especially pertinent given the nature of the Social Care Model, with the older person at the center involved in constantly changing patterns of support exchanges. Considerable gerontological research has been devoted to increasing our knowledge of both the nature of support exchanges within the informal social network—represented by the two innermost circles in the Social Care Model—as well as the way in which particular support elements are activated in times of need. We examine two heuristic models arising from this research, starting first with conceptualizations pertaining to the interpersonal relationships between elderly people and informal networks in general, and later examining social support preferences.

EXCHANGE THEORY/EQUITY THEORY

One approach to interpersonal relationships of a supportive nature stresses the notion of exchange and the necessity for an equilibrium between the needs of one party and the ability of the other person to fulfill such needs. Sussman (1976) notes that exchange provides the most viable explanation of primary group relations, and thus lies at the core of all assistance provided by members of informal networks. The components of these exchanges as specified by Sussman and later Dowd (1978) include cost, reward, profit, and reinforcement. Thus, in any given exchange, each person is interested in the avoidance of pain and the maximization of pleasure in the broadest interpretation. Rewards for members in interactions may not always be equal, though equality is clearly preferable. But individuals sometimes remain in the exchange situation because the relationship, although unequal, provides rewards that are considered more satisfying than the alternatives. Dependent elderly persons who are abused by family caregivers, but prefer to tolerate the mistreatment to continue dwelling in the community rather than face institutionalization are an extreme example of this situation. Sussman (1976, 1977) also emphasizes another important proposition of exchange theory—distributive justice—particularly as it applies to family situations. Distributive justice in exchange interactions is very pertinent to questions involving inheritance, as well as determining how family members share the burden of caring for frail and disabled elderly relatives. It should also be stressed that exchanges and the exercise of power are not limited to financial or instrumental forms of assistance, but are equally germane to exchanges based on purely emotional or psychosocial needs (Dowd, 1980).

Reciprocity is clearly basic to exchange theory and to other theories of social support as well. In the case of families, patterns of reciprocity are built over many years. And norms of filial responsibility and family cohesiveness play a large part in exchanges between the elderly and their kin (Bengtson & DeTerre, 1980; Bengtson & Treas, 1980; Horowitz and Shindelman, 1982; McCullock, 1990; Troll, 1971, 1987; 1989). In his extensive study of family and support relationships among the elderly of Australia, Kendig (1986) underscores the importance of such bonds between family members, but notes in a cautionary vein, that while such bonds may predispose, they by no means determine positive exchanges between children and their older parents. Furthermore, Reinhardt (1996) notes that, ". . . significant others may not only provide support, but also be a source of conflict and disappointment."

Thus, the difficulty and rarity of withdrawing from reciprocal bonds, particularly in the case of families, has both positive and negative aspects. On the one hand, such bonds open the possibilities for complex intergenerational relationships and exchanges, but on the other hand, reciprocal bonds used as levers in exchange situations can also engender feelings of guilt and disapproval in social care transactions. As a result, conflict and negotiations are as powerful forces as conscience and selflessness in any interpersonal exchanges (Kendig, 1986). Interestingly enough, there is a relative paucity of gerontological research on such negative feelings, most likely due to the difficulty on the part of both older and younger family members to express such socially unacceptable feelings, particularly in an interview with an outsider. But clearly, feelings of obligation and guilt, as well as affirmative expressions of emotional bonding, are critical bargaining tools in social exchanges involving not only family members, but also in those involving friends and neighbors.

Although reciprocity is most often associated in the literature with kin relationships, it is also certainly an operable factor in exchanges between older people and their friends and neighbors. The time span of the emotional bonds between older people and nonkin network members may be more limited, but reciprocity of need and assistance is still an underlying component of informal interactions of a supportive nature. As in the case of family support, the extent to which the needs of both parties in friend dyads are met will determine the level of equilibrium achieved and the success of the exchange.

In any given kinship social support exchange, empirical evidence regarding reciprocal helping patterns between generations consistently demonstrates that the person needing assistance and the person responding may be either younger or older (i.e., child to parent or parent to child assistance). Furthermore, findings from the 1970 "The Elderly in the Inner City of New York" (Cantor 1975a; 1975b), as well as the current study, "Growing Older In New York City in the 1990s" (Cantor & Brennan, 1993c) suggest that many older people have both younger and older friends and neighbors with whom they are in mutual exchange relationships.

The role of reciprocity in relationships between the elderly and family members and friends is particularly important in the light of the increasing powerlessness so often associated with old age. Dowd (1978) stresses the need in balanced exchanges for elderly to give as well as to receive. Empirical evidence suggests that reciprocity is an important element in successful aging (Ingersoll-Dayton & Antonucci, 1989). In a study measuring a variety of social support variables, reciprocity emerged as the most important predictor of happiness (Antonucci & Akiyama, 1987, 1989). Furthermore, Rook (1987, 1989) found that asymmetrical exchanges among friends within an older population resulted in feelings of loneliness and dissatisfaction with social relationships, while other data suggest that friendship relationships involving equitable exchanges are more satisfying and positive (Roberto, 1989). However, as is the case with family members, reciprocity among friends may not be judged on the basis of a single exchange, but rather may encompass longer periods of the relationship (Reinhardt, 1996).

Exchange theory, while acknowledging the long-term nature of emotional bonds within the informal social network, is an essentially static approach to understanding the operations of social networks and social care. It is particularly well suited to cross-sectional examinations of specific exchanges, and as a result, has been employed frequently in studies of social networks, caregiving, and social supports under varying conditions (Bengtson, Burgess, & Parrot, 1997).

THE LIFE COURSE PERSPECTIVE—THE CONVOY MODEL

The life course perspective offers another alternative approach to understanding how older people interact in situations involving the need for assistance and how a particular informal support element is selected to meet that need. Kahn and Antonucci (1980; 1984) and Antonucci (1985, 1990) employing a life course perspective, proposed a more inclusive model to describe the dynamics of social networks and the provision of social supports over the life course. This Convoy Model suggests that every person can be thought of as moving through the life course surrounded by a set of persons who provide emotional and instrumental support and to whom support is provided in return. According to Kahn and Antonucci (1980; 1984), the term *convoy* is employed to suggest a picture of a protective layer of family and friends surrounding the individual, who assist the person in navigating the challenges of life. Convoys are dynamic in nature and continue throughout the entire life span. Convoys change in some ways to meet evolving needs, but remain stable in other ways across time and situations. For example, parents and children remain in the convoy throughout life, but the nature of relationships between them may vary over time, as people age and have different experiences and needs (Antonucci, 1990; Antonucci & Akiyama, 1987). Like the Social Care Model, the Convey Model is a structural concept encompassing both individual and situational forces. Furthermore, the convey offers a dynamic approach in line with the life-course perspective, reminding us that the size, structure, and composition of informal social networks change over time in response to varying needs.

In their heuristic image of the convoy, Kahn and Antonucci (1980) designate a set of three circles, not dissimilar from the concentric circles envisioned in the Social Care Model (Cantor, 1975b; 1980; 1991). Each circle represents different levels of closeness to the focal point of the model—the older person. In the nearest circle are the most important informal support providers, persons to whom the individual feels closest and has relationships that transcend time and role requirements. Such relationships are seen as relatively stable and involve exchanges of a variety of types of social support over the life course. Members in this so-called inner circle are likely to be family and are therefore analogous to the persons found in the innermost circle in the Social Care Model.

Members in the second circle of the Convoy Model also represent a degree of closeness and relationships that transcend the simple fulfillment of role requirements. However, while members of the third and outermost circle are conceptualized as having some closeness to the focal point of the convoy (i.e., the older person), it is usually in a more role-prescribed manner. Thus, a coworker or coparticipant in a senior center with whom the older person may have a close relationship that does not transcend the work environment or the center, would be found in this third circle. In the case of elderly, those in the second and third circles of the Convoy Model, the so-called outer circles, are in all likelihood friends and neighbors subsumed in the second circle of the Social Care Model. Compared to outer-circle members, inner-circle members will probably include more family members and friends who are known over a longer period of time and who tend to be in more frequent contact with the older person (Antonucci, & Akiyama, 1987; Kahn, 1994).

Another important postulate of the Convoy Model is that, "structural and functional characteristics among convoy members vary in a normative manner by life-cycle stage, age, and feelings of closeness (circle placement) in a meaningful and predictive manner" (Antonucci & Akiyama, 1987). Because age is an important factor in understanding how these norms operate, the authors have proposed several hypotheses concerning the support convoys of older people:

1. Because of their greater likelihood of experiencing more losses of support members, older people will have smaller informal social support networks than younger people.
2. However, because of increased age, older people will know convoy members for longer periods of time and as a result have builtup more reciprocity in these relationships.
3. As older people tend to be less mobile, their close network members will be geographically closer and in more frequent contact than in the case of younger people.
4. Older people will receive more support than they provide, while the reverse will be the case among younger individuals.
5. Older people will receive support from fewer convoy members, but more support from each member than among younger people.

The first preliminary large-scale test of the Convoy Model was conducted by Antonucci and Akiyama (1987) using a national survey, "Social Networks in Adult Life" (Kahn & Antonucci, 1984), involving a sample of 718 men and women ranging from 50 to 90 years of age. The findings indicated that some, but not all, of the original hypotheses were supported. The most notable exception was that the relationships between age and circle placement in the structure and function of informal social supports was not always as consistent as predicted. However, the relatively enduring nature of perceived support reciprocity at different ages suggests that reciprocity may play a yet underestimated role in the well-being of people of all ages. Such a finding lends credence to the value of a life-span approach to social care as articulated in the Convoy Model. Antonucci and Akiyama (1987) emphasize that, ". . . for social supports to be a useful concept for scientist and service providers, it is necessary that we attain a better understanding of the process and mechanisms through which it operates throughout the life span."

Social support exchanges, particularly in the case of older people, are crucial to one's well-being and, at times, even survival. Such exchanges are often very complex, involving several actors, and frequently are based on long-term relationships covering the life-span, as well as more time-limited exchanges. Thus, the life-course Convoy Model would appear to offer a more comprehensive approach to social care than encompassed in the more time-limited, narrowly based exchange or equity theory perspective.

COMPARISON OF THEORIES OF
SOCIAL SUPPORTS IN LATER LIFE

In the previous sections we discussed three models of social support that have received attention in the gerontological literature. The Social Care and the Convoy Models have much in common. The Social Care Model (Cantor, 1975b; 1980; 1991) is a systemic approach describing how social care is provided and accessed by older people in the United States. As originally presented, it was a cross-sectional examination at a single time period. However, the approach could be easily be adapted to a longitudinal study describing how social care has been provided over time, with the relative importance of the various informal and formal components at different periods reflecting historic changes both in attitudes and social conditions. As previously noted, the Social Care Model envisions the older person at the center of a series of concentric circles. The inner two circles contain members of the informal support system: kin, friends, and neighbors. The two outer circles include other players in society, both mediating and formal sources of social support, whose actions impinge on the lives of elderly and whom the elderly influence in turn. Thus, the Social Care Model is inclusive of both formal and informal components.

In contrast, the Convoy Model (Antonucci, 1985; 1990; Kahn & Antonucci, 1980; 1984) focuses only on informal elements of the social care system and postulates in greater detail the nature of social relationships and networks found in the two inner circles of the Social Care Model. But the Convoy Model, like the Social Care Model, is a structural concept and encompasses a variety of actors with different roles and relationships to the older person, who, in both models, serves as the focal point. Encompassing a life-course perspective, the dynamic nature of the Convoy Model is illustrated by the changing nature of network membership as time and altering roles influence the size, nature, and composition of convoy membership. In the Social Care Model, on the other hand, the dynamic nature is suggested by exchanges between all sectors of society, as well as between players within each circle. Thus, in both cases, exchanges are not confined to single dyads, and there is a fluidity encompassing changing needs, as well as changing providers of support. On the other hand, the

Exchange Theory (or its outgrowth, the Equity Theory) is more static, particularly from a life-course perspective, and encompasses only the mechanism of discrete exchanges between two persons in specific situations.

Although all models emphasize different aspects of the reality of social care, they each, in their own way, contribute to our understanding of how older individuals needs are provided for as dependency increases with age. In a sense, they can be seen as providing a hierarchy of theoretical approaches to social care. The Social Care Model, the most comprehensive of the three, involves a system-wide approach, stressing the interaction of both informal and formal components of the social support system of older people. The Convoy Model is limited to describing the informal system, with an emphasis on how informal social support is provided over the life course. It postulates changes in the nature of informal networks in providing both instrumental and emotional assistance influenced by age and role relationships. The Exchange Theory focuses on the specific interactions occurring between people as they operate in dyadic relationships of an exchange nature. Depending on the nature of the question, all three theories offer important insights into the nature of social care and the mechanisms by which the needs of individual elderly are met.

Table 2.2 illustrates how each model or theory helps to illuminate the process of providing social care to elderly individuals by showing the focus of the respective models or theories and the major questions addressed by each approach.

PART II: PREFERENCES, SUBSTITUTION AND SPECIALIZATION: HOW OLDER PEOPLE SELECT PROVIDERS OF ASSISTANCE

INTRODUCTION

The foregoing discussion has presented three major theoretical models regarding the social relationships of older people involving social care exchanges. We now turn to the second level of analysis of the mechanisms of social care: How do older people decide which component of the Social Care Model (i.e., kin, friends/neighbors, or formal organizations) to turn to in time of need? The activation of specific providers of social care involves several issues, including the preferences of older persons regarding who should assist them in

TABLE 2.2 Comparison of Three Theories of Social Support to Elderly Persons

Model/theory	Focus	Major questions
Social Care Model Cantor (1975, 1980, 1991)	System-wide Informal and Formal Component Interactions Between Informal and Formal Components	Who is responsible for the care of the elderly? What is the role of informal and formal components? To what extent do informal and formal providers interact and complement each other in the provision of social care to the elderly?
Convoy Model Kahn & Antonucci, 1980 Antonucci, 1985, 1990	Informal Social Networks Over the Life Course	How does the informal system function over the life-course? What is the nature of the social networks of older people, their size, membership, and nature of support? What is the impact of time and social roles on such networks?
Exchange/ Equity Theory Sussman, 1976 Dowd, 1975	Individual Dyadic Exchanges	What are the principles underlying specific exchanges? How is maximum satisfaction of both parties to the exchange achieved? Is reciprocity of exchange always necessary for satisfaction? How does loss of power associated with aging affect the nature of supportive exchanges?

times of need; whom do they actually turn to in specific situations; and to what extent can kin, friends and neighbors, and community agencies substitute for each other; and how does the process of substitution occur?

In the following sections, we will describe the major theoretical models regarding support preferences, relationship specialization, and the process of substitution. This discussion will focus on whom older people turn to for assistance. Is this choice based primarily on normative and psychological notions of appropriateness and closeness as suggested by Cantor in her hierarchical-compensatory model (1979b; 1985) or are choices a function of the nature of the tasks involved and the characteristics endemic to the various types of support elements as postulated by Litwak (1965; 1985; Litwak & Messeni, 1989). And finally, to what extent is the choice of a particular element an issue of compensation or replacement and thus dependent on the availability of that element? It should be noted that a corollary question beyond the scope of the research reported in this book concerns the relative effects of different persons providing support in terms of health, well-being, and social functioning. Thus, as Rook (1996) notes, ". . . network replacements don't necessarily yield the same health related benefits as the network ties or functions that are missing."

In considering issues of whom older people turn to for help, it is important to remember that social networks are dynamic, and such fluidity is particularly evident in the case of the older person. As one ages, one suffers losses of kin and significant others through death and geographic dispersion, making it less likely that an elderly person will have the full array of informal support elements (i.e., spouse, children, siblings, other relatives, friends, and neighbors). In addition, there is a difference between having an element and having a *functional element*, defined by Cantor (1979b) as someone who is near enough or in frequent enough contact with the older person to make providing assistance reasonably possible. Thus the ability to substitute one support element for another is highly relevant to the smooth operation of any social support system. If an older person has a preference to turn to a spouse or child for help, and these individuals are absent from the informal network, the person to be relied on in times of need may be very different than in the case of an older person with a large network with all elements present and functional. It is with respect to substitution that age, degree of frailty, and above all, cultural and class norms make a crucial difference.

Additionally, there is the question of the degree of specialization of the tasks to be performed and to what extent can one network member easily substitute for another. The issue of specialization becomes particularly acute in times of greater frailty and dependency, when there is a greater need for technical skills, long-term commitment, and often physical strength and stamina beyond the reaches of a spouse or older friend. In such situations, older persons and their families are faced with a decision about whether to continue to rely on the informal system or to turn to formal providers of social care. But even in less extreme situations involving the everyday types of help ordinarily provided by family members, questions of substitution and specialization are an integral part of the process in which older people select who will assist them as needed.

SUPPORT PREFERENCES AND ACTUALIZATION OF ASSISTANCE

As noted previously, the social care system of elderly individuals is comprised of both informal and formal sectors. Looking first at the informal sector three major components can be identified: kin, close friends and intimates, and neighbors. In addition, there is the formal sector comprised of governmental and community agencies who help to insure that older people can retain independence as long as possible. It is possible to think of the support system and who is mobilized to assist in particular situations as operating according to four alternative models, outlined by Cantor (1979b):

Additive Model—each support element performs randomly chosen tasks that when added together increases the social care available to an older person.

Asymmetrical Model—one element dominates all forms of support, and no other element is considered appropriate or involved. Research findings to date support neither of these first two models.

Task-Specific Model—was postulated by Litwak (1965; Litwak & Szelny, 1969, 1985) as part of his theory of shared functions, addressed the difference between primary groups and formal organizations, their characteristics, and functions in terms of social support. Both were considered crucial to the well being of elderly persons, although they played different roles. According to this model the nature of the task and the characteristics of the various support elements determine who, in any given situation, will be involved. Preferences for specific providers receives minimal attention, and emphasis is placed on the match between structure and task, with bureaucratic organizations best able to perform tasks calling for technical skills, and primary social groups most suited to tasks that require geographic proximity, commitment, or face-to-face contact. Through such matches greater effectiveness and efficiency would be realized.

The kinship system is seen as most appropriately providing the traditional kin-associated support involving long-term history and intimacy. But given the geographic dispersion of many children, only those tasks not requiring proximity or immediacy would be appropriate for kin. Neighbors, on the other hand, can be expected to assist with tasks requiring speed of response, knowledge of the older person, and presence in the immediate area. Friends are uniquely able to deal with situations involving peer group status and similarity of experience, making them particularly well suited to provide companionship and emotional support. A spouse, although not specifically mentioned, would presumably be able to provide all types of assistance, limited only by personal resources and level of skill (Dono, Falbe, Kail, Litwak & Sherman, 1979).

It is important to note that the Task-Specific Model does not provide for substitutions, and if a particular element is absent, the extent to which another element could take its place is not specified. Thus, this model presumes a high degree of specialization and a limited degree of substitution. Litwak does suggest that if there is a group with some of the properties of the missing group, they may provide some of the support, but of a "variant" nature (Rook & Schuster, 1996).

The Task-Specific Model postulated by Litwak was originally based on a well-established tradition in sociology. This tradition classifies group structure along dimensions of proximity, length of commitment, commonality of life style, and size, in the case of primary groups and type of motivation, division of labor, and level of technical knowledge with respect to formal organizations (Messeri, Silverstein, & Litwak, 1993). Litwak (1985) tested his model with data from a 1978 study of 1,818 older adults, about one fourth of whom resided in institutions and three fourths in noninstitutional settings in New York and Florida. The findings revealed that different primary groups (neighbors, friends, modified extended family, and spouse) provided different types of services and support, such as, watching the house, providing companionship, care during illness, and housekeeping, according to their hypothesized structural competence.

In addition, substitutability by primary groups was limited, and those who lacked a particular group were likely to suffer because of this absence. For example, older people without friends were more likely to report having no one with whom to share leisure time activities (Rook, 1996). However, Litwak (1985) did find that other kin were more likely to provide services for childless older adults or for those whose children were unavailable, than was the case for older people with available children.

Hierarchical-Compensatory Theory of Social Supports—in this model the function of support provision is ordered according to the primacy of the relationship of the helper to the elderly recipient rather than defined by the nature of the task. This model postulates a hierarchical order of preference in the choice of support element in line with the value system of the current cohort of elderly persons. Kin are generally preferred as the most appropriate support providers, followed by nonrelated significant others (i.e., friends and neighbors), and lastly by formal organizations. When the initially preferred element is absent, other groups act in a compensatory manner as replacements. This theory specifically involves substitution, and suggests that if a particular person is unavailable the next person in the hierarchy of preferences will be called on by the older person for assistance. It is important to emphasize that the choice of support elements is based on both psychological feelings of closeness, normative values, such as filial responsibility and family solidarity, and the history of the relationships between the older person and other parties involved.

Cantor's Hierarchical-Compensatory Theory grew out of findings from the 1970 study, "The Elderly in the Inner City of New York" (see chapter I). In this study, 1552 older White, African American, and Hispanic older persons were presented with a series of 10 hypothetical critical incidents in which assistance might be needed. The situations were grouped according to the area of need under the broad rubric of instrumental (health, financial, tasks of daily living), affective (loneliness, talk about a family problem), and informational (assistance in filling out a form) domains. For each situation, respondents were asked to choose whom, other than spouse, they would most likely turn to for assistance. (Spouse was purposely omitted because of the closeness of the relationship and the presumption that they would be likely to be called on first in most circumstances.) The choice of helpers ranged over the full spectrum of the support system (with the exception of spouse) and included children, other relatives, friends, neighbors, formal organizations, or no one or self. The majority of respondents, regardless of the situation, evidenced a decided and clear preference for turning to kin when in need of assistance. Only a minority mentioned a friend or neighbor as first preference, while formal organizations were a choice of last resort. The same battery was repeated in the 1990 study, and the most recent findings will be compared with the original 1970 results in chapter 3.

To better understand the process of compensation and substitution involved in the Hierarchical Compensatory Theory, the 1552 respondents from "The Elderly In The Inner City" were further divided into four groups according to the nature and functionality of their informal support networks: nuclear—having a functional spouse or child; distant kin—without a functional spouse or child but with functional siblings and other relatives; family-less—without functional kin but having functional friends or neighbors; and those with *no functional support* (Cantor, 1979b). In the 10 critical incidents, those in the nuclear kin group usually preferred these close kin, followed by siblings or other relatives. Older New Yorkers with distant kin networks and those without functional family supports tended to turn more frequently to friends and neighbors for support. Thus, preferences for support elements appear to involve both the interaction of normative hierarchical preferences and the availability of preferred elements in times of need, with the nature of the task assuming a more secondary role.

Additional analyses of who took care of respondents during times of illness further illuminated the operation of the Hierarchical Compensatory Theory. Older New Yorkers with functional close kin were most likely to be cared for by a spouse or child, regardless of the duration of the illness. Virtually no one reported being without assistance when a functional spouse or child was present. Among those with only functional distant kin, responsibility for care during illness was shared initially between siblings and other more distant relatives (e.g., cousins, nieces, and nephews) and friends and neighbors. However, as the duration of the illness increased among older persons with functional distant kin, these family members became less involved, with the caregiving role shifted to friends and neighbors. But it is with respect to the family-less elderly that the compensatory role of friends and neighbors is most strikingly illustrated. In cases of illness of 1 week or less in duration, the family-less elderly reported caring for themselves, forgoing outside assistance. However, as illness increased in duration beyond 1 week, friends and neighbors, and to a lesser extent, formal organizations, assumed the bulk of responsibility for care.

In summarizing the Hierarchical-Compensatory Theory of Social Supports and the findings on which it was based, Cantor (1979b) notes:

> Among the present generation of elderly, kin are clearly considered the primary source of help, regardless of the task. Only

to the extent that family, particularly spouse and children, are not available, and with respect to certain well-defined tasks, do friends, neighbors, and formal organizations become important in the provision of informal supports. Thus, for example, in the arena of socialization and the provision of day-to-day companionship, friends and neighbors play a highly significant role. Likewise, friends and neighbors are helpful in providing short-term service of an emergency nature, such as shopping in inclement weather or help when one is taken ill. But their most important function appears to be as compensatory support elements when kin and children are non-existent or unavailable. The nature of the task, in contrast, though certainly a factor, appears of less importance in the determination of which primary group members are called upon. Rather the hierarchical nature of social preference and the replacement or compensatory role of non-kin seem to be paramount.

Although the Hierarchical Compensatory Theory of Social Supports was developed inductively based on empirical findings to account for regularities found in the social support systems of older people, its formulation rest on a strong theoretical basis in psychology. Most fundamental are the concepts of ego development and psychological bonding, which suggest that a person's definition of self is reflected in those with whom one is intimate. Notions of love, hate, affection, intimacy, nurturance, and the positive and negative ramifications of dependency are included in this broad concept of psychological bonding (Cantor & Hirshorn, 1989). A further extension of the psychological importance of intimacy and bonding is manifested in the notion that turning first to those one feels closest to for assistance, usually kin, inflicts the least damage to an older person's ego and sense of self-reliance. Closely related to, and perhaps overlapping with, this notion of psychological bonding is the concept of family solidarity as expressed by family sociologists (Bengtson, 1986; Rosenthal & Burton, 1990; Bengtson, 1985; Bengtson & DeTerre, 1980; Markides, Boldt, & Laura, 1986; Troll, Miller & Atchley, 1979; Troll, 1971).

RELEVANT RESEARCH ON PREFERENCE, CHOICE, AND
SUBSTITUTION IN SOCIAL SUPPORT NETWORKS

The mechanisms by which older people obtain the support they need, including their preferences for who should provide support, who actually performs the tasks, and the extent to which one support element is substitutable for another, has been a subject of much interest in gerontological literature. In the previous section we presented four possible models of how older people access assistance at times of need. The two models discussed in detail were the Hierarchical-Compensatory and Task-Specific Models, and it is these models that are most often referred to in gerontological literature on informal support provision to the elderly. Before reviewing the current research, it is important to reiterate that each model flows out of a different conceptual framework, uses different assessment approaches, and poses very different questions when drawing inferences about choice, specialization, and substitution.

The major thrust of the Hierarchical-Compensatory Theory is preference—who would older people choose, all things being equal, to assist them with a series of instrumental and affective needs. Furthermore, given the absence or inability of a preferred choice to provide assistance, whom are they next mostly likely to turn to and in what order? Thus the model involves a hierarchy of choices and presumes that support providers serve as generalists rather than as specialists and comes down firmly on the potential substitution of one element for another (Rook, 1996). The emphasis on preference was chosen both to better understand the mechanisms through which older people access help in different situations, and to probe the relative importance of primary groups and formal organizations in the operation of the broader system of social support postulated in Cantor's (1979b) Social Care Model. Validation of the Hierarchical-Compensatory Theory, in practice, would involve whether there appears to be a relatively well-ordered preference in the choice of helpers according to their social distance from the older person. In the absence of a preferred support element, would another element substitute, with the nature of the task being of secondary importance?

Litwak's (1965) Task-Specific model, in contrast, is concerned with the effectiveness of the match between the person and the task irrespective of preference or actual use. In the application of the model in Litwak's (1985) work, the emphasis is on the degree of congruency between the characteristics of the support element and the nature of the task. The model proposes that both tasks and groups can be classified along parallel sets of dimensions, and that the group most likely to be chosen by the older person to help with a particular task will have the structural features that match those of the task (Litwak, 1985). Based on this concept of match, different primary groups will perform different tasks, and the model presumes a high degree of specialization and minimum substitution. Empirical tests of the Task-Specific Model attempt to show that specific elements (spouse, child, other relatives, friends, and neighbors), in the main, perform specific and different instrumental and affective helping activities. Among the questions posed in recent research involving the application of these two models are:

1. Whom do older people prefer to turn to for instrumental and affective support? Is there a seeming order to their preferences?
2. In different situations of need, who usually provides help?
3. To what extent can different elements substitute or replace each other, or is the nature of the task the defining factor?
4. Do older persons' perceptions regarding the sufficiency and the adequacy of support vary depending on who provides the assistance?

Attempts to shed light on these questions tell us a great deal about how social care is provided to the elderly, whether in situations requiring short-term assistance in carrying out daily tasks of living or more extensive and long-term caregiving associated with greater levels of frailty.

RESEARCH ON SUPPORT PREFERENCES
AMONG ELDERLY PERSONS

Chatters, Taylor, and Jackson (1986) replicated Cantor's initial findings with a nationally representative sample of older Blacks. As was the case among inner city older New Yorkers, Blacks nationwide preferred spouse, children, siblings and other kin, in that order, as providers of support. Nonkin were more likely to be identified as potential caregivers in the case of unmarried elders. In a similar vein, Markides, Belt, and Pray (1986) in a study of three generations of Mexican Americans ($n = 1125$) reported that the older generation in five areas, including advice, instrumental, and emotional help, relied mostly on their sons and daughters.

Shanas (1979a) reporting on findings from a national probability sample of community-dwelling individuals 65 and older, with racial and age distribution in line with the U. S. Census, found that patterns of assistance are based on mutual expectations of each generation of the other. In a process Shanas labeled substitution, older people turn to their families for help because they expect families to help in case of need. When replacements for family are needed, they then turn to neighbors, and lastly to bureaucratic organizations and their representatives (i.e., social workers, ministers, and community agencies). Thus, Shanas found that the immediate close kin (i.e., spouse and children) were the mainstay of ill or homebound elderly, while visits from siblings and other relatives provided the links with the community. Although Shanas did not specify the hierarchy of substitution in as much detail as Cantor's (1979b) model, the emphasis on the primacy of the family, the compensatory role of formal organizations, and the foundation of support resting on intimacy and intergenerational norms of responsibility is very much in line with the postulates of the Hierarchical-Compensatory Model.

Consistent with the notion of compensation and the emphasis on spouse and children followed by distant kin and nonkin as the most preferred sources of support, Johnson (1983) and Johnson and Catalono (1983) found that married couples tended to rely on each other for support, and that in the absence of a spouse, widowed individuals turn to children and siblings, while childless unmarried and never-married elderly rely on siblings and more distant kin for assistance.

Peters, Hoyt, Babchuk, Kaiser, and Iijima (1987) attempted to test the Hierarchical Compensatory and Task-Specific models with a representative sample of 165 older adults residing in a midwestern, nonmetropolitan community by analyzing their support provision. They concluded that, ". . . certain network members are more likely to be selected regardless of whether the assistance needed is instrumental or affective." The elderly participants turned primarily to spouse, followed by adult children, friends, siblings, and other relatives, similar to, but not exactly as specified in, the Hierarchical Compensatory Model.

Another important finding from the Peters et al. (1987) research was that respondents often used multiple helpers both from within and between different primary groups. The authors concluded that the uniformity of their selections for assistance among significant others and the fact that those in the sample sought help from multiple groups for similar types of assistance casts some doubt on Litwak's Task-Specific Model. Rather, the Peters et al. findings emphasized the principle of selectivity in both seeking out and receiving support. This selectivity, conceptually similar to preference, operates in two ways according to the authors. First, some primary group members are more likely to be sought out, with network membership status taking predominance over type of support. Second, persons also select from a given pool of available others for instrumental and emotional support, both within and between primary group members.

Findings of this research suggest the presence of several operable factors in the choice of supportive elements. There is a clear preference for close kin (spouse and children) followed by more distant kin and nonkin regardless of the type of the support required. However, older people also use multiple sources of assistance, coming both from a particular element and between different elements. Although the primacy of preference, as opposed to the nature of the task, is stressed in this research, it is likely that factors such as proximity also affect who will be called on for help.

In a study examining the impact on network composition of changes over time in an older person's health and functional ability, Stoller and Pugliesi (1988) concluded that a pattern of network expansion occurs as frailty increases, consistent with both Antonucci and Akiyama's Convoy Model and the preferred hierarchy described by Shanas (1979a). Frail older people rely first on spouse, then on children and other family members, and finally on outside sources. Particularly significant are the findings that the network of older people in good health may include as helpers marginal or potential sources of support (the neighbors who picks up the mail or the friend who offers a ride), but such people are identified far less frequently in the helping networks of the more impaired elderly whose needs focus on actual provision of assistance with tasks of daily living. Again we see the complexity of choices and the interaction of several factors, including, in this case, preferences for closest kin and health status.

Further support for the order of preferences postulated in the Hierarchical Compensatory model is found in a cross-national study of 1056 community-based adults 60 and over residing in Australia (Kendig & Rowland, 1983). Consistent with the American findings, the study found that spouse and then children are the first recourse in times of need. Other sources serve primarily as supplementary helpers if spouse and children are unavailable, or as substitutes if there are none (Kendig & Rowland, 1983).

EMPIRICAL FINDINGS ON CHOICE OF HELPER
BASED ON NATURE OF THE TASK

As noted earlier, The Task-Specific model postulated by Litwak was originally based on a well-established tradition in sociology classifying group structure along dimensions of proximity, length of commitment, and commonality of life style. Several studies involving more narrowly defined populations and specific types of support lend some empirical support to the Task-Specific Model. Connidas and Davis (1990; 1992) sought in two studies to integrate both the Hierarchical-Compensatory and Task-Specific Models by comparing predictions about who would serve as confidants (i.e., persons whom one would confide in) versus companions (i.e., persons who are regular companions in activities or pastimes outside the home).

In the first study involving 400 older people, Connidas and Davis (1990) concluded that the lack of symmetry between the confident and companion network configurations reported provide some support for the Task-Specific Model. Children were more apt to be selected as confidants, while spouse and friends predominated as companions. In the second study involving married and widowed elderly with children, confidant, and companion networks of those groups who had the same ties were compared as the best way to address the issue of task specificity according to the authors. The most striking observations were: ". . . the greater dominance of a spouse in the companion rather than the confidant network among the married; the greater dominance of children in the confidant than companion network among those with children; the greater dominance of friends in the companion than confidant networks for all groups, and the greater dominance of siblings and other relatives in the confidant than in the companion networks for all groups" (Connidas & Davis, 1992).

Addressing the issue of compensation and substitution, Connidas and Davis (1992) found that when compared to confidant networks of married elderly persons, the networks of previously married contain friends, other relatives, and children to a greater extent. In the absence of proximate children, the companion network of previously married parents is dominated even more by friends.

SUMMARY OF EMPIRICAL FINDINGS PERTAINING TO CHOICE

In attempting to summarize the seemingly contradictory findings with respect to preference, specialization, and substitution that have emerged from the studies of social networks and the provision of support among the elderly population, it is important to reiterate that different conceptualizations of the processes are involved, as well as different ways of assessing support functions and services. Cantor's concern is with who older people prefer as providers of support and

who is most often tapped. Litwak focuses on the type of support provided by different network members and the match between the
nature of the task and the characteristics of the providers. In a thor-
ough review of the support literature, Rook (1996) notes that such conceptual and methodological differences make empirical comparisons
between the two models difficult. Not surprisingly, results of com-
parative studies have afforded evidence both for and against each
model (e.g., Connidas & Davis, 1990; 1992; Peters et al., 1987). In summarizing the literature Rook (1996) notes, "Spouses, children, and then
friends consistently emerge as the most frequent sources of support
in this work, as Cantor would predict based on the hierarchy of preferences. However, this does not necessarily favor Cantor's model over
all others, because some studies have yielded evidence, as well, that
different network members may perform different tasks, as Litwak
would predict."

The difference in who performs what tasks seems most pronounced between instrumental and affective support and is most
affected by the level of frailty of the older person. Instrumental support is more likely to be performed by kin, while friends and neighbors have a particular importance with respect to companionship and
the amelioration of loneliness. Thus Cantor (1979b) in the testing of
preferences regarding who should provide assistance notes that the
one task in which a large proportion of friends are preferred in addition to close kin involves "someone to talk with when you feel lonely."
In summary, with regard to the issue of preferences the evidence is
more conclusive, but with respect to relationship specialization, com-
parative studies in the gerontological literature do not consistently
favor one model over another (Rook, 1996).

But in actuality there is more that is complimentary between these
two models than is commonly assumed. Both the Hierarchical-
Compensatory and Task-Specific Models seem to represent two concurrent dynamics of how older people obtain assistance. Cantor's
theory of preferences is based internally on a person's ego-integrity
and internalized cultural and normative values. In contrast, the Task-
Specific Model is externally oriented and has more to do with the fea-
sibility and availability of particular helpers. Given these different
perspectives, it is logical that an older person's initial preferences
would generally be to turn to those with whom they are closest, with
task specifications being of lesser importance. However, the hierarchy
of choices does not vitiate Litwak's claims regarding the efficiency of
specific primary group members for performing certain tasks. As a

result, within the broad outline of preference, it is more than likely that a frail older person requiring immediate help in getting the mail would turn to a neighbor for assistance rather than to a child living at greater geographical distance. Thus in any given situation, the actual manifestation of support is probably a combination of both preferences for support elements as well as appropriate person matches for the task.

Further, it is important to note that both models perceive the spouse as the most important and inclusive source of social support, and that formal organizations are called on least frequently and only to perform specific functions. Litwak's model ascribes the shared role of informal and formal organizations to the nature of the two groups and their relative abilities arising from differences in the characteristics of primary groups and formal organizations. Cantor ,on the other hand, emphasizes that turning to formal organizations is a last resort for both older people and their families. This feeling that community-based organizations and other formal providers are regarded as a last resort is based on normative values of filial responsibility and culturally based notions of the relative role of family and society in the care of elderly persons. Although the reasoning is different in each model, the end result is that formal organizations are basically seen as replacements for primary groups. However, both Cantor and Litwak stress that the optimum social support for the elderly requires a shared functionality with regard to both informal and formal sources of assistance.

In conclusion, to understand the operation of social support in a given situation, it is probably necessary to consider multiple factors, including preferences about who should provide support, who is actually available to provide assistance, the state of health and functional ability of the older person, and the nature and level of needs. Of equal importance are the cultural and normative values regarding who should appropriately provide assistance to the elderly persons in time of need, as discussed in the following chapter. Furthermore, the needs of older people are fluid and change over time. The availability of helpers is also dynamic, affected by changing situations such as geographic dispersion, health, and family and work responsibilities. Thus, there is a need for longitudinal research to follow the provision of social support to older people over time. Only through such longitudinal investigations can we truly understand the complexity of preference, specialization, and substitution in the provision of social care for current and future cohorts of elderly persons.

In addition, it is important to reiterate that the most important aspect of the Hierarchical-Compensatory Theory of social supports is not merely the ordering of kin preferences, but rather its emphasis on the larger relationships between informal and formal support elements. Thus, it has relevance for social policy and practice, as well as theory building, and speaks to the optimal partnership between informal and formal members of the social care networks of older people. Such a partnership is best able to meet these social support needs, while at the same time it helps to preserve the older individual's independence and sense of personal integrity. In its concurrent examination of both informal and formal systems, while at the same time considering the preference for help from no one, the Hierarchical-Compensatory Theory highlights the primacy of kin and other informal supports without minimizing the need for formal assistance in a variety of situations; thus, it is both an outgrowth of, and an integral part of, the Social Care Model that is the focus of this book.

3

Preferences on the Part of
the Elderly for Assistance

To fully understand the operation of the social care system of the elderly population and the effects of ethnicity and class, it is necessary to know how older people perceive the various sources of assistance and the relative importance they place on the informal as opposed to the formal subsystems. The attitudes of the elderly regarding who should provide assistance in a variety of need situations has considerable relevance for how the social care system of older people in the United States is best structured from a policy and practice perspective.

In chapter 2, we presented the theoretical background regarding older people's preferences for social care. It is clear that elderly people do exercise preferences regarding appropriate sources of assistance, whether the Hierarchical-Compensatory Theory, the Task-Specific Model, or a combination of the two is employed to describe the processes involved. To discover more about the relative feelings regarding the informal and formal subsystems, considerable detail was elicited from respondents regarding support preferences in both the 1970 and 1990 studies of New York's elderly population. Because the identical battery of questions was used at both times, it is possible to not only ascertain the pattern of preferences among these two cohorts, but also to examine whether preferences have changed in the last 20 years. The question of the stability of support preferences among elderly people during the past two decades is particularly interesting in light of the explosive growth of formal community-based services for this population during the same time frame. Furthermore, both the 1970 and 1990 studies' representative samples contained respondents from a wide variety of ethnic groups and socioeconomic strata, with a variety of informal network configurations. This sample diversity permits the analysis of support preferences from several perspectives.

Our examination of support preferences will begin with a cohort comparison between elderly respondents in 1970 and 1990 on the choice of helper for the 10 critical incidents discussed in chapter 2 (see Table 3.1). It should be reiterated that these incidents covered all types of social support including instrumental, emotional, and informational assistance. Following this comparison, we will turn to the important corollary question: What is the impact of ethnicity, culture, and social class on elderly persons preferences for assistance?

PREFERENCES FOR ASSISTANCE: 1970 TO 1990

Table 3.1 presents each of the 10 critical incidents asked about, and the proportion of respondents in 1970 and 1990 choosing the different types of helpers, namely, child, other relatives, a friend or neighbor, a formal organization, or no one/myself as sources of assistance. Because there was considerable overlap in the two samples in the categories of friend and neighbor, these two types of helpers were combined into a single nonkin category.

Most strikingly, the responses of the older people regarding preferences for help in the 10 hypothetical critical incidents were virtually the same in 1970 and 1990. This stability occurred despite the passage of 20 years and the considerable expansion of community services for elderly persons during this period. Furthermore, the 1990 cohort of elderly individuals were better educated than those of 20 years ago, and many, particularly Whites and African Americans, were in improved economic situations relative to previous cohorts. Yet in both periods the majority evidenced a decided and clear preference for turning to kin when in need of assistance. Only a relative few mentioned a friend or neighbor as first preference, while formal organizations were still, in 1990 as in 1970, a choice of last resort. However, the strong feelings regarding the preservation of independence are suggested by the fact that in both periods a small, but not insubstantial proportion responded they would turn to no one/myself. This may, in part, represent social isolation. But for the majority, being self-reliant was, and continues to be, an important norm, particularly in incidents involving money and filling out forms. The extensive public transportation system in New York City (including buses that kneel and accommodate wheel chairs) allows more freedom in getting to doctors or clinics, and is probably reflective of the somewhat higher proportion of no one/myself responses to the item "Someone to take you to the Doctor," than might be found among other older populations in rural or suburban areas.

As noted previously, social support is generally conceptualized as involving three separate types of assistance: instrumental help with tasks of daily living, emotional or affective support, and informational assistance (Kahn & Antonucci, 1980; Lopata, 1975; Tolsdorf, 1976). We will first examine situations requiring instrumental assistance, such as the onset of sudden illness, escort to the doctor, someone to check on apartment or house when you are in the hospital, need for assistance with bathing or taking medicine, and two items involving money (short-term borrowing until the next check and money for a large medical bill). Members of the kin network were clearly the preferred source of assistance in this domain in both periods. Between 40 and 60% of respondents, both in 1970 and 1990, reported they would turn to kin, usually a child, for such instrumental assistance. In fact, if anything, the 1990 respondents reported a slightly stronger preference for support from kin than did their peers 20 years earlier.

The one item of instrumental support in which families were not seen as the primary source of support involved help changing a light bulb in the ceiling. New York City is mainly a rental or co-op market, and it is not uncommon for both older and younger people to request assistance from building personnel for chores involving their dwelling units. Thus, both in 1970 and 1990, over one half of elderly respondents indicated that they would turn to a formal source (the superintendent) or rely on themselves to change a light bulb in the ceiling. But even in this situation, close to one third of both cohorts named as their preferred helper a child or other family member. With respect to instrumental care, friends and neighbors play a minor role, and are rarely mentioned as a preferred source of support (see Table 3.1). The two exceptions, with as many as 25% of the respondents choosing friends or neighbors, included assistance when suddenly feeling dizzy and checking on the apartment. Both of these situations involve proximity and limited assistance.

Two small but discernible shifts in preferences for instrumental assistance that occurred between 1970 and 1990 are noteworthy because of their implications for the future of social care. In 1990, financial assistance with a large medical bill was far less likely to be

TABLE 3.1 Preferred Sources of Assistance (Other than Spouse) at the Elderly of New York City in 1970 and 1990 (Valid Percent[a])

Type of Assistance	Informal		Formal	Myself-No one
	Kin	Nonkin	Formal	No one
Instrumental help				
Suddenly feel sick or dizzy				
NYC Elderly-1970	42	25	15	18
NYC Elderly-1990	[46]	[24]	[14]	[17]
Borrow money until next check comes				
NYC Elderly-1970	40	19	6	36
NYC Elderly-1990	[45]	[13]	[2]	[41]
Change lightbulb in ceiling				
NYC Elderly-1970	27	14	17	42
NYC Elderly-1990	[29]	[10]	[24]	[38]
Someone to take you to the doctor				
NYC Elderly-1970	42	27	11	18
NYC Elderly-1990	[47]	[16]	[12]	[24]
Need money for large medical bill				
NYC Elderly-1970	34	9	21	35
NYC Elderly-1990	[38]	[4]	[14]	[45]
Someone to check apartment if in the hospital				
NYC Elderly-1970	49	14	17	42
NYC Elderly-1990	[59]	[24]	[4]	[13]

TABLE 3.1 (continued)

Type of Assistance	Kin	Informal Nonkin	Formal	Myself-No one
Someone to bathe you or help with medication				
NYC Elderly-1970	46	25	15	18
NYC Elderly-1990	[47]	[11]	[21]	[20]
Emotional support				
Lonely and want to talk				
NYC Elderly-1970	38	40	2	20
NYC Elderly-1990	[38]	[34]	[6]	[17]
Information				
Talk about child or family problem				
NYC Elderly-1970	41	27	4	26
NYC Elderly-1990	[41]	[23]	[4]	[24]
Help filling out a form				
NYC Elderly-1970	45	21	5	28
NYC Elderly-1990	[45]	[10]	[7]	[35]

[a]Totals equal 100%.
[b]Elderly of Inner City of New York-1970 ($n = 1552$); Growing Older In New York City-1990 ($n = 1577$).

seen as falling within the province of the formal system than was the case in 1970. The desire for financial independence among older people in the 1990 sample was very strong. Most respondents indicated that they would prefer to handle the bill themselves, or if necessary, turn for help to a child or other relative. However, it is also important to note that a larger proportion of the 1990 cohort were more financially secure than was true in 1970.

The second trend in changing attitudes between the two cohorts concerns the willingness to turn to community agencies with respect to care in the home ("someone to come in and bathe you and help you with your medicine"). Although most of the older persons in both cohorts preferred help from family in this situation, in 1990, 21% indicated a willingness to consider assistance from a formal agency as compared with only 15% in 1970. Other than changing a light bulb in the ceiling, in-home care was the only critical incident reflecting even a minimal preference for a formal agency in the provision of instrumental assistance. This attitudinal shift toward a greater willingness to rely on formal in-home care in 1990, although far from universal, was also reflected in the increased use of home care services reported in 1990 as compared with 1970.

With respect to the two other types of social support asked about—emotional support and informational assistance—in both 1970 and 1990 the overwhelming preference for support from the informal as opposed to the formal system was clearly evident. The preference for kin (see Table 3.1) is particularly striking, both with respect to the need for someone to talk with about child or family problems and help in filling out forms. Both of these needs often require specialized expertise and are often considered to be within the domain of formal organizations. Yet less than 10% of New York City's elderly population think in terms of assistance from community agencies when having such needs, with clear preferences for either children or other relatives as sources of support. Furthermore, in 1990 about one third felt they could handle filling out forms themselves, as compared with a somewhat smaller group in 1970, which may reflect the higher educational level of the current cohort of older people.

The one area in which friends or neighbors are seen as playing a more important role is in providing assistance as buffers against loneliness. Slightly over one third in both 1970 and 1990 indicated a preference for turning to a friend or neighbor when lonely and wanting companionship. However, even in this area, which is so appropriately the domain for friend or confidant involvement, almost as many respondents in both cohorts selected a family member (e.g., a child or other relative) as their preferred choice for emotional support. The crucial role of children in addition to spouse as the cornerstone of family support systems is illustrated when the kin choices are dichotomized into children and other relatives. In the case of all seven instrumental incidents and one of the two informational situations (i.e., filling out forms), children clearly outranked other relatives as preferred sources of assistance in both 1970 and 1990. Therefore the closeness of the parent-child bond, coupled with the fact that many other relatives such as siblings may themselves be older and unable to provide much direct assistance, places children and spouse at the center of the informal support system of older people. However, in addition to the marital relationship and factors of intergenerational bonding and reciprocity, the nature of the task is also a consideration for some elderly respondents. As previously noted, when respondents were lonely and wanted someone to talk with, about 40 percent of the respondents in both time periods mentioned a friend or neighbors. Problems with children and family are shared primarily with other relatives or with friends, although even in this area 18% in 1990 and 23% in 1970 named a child as their first choice. The foregoing underscores the hierarchical order of preference with respect to avenues of social support, starting with the close-kin bonds, and radiating out in some situations to involve friends or neighbors, and rarely, if ever, including formal organizations, except as a choice of last resort.

THE EFFECT OF RACE AND ETHNICITY ON PREFERENCES FOR SUPPORT

With the increased recognition of the diversity of the elderly population has come a greater interest in how ethnicity and culture affect the nature and operation of the informal social support system. If in 1990, as was the case in 1970, older New Yorkers evidenced a hierarchical-compensatory pattern of preference, starting with close relatives, particularly children in addition to a spouse where present, and then moving outward to nonkin and formal organizations if needed, is this pattern equally applicable to the three major ethnic subgroups in the sample, namely, White, African American, and Latino elderly? The overall pattern of choices was similar among all three groups, with children and to a lesser extent other relatives being clearly dominant, particularly with respect to the instrumental tasks (see Table 3.2). But even with respect to emotional and informational assistance, where the proportion of respondents regardless of ethnicity mentioning friends or neighbors increases somewhat, kin were still the primary choice of a most older New Yorkers. Among all three groups only a relatively few older people indicated that they would turn to the formal system except in such instances as changing a light bulb, or, in the case of Black and Hispanic elderly among whom poverty is more prevalent, help with money for a large medical bill. In contrast to their minority counterparts, White elderly respondents were somewhat more likely to consider formal providers as appropriate sources of assistance when needing personal care, such as help with bathing or taking medicine (see table 3.2).

Although the overall pattern of preference was similar among all three groups, there were some notable differences with regard to the importance of children, versus other possible support elements among the Latino compared to Black and White older New Yorkers. In all 10 critical incidents, Latino elderly respondents were significantly more likely to mention a child as the preferred source of assistance than were either Whites or Blacks, and the proportion choosing a child in each case far exceeded the proportions found among the other groups. Thus, in all 10 situations, children were chosen most frequently by Latinos as their preferred source of help. African Americans selected a child most often in five situations involving mainly instrumental help, such as checking on an apartment when ill, providing personal care during times of frailty or illness, and assistance filling out forms. In three situations (two of which involved money matters), as well as in the remaining two areas involving need for emotional support and someone to talk with about family problems, Blacks chose other relatives or friends as their most preferred source of help.

White elderly respondents, on the other hand, were the least likely to select a child, choosing a child most frequently in only four situations. Again, similar to the Black elderly, all such situations involved sudden illness or needing personal care and assistance because of frailty. In four situations, Whites preferred to rely on no one or themselves most often, the first two involving money matters, the next regarding help changing a light bulb, and lastly for help with filling out forms. Presumably, the relatively higher educational level of the White respondents made independence in this final area a more likely choice. Among White elderly, friends, neighbors and other relatives were the preferred choice for emotional assistance and someone to talk with about problems pertaining to the family. Among African American and White

TABLE 3.2 Preferred Sources of Assistance (Other than Spouse): Comparison Among White, African American and Latino Older New Yorkers in 1990 (Valid Percent[a,b])

Type of assistance		Informal			Myself-no one	No response
		Kin	Nonkin	Formal		
Instrumental help						
Suddenly feel	White	44	24	15	12	6
sick or dizzy	African American	48	26	11	10	6
	Latino	55	19	8	13	5
Borrow money until	White	45	13	2	32	10
next check comes	African American	42	17	2	34	7
	Latino	53	10	1	32	5
Change lightbulb	White	25	11	25	37	4
in ceiling	African American	35	9	21	32	4
	Latino	47	8	25	17	4
Someone to take	White	46	15	15	22	3
you to the doctor	African American	48	9	9	15	6
	Latino	54	7	6	16	4
Need money for	White	30	4	12	33	13
large medical bill	African American	31	5	21	25	18
	Latino	41	3	16	23	18
Someone to check	White	56	27	4	8	5
apartment if	African American	64	19	3	6	8
in the hospital	Latino	69	14	3	8	6

TABLE 3.2 (continued)

Type of assistance	Informal		Formal	Myself-no one	No response
	Kin	Nonkin			
Someone to bathe you or help with medication					
White	45	11	24	9	12
African American	51	15	15	7	13
Latino	58	10	13	8	12
Emotional support					
Lonely and want to talk					
White	47	34	2	16	1
African American	42	39	4	10	5
Latino	56	27	2	9	6
Information					
Talk about child / family problem					
White	49	23	4	18	6
African American	45	27	6	16	6
Latino	54	20	2	18	6
Help filling out a form					
White	46	10	6	35	4
African American	55	10	8	24	4
Latino	61	13	9	14	3

[a]Totals equal 100%.
[b]Growing Older In New York City-1990 (*n* = 1577).

elderly persons, in situations where no one/self was the most frequent response, a child was usually the second most often preferred source, again emphasizing the primacy of children in the support hierarchy of all three ethnic groups.

Findings on support preferences in 1970 and 1990 suggest that there may be differing cultural assumptions regarding the appropriate support element in the case of the Latino elderly respondents compared to those underlying the preferences among African American and White older New Yorkers. Although all three groups reported a child as the principal support preference, among Latinos there was virtually no other choice made beyond children and other family members, regardless of the situation or the suitability of children or kin to perform the tasks involved. Receiving help from children, and to a lesser extent from other relatives and sometimes neighbors, is strongly sanctioned and is an integral part of the extended family culture brought from Puerto Rico, the Dominican Republic, and other parts of Central and Latin America from which the majority of New York's Latino older persons originate, particularly the more recent arrivals. The strength of cultural expectations regarding the role of children (and other kin when children are not present) was clearly evident among Latino elderly respondents, and only rarely was turning to formal agencies considered to be an option.

Among the other two groups an interesting duality appears to exist. On the one hand, among a small but not insignificant group of Black and White elderly, there is a clear preference for self-reliance whenever possible. On the other hand, if assistance is required, especially at times of illness or to provide opportunities for socialization and sharing of personal problems, it is clearly considered appropriate among Black and White elderly to turn to children, other relatives, and friends or neighbors for help. Further, there are some situations when turning to the formal system may be considered the better choice, particularly if such assistance contributes to continued independence (e.g., assistance in the home in the face of incapacity or the need for help to get to a doctor or clinic). But for all three groups of older New Yorkers, both in 1970 and 1990, turning to community agencies was generally the least preferred choice. However, among older people there appears to be a recognition that the level of skill provided by the formal sector was sometimes needed, and there may come a time where help from community agencies may be desirable, albeit not preferable.

The findings from 1990 reinforce the earlier 1970 findings, suggesting that for elderly persons of all ethnic and cultural backgrounds, the Hierarchical-Compensatory Theory of Social Supports has validity in explaining the operation of the social care system of older people. Given the universal cultural norms regarding the role of family, it is not surprising that in generation after generation, the family is perceived as the first avenue of support, followed by friends and neighbors. Preferences for formal organizations are rarely expressed, occurring most often when family is not available, when relationships within the family are not functional, or when a high level of skill is required beyond the capacity of the average family.

PART II

The Practice of Social Care:
Three Case Studies of Older New Yorkers

4

Introduction to the Case Studies

In Part 1 of this book we presented a full examination of the Social
Care Model, the theories regarding exchanges between the elderly
and those around them, as well as the preferences of older people for
who should help them in a variety of instrumental, emotional, and
informational social support situations based on studies of New
York's older population in both 1970 and 1990. That discussion provides the conceptual basis on which the empirical findings of the next
sections rest.

We now turn in Part 2 to three case studies that illustrate the operation of the social care system among three important subgroups of
older New Yorkers: White-Jewish, Latino, and African American. Each
case study will examine in detail the informal networks of each group
and the extent to which these networks respond to the needs for assistance among their older members. Of particular interest will be the
impact of ethnicity and class on the operation of the informal system.
In the second part of each case study, we will turn to the other crucial
part of the social care system of older people—the formal service network and its role in the provision of social care. Our interests here will
include the extent to which Black, Latino, and Jewish elderly persons
avail themselves of the services from the formal sector, the barriers to
service use, and the nature and extent of unmet needs expressed by
these three groups of New York City elderly in the closing decades of
the twentieth century.

Race and ethnicity have been factors in American life since the
time of the founding fathers. Although anti-immigrant sentiment has
always been prevalent, the accepted view by both the public and academics was that the particular strength of the United States was its
function as a melting pot, where people from all parts of the globe

could merge their distinctive ethnic and cultural identities and become Americans. More recently, this view has been challenged, and there is a growing recognition that, in actuality, the United States is a culturally pluralistic society in which racial and ethnic groups retain their uniqueness and still participate in the economic, political, and social life of this country (Harel & Kart, 1994). To encompass this broader reality, Andrew Greeley (1974) has postulated the concept of *ethnogenesis* to describe a model of ethnic relations in which there is both a pull toward assimilation and at the same time an attempt to maintain ethnic and cultural identity.

In line with the newer emphasis on cultural pluralism, there has come increased interest in the role played by both ethnicity and social class in a variety of aspects of American life, including adherence to social norms, political behavior, residential choices, educational and occupational aspirations and status, and most germane to the purpose of this volume, family life and informal supports (Mindel & Habenstein, 1981). As noted by Markides and Mindel (1987), in the early beginnings of gerontology there was only limited interest in the effects of ethnicity on aging and attention to diversity. However, the relationship between aging and ethnicity has become an important focus of gerontologists in the decades since the 1970s. As a result, there is emerging literature concerning various racial and ethnic groups in the aging population of this country, particularly historically disadvantaged minorities such as African American, Latino, Native American, and more recently, Asian American elderly populations (Cantor, 1978; Gelfand & Kutzik, 1979; Harel, 1986; Jackson, 1985; Markides, 1983; Markides, Liang & Jackson, 1990). Somewhat more limited attention has been directed to elderly Americans of European origin (Cantor, Brook, & Mellor, 1986; Gelfand & Berreci, 1987; Harel, 1986; Harel, Biegel, & Guttman, 1994; Hayes, Kalish, & Guttman, 1986).

Given our interest in the effects of ethnicity and culture on the provision of social care for the elderly in the United States at present, the selection of African American and Latino elderly persons as the focus of two of our case studies in this book is obvious. Minority elderly are the fastest growing segment of the older population in New York City and in most urban areas across the country. Although Blacks and Latinos have differing cultural and historical backgrounds, both have suffered from discrimination and have strong cultural norms regarding the role of family in support of its older members. In addition, among African Americans in New York City there has been recent evidence of an emergent middle-class, both among younger adults and current retirees. As a result, the case study of Black older New Yorkers offers an unique opportunity to examine race/ethnicity and social class factors in the patterning of informal and formal social supports. Hispanic elderly, in contrast, are the largest group of recent immigrants to New York City. As such, older Latinos provide an opportunity to study the impact of immigration and assimilation pressures on the traditional extended family culture brought with them from their homelands in the Caribbean and Central and South America. To what extent does such a cultural heritage survive in New York City in the late twentieth century, and what barriers, if any, does it pose to the use of community-based services on the part of Latino elderly?

The choice of Jewish elderly as the focus of a case study was based on several factors. Jews, although highly integrated into mainstream United States, both racially and culturally, are illustrative of another important emphasis in ethnic studies—the effects of common culture, religion, and group identity on behavior and social norms. Specifically, the Jewish elderly population of New York City and their children form a very substantial proportion of the city's White population in the five boroughs and surrounding metropolitan area. Further, while there has been a decline from 1970 to 1990 in the total White non-Hispanic elderly population in New York City, the decline in the proportion of Jewish elderly was less compared to other groups.

Perhaps the most important reason for the selection of the Jewish elderly population for a case study was that, despite assimilation into American mainstream culture, Jews have generally maintained a strong sense of group identity and an emphasis on the importance of family and communal responsibility. These tendencies can be viewed as an outgrowth of both religious orientation, centuries of anti-Semitic persecution, and in many countries either *de jure* or *de facto* segregation. As a present day testament to the historic emphasis on community, the Jewish community in New York maintains a wide array of community services. These services, available to both Jews and non-Jews alike under the aegis of the United Jewish Appeal-Federation of Jewish Philanthropies, have historically been an integral part of formal social supports for all older New Yorkers. Although Jewish older people in New York City are not separated from their peers in most aspects of life, this heightened sense of the appropriateness of community intervention and strong ties to family, on both religious and cultural grounds, makes them a particularly interesting focus for an examination of the effects of ethnicity and culture on the operation of the social care system of older people. And last, but certainly not least, the demographic profile of the Jewish elderly, including their somewhat greater age, higher levels of education, greater economic resources, and greater geographic dispersion of children, suggests this group as a prototype of future cohorts of types of social care systems that may be required in the decades ahead.

5

Growing Older and Jewish in New York City in the 1990s

INTRODUCTION: THE JEWS IN THE UNITED STATES

As a prelude to examining the social support system of the Jewish elderly of New York City, it is helpful to know something in the way of context about the American Jewish population both nationally and in the New York City Metropolitan area. Discussions of ethnic group identity typically take one of two approaches, the first in terms of demographic characteristics, and the second in terms of cultural values and norms. Clearly, it is important to know characteristics of the American Jewish population; the numbers involved, their economic, educational, and health status, as well as length of residency in the United States and level of acculturation. But perhaps equally, if not more important, is some idea of the shared history of the Jewish population and cultural themes that help to unite them as a distinct ethnic entity.

THE JEWISH POPULATION IN THE UNITED STATES

To begin, a demographic overview of American Jewry in the late twentieth century will be presented to understand how the Jewish elderly fit into the larger picture. Information on American Jewry and those living in the New York City metropolitan areas come from two recent major studies: "The National Jewish Population Study" (Kosmin et al., 1991) and its companion, "The 1991 New York Jewish Population

Study" (Horowitz, 1993). According to the national study (timed to coincide with the 1990 U.S. Census, which asked no information on religious affiliation), the core Jewish population in the United States in 1990, both community and institutional dwelling, comprised 5.5 million persons. This core includes persons reporting themselves to be Jewish by virtue of religion, ethnic origin, up-bringing, or parentage. Additionally, if all individuals living in a household in which at least one person was identified as Jewish are included, the study estimates that as many as 8.1 million persons live in a household with some Jewish identification.

The core Jewish American population has shown only a small increase in size from 5.2 million in 1970, 5.5 million in 1990, influenced by low fertility and rising rates of intermarriage. However, the small increase is likely due to recent immigration from Israel and the former Soviet Union, more people willing to identify themselves as Jewish, and the more sophisticated sampling methods used in the 1990 study, which helped to insure fuller coverage of the eligible population (Kosmin, 1991). Based only on the core Jewish population (5.5 million) in 1990, American Jewry comprised 2.3% of the total United States population (Kosmin, 1991; Horowitz, 1993), but nearly one-half (45%) of the world's Jewish population (Singer & Seldin, 1994).

ORIGINS OF AMERICAN JEWRY

The Jewish population in the United States is comprised of persons who have come from every part of the globe. As such, it reflects the history of the Jewish *Diaspora*, buffeted by forces of anti-Semitism. Although a small proportion of current American Jews are descendants of *Sephardic* Spanish Jews who trace their origins to the middle seventeenth century, most Jews in America arrived during the middle nineteenth to late twentieth century. Three separate waves of this recent Jewish immigration are identifiable: Jews immigrating primarily from Germany in the middle nineteenth century; vast numbers who fled from Eastern Europe as part of the sustained immigration to the United States from the turn of the century to World War II; and the nearly 300,000 Jews arriving from the former Soviet Union (Rosen & Weltman, 1996).

The majority of American Jews have roots in Eastern Europe. Some of the oldest are first generation Americans, but increasingly Jews of all ages are second, third, and even fourth generation descendants of those seeking refuge in the United States at the beginning of the twentieth century (Harel & Kart, 1994). Currently, the vast majority of Jews are concentrated in large urban areas (Goldstein, 1993). Although Jews have migrated to all parts of the country, large population centers are found principally on the East and West coasts with New York and California alone home to half the U.S. Jewish population (2.5 million) (Rosen & Weltman, 1996). However, this picture is changing as younger generations of Jewish Americans move to other parts of the country in response to career and lifestyle opportunities. Not only does this increased willingness to move sometimes result in enormous distance between American Jewish elderly and their adult children, but many younger Jews find themselves moving to smaller communities that have historically had fewer resources to care for the aged population (Klaff, 1987).

THE JEWISH COMMUNITY OF
NEW YORK CITY AND ITS ENVIRONS

To place our examination of the Jewish elderly population of New York City in perspective, some salient facts about the Jewish community in the New York Metropolitan area are helpful. Like all Jewish communities, the Jewish population of this region is diverse, and its members have differing opinions, beliefs and religious practices depending on age, income, social class, and national background. But as is the case of nearly all Jews, Jews in New York perceive themselves to be both coreligionists and part of a cultural and ethnic corpus, whose membership is bestowed by birth rather than by religious belief or practice (Cohen & Rosen, 1992; Rosen & Weltman, 1996).

The 1991 New York Jewish Population Study (Horowitz, 1993), provides a comprehensive picture of the New York Jewish community. The study area encompassed the five boroughs of New York City as well as three suburban counties surrounding the City. Thus, in the greater New York City Metropolitan area are found not only the older Jews of New York City, the focus of this Chapter, but many of their adult children, grandchildren, and other relatives as well. The New York City Metropolitan area contains a core population of 1.4 milliom persons who identify themselves as Jewish in either religious or secular-ethnic terms (Horowitz, 1993). In addition, there are another approximately 200,000 persons who are more marginally connected to the Jewish population, but do not identify themselves as Jewish, for a total of 1.6 million persons.

The vast majority of these Jewish or Jewish-connected New Yorkers (83%) describe themselves as Jewish based on religious affiliation, although not all are formal members of synagogues or temples. In fact, a significant number of American Jews identify themselves as secular or nonreligious but retaining a Jewish identity, resulting in a wide continuum of Jewish commitment (Rosen & Weltman, 1996). Of the total Jewish population in the New York City Metropolitan area, more than 1 million live within the five boroughs. The concentration of Jews in the New York City metropolitan area is illustrated by the fact that one in eight persons in this eight-county area is Jewish, compared to about one in ten statewide, and one in twenty nationwide (Horowitz, 1993).

Jews in the New York City area tend to be native born (83%), and except for the oldest, most are third and fourth generation Americans. Most adults are married, although there has been an increase in the percentage of never-married Jewish Americans in recent years (15% in 1981 to 23% in 1991), a factor that has consequences for the care of Jewish elderly in the not too distant future. With respect to age, about 24% of the Jewish population in the New York City area are 19 years or younger, while about the same proportion (22%) are 60 years or more. Most Jewish New Yorkers are well-educated, almost two-thirds of males and over half of females are college graduates (Horowitz, 1993).

While 18% of the sample did not provide information on income, which is typical of most survey research, the median 1990 annual income for Jewish households in the New York City Metropolitan area was over $50,000, with considerable variation by county. Kings County (Brooklyn), with the highest proportion of Jewish elderly persons, had the lowest median income ($29,700), while median incomes in the suburban counties of Westchester and Nassau ranged from $60,000 to $65,000. Findings on income suggest that the majority of Jews in the greater New York City area are middle- to upper middle-class. Only 3% of New York Jewish households reported incomes at or below poverty, but this triples to 9% if one considers near-poverty (up to 150% of poverty level) incomes. Jewish poor are mainly concentrated within the five boroughs of New York City, where 92% of poor Jewish households are found (Horowitz, 1993). (We will readdress the question of poverty among the Jewish elderly population later in this chapter.)

THE JEWS OF NEW YORK CITY

At present, Jews constitute 14% of the total New York City population. The 1950s were the peak years of Jewish population in the City , but in the intervening decades there has been a steady flow from the New York neighborhoods first settled by immigrants to the suburbs and other parts of the country on the part of successive generations. Since the post-World War II era, the Jewish population in New York City has declined from 2.1 million to 1.1 million in 1981, and 1.03 million in 1991. Horowitz (1993) notes that this decline during the 1980s is clearly a continuation of an historic trend, but at least with regard to New York City, Jewish out-migration has slowed and may be reversing. In Manhattan, this reversal has actually occurred, with a growth in the Jewish population in this same period due primarily to two factors: baby-boomers who have chosen to remain in Manhattan and older Jews from the suburbs with grown children who are coming back. Thus, in the last decade, the out-migration of Jews from New York City has been slower compared to other non-Hispanic Whites, a decline of 8% and 18%, respectively.

With respect to elderly Jews, Horowitz (1993) reports a total of almost one quarter of a million Jews 60 years and older (240,800), with a slightly greater proportion of individuals 70 years or more (131,200) compared to those 60 to 69 years (109,600). Elderly persons 60 years and older comprise a greater proportion of the population of Jews in New York City, compared to other non-Hispanic White groups such as Irish and Italians (24% and 18%, respectively).

CULTURAL THEMES OF THE JEWISH COMMUNITY

Jewish elderly, as a distinct ethnic and cultural subgroup of older New Yorkers, are part of the larger Jewish community. Thus, our discussion of the attitudes toward, and manifestations of, social care must consider the larger cultural themes and norms that permeate the Jewish community in the United States and provide a sense of group identity. Rubenstein (1994) notes that Jewish communities, regardless of structure, practice or geographic location, possess, ". . . an undefinable oneness to Jewish identity reflected in the notion of 'one people' and of homeland.'" Aging and ethnicity can be examined from at least three perspectives: cultural content or that which defines Jewishness; generation and changes in ethnic identity with age; and the perspective of the cohort or historically-bound birth group (Rubenstein, 1994). For the purpose of understanding the effect of culture, class, and ethnicity on the social support system of older Jewish New Yorkers, one must remember that future cohorts of American Jews will have different experiences and characteristics compared to the current group of Jewish elderly people discussed in this chapter (Harel, Biegel & Guttman, 1994).

Cultural and ethnic identity of all groups is a complex amalgamation of attributes, beliefs, and practices, as well as basic norms passed down from generation to generation. Herz and Rosen (1982) describe several themes that pervade Jewish cultural, social, and religious life: the significance of family; suffering as a shared value; the goal of intellectual achievement; and unique patterns of life rituals and values, including and most central to our discussion, the centrality of the parent-child bond throughout the life course. Rubenstein (1994) suggests two additional defining norms—the notion of community or communal services for those needing assistance and the idea of the oneness of the Jewish people.

CENTRALITY OF FAMILY AS A JEWISH CULTURAL NORM

To understand the aged person in the Jewish community, one needs to understand the role of family in Jewish life, and the role of the elderly in Jewish families (Climo, 1987). The centrality of family is an essential aspect of Jewish cultural dynamics. The first commandment in the Torah is, "You shall be fruitful and multiply." Today, Jews still have a higher rate of marriage and a slightly lower rate of divorce than the general population. This is reflected in the relatively lower proportions of never-married persons among older Jewish New Yorkers. In addition to the Torah, other factors noted by Rosen and Weltman (1996) for the strong emphasis on marriage and family life among Jews include the child-focused nature of Jewish life, with children and grandchildren the very essence of a meaningful and happy existence, the history of suffering and persecution, which makes family a safe haven in the face of unreliable and often dangerous social institutions, and the connection between past and future generations of Jewry and the obligation to preserve Jewish heritage.

Jewish elderly have a well-defined place in the family, given the key social roles played by mothers and fathers in Jewish culture. This sense of family and veneration of the older generation is reinforced through rituals and expectations regarding familism in celebration of major religious holidays. Although cross-generational separation has played an important part in American Jewish life, both in terms of separation resulting from immigration to the United States, as well as more recent migration to other parts of the country by younger generations, the family remains a basic value of Jewish life.

According to Jewish tradition, the marriage of children becomes an extension of parental worth (Rosen & Weltman, 1996; Zborowski & Herzog, 1952). Jewish theology does not espouse an afterlife, and the path of achieving immortality is through family and children. Success, and its public recognition, is also vitally important to the Jewish family ethos, reflecting a central family value of education and professional achievement (originally exclusively on the part of sons, but in recent cohorts extending to daughters as well). This emphasis on learning stems from the history of Jews as People of the Book (i.e., the *Torah*). In addition, learning was a portable means of earning a living, and often an advantage for Jews who were so often forced to flee from persecution. However, success can also mean sacrificing closeness to family and community, and thus we see a conflict between two highly valued norms in Jewish culture. As Myerhoff (1978) noted in her seminal ethnographic study of Jewish elderly, many older Jews feel a mixture of both pride and grief when children move away in pursuit of achievement and success.

Historically, the mother has been the nurturer of both children and husband in the Jewish nuclear family. No sacrifice is considered too great for the Jewish mother, especially if it is for the sake of her children. In return, this may engender guilt on the part of children who may feel that nothing they do is adequate to repay their mother's efforts. Parental sacrifice, suffering, and solicitude generate filial indebtedness, which is repaid by children through expressions of caring and respect (Rosen & Weltman, 1996). A related concept is that of providing *nachis*, a Yiddish word denoting pleasure or pride that can be delivered through achievement, financial success, marriage, or children. According to Rosen and Weltman, ". . . the Jewish family is bound together by both religious precedence and cultural expectation of each generation in turn helping each other."

STRESS AND STRAIN IN JEWISH FAMILIES

Although multigenerational Jewish families sometimes co-reside, living arrangements among American Jews mainly involve separate households. In some situations, generations live in close proximity, and in other cases there is considerable distance between adult children and Jewish older parents. However, geographic distance is not considered a valid excuse for failing to fulfill family obligations. Given the centrality of the family in Jewish life, the respective roles assumed by parents and children, and the complications raised by geographic dispersion, it is not surprising that there are often intergenerational tensions between obligations and independence that are frequently difficult to resolve (Glicksman & Koropeckyj-Cox, 1994; Rosen & Weltman, 1996; Rosenthal, 1984; Rubenstein, 1994; Sanua, 1981).

In addition to the desire to live independently typical of most older people, Jewish elderly place a strong value on not being a burden on one's children and becoming a hindrance to a child's advancement and success. As noted previously, this may entail children moving away from parents in both a geographic as well as a social sense. On the other hand, among adult Jewish children, there is a strong commitment to respect parental independence and yet provide help as needed in concert with their own needs for autonomy and sometimes conflicting lifestyle demands. But to see this tension only in terms of conflict would ignore the great satisfaction Jewish parents experience in the success of children and grandchildren. Thus, older parents often encourage children to move because they want their offspring to succeed (Glicksman & Koropeckyj-Cox, 1994). Kahana and Kahana (1984) suggest that a large part of the success of Jewish children, particularly immigrants, can be traced to both moral and financial parental support and encouragement for mobility in every sense of the word. Glicksman and Koropeckyj-Cox (1994) summarize this ambivalence in Jewish families: ". . . the relation...cannot be described as simply positive or negative, but there is a constant tension between independence and responsibility, between the need for privacy and the need for strong links, between the twin values of taking care of one's parents and being successful in life." While none of these tensions is unique to the Jewish family, given the importance of reciprocity in intergenerational relationships as a lasting feature of Jewish tradition and notions of social justice, as well as the cohesion of the Jewish community, these cultural value conflicts are very important when considering the dynamics of social care in the case of the Jewish elderly.

THE IMPORTANCE OF THE JEWISH COMMUNITY
AND COMMUNITY SERVICES

Social institutions are rooted in both need and ideology. The extensive network of services developed by the Jewish community in America reflects both cultural values and historic realities. As Rubenstein (1994) notes, a major Jewish cultural theme is the notion of communal and community services. This strong sense of community and prevailing norms regarding the responsibility of each individual to the larger community is related to both important cultural and religious themes in Judaism as well as the history of the Jewish people.

Historically, Jews have been persecuted and marginalized in country after country, forcing them to create both the religious and secular institutions necessary for their survival as a people. Despite the widespread assimilation of Jews in the United States into American culture, the prevalence and impact of anti-Semitism, which was most starkly expressed in this century with the Holocaust, cannot be underestimated in assessing the nature of the Jewish people (Rosen & Weltman, 1996; Rubenstein, 1994). The sense of marginalization over generations has given urgency to the importance of building a sense of community and underscored the cultural values associated with the norm of mutual self-help. Although the ethos of suffering is a fundamental theme of Jewish culture, it is balanced by a belief in the survival and longevity of the Jewish people, based on the successive generative actions of each generation. Most Jews, whether religiously inclined or not, feel a sense of oneness with the Jewish people and the special nature of Jewish identity. Thus, the cultural emphasis on shared responsibility between individuals, families, and community is consistent with the idea that the actions taken by each of these players affects not only those involved but the survival of the Jewish people as a whole. Rubenstein (1994) expresses this by stating, ". . . among American Jews, each person and family has issues that are experienced individually, but each issue is bigger than the individual and the individual family, ramifying out to the Jewish people as a holistic entity, a community."

Along with the religious belief of the oneness of the Jewish people, the strong norms regarding shared responsibility between groups and individuals, and the need to care for one's own in often hostile circumstances, is the high regard in the Jewish community for intellectual and professional achievement. Rosen and Weltman (1996), based on clinical examples, note the preoccupation among many Jewish families to find the right doctor or specialist in times of crisis. In the same light, willingness to turn to community agencies on the part of both Jewish elderly and their families can be interpreted as stemming from a recognition of the superior level of skill that can be best provided by professional staff from formal health care and social service agencies.

As a result, from its beginning the Jewish community in the United States has developed and supported a professional network of hospitals, social service agencies, and institutions for children, families, and older people in need. The strong sense of social justice in Jewish culture is the foundation for this notion of communal responsibility. Thus, among Jews, turning to the community for assistance does not carry the same stigma as among many other non-Hispanic White and minority ethnic groups. This contrast in attitudes concerning receipt of assistance from the community is particularly distinct from traditional "Yankee" values of self-sufficiency as the measure of self-worth. It will be interesting to see if this greater willingness to utilize assistance provided by formal community-based agencies is manifested in the use of these supports among the Jewish elderly population of New York City.

WHO ARE THE JEWISH ELDERLY
PERSONS OF NEW YORK CITY?

An examination of the demographic profile of New York's Jewish elderly population, their economic and work history, and the comparisons between older Jews and older New Yorkers in general underscores the crucial theme of heterogeneity among older people. Like all older Americans, Jewish elderly are young-old and old-old, functionally vigorous and frail, living in a variety of household arrangements and with incomes ranging from at or below poverty to affluence. Furthermore, in many respects the Jewish elderly people are similar to other older New Yorkers, but there are some significant differences that may affect the assistance provided by the informal system as well as their use of formal services.

PERSONAL CHARACTERISTICS OF
NEW YORK CITY'S JEWISH ELDERLY

The major demographic and socioeconomic characteristics of the Jewish elderly population of New York City are summarized in Tables 5.1 and 5.2, below. In the following section, we will discuss the major highlights of these characteristics as well as compare older Jews to the elderly population of New York City in general.

AGE DISTRIBUTION

First, and perhaps most important, Jewish elderly tend to be older on average (77.3 years) as compared with older New Yorkers in general (74.3 years), with correspondingly higher proportions of the oldest-old (85 years or more). Thus, about two-thirds of Jewish elderly in the sample were 75 years or older, as compared with only about one-third of New York City's elderly population overall. And 17% of the Jewish elderly are among the oldest-old compared to 10% among older New Yorkers in general. Equally important from a planning perspective is the relatively smaller proportion of Jews in the cohorts of the young-old (65 to 74 years of age, 17%), as compared with almost double that proportion (30%) among the City's older population as a whole. Therefore, there is a definite tilt among the current Jewish elderly population toward advanced age, when increased frailty and the need for supportive and health services are most likely. Given the relocation to suburban areas during the 1940s and 1950s of Whites, including Jews, and the tendency to out-migration among younger retirees, it is likely that the age distribution of the current cohort of Jewish elderly is probably a preview of the future cohort of New York City's White elderly population. But these findings clearly suggest that issues of health, long-term care, chronic frailty, and social support will continue to be germane to the older Jewish population both today and in the future.

RATIO OF MEN TO WOMEN

Although women tend to outnumber men in virtually all elderly populations, the gender gap is somewhat less in the case of the Jewish elderly of New York City. Among older Jews, 56% are female, and 44% are male, a much more equivalent distribution than among the city's older population as a whole (61% female, 39% male). The narrower

TABLE 5.1 Demographic Characteristics of the Elderly Jews of New York City

Characteristic		Valid Percent[a][b]
Age group (years):	65 to 69	17.3
	70 to 74	19.4
	75 to 79	25.1
	80 to 84	20.9
	85 or more	17.3
Average age:	77.3 years	
Gender:	Female	56.1
	Male	43.9
Current marital status:	Married	51.3
	Widowed	39.7
	Divorced/separated	4.2
	Never married	4.5
Nativity:	Born in United States	62.7
	Foreign born	35.5
Education:	8th Grade or less	19.4
	Some high school	11.9
	Completed high school	29.9
	Some college	14.3
	College graduate	10.7
	Postgraduate	9.6
Self-perceived health:	Excellent	17.3
	Good	37.6
	Fair	31.6
	Poor	12.8
Living arrangements:	Alone	40.6
	With spouse	49.9
	With others but no spouse	9.9

[a] $n = 335$.
[b] Totals equal 100%.

gender differential in the case of the Jewish elderly cohort occurs despite the greater average age of this group and suggests that more older Jewish males are living longer in comparison to their counterparts in New York City. Past research has underscored the positive relationship between income and health in later life, which undoubtedly contributes to the increased longevity of older Jewish men.

CURRENT MARITAL STATUS

Partly as a result of the increased survival of elderly Jewish men noted above, older Jews are more likely to be married (51%) compared to older New Yorkers in general (43%). The proportion of widows in the Jewish elderly population is similar to that of the general population (approximately 40%), but there are fewer Jewish elderly who reported being divorced, separated, or never married. The likelihood of being currently married among the Jewish elderly persons decreases steadily with advanced age. By the age of 85 years or older, only 26% are still married as compared with 85% of those 65 to 69 years of age. Furthermore, given the longer life expectancies of women, there is a strong relationship between gender and marital status. Two-thirds of older Jewish males are still married, as compared with only 38% of females, while 54% of Jewish elderly women reported being widowed as compared to 21% of older Jewish men. Finally, those with incomes below 150% of the poverty level were far less likely to be married than those more economically secure. Again, this partially stems from the higher proportion of women and the oldest-old who are without a living spouse and also have lower incomes.

NATIVITY AND LANGUAGE SPOKEN AT HOME

Unlike past cohorts, the majority of Jewish elderly persons in the study sample were born in the United States (63%), with only the oldest-old (85 years or more) containing a substantial proportion of foreign-born elderly (57%). The heavy concentration of native-born Jewish elderly persons in the cohort translates into the vast majority of them speaking only English at home (85%), with only 2% speaking only a foreign language at home, usually Yiddish, and 12% speaking a combination of English and another language. Poverty level incomes were associated with an increased likelihood of speaking only a foreign language at home, likely a reflection of the recent heavy immigration from the former Soviet Union and other Eastern European nations. With the exception of Latino elderly, most other older New Yorkers are similar to their Jewish counterparts in that most are native born.

EDUCATION

The average level of education among the Jewish elderly (12.2 years) is somewhat higher than among older New Yorkers in general (11.0 years), despite the rise in education level among all groups of elderly in the cohort. The higher level of education among older Jews reflects two trends: Jewish elderly are less likely to have only a grade-school education; and they are more than twice as likely to have completed college or postgraduate courses than older New Yorkers in general (28% and 12%, respectively). As expected, younger age is associated with greater educational attainment among the Jewish elderly, as are higher incomes.

SELF-REPORTED HEALTH

Self-reports of health status also bear out the relatively advantaged position of the Jewish elderly. Like most older people, Jews and older New Yorkers in general tend to rate their health as either good or fair. But what is surprising is that, despite the heavier concentration of Jews over 75 and even 85 years of age when poorer health and increased frailty become more likely, Jewish elderly were only slightly more likely to rate their health as poor compared to New York's older population as a whole. In fact, a slightly higher proportion of the Jewish group rated their health as excellent compared to older New Yorkers in general. Among Jewish elderly, rating one's health as poor was associated with increased age, being female, and reporting poverty level incomes. Thus, the somewhat better economic circumstances of many Jewish elderly seems to mitigate and even postpone the onset of frailty and poor health that increase with prevalence among older ages. This finding, which is congruent with the earlier discussed greater longevity of older Jewish males, suggests that service needs resulting from age-related frailties among Jewish elderly may be deferred until very late in life (i.e., late eighties and beyond), while these challenges are likely to have an earlier onset among New York City's older population as a whole, particularly among Latinos and Blacks.

LIVING ARRANGEMENTS AMONG JEWISH ELDERLY

Not having others in the household has implications for the provision of assistance in times of need, and Jewish elderly persons were just as likely as older New Yorkers as a whole to report living alone, (approximately 40%). However, the Jewish elderly, as a reflection of their greater tendency to be married, were more likely than their peers city-wide to be living with a spouse (50% and 42%, respectively). Furthermore, they were less likely to be living in households with others (usually children) and without a spouse (10%), compared to nearly double that proportion among the City's older population as a whole (19%).

Living arrangements varied significantly by age among the Jewish elderly, advanced age being associated with less likelihood of living with a spouse and a greater likelihood of living alone or with others but no spouse. It is noteworthy that only among Jewish elderly 85 years and older do any sizable proportion report living with others but without a spouse; nearly one-fifth live in such households, usually with children, as compared to only 2% who report living with others among 65 to 69-year-olds. Thus, Jewish older persons like most older persons, clearly prefer independent living, either with spouse or alone, unless increased frailty or economic difficulties make independent living too difficult.

ECONOMIC WELL-BEING OF
NEW YORK CITY'S ELDERLY JEWS

An equally important factor in the maintenance of independent living and a positive quality of life for older people is the possession of sufficient economic resources to maintain one's standard of living and have the ability to purchase needed goods and services. Table 5.2 summarizes the economic position of the Jewish elderly population of New York City.

SOCIOECONOMIC STATUS

As a whole, New York City's Jewish elderly comprise a middle-class population according to Hollingshead's (1957) Index of Social Position (ISP), with the majority clustered in the medium to high socioeconomic strata. Jewish elderly are much more likely to be classified in these higher levels compared to older New Yorkers in general. Furthermore, only 14% of the Jewish elderly were classified in the lowest level of the ISP, which is based on educational and occupational attainment, as compared with 25% of older New Yorkers in general.

TABLE 5.2 Economic Characteristics of the Elderly Jews of
New York City

Characteristic		Valid Percent[ab]
Socio-economic status:	High	15.3
	Medium-high	10.7
	Medium	28.4
	Medium-low	31.8
	Low	13.8
Total 1989 income:	$6000 or less	6.3
	$6001–$8500	7.2
	$8501–$10,000	6.0
	$10,001–$15,000	15.3
	$15,001–$25,000	14.6
	$25,001–$35,000	9.0
	$35,001–$50,000	8.7
	$50,001 or More	11.1
Average income:	$26,345	
Median income:	$20,001	
Poverty level:	At or below poverty	10.0
	Near poverty (101%–150%)	19.5
	Over 150% poverty	70.5
Sources of income (independent items):	Social Security	96.7
	Interest or dividends	74.0
	Pensions	45.4
	Wages/Salaries/ Commissions	17.3
	Supplemental security income	8.4
	Family or friends	5.4
	Other	5.4
Perception of economic well-being:	Cannot make ends meet	2.1
	Just manage to get by	33.4
	Enough money with a little extra	35.2
	Money is no problem	28.1

[a] $n = 335$.
[b] Totals equal 100%.

LEVELS OF 1989 HOUSEHOLD INCOME

Given their generally higher socioeconomic class, it is not surprising that the median annual income of Jewish older New Yorkers ($20,001) far exceeds that of the city's elderly population as a whole ($13,751). This differential occurs at both the low and high ends of reported income. One quarter of all older New Yorkers reported 1989 incomes below $8500, while among older Jewish persons, only 14% reported incomes in this low range. Additionally, 29% of the Jewish elderly population reported 1989 incomes exceeding $25,000, compared to only 19% for older New Yorkers in general, while older Jews were twice as likely to report incomes above $50,000 compared to their peers (11% and 5%, respectively).

Despite the higher median income of Jewish elderly compared to their counterparts in New York City, most are far from affluent. Like older New Yorkers in general, the largest single group of Jewish elderly reported 1989 annual incomes in the moderate range of $12,500 to $25,000. Given the high cost of living in New York City and the ever present specter of costly long-term illness, most elderly Jews and older New Yorkers alike are far from being economically comfortable. Furthermore, while there is a small but not insubstantial group of well-off older Jews (i.e., 9% with incomes $50,000 or greater and 2% with incomes of $100,000 or more in 1989), a much more numerous group is comprised of the nearly one-third (30%) reporting incomes at or below poverty or near poverty (101% to 150% of poverty) in 1989. The poverty rate for the Jewish elderly population (10%) is very close to that for older Whites nationwide (12%) (U.S. Census Bureau, 1990). But the level of poverty and near poverty among Jewish older New Yorkers is much lower than that found among older New Yorkers in general (20% and 23%, respectively).

Gender, age and living arrangements were all associated with 1989 incomes reported by Jewish older persons: males reported higher average annual incomes compared to females ($33,269 and $19,981, respectively); 65- to 69-year olds reported the highest average incomes ($36,245), which steadily decreased to $17,384 among the 85 and older group; and Jewish elderly persons living with a spouse reported greater average incomes compared to those living alone or with others but no spouse. As an illustration of the problems faced by older women living alone, the poverty rate among the Jewish elderly living by themselves was 10% in the case of men, but nearly doubled to 19% among older Jewish women living alone.

USE OF NEEDS-BASED ENTITLEMENTS

Despite the extent of poverty among New York City's elderly population, the utilization of needs-based entitlement programs is lower
than would be expected, particularly in the case of White older persons. Among Jewish elderly reporting poverty-level incomes, only 39%
participated in Supplemental Security Income (SSI), 50% reported
Medicaid enrollment, and only 19% were receiving food stamps.
Among all older New Yorkers in poverty, the proportions were 52%,
58%, and 32%, respectively. Thus among all older New Yorkers in
poverty and particularly among Jewish older persons, the very programs designed to assist older people in economic need are underutilized. This finding suggests the need for careful evaluation of why
older New Yorkers in poverty, including Jews, fail to take advantage
of these important programs, with particular emphasis on attitudes
toward governmental assistance and the role of asset limitations in
determining program eligibility. However, it is likely this need for
evaluation will remain unmet in the current political climate of welfare reform and devolution.

SOURCES OF INCOME

In general, the major sources of income for older Jewish New Yorkers
are similar to those of older people nationally. Social Security is of crucial importance, and virtually all Jewish older people (97%) reported
this source of income, as was true for the city overall (93%). Pensions
and income from interest and dividends also play a significant role in
supplementing the incomes of elderly Jews. A slightly higher proportion of New York City's older population in general reported receiving pensions (50%), as compared with the Jewish elderly (45%).
However, reflecting their higher socioeconomic status, Jewish elderly
were far more likely to report income from investments compared to
the older population as a whole (74% and 55%, respectively). Only
17% of Jewish respondents reported receiving income from wages,
which was not surprising, given that the vast majority reported being
retired from work (79%), a finding also true for older New Yorkers as
a group.

   Despite the high proportions reporting income from investments
or pensions, Social Security was reported as the principal source of
income for the majority of older Jews (55%) and an even greater proportion of older New Yorkers in general (62%). Furthermore, depen-

dency on Social Security as the primary income source among elderly Jews was associated with greater age, female gender, and living alone. The second most frequently reported source of income among the Jewish elderly was interest or dividends (18%), while among the City's older population as a whole, pensions followed Social Security as the second most frequently cited primary income source.

PERCEPTIONS OF ECONOMIC WELL-BEING

Given the relatively high levels of income among Jewish older people in New York City, it is not surprising that only slightly more than one-third (36%) reported economic pressures, such as, not managing to make ends meet or just managing to get by. Another one-third perceived themselves as having enough money with a little extra, while the strong economic position of a minority of Jewish elderly was reflected in the 28% who reported that money is no problem at all. Perceptions of income adequacy were far less sanguine among New York City's elderly population in general, with nearly double the proportion of Jewish elderly reporting that money was no problem compared to the City's elderly as a whole.

SUMMARY OF ECONOMIC WELL-BEING

As is the case with all elderly populations, there is considerable diversity of economic resources among elderly Jews despite their relatively advantaged position as compared with older New Yorkers in general. There is a small but substantial group of wealthy older Jews as well as a much more sizable group of Jewish elderly with poverty or near poverty incomes. It is noteworthy that the majority of older Jews in New York City have moderate annual incomes ranging from $12,500 to $25,000, and they appear to be managing on a day-to-day basis. But in the advent of long-term illness or other crises, the situation of many of them is likely to worsen. In the continuing absence of affordable long-term care insurance through Medicare or other carriers, social care assistance from the family and the community will be essential to prevent a sharp deterioration in the economic circumstances of such moderate income elderly persons.

JEWISH CONTINUITY AND INVOLVEMENT WITH RELIGION

At present, the Jewish community is very concerned with issues of Jewish continuity. The attitude of the Jewish elderly toward the importance of religion and the extent of involvement in Jewish religious rituals and activities is very germane to our discussion of the effects of culture on the provision of social care to older people. Although "Growing Older In New York City" was not designed as an in-depth exploration of religious values and beliefs, two items provide some minimal background to this discussion. Respondents were asked to indicate their frequency of attendance at religious services, as well as to rate the importance of religion in their lives.

ATTENDANCE AT SYNAGOGUE/TEMPLE

In the main, Jewish elderly respondents reported attending the synagogue or temple only occasionally. Although almost one-half (48%) of older Jews indicated they attended religious services at least several times per year, the proportion of regular attendees was small, with only 10% attending at least weekly, and 7% at least monthly. Furthermore, close to one-quarter (22%) attended services only once per year or less often, probably at the High Holy Days, while one-third reported never attending services.

IMPORTANCE OF RELIGION

Responses regarding the importance of religion also are suggestive of a trend toward secularism. Slightly over one-quarter (28%) of Jewish elderly in New York City reported that religion is very important, while two-fifths (40%) indicated that religion was somewhat important. One third of older Jewish New Yorkers indicated, however, that religion was either not very important or not important at all. Among older New Yorkers in general, religion appears to play a more central role. Nearly twice as many older New Yorkers overall (52%) report that religion is very important compared to the Jewish respondents (28%). Furthermore, older Jews are twice as likely to indicate that religion is not important compared to older New Yorkers in general (30% and 16%, respectively). Trends regarding attendance at services are similar, with the City's older population overall more likely to attend services on a regular basis as compared with Jewish elderly.

Thus, the increased secularism among older Jews is manifested both in terms of feelings about the importance of religion as well as less frequent attendance at religious services. But it is important to note that these findings do not preclude a sense of Jewish identity; all elderly who are the focus of the present chapter self-identified themselves as Jewish. It is of further interest that "feeling religion was not important" was related to both higher education and higher income. For example, Jewish elderly persons with incomes over 150% of poverty were much more likely to report religion was not important at all (16%), compared to 2% of older Jews with poverty or near poverty incomes.

Having discussed the contextual factors influencing the Jewish experience of growing older in New York City, we will return to our major focus, the provision of social care. In line with the social care model presented in the second chapter, we turn now to the system in closest proximity to older people, namely, the informal social network.

THE INFORMAL SOCIAL NETWORKS OF JEWISH OLDER NEW YORKERS

INTRODUCTION

Jewish family life, in so far as it affects older people, seems strong and vibrant. The Jewish elderly population of New York City is embedded in sizable social networks, and most older Jews, by their own evaluations, appear to receive the emotional and instrumental support they need. Assistance comes mainly from kin and nonkin significant others, supplemented when needed by services from the formal system. If, as suggested throughout this chapter, the Jewish elderly population of New York City can be considered prototypes of future older Americans, the findings on the role of family, friends, and neighbors suggest important directions for a meaningful partnership between the informal and formal systems of social care.

Informal social networks and their role in support of older people are greatly influenced by factors such as group history, culture, class, and level of acculturation. Previous research has suggested that the African-American and Latino minority elderly of New York have somewhat different social networks and patterns of assistance than their White peers (Cantor & Brennan, 1993c). In examining the family life of the Jewish elderly it, therefore, seems most appropriate to limit comparison to those older New Yorkers whom they most resemble, their non-Jewish White peers. However, even between Jewish and non-Jewish White elderly, there are some demographic differences, which although not major, need to be considered when comparing the helping patterns of Jewish families with non-Jewish White families. Briefly, on average, the Jewish elderly are slightly older, more likely to still be married, and have slightly higher annual incomes and a lower incidence of poverty compared to their non-Jewish White peers. Reflecting this tendency to be more likely to be in middle to upper-middle socioeconomic strata, older Jewish New Yorkers have higher educational levels as compared with their White peers, an important factor in attitudes about appropriate sources of social care. However, the proportions of Jewish and non-Jewish White elderly persons who live alone are similar, although elderly Jews are less likely to move in with children following loss of spouse or increased levels of frailty.

With these differences in mind, we look first to the nature of the informal support system of the White elderly of New York City, comparing Jewish and non-Jewish White elderly, and then recapitulating findings on the flow of assistance between them and their children, and the perceptions of older persons regarding the availability and adequacy of social support. As noted previously, the six elements of the informal support system include four members of the kinship network (i.e., spouse, children, siblings, and other relatives) and two members of nonkin significant others (i.e., friend-confidants and neighbors). Most older Jews in New York City have the majority of these components in their networks, and some have networks with all six elements. Only 1% of Jewish elderly respondents reported being without any of these six social support elements. Table 5.3 summarizes and compares the major informal social network components of Jewish and non-Jewish White elderly in New York City.

SPOUSES

For most older people, a spouse, when present, serves as the base of the social support network, providing intimacy and the immediate availability of assistance in times of need. However, loss of spouse through death is common with increasing age, especially for older women. When a spouse is present, much of the needed assistance is likely to be supplied within the marriage dyad, with secondary support from children. For widows and widowers, single persons, as well

TABLE 5.3 Informal Social Network Characteristics of the Elderly Jews As Compared with Non-Jewish Elderly Whites of New York City (Valid Percent[ab])

Respondent has at least one . . .	Elderly Jews	Non-Jewish Elderly Whites
Spouse***:	51.3	38.5
Child:	80.0	75.0
Average number of children++:	1.6	1.9
Sibling:	72.8	71.3
Other relative in New York City***:	56.7	40.6
Friend—Confidant:	37.3	37.1
Neighbor known well:	62.7	67.4

[a] Totals equal 100%.
[b]. Jewish ($n = 335$); Non-Jewish White ($n = 512$).
* $p < .05$, ** $p < .01$, *** $p < .001$, Chi-square tests of significance.
++ $p < .01$, One way analysis of variance.

as childless older individuals, other relatives, friends, and neighbors assume a more important role.

The vast majority of Jewish elderly (95%) have been married at some point in their lives. However, in 1990, slightly over one half (52%) were married and had a living spouse (see Table 5.3). Of those remaining, 40% were widowed, 4% were divorced or separated, and 5% had never married. As expected, among older Jews the presence of a living spouse was strongly related to both age and gender, with the oldest-old and women being far less likely to have a spouse than either the younger-old or men. The proportion of married Jewish elderly was 85% among 65 to 69 year-olds, falling in a linear fashion to 25% among those 85 years old and older, while 69% of Jewish men were currently married as compared to 38% of older Jewish women. Jewish older New Yorkers were considerably more likely than their non-Jewish White counterparts to have a living spouse (52% and 39%, respectively), in part reflecting the somewhat greater longevity of Jewish men and the lower proportions of Jewish elderly who never married (5% and 10%, respectively).

LIVING CHILDREN

As noted previously, following spouses, children comprise the most crucial component of an older person's social network. Those without children or with children unable or unwilling to provide assistance are seriously disadvantaged in the face of increased frailty and must turn to more distant elements of the informal network for needed assistance (e.g., siblings, friends, or neighbors) or to formal community agencies. Four fifths of Jewish elderly respondents (80%) reported having at least one living child, including both biological children and other children raised by the respondent (see Table 5.3). On average, Jewish elderly reported 1.6 living children, though nearly two-thirds (64%) reported two living children. While most older Americans have at least one living child, Jewish elderly were somewhat more likely than their non-Jewish peers to have this support element (80% and 75%, respectively). Thus, elderly Jews are in a somewhat advantaged position relative to their non-Jewish counterparts in the availability of both a living child and a living spouse.

Although Jewish elderly individuals are more likely to have at least one child, those with children report fewer on average (1.6) as compared with non-Jewish White elderly parents (2.5). It is noteworthy that among White elderly persons regardless of religious affiliation, the mean family size was 2.4 children, very different than the situation found among minority families in which the average number of living children is much greater (2..9 among African Americans and 3.7 in the case of older Latino New Yorkers). Although more than two thirds of Jewish elderly living alone reported a living child (71%), it is among live alones that the greatest proportion of childless elderly is found, 29%, as compared to approximately 15% in the case of both older Jews living with a spouse or with others.

PROFILE OF THE CHILDREN OF THE JEWISH ELDERLY

To better understand the relationships between generations and the potential for intergenerational exchanges of assistance, both in times of crisis as well as in more ongoing situations, detailed information was collected from older parents regarding the characteristics of each living child (age, gender, geographic location, and degree of closeness) as well as the frequency of both face-to-face and telephone interaction (n = 530 children).

Age and Gender of Children

Jewish elderly in New York City reported that the majority of their children (55%) were middle-aged (i.e., 41 to 59 years of age), followed by young adults 21 to 40 (33%). Less than 1% of the children were minors under 21. But a not insubstantial proportion of the children were 60 years or older (7%) and entering the aging cohort themselves. It is particularly worth noting that among Jewish parents 85 years and older, 40% of their children were aged 60 years or more. Such older children may not be in a position to provide assistance to their older parents as their own health and functional limitations increase with age. The fact that older Jewish parents tend to have children who are themselves entering the aging cohort underscores the importance of the availability of formal services for the oldest-old. In terms of gender, children of the Jewish elderly were nearly equally divided between males and females (52% and 48%, respectively).

Geographic Location of Children

The ability to provide assistance in times of need is closely tied to the geographic proximity and hence availability of children for contact with the older person. Approximately one-third of the children of Jewish elderly individuals live within the five boroughs of New York City, with 13% being in walking distance of their older parents. Approximately one-quarter (27%) live in surrounding suburban areas and could be with a parent in 1 to 2 hours. However, two of five children of Jewish elderly respondents (41%) live beyond the New York Metropolitan area, requiring both time and expense to return to assist a parent. The pattern of older parents having at least one child in close proximity despite the dispersion of other children across the country has been noted previously (Cantor, 1975a; Shanas et al., 1968). This pattern is also true of older Jewish parents in New York City, 60% of whom report having at least one child in the Metropolitan area.

However, when compared to the children of non-Jewish White elderly, children of elderly Jews tend to be more dispersed, with fewer living within New York City, and only half as many reported living within walking distance (13% and 24% among the children of Jewish and non-Jewish Whites, respectively). This greater geographic dispersion of the children of the Jewish elderly has implications both for intergenerational assistance patterns and perceptions of adequacy and availability of social support discussed below.

Functionality of the Older Jewish and Child Network

Research on the informal networks of older adults has suggested repeatedly the importance of children as sources of both instrumental assistance with tasks of daily living, as well as affective and emotional support. While the geographic proximity of children is in many ways a necessary condition for support availability, it is not a sufficient guarantee that older parents will receive needed assistance from children. More indicative of the potential to provide assistance in times of need is the extent to which children are functional, that is, in regular contact with their older parents, and can thus be more reasonably assumed to be available helpers. As noted earlier, Cantor (1979b, 1980) refers to this concept as the functionality of the kin system. To examine the nature of the interaction between older parents and children, respondents were asked how often they were in face-to-face contact with a child, as well as the frequency of telephone interaction. In this context, a functional child was defined as one who was in at least monthly face-to-face contact, or was in touch by telephone on a weekly basis.

Frequency of Face-to-Face Contact with Children

Confirming the often-reported closeness of many Jewish families, older Jewish parents in New York City reported relatively frequent contact with children. The majority of children (65%) were seen by parents on at least a monthly basis, if not more often, thereby fitting the definition of functionality. More than one-third (36%) were seen either daily or weekly, while more than one quarter (28%) were seen at least monthly. However, in line with the finding that two of five children live beyond the New York Metropolitan area, one-quarter (25%) of children see their parents only several times per year. Only one of ten children (10%) see a parent once per year or less often, while very few (1%) are never in face-to-face contact with their parents.

Comparison of frequency of face-to-face contact with children between Jewish and non-Jewish Whites points to geographic proximity as an important factor in the proportion of children who are seen on a regular basis. Among non-Jewish White older New Yorkers, who have nearly double the proportion of children living within walking distance, greater proportions of children are seen on at least a weekly basis (44%) as compared to the children of Jewish elderly (36%). In contrast, children of Jewish elderly are more likely to have been in face-to-face contact on a monthly basis or less often with their parent (64%) as compared to the children of non-Jewish older New Yorkers (43%).

Telephone Contact with Children

Although not all children are able to see parents frequently, often because they live some distance from their parents, ongoing contact is possible through the telephone. It appears that the children of Jewish elderly compensate for their geographic dispersion and resultant difficulties in frequent face-to-face contact through very frequent use of the telephone to stay in touch with older parents. Nearly one-third (30%) of the children of Jewish older New Yorkers are reported to be in daily contact with their parents by phone, while nearly half (49%) speak to parents at least weekly. Thus, nearly four-fifths (79%) of the children of elderly Jews maintain at least weekly telephone contact with their older parents. Of the remaining one-fifth of Jewish children, 8% are in at least monthly phone contact with parents, 7% speak to parents on the phone several times per year, and only 7% speak to parents on the phone once per year or less often.

The importance of the telephone for elderly Jews as a means of keeping in contact with children and compensating for geographic distance is underscored when patterns of phone usage between Jewish and non-Jewish White elderly persons and children are compared. While approximately 79% of Jewish children are in at least weekly phone contact with their parents, this proportion falls to 68% among the children of non-Jewish White older New Yorkers. Furthermore, Jewish children were only half as likely to speak to parents on the phone infrequently (i.e., once per year or less often) as compared to children of their non-Jewish White peers (7% and 15%, respectively). Thus, the functionality of the children of Jewish elderly rests far more heavily on frequent telephone as opposed to face-to-face visits.

The high levels of contact between both Jewish and non-Jewish White older New Yorkers and their children reinforces the notion of the solidarity of the families of these elderly, regardless of religious or national backgrounds. And it should be noted that these same family strengths are equally apparent in the case of older African Americans and Latinos in New York City and their children. However, if keeping in regular touch with parents is a central cultural norm and valued by the Jewish community, findings suggest that the telephone is a crucial vehicle for making such contact possible, particularly in the fast-paced and geographically dispersed society of the late twentieth century.

Degree of Closeness to Children

While the extent to which older people have children, where these children are located, and frequency of contact with parents are important determinants of support received from the informal social network, of equal importance and often omitted from social network research are the affective bonds between elderly individuals and their children. Clearly, it is possible to see children frequently but not have meaningful contact with them. To ascertain the extent of affective bonds between older people and their children, older parents were asked to rate the degree of closeness to each child, from very close to not close at all, and then to indicate for children, in general, whether they desired to see them more or less often.

While it is recognized that it may be difficult for a parent to admit a lack of closeness to a child, the overwhelmingly positive responses to the question regarding closeness between parents and children was consistent with the high frequency of contact reported between children and Jewish older New Yorkers. Nearly four of five children (77%) were reported as being very close to their parents, with an additional 15% somewhat close. Only 7% of the children of Jewish elderly were reported to be not very close or not close at all to their parents.

A further illustration of the close emotional bonds between Jewish elderly persons and their children is apparent in that the majority (54%) would like to see their children more often, while 42% were satisfied with the current level of contact with their offspring. Only a small group (4%) of older Jewish parents said they would like to see children less often. Fewer non-Jewish White older New Yorkers indicated a desire to see children more often as compared with their Jewish peers (42% and 54%, respectively). Thus, geographic dispersion appears to influence the desire to see children more often. However, in the case of the elderly Jews of New York City, who highly value close family relationships, cultural factors may also account for the greater expressed desire to see children more often.

The foregoing findings regarding high levels of contact between older Jewish New Yorkers and their children, as well as the positive appraisals of closeness and desire to see children even more often suggests a high degree of generational solidarity, in the Jewish community. The behavioral manifestations of this solidarity in provisions of social care will be apparent in the following sections, which describe patterns of intergenerational assistance between older Jewish parents and their children.

INTERGENERATIONAL ASSISTANCE AMONG JEWISH ELDERLY PARENTS AND CHILDREN

Elderly parents are often involved in reciprocal exchanges of assistance with their offspring. Among the younger, healthier older parent, intergenerational assistance between parent and child tends to flow in both directions, in a generally reciprocal manner. Although contact between elderly individuals and their families clearly involves socialization, instrumental assistance is often involved. This instrumental help commonly includes crisis intervention, such as help during times of illness, gift giving and monetary assistance, as well as assistance with everyday activities, such as shopping, running errands, housekeeping, home repairs, child care, and help with transportation. However, as parents become older and often frailer or in circumstances of diminished financial resources, the flow of assistance from children increases proportionately to meet the greater need on the part of older parents (Cantor & Little, 1985). Furthermore, the flow of assistance tends to become less reciprocal, with greater provisions of support by children relative to their elderly parents.

To ascertain the nature and flow of assistance between older New Yorkers and their children, respondents with one or more living children (80% of elderly Jews) were presented with a series of common types of intergenerational assistance and asked which types they provided to children and which were provided by children in return. Areas of assistance covered four broad categories: crisis intervention; activities of daily living; financial assistance; and advice or information.

PARENTAL ASSISTANCE TO CHILDREN

It is important to keep in mind, as findings on patterns of instrumental help are presented, that a sizable proportion of the children of the

Jewish elderly live beyond the New York City Metropolitan area, rendering direct assistance on a daily or more ongoing basis somewhat problematic. However, most elderly parents, regardless of Jewish heritage, provide some assistance to their children. Thus, the proportion of parents within each group providing no assistance is small and not markedly different between Jewish (10%) and non-Jewish White (7%) elderly respondents.

Types of Parental Assistance From Jewish Elderly Parents to Children

Looking first at the types of help provided by Jewish parents to their children, two areas stand out as significant—assistance in times of illness or other crisis and financial assistance in the form of both gifts and money. The most frequently reported type of assistance was in the financial area; 86% of parents reported giving gifts and 42% reported giving money to children. Following financial assistance, crisis intervention was the next most frequent type of assistance given to children, with 49% of Jewish older parents reporting helping children in this way.

In the areas of assistance with activities of daily living and advice giving, the proportion of Jewish older New Yorkers involved in helping children drops sharply, with no more than 30% of parents reporting assistance to children in either area. Babysitting for grandchildren was the most frequently reported instrumental help (30%), while about one-fifth (22%) reported shopping or running errands for children. Help with home repairs and with housekeeping were rarely reported (11% and 5%, respectively). Jewish older New Yorkers were somewhat less likely than their non-Jewish White counterparts to be involved in providing instrumental assistance to children. Fewer Jewish, as compared with non-Jewish White older New Yorkers babysit for a grandchild (30% and 38%, respectively), help with housekeeping (5% and 15%, respectively), or help with home repairs (11% and 22%, respectively).

An interesting finding is the lack of involvement on the part of older Jewish parents in giving advice to children whether on job or business matters (25%), large purchase decisions (20%), or on running the home and raising children (16%). This lack of involvement in giving advice and decision-making suggests an erosion of the role of elders in our society as traditional sources of wisdom and authority, and this was generally true of both Jewish and non-Jewish White older New Yorkers. Reflecting their greater involvement in the day-to-day lives of their children (including both more frequent face-to-face contact and greater provision of instrumental assistance), non-Jewish White elderly individuals were twice as likely (22%) to provide advice on the home or raising children as compared with Jewish elderly parents (11%). But with respect to advice giving in the domains of jobs and businesses or large purchase decisions, there were no notable differences between these two groups.

Although the patterns of parent to child assistance between Jewish and non-Jewish Whites are more similar than different, the differences that are apparent are likely influenced by issues of social class, geographic dispersion of children, and advanced age and concomitant frailty. It would appear that parental help may still be welcomed in certain crisis situations, particularly illness, or in terms of financial help. But the independence of the younger generation is increasingly the norm, whether such decisions involve how grandchildren are raised, financial decisions, or when career and business matters are at stake.

ASSISTANCE FROM CHILDREN TO OLDER PARENTS

As was found in both the 1970 and 1990 studies of New York City's elderly population, the pattern of assistance from children to their older parents closely parallels that provided from parents to children, although in most cases the level of child assistance to the parent is greater (Cantor, 1979a; Cantor & Brennan, 1993c). This is equally true for the Jewish elderly of New York City and their children. The vast majority of children of White older New Yorkers, both Jewish and non-Jewish, were reported to help their parents in one or more ways. Only 9% of Jewish parents and 6% of non-Jewish White parents reported receiving no assistance from children in any of the four areas inquired about (i.e., crisis intervention, instrumental assistance with activities of daily living, information and advice, and financial assistance). But overall, Jewish older persons received somewhat less assistance from children than did their White non-Jewish peers, particularly in the area of instrumental assistance, as discussed below.

Types of Assistance Provided by Children to Jewish Elderly Parents

The most frequently reported type of intergenerational help from children was in the domain of financial assistance: 87% of older Jewish parents reported receiving gifts from children, as compared with the 86% who gave gifts to children. Suggestive of the notion that need plays a role in gift-giving, older Jewish mothers were more likely to receive gifts from children than were fathers (91% and 81%, respectively). Compared to non-Jewish White older New Yorkers, Jewish elderly parents were equally likely to report receiving gifts from children (90% and 87%, respectively).

The relatively affluent financial circumstances of many Jewish older persons in New York City is reflected in the finding that the flow of money between generations is more likely to be from parent to child; while only 15% reported receiving money from children, 42% reported providing money to children. However, like most children, those of the Jewish elderly appear to respond to increasing economic need on the part of parents, and receiving monetary help was much more likely among Jewish parents with poverty or near poverty incomes (32% and 29%, respectively) than in the case of parents with incomes over 150% of poverty (7%). This interpretation is also bolstered by the finding that non-Jewish White elderly individuals, who reported lower average incomes as compared to their Jewish counterparts, were more likely to report receiving direct monetary help from children (25% and 15%, respectively). However, among Jewish elderly in other areas of child to parent help (e.g., instrumental assistance), parental income was not significantly related to the amount of help received.

Intervention during illness or other crisis was the next most frequently mentioned type of child to parent assistance among Jewish older New Yorkers, with 62% of parents reporting the receipt of this type of help. As a reflection of the fact that older women are more likely to be widowed and lack a spouse, Jewish elderly mothers were more likely (70%) to report help in terms of crisis intervention from children compared to elderly Jewish fathers (51%). Given the more proximal location of the children of non-Jewish Whites, it is not surprising that these parents were more likely to report receiving crisis intervention from children (72%) as compared with 62% of Jewish elderly parents, whose children tend to live farther away, making the provision of direct assistance more difficult.

With regard to instrumental assistance with tasks of daily living, about two-fifths of older Jewish parents reported children did shopping or ran errands or provided transportation or escort assistance to places like a doctor's office or clinic. Again, older Jewish women were more likely than men to receive this type of assistance (44% and 29%, respectively). Further, over one-third (35%) of older Jewish parents reported that children helped with home repairs. However, the remaining areas of instrumental assistance from children to parents involving other daily activities were rarely mentioned; (e.g.: cooking or preparing meals (9%) and housekeeping (7%)). Similar to findings with regard to crisis intervention, older Jewish parents were less likely to receive instrumental assistance from children as compared with their non-Jewish White peers, for example, in the areas of shopping or running errands (37% and 58%, respectively). A similar pattern emerged in terms of housekeeping and home repairs. Only with regard to transportation assistance from children, were the proportions of Jewish and non-Jewish White elderly responses the same (both 37%).

The final domain, information and advice from children to parents, was at similarly low levels as found with respect to the provision of advice from parent to child: 27% of older Jewish parents reported receiving help with decisions on large purchases, while 25% received financial advice from children. Again, reflecting the greater face-to-face contact between non-Jewish White elderly parents and their children relative to their Jewish peers, non-Jewish older New Yorkers were more likely to receive advice on finances or large purchase decisions: approximately one-third of non-Jewish White older parents reported receiving both types of advice as compared to about one-quarter of Jewish parents. However, as noted earlier regarding parental advice to children, the proportion of parents in either group receiving such assistance was not very high. This finding supports the earlier observation that despite a high degree of closeness between older parents and children, the generations appear to operate independently with respect to giving and receiving advice. If old age encompasses the passing on of wisdom to younger generations, it seems not to be appropriate to interfere with the decision-making process of the other generation, unless such help is specifically requested.

Conclusions Regarding Intergenerational Assistance Among the Jewish Elderly

Previous research on New York City's elderly population has shown that concrete help from children, in contrast to emotional support, is related to the level of need on the part of the older parent, especially in terms of economic resources and level of frailty (Cantor, 1979a; Cantor

& Little, 1985; Cantor & Brennan, 1993c). Thus, it is not surprising that Jewish elderly persons receive less monetary assistance than their non-Jewish White peers, given their somewhat more affluent economic position. Because they are older on average, it is less easy to understand why the Jewish elderly receive less concrete help of an instrumental nature from children. One factor that undoubtedly limits the ability of children of Jewish elderly New Yorkers to provide such hands-on assistance is the greater geographic dispersion of Jewish children; two of five live beyond the New York City Metropolitan area. But, as we will discuss below, there is an indication that elderly Jews are more likely to turn to community agencies and paid helpers for instrumental help compared to their peers. Such willingness is probably influenced by strong cultural norms in the Jewish community about independence and not burdening one's children. In addition, persecution and segregation, as well as religious beliefs, have historically sanctioned reliance on others in the Jewish community for help in times of need. And not coincidentally, the Jewish community of New York City supports a wide array of health and social welfare services for both Jews and non-Jews alike.

GRANDCHILDREN AND GREAT-GRANDCHILDREN OF
JEWISH OLDER NEW YORKERS

With increases in life expectancy, three- and even four-generation families are becoming more common. The presence of grandchildren and great-grandchildren can be one of the most emotionally enriching experiences in the lives of older people. Additionally, as these children grow into adolescence and young adulthood, they too may become important sources of not only emotional, but also instrumental support to their grandparents. Concurrently, there is evidence that grandparents are becoming increasingly involved in the regular day-to-day care of grandchildren, and greater proportions of grandparents are responsible for raising grandchildren. Thus, respondents with children were asked both about the presence of grandchildren and great-grandchildren, as well as the extent to which they were involved in regular ongoing care of a grandchild.

Among Jewish respondents with children, the vast majority (85%) reported having one or more grandchildren, with 3.2 grandchildren on average. Additionally, one-quarter reported having at least one great-grandchild, having approximately one such descendant on average. With regard to the regular care of grandchildren and great-grandchildren, nearly one-third (30%) of Jewish grandparents were involved in such care, most often because parents were working.

SIBLINGS AND OTHER RELATIVES OF JEWISH OLDER NEW YORKERS

In addition to nuclear families, the social networks of older people normally include brothers and sisters and a variety of other, more distant relations (i.e., cousins, nieces and nephews, etc.). However, as people age, their siblings age as well, often resulting in functional limitations among brothers and sisters that may limit their ability to provide meaningful amounts of hands-on assistance. Findings from the 1970 study, "The Elderly in the Inner City of New York", revealed that while siblings and other relatives were less central in the provision of instrumental assistance to elderly individuals as compared to either spouses or children, they were, however, considered important sources of emotional sustenance and companionship by older New Yorkers, even if contact was limited to the telephone.

Presence of Siblings

Close to three-quarters (73%) of older Jewish New Yorkers reported having at least one living brother or sister, but only 41% reported having a sibling living in New York City (see Table 5.3). Among those with a sibling in the five boroughs, the modal number was one to two siblings. As might be expected, greater age was associated with the decreased likelihood of having a living sibling; those 85 years or more were the least likely to report a living sibling (53%), as compared with 79% among the youngest elderly group (65 to 74 years old) and about three-quarters of those in their late seventies and early eighties. The proportion of Jewish and non-Jewish Whites who reported the presence of a living sibling was nearly identical (73% and 71%, respectively).

Contact with Siblings

Reflecting increasing age, geographic dispersion, and potential frailty among siblings, frequent face-to-face contact between older Jewish New Yorkers and their siblings was somewhat limited. Only 40% reported seeing a sibling at least monthly (18% weekly and 22% monthly), while another 27% had face-to-face contact with a sibling only several times per year. The remaining one-third reported seeing a brother or sister only once per year or less, while 8% reported that they never saw their siblings. However, similar to the findings regarding contact with children, the telephone appears to operate as a compensatory mechanism, providing an alternative means of maintaining closeness and providing emotional support. Whereas only 14% of older Jewish New Yorkers with siblings see a brother or sister weekly, over half (56%) speak to a sibling on the phone on either a weekly (44%) or daily (12%) basis. Another 18% speak to a sibling on the phone on at least a monthly basis. Thus, the closeness between siblings and the potential for providing emotional support is manifested more through use of the telephone rather than face-to-face contact, with three-quarters (74%) speaking to siblings on the phone at least monthly if not more often. Only a small group, 11%, speak infrequently on the phone to siblings or not at all (5% once per year or less and 6% never).

Economic circumstances and the high cost of long distance phone services appear to affect the frequency of telephone contact with siblings among the Jewish elderly. Only about one-fifth reporting poverty level incomes speak to siblings on at least a weekly basis as compared to 52% of those in near poverty and 61% of those with incomes above 150% of poverty.

When comparing Jewish with non-Jewish White older New Yorkers' patterns of contact with siblings, the picture was very similar to that involving children. Non-Jewish Whites reported more frequent face-to-face contact with siblings compared to their Jewish counterparts; 27% of older Non-Jewish Whites were in face-to-face contact with a sibling on at least a weekly basis as compared with 18% of Jewish elderly respondents. But reflecting their relatively greater affluence and compensating for a lack of face-to-face visits, Jewish elderly individuals were more likely to be in regular (at least weekly) phone contact with a brother or sister as compared with their non-Jewish White peers (55% and 42%, respectively).

Other Relatives in New York City

Well over half (57%) of older Jewish New Yorkers reported the presence of at least one more distant relation, such as a cousin, niece, or nephew, with 3.3 such relations on average (see Table 5.3). However, only 38% of Jewish elderly persons reported having frequent contact with these other relatives, and the average number of distant relatives in frequent contact decreased to 1.1. Interestingly, older Jews were much more likely to report having one or more distant relatives in the five boroughs of New York City compared to non-Jewish White older

New Yorkers (57% and 41%, respectively). This difference is likely the result of immigration patterns among Jews, with heavy settlement of early Jewish immigrants tending to cluster in large urban areas, especially New York City. As a result, the concentration of distant relations in the five boroughs is today greater for Jews compared to their non-Jewish peers.

CONFIDANTS, FRIENDS, AND NEIGHBORS OF THE
JEWISH ELDERLY

While family members, particularly spouse and children, form the core of the social networks of older people, friends and neighbors often play important secondary roles, and may assume primary roles in the case of elderly persons without kin (Cantor & Johnson, 1978; Cantor & Little, 1985). Such persons have been found to provide important emotional, and in some cases, instrumental support to the older person (Reinhardt, 1996). Furthermore, having intimate relationships with friends positively contributes to higher morale and emotional well-being in late life (Troll et al., 1979). Some research has suggested that having a friend or confidant may be more important than kin in contributing to positive mental health among elderly persons (Cantor & Brennan, 1993c; Reinhardt, 1996). With this in mind, we now turn to the role of friends, confidants, and neighbors in the informal support networks of the elderly Jews of New York City.

Confidants

To learn more about the roles of friends and confidants, respondents were asked, "Is there anyone that you feel very close to, such as a friend, relative or neighbor? This would be someone you share confidences, feelings or problems with." For each person named, the respondent was asked to indicate the nature of the relationship, their relative age, geographic location, and frequency of both face-to-face and telephone contact with the respondent. The majority of Jewish elderly in New York City (57%) reported having at least one confidant, with the number of confidants being relatively small, usually one or two such individuals. Furthermore, over one-half of named confidants (56%) were kin (e.g., spouse, child). Social class was found to be an important indicator of the likelihood of having a confidant, with the presence of such an individual more prevalent in upper rather than lower socioeconomic strata among older Jewish New Yorkers.

Friends as Confidants

Because so many confidants were relatives, it was deemed important to differentiate between kin and nonkin confidants. As a result, kin confidants were set aside, and a more limited category of friend-confidant was created (hereafter referred to as "friends"). This procedure limited somewhat the proportion of elderly respondents with a confidant, but provided information on a more conceptually discrete category of friends as a separate component of the informal social care network.

Thus, while almost 60% of Jewish elderly persons designated at least one confidant, the proportion having a nonkin close friend fell to 37%, similar to older New Yorkers in general both in 1990 and in 1970 (see Table 5.3) (Cantor, 1979a; Cantor & Brennan, 1993c). On average, the number of friends reported by Jewish elderly individuals was one. Social class was found to be related to the likelihood of having a friend-confidant, with those in upper and middle strata more likely to have this support element as compared with those in lower socioeconimic strata. It is likely that for this latter group, the family plays a more central role than non-related outsiders, similar to the situation for many Latino older New Yorkers. There was no difference in the likelihood of having a close friend-confidant between Jewish and non-Jewish Whites in New York City: approximately one-third of each group named one such person in their social networks, and both groups reported approximately one friend, on average.

Geographic Location of Close Friends of Elderly Jews

Friends, by and large, tend to live nearby. One-half of the friends of the Jewish elderly lived in close proximity; 26% live in the same building, and another 27% live within walking distance. Although over half of the friends of the Jewish elderly could also be designated as neighbors given their close proximity, the two categories are not synonymous. It is the degree of intimacy and interdependence, the regularity of interaction, and personal choice in the formation of the relationship that distinguishes friends from neighbors. In addition to friends in the immediate vicinity, 21% of the friends of elderly Jews lived within the five boroughs of New York City and would be reachable with public transportation. However, a small though substantial proportion of friends (18%) live outside the city, with 10% living beyond the New York Metropolitan area. This finding suggests that although one's life space tends to shrink with advancing age, thus producing a greater tendency for friendships to be concentrated within the immediate neighborhood, older Jews do continue to maintain contact with friends that involve greater distance, assisted no doubt by the telephone and written correspondence. As was true in the case of children, the friends of Jewish elderly tended to be more geographically dispersed compared to the friends of non-Jewish White elderly. The difference between these groups in the extent of neighborhood-based friendships may be a reflection of the somewhat higher incomes and educations reported by Jewish elderly respondents, making continued contact with distant friends through the telephone, correspondence, and visiting more feasible.

Level of Interaction with Friends

Given the tendency for many friends to be neighborhood based, it is not surprising that older Jews in New York City and their friends are in frequent face-to-face contact. Most friends are seen on either a daily or weekly basis (27% and 37%, respectively). Thus, they are in at least weekly face-to-face contact with nearly two-thirds (64%) of their friends. One-fifth (22%) of the friends of Jewish elderly are seen with moderate frequency on a monthly basis, while only 14% are seen infrequently, that is, several times per year or less, with distance probably the main barrier in such cases.

Even given the high level of face-to-face visits, Jewish elderly individuals and their friends are in even more frequent contact over the telephone. Nearly three-quarters of friends are in telephone contact with respondents on at least a weekly basis (23% daily and 49% weekly). Of those in less frequent contact, 15% of friends are in telephone contact at least once per month, while only 13% are in phone contact several times per year or less often. This high level of both face-to-face and telephone contact between older Jews and their friends suggests the importance of friendship ties in old age. Such relationships appear to provide important avenues for emotional intimacy and socialization over and above the existence of strong family ties.

Age of Friends

The final aspect of the friendship patterns of the Jewish elderly worth particular note is that age does not appear to be a limiting factor in the formation of intimate nonkin relationships. Thus, the majority

(59%) of the friends of the elderly Jews of New York City were reported to be younger than the respondent, with the remaining two-fifths nearly equally divided between friends of the same age (22%) and friends older than the respondent (20%). The higher proportion of younger friends was equally true among both Jewish and non-Jewish White respondents (59% and 62% of friends, respectively).

Summary of the Friendship Patterns of the Jewish Elderly

In the foregoing discussion of friendship among the Jewish elderly, several points emerge. The tendency for friends to be located in the neighborhood or nearby suggests that most older people (except perhaps the physically vigorous and those who are well-to-do) tend to be neighborhood-bound. A neighborhood, as defined by the elderly persons themselves, usually encompasses a radius of about 10 blocks (Cantor, 1979a; Cantor, 1981; Cantor & Brennan, 1993b). This geographic restriction, when combined with loss of friends through death or out-migration, may explain the somewhat restricted friendship networks of Jewish elderly persons, which rarely involve more than one or two nonkin intimates. Furthermore, nearly two-thirds (63%) of Jewish older New Yorkers did not report this often vital support element in their social networks. However, age does not appear to be a barrier to friendship in the case of the elderly, and those who do have friends appear to benefit from close relationships characterized by high levels of both face-to-face and telephone contact. Finally, although the pool of friends may be limited, the location of the majority of friends in the neighborhood is of considerable compensatory significance with respect to the potential for emotional social support and the intimacy involved in a confidant relationship, as well as more limited instances of instrumental assistance.

NEIGHBORS KNOWN WELL

In general, the Jewish elderly of New York City have substantial kin networks comprised of spouse, children, siblings, and other relatives. However, some have only limited kin networks (18% report two or fewer kin support elements), and others may have relatives that live some distance from themselves. For these older people, friends and neighbors could, if present, substitute as primary social supports, particularly in case of emergencies. And even for those with vigorous kin support networks, there are important socialization and types of assistance that are particularly suited to friends and neighbors (Litwak & Szelenyi, 1969). New York City's neighborhoods have always been characterized by high levels of diversity, including a wide range of age groups and ethnic backgrounds (Cantor & Brennan, 1993b). Therefore, it is of particular interest to examine the extent to which the Jewish elderly New Yorkers know their neighbors well and the amount and types of support that they and their neighbors may provide for each other.

Among the Jewish older New Yorkers, nearly two-thirds (63%) reported knowing one or more neighbors well, a proportion substantially exceeding the 37% reporting a friend (see Table 5.3). Not only were Jewish elderly persons more likely to know neighbors, but they knew more than twice as many neighbors, (on average 2.2) compared to the average number of friends (0.7). Jewish elderly respondents in lower socioeconomic strata were much more likely to know neighbors well as compared with their upper-class peers, ranging from 72% in the lowest group to between 43 and 55% in the highest strata. Thus, it would appear that embeddedness in the neighborhood is more characteristic of low income and working class elderly persons than for those at the opposite end of the economic spectrum, for whom friends play a more important role.

Types and Extent of Assistance Between Jewish Elderly and Their Neighbors

Knowing a neighbor well does not, in and of itself, guarantee that a helping relationship exists. Therefore, respondents who reported knowing at least one neighbor well were asked to indicate the extent of assistance exchanged between themselves and their neighbors either a lot, only in emergencies, or not at all. Responses indicated that there was a considerable amount of help exchanged between older Jews and their neighbors, with nearly one-third (31%) reporting that they and their neighbors helped each other a lot, while nearly half (47%) said they and their neighbors helped each other at least in emergencies. Only 19% of Jewish older New Yorkers knowing neighbors well indicated that they and their neighbors never helped each other, even during crisis situations.

To better understand the flow of assistance between elderly persons and their neighbors, respondents who were involved in a helping relationship with their neighbors were asked about the nature of

social support provided. Of the six types of help asked about, two pertained to health (i.e., help if someone is ill and escort to the
doctor/clinic), two involved everyday activities (i.e., shopping and
picking up mail), one involved lending money, and the final item pertained to socializing in each other's homes or apartments.

Socialization was the most frequently mentioned type of activity
shared between Jewish elderly New Yorkers and their neighbors—79%
reported visiting each other at home. Following socialization, everyday instrumental assistance in the form of picking up mail (64%) or
shopping (55%) was the next most frequently reported activity, closely
followed by health related assistance (help during illness, 61%; escort
to doctor/clinic, 39%). With respect to neighbor assistance during
times of illness, findings about older New Yorkers in general (Cantor
& Brennan, 1993c) suggest that much of this assistance given by neighbors was of a short-term and emergency nature, often provided when
children or other kin were not available. As noted in chapter 2, where
the need for assistance persists, health-related care is more typically
provided by close kin or formal providers. Finally, as is true for the
vast majority of elderly people and their neighbors, lending money to
each other was reported only infrequently between Jewish older New
Yorkers and their neighbors; only 14% reported this type of exchange.
Financial assistance, when it occurs, is more likely provided by family members or occasionally close friends.

Comparing patterns of assistance with neighbors between Jewish
and non-Jewish White older New Yorkers revealed no real differences,
both in terms of the level of help exchanged as well as the types of activities comprising this assistance. Approximately four-fifths of both groups
who reported knowing neighbors well also reported that they either
exchanged a lot of help with neighbors or at least did so during emergencies. Socialization was the most frequently reported activity shared
with neighbors by both Jewish and non-Jewish White elderly respondents, underscoring the importance of neighbors in providing emotional
support. In addition, both groups were involved in providing help during times of illness or escorting to the doctor/clinic or limited instrumental assistance in terms of shopping or picking up mail.

Summary of Relationships Between Jewish
Elderly and Neighbors

Most White older New Yorkers, including Jews, have in addition to
kin, one or more neighbors as part of their informal social support sys-

tem. In addition, a smaller but substantial group have friend as well. It would appear that the high population density found in large cities such as New York offer many opportunities for continued relationships between older people and nonrelated significant others, particularly in the case of individuals living within the immediate neighborhood. Such relationships can be of considerable significance to the older person for ongoing emotional support as well as instrumental assistance during times of illness or other crisis.

PERCEPTIONS OF INFORMAL SOCIAL SUPPORT
AVAILABILITY AND ADEQUACY

The previous sections on the nature of the social networks of the Jewish elderly of New York City revealed that they are well-endowed with both kin and nonkin, and that a considerable amount of interaction, both social and of a helping nature, occurs between them and members of their informal networks. While these findings suggest that older Jews are not isolated and have someone to turn to in times of need, it is important to determine the extent to which individuals perceive support from the informal social network to be both available and adequate.

Thus, after providing information on the extent and composition of their informal networks, respondents were asked to rate the availability and adequacy of social support received in the two major areas, namely, instrumental help with tasks of daily living and emotional support. The question pertaining to availability asked, "If you need some extra help (with tasks of daily living/emotional support), do you have someone you can count on to help you: (a) most of the time; (b) some of the time; (c) only occasionally; or (d) not at all?" The second item dealing with adequacy of support asked, "During the past year, could you have used: (a) a lot more; (b) some more; (c) a little more (instrumental help/emotional support); or did you (d) get all the (help/support) you needed? Because these four items immediately followed the section on the informal network and before any reference to formal service utilization, it is fair to assume that perceptions regarding availability and adequacy of support pertained for most respondents to help from kin or nonkin, rather than formal service providers.

Perceived Availability of Instrumental Help

Nearly two-thirds (65%) of Jewish older New Yorkers reported relatively high levels of availability of instrumental helpers: one-half (52%)
said they had a person to count on most of the time, and 13% reported
someone was available at least some of the time. However, one-third
of Jewish elderly respondents were less sanguine about the availability of someone to count on for help with instrumental activities of
daily living: 13% reported such help to be available only occasionally,
and fully one-fifth (20%) indicated they had no one to help with instrumental tasks. The sizable number who had their doubts about their
ability to access instrumental help from the informal system underscores the importance of formal community-based services for many
elderly individuals, even those with kin, friend, and neighbor support
elements present.

    As might be expected, there was a trend among those living
alone to be more likely (36%) to report that instrumental help was
available only sporadically, that is, some of the time or only occasionally in comparison to elderly living with a spouse (17%) or living with others (mainly children) (24%). However, among those
reporting that they had no one to count on for instrumental help, living arrangements per se did not appear to be a determining factor.
Thus, 21% of elderly persons living alone, 20% of those living with
a spouse, and 18% of those living with others, but without a spouse,
reported no one was available to provide instrumental help. This
finding clearly suggests that older people needing help with instrumental tasks may be found in all types of households, including
those in which children and even a spouse is present.

    Despite the fact that the children of elderly Jewish parents tended
to be more dispersed than the children of non-Jewish White elderly
parents and were also less involved in the provision of instrumental
assistance, there were no statistically significant differences in perceptions of the availability of instrumental help between these two
groups. Although non-Jewish Whites were somewhat more likely than
Jews to report they had someone to count on for instrumental help
most of the time (57% and 52%, respectively), about two-thirds of both
groups reported someone available at least some of the time. There
was a slight trend for Jewish elderly to be more likely to report they
had no one to count on for instrumental assistance compared to non-
Jewish White elderly respondents (20% and 17%, respectively).

Adequacy of Instrumental Support.

With regard to the adequacy of instrumental support received during the past year, the picture was even more positive, with nearly three-quarters (72%) of Jewish elderly individuals indicating that they had received all the help they needed. This positive appraisal seems to be at odds with the earlier finding that 20% reported they had no one to turn to for help with instrumental tasks, but it is likely some of these elderly persons did not need help in the past year and were managing on their own. Of the approximately one quarter of older Jews who needed more instrumental help, 8% reported needing a little more help; 12% said they needed some more help; and only 6% indicated needing a lot more help. Again, the need for additional instrumental help was significantly related to living arrangements of the Jewish elderly; over one-third of those living alone indicated the need for more help in the past year as compared with one-quarter of older Jews living with a spouse or others. Need for instrumental assistance was also related to income, with a substantial proportion of those with poverty or near-poverty level incomes (46% and 41%, respectively) indicating the need for additional help, as compared to half that proportion (21%) among those with incomes over 150% of poverty level. Older Jewish women were also more likely (33%) to report needing more help as compared to older Jewish men.

Despite the trend for non-Jewish White elderly respondents to perceive greater levels of instrumental help availability relative to their Jewish counterparts, it was Jewish older New Yorkers who were the more positive regarding the adequacy of this type of assistance during the past year. While almost three-quarters of the Jewish elderly indicated they had received all the help they needed, this proportion fell to two-thirds in the case of the non-Jewish White elderly. This finding is consistent with the hypothesis that elderly Jews in need of assistance may be obtaining this help from outside their informal networks, although it is also possible that their level of expectations for receipt of assistance with tasks of daily living may be lower than their non-Jewish White counterparts. Given the fact that the members of Jewish elderly group tended to be older and somewhat frailer than their non-Jewish White peers, it is unlikely that this more positive perception of instrumental support adequacy is the result of relatively reduced need between the two groups.

Perceived Availability and Adequacy
of Emotional Support

When asked if someone was available to provide emotional support in the past year, elderly Jews of New York City were even more positive in their ratings than those for instrumental help. Over two-thirds (69%) reported that emotional support was available most of the time, while approximately one-fifth indicated such support was available either some of the time (12%) or at least occasionally. Only one of ten older Jews indicated that they had no one available to provide emotional support. As was the case with instrumental support, the living arrangements were significantly related to perceptions of emotional support availability; those living with a spouse were the most likely (76%) to report such support was available most of the time, illustrating the central role of the marriage dyad in meeting emotional needs. Jewish elderly individuals living with others, but without a spouse, were the next most likely (70%) to report emotional support availability most of the time, followed by those living alone (60%). Taken with the earlier findings on instrumental help availability, Jewish elderly living alone appear to be disadvantaged in terms of informal assistance in both domains. Advanced age was also related to a decreased likelihood of having someone for emotional support most of the time, from a high of about three-quarters among those in their late sixties and early seventies, to 60% of those 80 years and older.

As was true for perceptions regarding instrumental help adequacy, nearly three-quarters (72%) of Jewish elderly respondents reported that they had received all the emotional support they needed during the past year. But slightly more than one-quarter of Jewish older New Yorkers reported they could have used from a little to a lot more emotional support in the past year. Again, Jewish elderly persons living with a spouse were the most likely (80%) to report receiving all the emotional support they needed in the past year, followed by those living with others but without a spouse (70%), and lastly those living alone (63%). Older Jewish women were more likely to indicate the need for more emotional support (30%) as compared with males (17%), not surprising given the greater likelihood of males to be living with a spouse, as compared to females who are more likely to be widowed and living alone.

With respect to perceptions regarding the availability and adequacy of emotional support, there were no substantial differences between Jewish and non-Jewish White older New Yorkers. Both groups were equally likely to indicate emotional support was available most of the time (69% among Jewish and 69% among non-Jewish White), some of the time (12% and 12%, respectively), only occasionally (7% and 9%, respectively), and not at all (9% and 8%, respectively). Findings were similar concerning the adequacy of emotional support, where 72% of Jews and 75% of non-Jewish Whites indicated they had received all the support they had needed in the past year. It is clear that the vast majority of White elderly in New York City, Jewish and non-Jewish alike, perceive that emotional support from members of their informal networks is both highly available and very adequate.

THE USE OF FORMAL COMMUNITY-BASED SERVICES AMONG THE JEWISH ELDERLY OF NEW YORK CITY

The previous sections have revealed that the Jewish elderly population of New York is well endowed with an extensive informal network that involves interaction on a regular basis. Jewish older New Yorkers, like most older persons, provide support to children and receive assistance from them in return. In addition, they have other kin, friends, and neighbors for both socialization and, in some cases, instrumental assistance of an ongoing nature and during times of crisis. But we have also seen that the children of Jewish elderly parents are more likely than children of other older New Yorkers to live outside the City, not only in the suburbs but beyond the metropolitan area. Thus, the Jewish elderly, despite their greater average age, tend to receive less hands-on assistance compared to other groups of older New Yorkers. However, this is not to say that as a group older Jews are without informal supports, and satisfaction with the availability and adequacy of these supports is at similarly high levels as other groups of elderly people in New York City.

Throughout this book we have conceptualized the social care system of older people as involving a partnership of both formal and informal social support components. It is, therefore, likely that for those Jewish elderly respondents who reported that assistance from informal sources was either unavailable or inadequate, community agencies may be filling the gap between the desire and ability to maintain independence. Thus, it is critical to know more about the extent to which Jewish elderly turned to formal providers in the past year for assistance and which components of the formal system were used most extensively to compensate for help not provided by family, friends, and neighbors. In the following sections, we will examine the extent of the use of community services among the Jewish elderly as compared with older New Yorkers in general. What makes such a comparison particularly informative is that Jewish older New Yorkers, with their higher levels of education and , as we shall see, greater use of community agencies, are in many ways prototypical of future cohorts of older Americans, especially as the baby-boomers enter their later years.

NEED AND UTILIZATION OF FORMAL SERVICES

While most Jewish older New Yorkers receive help from informal sources, there are circumstances in which kin are unavailable or cannot carry the burden of care because they lack the skills to provide the help required. The bulk of previous research, including the larger study from which the Jewish elderly respondents were drawn, indicates that the best predictor of whether a person will turn to the formal system for assistance is the level of need (Cantor & Brennan, 1993c). Past research on service utilization by older persons has used several measures of need, including chronological age, degree of functional incapacity with tasks of daily living and personal care, and adequacy of financial resources. In addition, gender, living arrangements, and the availability of informal support (usually from children) are frequently hypothesized factors in the utilization of formal services. As we examined the use of formal services among the Jewish elderly, we also examined the influence of these factors, paying careful attention to age, functional ability and economic status as they related to service utilization, both overall and with respect to specific services.[1]

Need for Social Care Assistance Among the Jewish Elderly

As indicated earlier, older Jews in New York City tended to be 3 years older on average (77 years) compared to older New Yorkers in general, and nearly 40% were 80 years old or older. In addition, 10% of Jews reported annual incomes at or below poverty and an additional 20% were in near-poverty. Although self-appraised health status is an

---

1. It should be noted that in the following section on service utilization, we return to comparisons between Jewish elderly and older New Yorkers, in general.

acceptable measure of the physical capacity when evaluating the need for services, a person's level of functional ability is perhaps even more important. To appraise the functional capacity of the Jewish elderly to perform tasks of daily living, a modified version of the Townsend Index of Functional Ability was employed (see Cantor & Brennan, 1993c; Townsend 1963, 1968). Six representative aspects of independent living were assessed for the ability to perform without assistance: dressing, climbing one flight of stairs, going outside, walking, bathing/showering, and cutting toenails. Respondents were classified into one of three categories based on their item scores: (a) active (no reported impairments); (b) limited (difficulty in one area but normal day-to-day functioning); and (c) frail (two or more areas of functional incapacity). Despite their greater average age, Jewish elderly were no more likely than older New Yorkers in general to be classified as frail in terms of functional ability with tasks of daily living (23% and 22%, respectively). Among elderly Jews, slightly over half (53%) were classified as active and thus were without any significant levels of functional disability. In the case of the remaining 24% classified as limited, it is likely that these individuals suffer activity restrictions but not severe enough to preclude independent living with only minimal assistance.

As is true for all elderly, frailty is more likely to occur with increasing age among Jewish older New Yorkers, and half of Jews 85 years and older were classified as frail, as compared with approximately one quarter of the 75 to 84 year olds, and 17% of those 70 to 74 years old. However, even among the youngest group (65 to 69 years old), nearly one in ten reported two or more functional limitations and were classified as frail. In addition, Jewish older women were more likely than men to suffer from functional limitations, a factor of both their greater average age, as well as their greater likelihood to suffer from chronic, as opposed to acute, illnesses. There was also a significant relationship between functional ability and poverty, with frail elderly persons far more likely to report poverty or near-poverty incomes than either limited or active Jewish older New Yorkers. These findings illustrate the interrelationship between advanced years, female gender, poverty, and functional disability among elderly persons, irrespective of ethnicity or culture. Furthermore, they suggest a need for social care assistance among a small but significant segment of the older population.

UTILIZATION OF FORMAL SERVICES BY
JEWISH OLDER NEW YORKERS

To ascertain the extent of the use of community-based services, respondents were presented with a list of special groups or agencies in New York City that help older people with any difficulties they might have, and were asked to indicate which, if any, agencies they had turned to in the past year for help. It should be noted that the question was purposely worded to exclude mere contact with an agency, and to elicit responses concerning the more positive concept of seeking help in times of need. The list encompassed a broad spectrum of community services, including the offices responsible for basic entitlements (i.e., Social Security, Medicare, Medicaid), in-home services (i.e., homecare agencies, visiting nurse), health care (i.e., nursing home, Veterans Administration Hospital), local government agencies (i.e., New York City Department for the Aging, Department of Social Services, Police, Housing Authority), religious leaders (i.e., rabbi, minister, or priest), and senior centers[2] (Table 5.4).

Extent of Formal Service Utilization

Almost three-fifths (59%) of Jewish older New Yorkers indicated turning to one or more community agencies during the previous year, a proportion only slightly higher than that found among New York's elderly population overall (56%). Most elderly Jews, as well as older New Yorkers in general, who reported formal service utilization in the previous year indicated turning to one or at most two agencies. The average number of agencies turned to by the Jewish elderly was 1.3, only slightly higher than the average for the city's older population as a whole (1.2), reflecting to some extent their greater tendency to use homecare and health-related services, as will be discussed below.

Types of Formal Services Used by the Jewish Elderly

Table 5.4 provides a list of community services inquired about and the proportion of Jewish elderly and older New Yorkers in general who reported turning to each agency during the previous year. The extent of utilization of formal agencies varied considerably among both

---

2. Due to the structure of the questionnaire, information on senior center use pertained to attendance in the past month.

TABLE 5.4 Extent of Formal Service Utilization in Past Year by Type of Assistance: Comparison of Jewish Elderly and All Older New Yorkers (Percent[a])

Type of service	Jewish elderly Percent	Rank	All New York City elderly Percent	Rank
Entitlements				
Social Security	16.7	5	19.1	2
Medicare	22.7	1	18.2	3
Medicaid	3.6	14	4.6	14
Department of Social Services	6.5	11	6.4	11
In-home services				
Homecare (all types)	14.9	6	10.3	6
Visiting nurse service	11.9	7	6.8	10
Health services				
Nursing home	3.0	15	1.2	15
Veterans administration /V.A. hospital	5.4	12	7.4	9
Emergency room	21.2	2	19.8	1
Inpatient hospital	18.8	4	16.8	5
Local community services				
Senior center	20.0	3	17.3	4
NYC Department for The Aging	6.6	10	5.5	12
NYC housing authority	5.1	13	5.2	13
Police department	9.0	8	7.5	8
Rabbi/minister/priest	8.4	9	9.2	7

[a] Independent items, totals do not equal 100%.
[b] Jewish (n = 335); total New York City (n = 1577).

elderly Jews and older New Yorkers overall, and the proportion turning to any one agency rarely exceeded about 20%. Table 5.4 also contains utilization rates for two types of acute medical services: inpatient hospital and emergency room care, although these questions were not presented at the same time as the other 10 agencies. They were included because of their importance in the maintenance of positive quality of life and independent living in the community.

Among Jewish older New Yorkers, four types of service utilization were the most frequently reported. In order, these services were
the basic entitlement offices (Medicare, 23%; Social Security, 17%);
acute health care services (inpatient hospital, 19%; emergency room,
21%), socialization and nutrition services (senior center, 20%); and
finally homecare services (homemaker/housekeeping, 15%; visiting
nurse, 12%). Use of the remaining agencies was infrequent, with only
4% to 9% of Jewish elderly respondents reporting turning to any in
this group in the previous year.

An interesting finding was that the general pattern of utilization
was similar when comparing older Jewish New Yorkers with elderly
persons in general, although differences did emerge in the order of
importance of the most frequently used types of service (see Table 5.4).
The four most frequently utilized types of service were the same in
either case, namely, basic entitlement offices, acute health services,
senior centers, and lastly, in-home services. There was also little difference in the rate of inpatient hospitalization and emergency room
use between older Jewish persons and older New Yorkers in general,
with about one-fifth of each group reporting using either service (inpatient hospital, 18% and 19%, respectively; emergency room, 21% and
20%, respectively).

However, the most notable difference in service utilization between
Jewish elderly and older New Yorkers as a whole was apparent in the
use of in-home services. Almost twice the proportion of Jewish elderly
respondents reported visiting nurse utilization, compared to the City's
older population overall (12% and 7%, respectively). In the case of
homecare and housekeeping services, 16% of elderly Jews reported
using these services in the previous year, as compared with 10% among
older New Yorkers overall. A fuller discussion of utilization patterns of
in-home services and reasons for higher rates of utilization among
Jewish elderly persons will be found later in this chapter.

AN IN-DEPTH EXAMINATION OF THE USE OF SPECIFIC
SERVICES BY THE JEWISH ELDERLY

Although a proportion of Jewish older New Yorkers reported turning
to all 10 services inquired about during the previous year, some services are more germane than others to our examination of the role of
the formal sector as a substitute or complement for assistance provided by the informal network, particularly close family. For this reason, we undertook to thoroughly explore formal service utilization in

three crucial areas: (a) emergency room use, (b) in-home services (homecare and visiting nurse), and (c) senior centers, where in addition to the nutrition program and opportunities for socialization, assistance in securing entitlements and needed services is often provided.

Use of the Hospital Emergency Room

As noted earlier, about one-fifth of both Jewish elderly respondents and older New Yorkers in general reported turning to the hospital emergency room in the previous year. In the minds of many people, emergency room utilization is associated with low-income minority communities, where private doctors and clinics are unavailable. Thus, it was surprising to find that Jewish elderly, who as a group are in a stronger financial position, as compared with their peers citywide, were equally frequent users of the emergency room. This finding suggests that such usage is not necessarily limited by income or the availability of private doctors. While it is reasonable to assume that some of the emergency room utilization by older Jews was by those who lacked a private physician, one must also infer that many other Jewish elderly who had private doctors utilized emergency rooms as well. One possible explanation for this relatively high utilization by Jewish older New Yorkers may be that, among those with a private doctor, circumstances arise when that doctor may not be available (late night, weekends) or the doctor may be directing them to the emergency room for immediate or specialized treatment.

Another explanation is that financial advantages that would generally tend to mitigate against emergency room use by older Jews is counterbalanced by their greater age and concomitant increased frailty and need of medical care as compared with older New Yorkers overall. Within-group analyses tend to support this hypothesis. Thus, among the Jewish elderly, there was a trend for greater emergency room use with increased age; reported by 33% of Jews 85 years old or more, compared with only about one-fifth of those 70 to 84, and less than 10% of the youngest group (65 to 69 years). Frailty was also significantly related to emergency room use: 31% of frail elderly Jews reported such utilization, as compared with 21% among limited and 17% among active older Jewish New Yorkers.

Living arrangement was significantly related to emergency room use among Jewish elderly persons as well. Those living alone or with others, but not spouse, were twice as likely as married couples to report emergency room use. Because older Jewish women were more likely to be living alone or with others, but without a spouse, tend to be older, and report greater levels of frailty, it follows that they were also more likely to have used an emergency room in the previous year, compared to their male counterparts. But perhaps most interesting, was the finding that, unlike most other services, emergency room use was related to neither income nor poverty level, suggesting Jewish elderly use emergency rooms for immediate care, rather than as a substitute because they lack funds for a private doctor.

Findings that frailty and advanced age are related to emergency room use among the Jewish elderly, but that income does not appear to play a role, have important implications for health care delivery in the near future. As we posited earlier, the Jewish elderly are prototypical of future cohorts of older Americans, with greater proportions of the oldest old (80 years or more) as compared with the current elderly population, (especially in urban areas like New York City with large proportions of generally younger minority elderly.) There is a general recognition that the projected increases in the oldest-old will result in greater need for long-term care in the future. Less attention, however, has been paid to the impact on emergency room utilization of increasing numbers of persons in their eighth decade and beyond, with increasing incidence of frailty and morbidity. For them, it is essential that services are available for the immediate diagnosis and relevant treatment of medical problems, whether they are located in the emergency room or neighborhood clinics, so that what may be an initially minor medical episode does not develop into a serious life-threatening illness. It would appear, based on the emergency room utilization patterns among the Jewish elderly in New York City (i.e., the high use by the very frail and very old), that in the future emergency room services can be expected to increase in importance among all older people, regardless of the availability of private physicians or health maintenance organizations for general medical care.

Use of In-Home Services

As noted earlier, Jewish elderly respondents were more likely than older New Yorkers as a whole to use both homecare (15% and 10%, respectively) and visiting nurse services (12% and 7%, respectively). The need for long-term care can ensue as a result of an acute medical illness, but may also arise as a result of gradual decline in functional ability, often accompanying advanced age, chronic illness, or mental decline.

As was the case with emergency room use, utilization of in-home services (i.e., homecare and visiting nurse) by older Jewish New Yorkers was related to both age and functional ability. With respect to age, approximately one-third of Jews 85 years old or more reported using in-home services in the previous year, followed by close to one-fifth of those 80 to 84 years of age. Among Jews in their eighth decade, the proportion using in-home services fell to less than 10%, and only very few (0% to 2%) of those 65 to 69 years old indicated the use of such assistance. Findings in terms of functional ability were even more robust. Nearly two in five (38%) older Jews who were classified as frail reported having used homecare in the previous year, compared to one in ten (11%) among the limited, and 6% of elderly persons who were classified as active. With regard to visiting nurse utilization, about one-quarter of frail, 13% of limited, and only 5% of active elderly persons reported using these in-home services.

Living arrangement and gender were also related to homecare use among Jewish elderly respondents. Those living alone were almost twice as likely to use homecare as those living with a spouse, or others but without spouse (21%, 12%, and 12%, respectively). The greater likelihood of older men to be cared for by a spouse, and the greater tendency for women to live both longer and alone are the most probable explanations for the finding that Jewish elderly women were more than twice as likely than men to report homecare service utilization (21% and 8%, respectively).

Generally, these findings parallel the relationships with respect to emergency room use. However, in the case of homecare utilization, poverty level was significantly related to homecare usage. Community-based homecare services were used by about one-quarter of Jewish elderly with poverty or near poverty incomes, as compared with only 9% of those with incomes over 150% of poverty. Because long-term, community-based homecare is generally financed by Medicaid, which has income and asset eligibility limits, the proportion of Jewish elderly individuals with incomes over 150% of poverty utilizing homecare may be underestimated; some of these elderly may be paying for homecare out-of-pocket. Patterns in visiting nurse utilization among Jewish older New Yorkers were similar to those observed for homecare, with a greater likelihood of use associated with being female, living alone, and having poverty or near poverty income.

In addition to the traditional need-based reasons for turning to in-home services (e.g., greater frailty), in the case of Jewish elderly other factors would appear to operate as well in explaining their greater utilization, as compared to older New Yorkers in general. The fact that a greater proportion of the children of Jewish elderly live far away from their parents and are less likely to be involved in the provision of instrumental assistance undoubtedly plays a role. Thus, the greater use of in-home long-term care in many situations may be encouraged by children who are concerned for a parent's well-being and who may arrange for and even reimburse providers of needed in-home services. The relatively greater affluence of older Jews and their children makes the procurement of such assistance all the more feasible.

A second important factor involves the values and norms regarding the relative role of family and community in providing care to its members, an integral part of the mosaic of Jewish culture. Jewish communal life, both historically and presently, places a high value on supporting a vast array of community-based health and social services, and on turning to the formal sector in times of need is clearly countenanced by both older and younger generations. Thus, elderly Jews express a greater willingness, compared to their peers, to utilize formal helpers, particularly with respect to in-home services. In part, this may also be a manifestation of the cultural value in the Jewish community of not burdening children or impeding their advancement.

The greater use of in-home services among Jewish older New Yorkers appears to stem from an amalgam of both objective needs and cultural values cherished by Jews regardless of age. It is likely that the willingness to use formal in-home, long-term care services will increase in the future, among both older Jews and other emerging elderly cohorts of better educated, more financially secure older people, particularly if families in the United States continue to be geographically dispersed.

Use of Senior Centers by Jewish Older New Yorkers

Aside from the major entitlement offices, and health-related and in-home services, senior centers were the most frequently reported community service used by both Jewish elderly and older New Yorkers in general. A comparison of rates of senior center utilization in New York City between 1970 and 1990 suggests stability, such attendence being reported by about 17% of older New Yorkers at both times (Cantor & Brennan, 1993c). The substantial proportions of New York City's elderly population who report going to a senior center over the past two decades attests to their importance as places for socialization, information and referral, and for many, the opportunity for the only hot meal of the day.

Jewish elderly respondents reported using senior centers only slightly more than their older New Yorkers as a whole (20% and 17%, respectively). For Jewish elderly with geographically dispersed children, the need for companionship possible in a senior center environment may take on greater importance. However, rates of senior center utilization among Jews differed sharply by age group, which has important implications for future senior center program planning. Among the young-old (65 to 74 year of age), who tend to have higher education levels and incomes, as well as better health, only 7% reported attending a senior center in the previous month. Attendance rose to 31% among the middle-old (70 to 74 years), but decreased to 16% among 75- to 79-year-olds. Usage among the oldest-old, however, rose again, with between 22% and 24% of those in their ninth decade and beyond attending a senior center in the past month.

Clearly, the oft-noted aging-in of senior center membership is apparent in the utilization rates of Jewish older New Yorkers. But equally important is the low rate of participation among younger Jewish elderly, suggesting that the age-segregated nature of current programs in many of these centers may not be attractive to current and future cohorts of better educated and more affluent elderly possessing other avenues for community participation, socialization, education, and leisure pursuits. A similar finding was noted among suburban elderly Jews (Cantor, Brook, & Mellor, 1986), suggesting that the senior centers of the future will need to broaden their programming if they are to continue to attract the younger elderly population.

The finding of increased utilization among Jewish older persons in their early seventies is important to note and may reflect the need for opportunities for socialization and information among those who age in-place after retirement. For such older people, reductions in social networks due to loss of spouse, family and friends through death or relocation, coupled with an increased recognition of one's aged status, may play a role in the greater senior center participation of 70- to 74-years-olds. The increasing diversity of incoming senior center members, combined with the heavy concentration of members who are aging-in and becoming both older and frailer, poses difficult questions regarding program priorities in the future.

For the current generation of older people involved in the senior center movement, the value of this program seems clear, particularly among older Jews living alone or with spouse, and those with sufficient functional ability to travel to, and participate in, activities and programs. Thus, aside from age, the most salient factor associated with senior center participation is frailty, and among the Jewish elderly, low levels of participation were found for those who were frailest or those living with children (often due to frailty). This finding would suggest that in the continuum of community-based services for independent living, attending a senior center requires a minimum level of health and functional ability. With decreasing rates of disability among the incoming cohorts of older people, along with growing availability of adult day care for the very frail, the future may witness a generally more vigorous senior center membership, offering increased opportunities for diverse programming. Along with family, friends, and neighbors, participation at senior centers clearly provides opportunities to form meaningful relationships that are basic to maintaining quality of life.

NEED FOR ADDITIONAL FORMAL SERVICES
AMONG JEWISH ELDERLY

The finding that approximately 60% of Jewish older New Yorkers had turned to the formal system during the previous year provides only part of the picture with respect to the importance of community-based agencies in maintaining quality of life for New York City's elderly population, regardless of religious affiliation. Analogous to the questions regarding adequacy and availability of informal support, is the extent to which older people report unmet need in the provision of formal care. Some elderly people may have developed needs that are beyond the capacities of their informal networks and may not possess knowledge or linkages to formal services. For others, psychological or cultural barriers may stand in the way of obtaining needed assistance. Thus, any analysis of the role played by formal agencies in providing help to older people must take into account the perceptions of unmet need, in addition to patterns of service utilization.

Following the section on use of community-based agencies, respondents were asked about the extent of unmet need with respect to a list of 11 commonly-used, community-based services, as well as any other areas in which they could have used assistance during the previous year. Types of assistance needed fell into five domains: (a) tasks of daily living; (b) health care; (c) socialization; (d) personal and job counseling; and (e) assistance in obtaining entitlements/benefits (a list of services covered is provided in Table 5.5). While these domains generally paralleled those covered in the section on service utilization, they were not identical.

Extent and Types of Unmet Need
Expressed by the Jewish Elderly

While the extent of service utilization was similar in the case of Jewish elderly and older New Yorkers in general (about 60% among each), Jewish elderly were much more likely than the City's elderly as a whole to report needing one or more additional services. Jews also reported a greater number of unmet needs, on average 1.5, as compared with other older New Yorkers (1.3 on average). This finding was somewhat surprising in light of earlier results that showed Jewish elderly more likely than their peers to report receiving all the informal assistance they required. Here again, their greater relative age, the greater likelihood for the children of Jewish elderly to be living some distance from parents, as well as cultural values may play a role in the greater reported unmet needs among these older New Yorkers.

The type of additional needs reported by the Jewish elderly mirrors the agencies they had utilized most frequently in the previous year. The greatest reported unmet need was, first and foremost, help with everyday tasks of living (see Table 5.5). Help with housekeeping or personal care was the most frequently mentioned unmet need among older Jews (37%), followed by help with home repairs (33%). Unmet needs for transportation were also considerable, with 28% reporting needing "someone to take you to the doctor or clinic." Furthermore, one in ten older Jewish New Yorkers (10%) reported needing help with personal care following a stay at the hospital or visiting nurse services. However, the proportion expressing an unmet need for home-delivered meals was relatively low (6%), partially due to the extensive Meals-on-Wheels programs in New York City.

Findings on the reduced likelihood for the children of Jewish elderly parents to provide direct instrumental help to parents, coupled with the greater average age of the older Jews, suggest that many in this population may suffer from an insufficiency of needed in-home assistance. These findings may also be influenced by a strong sense of independence among the Jewish elderly, as well as their desire not to burden children. These factors may lead older Jews to conceal unmet needs even from their closest family members. However,

TABLE 5.5 Extent of Need for Additional Assistance in Past Year by Type: Comparison of the Elderly Jews With All Older New Yorkers (Percent[a])

Type of Need	Jewish Percent	Rank	All older New Yorkers Percent	Rank
Activities of daily living				
Homemaker/				
personal care	37.3	1	25.0	3
Home repairs	33.4	2	26.9	2
Escort or ride to doctor	29.3	3	28.3	1
Home-delivered meals	5.7	8	5.1	8
Health care				
Assistance after				
hospital stay	9.6	5	10.1	5
Visiting nurse service	11.0	4	7.2	7
Socialization				
Someone to call or visit				
regularly	8.4	7	9.5	6
Personal/job assistance				
Help finding a job	1.2	10	1.1	10
Personal/family counseling	4.2	9	2.4	9
Advocacy				
Help with entitlements	9.3	6	11.7	4

[a] Independent items, totals do not equal 100%.
[b] Jewish (n = 335); total New York City (n = 1577).

both the greater utilization of in-home services among Jewish elderly and their reports of unmet need in this domain underscores the importance of formal services in mitigating the unmet needs of older people.

In comparison to older New Yorkers as a whole, the reported areas of unmet need among elderly Jews are very similar. There is a difference, however, in the order of importance of need in specific areas, which can be largely attributed to the characteristics of those involved. Whereas the need for help with activities of daily living is more often reported by Jewish older New Yorkers than the population as a whole

(37% and 25%, respectively), Jewish elderly are less likely than the City's older population in general to report needing help to obtain benefits and entitlements. In this instance, the generally higher levels of income and education among older Jews, compared to their peers, (particularly minority elderly,) not only minimizes the need for such services, but enables one to more successfully negotiate the often cumbersome bureaucracy. Thus, the influence of both family structure and assistance patterns, as well as socioeconomic factors appear to be distinguishing variables with respect to the level and nature of request for help from the formal system on the part of older New Yorkers.

CHARACTERISTICS OF JEWISH ELDERLY
EXPRESSING HIGH LEVELS OF NEED FOR SERVICES

Given the nature of service needs most frequently reported by older Jewish New Yorkers, with the emphasis on in-home assistance for instrumental tasks of daily living and health-related care, it is not surprising that certain demographic characteristics distinguish persons expressing high levels of need for service from those with minimal needs. For the following analyses, Jewish elderly who reported moderate to high levels of need (i.e., two or more unmet needs) were compared with elderly who did not express any unmet need. Demographic characteristics employed in these analyses included age, gender, living arrangements, socioeconomic status, income, and functional ability. In addition, because of the importance of having children living nearby to provide informal assistance, two measures of the availability of children to provide help to parents were included. The first was the presence of at least one child in the New York City Metropolitan area. Such a child could reasonably be assumed to be able to travel to assist a parent with relative ease. The second measure was the number of functional children, namely, those who were in frequent enough face-to-face or telephone contact to be considered probable sources of support (see Table 5.6).

The profile of Jewish older New Yorkers indicating moderate to high levels of unmet need for services illustrates the crucial role of health and functional ability in the maintenance of quality of life and the ability to remain independent with advanced age. Poor health, limited functional ability, and greater age were all significantly more likely to be found among those with moderate to high levels of unmet need. Thus, 43% of the Jewish elderly with greater unmet needs were

TABLE 5.6 Characteristics of Jewish Elderly Expressing Moderate to High Levels of Need for Additional Assistance in the Past Year (Percent[a])

Characteristic		Services not needed	Moderate to high service needs
Age group (years)**:	65 to 69	22.0	10.1
	70 to 74	25.0	13.8
	75 to 79	26.5	24.6
	80 to 84	16.7	23.9
	85 or more	9.8	27.5
Average age**:		75.5 years (6.7)	79.7 years (7.4)
Gender**:	Male	57.6	32.6
	Female	42.4	67.4
Functional ability**:	Active	67.4	34.1
	Limited	20.5	23.2
	Frail	12.1	42.8
Living arrangements**:	Alone	30.3	51.4
	With spouse	62.1	35.5
	With others but no spouse	7.6	13.0
Socioeconomic status*:	High-medium high	22.8	30.4
	Medium	31.1	24.6
	Medium low-low	46.2	44.9
Poverty level**:	At or below	2.8	17.1
	Near poverty	10.4	31.4
	Above 150%	86.8	51.4
One child in metropolitan area:		56.1	61.6
Average number functional children:		1.4	1.3

Note. A functional child is one who sees older parents at least monthly or is in phone contact at least weekly.
[a] No service needs ($n = 132$); moderate to high service needs ($n = 138$).
* = $p < .05$, ** = $p < .01$:Chi-square and analysis of variance tests of significance.

frail, and about one-half were 80 year of age or older. Among Jewish elderly persons reporting no need for additional assistance, only 12% were frail and slightly over one-quarter were 80 years old or more.

Given the interrelationship between age, frailty, and female gender in the elderly population, it is not surprising that older Jewish women comprised the largest proportion (67%) of those expressing moderate to high service needs, while elderly men were more prominent in the group indicating no need for additional services (58%). The lower level of expressed need on the part of elderly Jewish males is influenced by the fact that men are more likely to be married and hence have a spouse available to provide support. Also, older men, as a group, may be less willing to express need for assistance compared to women.

In the case of living arrangements, Jewish elderly living alone, and those living with others but without a spouse, were disproportionately found among those expressing moderate to high service needs, while those living with a spouse were more likely to indicate no additional need for help. It is clear that the presence of a spouse in the household acts to mitigate the need for formal assistance. The relationship between persons living alone and moderate to high levels of service needs is not surprising, given that these individuals tend to be older, and informal support received must be provided by non-household members. In the case of Jewish elderly persons living with others, usually children, but without a spouse, poor health or a lack of financial resources was probably a precipitating factor. Thus, even the availability of informal support within the household from children may be counterbalanced by the greater frailty and increased need for additional assistance over and above that provided by children. However, it is important to note that although most married Jewish elderly expressed few or no unmet needs, 36% of those with moderate to high levels of need were living with a spouse. Such situations among older married couples are illustrative of the double jeopardy arising from the combination of advanced age and frailty, with neither partner able to provide for the needs of the other without home-care or help from family members.

The relationship between unmet need and social class and income among the Jewish elderly is somewhat more complex. Although moderate to high needs for service are found among all socioeconomic groups and income levels, the unmet need for service may be stronger among middle-income elderly Jews, compared to those at the lowest end of the income-class continuum. For example, 50% of those in the medium to high socioeconomic status categories reported unmet needs, as compared with 45% of those in the two lowest strata. With regard to income, 17% of those with incomes at or below the poverty level expressed moderate to high unmet service needs, as compared with 31% of those with near-poverty incomes, and 51% of Jewish elderly persons with incomes over 150% of poverty. These seemingly contradictory findings probably reflect the role of the public sector in providing in-home services. It is likely that many Jewish elderly persons with poverty level incomes who are in need of homecare receive assistance from providers reimbursed by Medicaid and thus may be less likely to report unmet need. But among Jewish elderly individuals with moderate to high retirement incomes over 150% of poverty, it is difficult to qualify for the Medicaid homecare program without significant spending-down and liquidation of assets. Thus moderate income elderly as well as even some of the more financially secure Jewish older New Yorkers, may have more unmet long-term care needs, if help cannot be obtained from children and other family members, or if services cannot be privately paid for by insurance or savings.

It was interesting that the functionality of a key component of the informal social network of older people, one's children, was not related to unmet needs among Jewish older New Yorkers. In terms of geographic dispersion, there was a trend for older Jews with moderate to high levels of unmet needs to be more likely to have at least one child in the metropolitan area (62%) as compared with those with no service needs (56%), but this difference was not significant. In terms of child functionality, the average number of functional children in both groups was nearly identical at slightly more than 1 functional child (see Table 5.6). The implication of these findings is clear. The need among Jewish elderly for additional services appear to be more closely related to underlying physical and socioeconomic characteristics rather than the sufficiency of informal supports, as such, suggesting a continued and growing need for community-based services for the elderly, both currently and in the foreseeable future.

CONCLUSIONS AND IMPLICATIONS REGARDING
JEWISH OLDER NEW YORKERS

The Jewish elderly of New York City, although not necessarily involved in organized religion, are clearly influenced by the cultural and religious values of the Jewish community. To understand the patterning of social care in the case of Jewish elderly, several important themes are worth noting, stemming not only from the history of the Jewish people as a segregated and persecuted minority, and the values of Judaism, but also the sociodemographic characteristics of the current cohort of older Jews. American Jews are for the most part highly acculturated, sharing many values with other White and minority elderly groups. However, there are some differences between the Jewish elderly, when compared to some of their peers, in attitudes toward intellectual pursuits and career advancement and the role of family and community, based on the shared experiences of the Jewish people over the centuries.

As noted in the introduction to this chapter, the central focus on family that typifies Jewish culture resulted not only from the family as a refuge in a hostile world, but equally important from the role of the family as a source for joy, encouragement, and intergenerational support. At the same time, a high value was placed on both intellectual pursuits and professional and business attainments. In previous generations, both before and after immigration to the United States, Jewish families stayed together, and there was a minimum of conflict between themes of family solidarity and learning and advancement.

In America today, Jewish families sometimes find the consequences of these two themes hard to reconcile. Close relationships with children and other kin are still of central importance to most Jews, and from the standpoint of Jewish elderly, still operable and durable. However, the emphasis on education and upward mobility has often resulted in the greater geographic dispersion of the children of the Jewish elderly. Thus, older Jews are less likely than their peers to have children living nearby; fewer live in the immediate neighborhood, and a sizeable proportion live beyond the New York City Metropolitan area. This can often be a double-edged sword: being supportive of their children's' need to migrate in search of career opportunities and having pride in the success of their children, while at the same time being the most likely of any older New Yorkers to express the desire to see their children more often. And as evidenced by their preferences for whom they would turn to for assistance, Jewish elderly parents tend to feel strongly about not becoming a burden to their children and maintaining their independence. High aspirations for children can sometimes result in loneliness as well as a greater willingness to be cared for by paid helpers, in order not to interfere in the educational or career advancements of children. While this attitude was largely associated in the past with sons, the gains made by women in the workplace have seen the attitude extended to daughters as well.

Given the tendency for greater dispersion on the part of children of the Jewish elderly, child-parent contacts are more frequently made over the telephone than is the case among non-Jewish counterparts. However, Jews are as likely as non-Jewish Whites to have at least one child living at least in the New York Metropolitan area. And although hands-on help from children with tasks of daily living is less frequently reported by Jewish elderly parents, compared with their peers, with respect to economic assistance and help during a crisis like a sudden illness, children of Jewish elderly parents respond to the same degree as the children of other older New Yorkers. Additionally, the greater affluence of many elderly Jews and their willingness to consider the use of community-based agencies may result in children assuming the role of a case manager, arranging services and care for an older parent as necessary, without direct provision of assistance. Despite this pattern of intergenerational assistance between parents and children, Jewish elderly respondents reported a high degree of satisfaction with the adequacy of help received from informal sources.

Another factor that likely contributes to the lower levels of direct care provided to parents by Jewish children is the extensive infrastructure of Jewish community services and the role of this community in caring for its members in need. The historic role of the Jewish community in providing assistance is reflected in the greater willingness on the part of Jewish elderly to consider turning to formal providers of health and community services when the need arises. As is true for the earlier-discussed themes of family solidarity and career advancement, the role of Jewish community services is rooted in both religious belief and historical experience. The stigma of turning outside of one's family for help is not part of the Jewish cultural landscape. It is not surprising, given the history and values of Jewish culture, that the Jewish community in New York City and across the nation is deeply involved in providing health and social services for not only Jewish elderly but anyone in need of assistance.

Thus, for the Jewish elderly of New York, there is a foundation of social support provided by the family and augmented by assistance from the Jewish community that is not hindered by psychological barriers to formal service use, such as found among many Latino elderly persons. The family, though strong and playing a central role for older Jews, often shares responsibility for providing support with the formal sector, permitting the freedom to maintain daily activities while ensuring that the needs of older parents are adequately met. The relative affluence of many Jewish elderly people also translates to the ability to pay for needed assistance without burdening children. Given the increasing number of dual-income families along with the greater geographic dispersion of children among American families, it is likely that this partnership between families and formal service providers illustrated in the case of Jewish older New Yorkers, may be a prototype for increasing numbers of older Americans, regardless of religious or ethnic background. In the continuum of social care that spans from informal to formal providers, there appears to be a balance between these two subsystems in the case of Jewish elderly individuals that maintains family solidarity while at the same time utilizes the services of the community to ensure adequate levels of care.

Although the Jewish elderly of New York City and their families appear to have arrived at a social care system based on cultural norms and expectations of each generation, there are several implications for the future based on demographic projections and programmatic considerations.

First are implications based on projected vulnerability and frailty. Although as a group, older Jews are somewhat better-off financially than their peers, especially in comparison to New York City's minority elderly population, there is still considerable vulnerability and frailty in the older Jewish population that requires community intervention. Ten percent of Jewish elderly respondents reported poverty-level incomes, while another one-fifth have near-poverty incomes (i.e., 101% to 150% of poverty). Many of the poor Jewish elderly are not currently covered by income enhancing programs directed at low-income elderly, namely Supplemental Security Income, Food Stamps, or Medicaid. It may be that in some cases program asset limitations may render some of them ineligible. However, it is likely that these means-tested entitlements are underutilized as well. Furthermore, it is important to continue to advocate for more realistic eligibility requirements, as well as to consider attitudinal barriers to use of these programs when working with the Jewish elderly in poverty or near-poverty.

Given the higher proportion of the oldest-old, it is obvious that there is considerable social and functional frailty among the Jewish elderly of New York City. In our analyses both of high service users as well as those expressing high levels of need for service among older Jewish New Yorkers, the same factors repeatedly emerged as predictors: poor health, impaired functional ability, poverty level income, and being female, widowed, and living alone. These factors tend to be intertwined, producing multifaceted challenges to the ability of these Jewish elderly individuals to maintain a decent quality of life without assistance from family and community. However, it must be noted that frailty and vulnerability occur among older persons of all ages, at both low and moderate income levels, and in a variety of living situations.

The second implication pertains to the role of family and other informal sources of social support. Given the increased life expectancy of the current and future elderly cohorts and the trend for decreased disability until near the end of the lifespan, the point of need in the caregiving cycle between elderly and their adult children must be noted. These adult children, who are often themselves in their fifties and sixties and facing their own retirement transitions, may not be able to provide the level of assistance necessary to insure adequate care for their older parents when need arises. This trend argues for a more well-articulated partnership between formal organizations and families, with community services playing a more active role as back-up and in supplementation of family efforts to care for elderly Jewish and non-Jewish parents alike.

Finally, with respect to age composition, the Jewish elderly tend to be older on average than New York City's elderly population in general, and there are substantial numbers who are very old and nearing the end of the life span. At the same time, due to earlier migration to the suburbs and out-migration of young elderly persons at retirement, the proportion of those 65 to 74 year of age is smaller, and the proportion of this age group will probably remain relatively small in the future. Thus, it appears that the Jewish elderly population may be composed of two very different groups, both in terms of relative prevalence in the population as well as their needs. Services needed by younger elderly persons, who tend to have higher educational attainment, and income, better health and mobility, and are more often living with a spouse, will be very different from those needed by their counterparts in their eighties and nineties in whom frailty is most concentrated, where economic resources may be depleted, and far greater proportions of whom are widowed and often living alone. As a result, planning by the Jewish community in the future may require a bipolar focus to encompass differing age cohorts of elderly persons.

With respect to the role of the Jewish community in providing social support for its older members, it seems clear that such a role can only increase in importance in the future. But community-based services must be more clearly targeted to the differing age cohorts. For the oldest elderly, needs for social support, in-home supportive services, and institutional care will become ever more important in the light of the increased age at which frailty is projected to occur. In addition, with the proportion of working women projected at near 80% in the coming decades, the ability for these traditional providers of hands-on social care to older family members will be in serious jeopardy without assistance from the larger community.

For younger elderly, with greater personal financial resources, challenges to the productive use of time will be paramount. The Jewish community will need to consider how to meet their educational and recreational needs in nonsegregated environments. The knowledge and vitality of these younger elderly should also be tapped in expanding volunteer opportunities in the community, which not only helps society at large, but does much to further the psychological well-being of older volunteers.

Opportunities for meaningful volunteerism, broadening horizons through educational experiences, and occasions to socialize with persons of all ages with shared interests are as equally important to the younger elderly as the need for in-home services are for the frail oldest-old. Furthermore, it is important to recognize that many relatively well-off middle-income elderly persons may become poor overnight when faced with a serious illness and the enormous medical expenses that are frequently incurred. Thus, the boundaries between those who can maintain their independence and those who fall into need are constantly in flux. Clearly, priorities must be set in service planning and delivery, but attending to the differing program needs and levels of assistance required by both healthy and frail Jewish elderly is a challenge for the future if the older Jews of New York City are to continue to have a decent quality of life in their later years. To the extent to which the current Jewish elderly of New York City are prototypical of future cohorts of elderly persons, particularly in terms of educational background and economic security, the implications of this case study have wider relevance to older people in general in the twenty-first century.

6

The Older Latinos of New York City in the 1990s

INTRODUCTION

New York City stands at the threshold of two emerging trends that have implications for both the city and the nation in terms of public policy decisions and the allocation of all too scarce taxpayer dollars. These two trends are the projected continued increase in the number of older persons as well as an increase in the proportion of persons of Hispanic origin in the United States (Torres-Gil, 1990). While Latinos are perceived as being a relatively young group, as of 1990, 6.4% of Latinos (1,330,000) were aged 65 and older (Rodriguez & Mahard O'Donnell, 1992), and the number of Latino elderly persons is projected to increase to almost 8 million by the year 2050 (Angel & Hogan, 1991).

During the 1980s, the number of Latinos 65 years or older in New York increased by 60%, with Latinos comprising nearly 10% of the elderly population in the city by 1990 (Hanreider, 1992b). Because Latinos are expected to continue to immigrate to this country in large numbers and because New York serves as a port of entry for many Latinos, Latino elderly can be expected to have an increasingly important presence in New York City. Thus, New York, as well as other localities with large Latino populations, such as California and Texas, must develop new strategies in service implementation and delivery targeted at older persons to reflect the special circumstances of being older and Latino in the United States.

135

Policy and planning decisions affecting the elderly Latino population should ideally be based on up-to-date, current information. However, where research on minority elderly population does appear, it is often in the form of cross-group comparisons between minority and majority elderly groups. There has been increasing recognition of the need for detailed within-group analyses of minority populations by gerontologists and others with minority concerns, especially with regard to the current and future status of Latinos in the United States (Romo, 1990).

It is especially imperative that such in-depth research be conducted on Latino elderly given the diversity of the persons who fall into this category. In fact, the appropriateness of labeling these many differing individuals with the single term Latino has itself been the subject of debate (Torres-Gil, 1990). The heterogeneity of the Latino population has been described in terms of different national origins (i.e., Mexican, Cuban, Puerto Rican, etc.), differences in nativity and immigration patterns, differences in the use of the Spanish and English languages, and the varying multiracial background of persons of Latino descent (Romo, 1990). With regard to national origin among Latino elderly in United States, the largest group are Mexican Americans (48%), followed by Cuban Americans (18%), Puerto Ricans (11%), and Central and South Americans (8%), with 15% classified as other (Angel & Hogan, 1991).

Each of these groups have had varied immigration patterns, with some groups like Mexican Americans being among the United State's earliest immigrants, while others are relative latecomers, particularly Cuban Americans and present immigrants from Central and South America (National Council of La Raza, 1992). While these various Latino groups have the cultural bonds of the Spanish language and religion (Roman Catholicism), they have immigrated from different areas of the world that have particular economic and political structures and have immigrated for different reasons at different points in their lives during different historic periods (Commonwealth Fund, 1989a). For example, many Mexican Americans have been in this country since colonial times or became citizens by conquest with the annexation of the northern part of Mexico by the United States in the mid-nineteenth century (National Council of La Raza, 1992), while the Cold War era brought about substantial immigration from Cuba in the 1960s. In New York City, the largest group of Latinos has traditionally consisted of Puerto Ricans. While this is still true, sizable numbers of new immigrants from the Dominican Republic and Central and South

America, as well as immigrants from Cuba have resulted in the considerable diversification of the Latino population in New York City.

Puerto Ricans, the largest Latino group in New York City, have been citizens of the United States for nearly a century, and there is an extensive two-way migration between the island and the New York metropolitan area (Torres-Gil, 1990). On the U. S. mainland, Puerto Ricans are mainly found in highly urban environments (e.g., New York City) and have often been limited to low-wage and low-status jobs in the service economy. Thus, issues of unemployment and underemployment both on the mainland and in Puerto Rico have been the subject of attention of the relatively well-organized political organizations of these Latinos. Puerto Ricans are among the youngest of the Latino groups in terms of average age (Torres-Gil, 1990), and those born on the island were among the youngest to migrate to the U.S. mainland, with half coming before the age of 34 (Commonwealth Fund, 1989a). While Puerto Rican elderly tend to be among the youngest of the Latino elderly population, even after adjusting for age older Puerto Ricans report the worst health status compared to other Latino groups (i.e., Mexican Americans and Cubans) and the lowest levels of education (Commonwealth Fund, 1989b).

Dominicans comprise the second largest group of Latinos in New York City (Georges, 1990), but are relatively recent arrivals compared to other groups, particularly Puerto Ricans. However, despite their large numbers, Dominicans have often been lumped together with Puerto Ricans in political circles, which has led to an increase in political activism and visibility among these Latinos. Like the Puerto Ricans, Dominicans often face limited opportunities in terms of low status jobs or unemployment and resultant low incomes. Dominicans have responded to the challenges of a foreign culture and difficult environment by creating their own ethnic communities, particularly in the Washington Heights section of Manhattan, and by forming numerous ethnic associations that provide many services to the Dominican community (Georges, 1990).

Cuban-Americans constitute a small, though important Latino group. Though tending to settle in the southeastern United States, some Cubans have settled in New York City, and there is a large and vital Cuban community in West New York, New Jersey (Cuban American National Council, 1989; Rogg & Cooney, 1980). There have been two major waves of Cuban immigration into the United States: the first during the 1960s to flee the Castro regime and the second during the 1980s with the Mariel boatlift (Angel & Hogan, 1991; Torres-

Gil, 1990). These two waves of immigrants were markedly different. Those who were refugees from the Castro regime tended to be well-educated, middle-class individuals who came to this country in middle-age or young adulthood with intact families, while the latter wave consisted mostly of poorly-educated single males who came to this country alone (Torres-Gil, 1990). Thus, on the national level, Cubans tend to fare better in terms of income and occupation than other Latino groups. Because of their late age of immigration, Cuban elderly tend to be among the oldest of the Latino groups, with nearly half (45%) being age 75 or older (Commonwealth Fund, 1989b; Rodriguez & Mahard O'Donnell, 1992).

In addition to the three Latino groups detailed above, New York City also has a large number of other Latinos who have immigrated from the Caribbean and Central and South America. Not only heterogeneous with respect to national origin, there is also a great deal of diversity among these other Latinos in terms of education, social class, immigration patterns, and so forth. Although numerous, these Latino groups have rarely been studied in this country due to their relatively small numbers compared to Mexican Americans or Puerto Ricans, although these other Latinos now comprise nearly 20% of the Latino population in the United States (Torres-Gil, 1990).

When considering the Latino elderly population in New York City, the differences in immigration patterns described above yield important implications with regard to both the relative age of these groups of older persons, as well as issues of acculturation in terms of length of residency and language use. With respect to age, older Latinos tend to be younger than the elderly population as a whole (Commonwealth Fund, 1989b). But as noted previously, there is a greater proportion of elderly Cubans who are age 75 and older than is the case in other Latino groups, due mostly to their late age at immigration (Angel & Hogan, 1991; Torres-Gil, 1990; Commonwealth Fund, 1989b).

Age at immigration also has an important impact on the levels of acculturation of these groups of older Latinos. Puerto Ricans are among the earliest arriving Latinos, with about one-quarter coming to the mainland before age 25 and another quarter arriving between the ages of 26 and 34 years. Cubans and Latinos from other parts of Central and South America tend to arrive at a later age, with almost 80% arriving after the age 35 (Commonwealth Fund, 1989a). Because of these differences in age of immigration and length of residency in the United States, the rate of acculturation also varies among these different groups of Latino elderly. Presumably, Latinos who arrived in the United States at an earlier age and those who have resided in this country for a long time will have adopted more of the values of the mainstream American culture and have greater facility with the English language. Acculturation and cultural barriers have far-reaching implications for elderly Latinos, ranging from poor job opportunities because of lack of English fluency, which may lead to poverty and health problems in old age (Commonwealth Fund, 1989b), to the underutilization of community-based services due to long-established patterns of informal assistance from family and friends and Latino cultural barriers, which predispose against turning to formal, community-based agencies for assistance (Rodriguez & Mahard O'Donnell, 1992; Rodriguez, 1987).

Due to the diversity of the elderly Latino population of New York City and the projected increase in the proportion of older New Yorkers who will be of Latino descent in the coming years, it is imperative that more information about this group is explored in detail to determine the similarities and differences that exist among the major groups of New York's Latino elderly population. This work is designed to provide such detailed information for elderly Puerto Ricans, Dominicans, Cubans, and Latinos of other nationalities who are residing in New York City.

LATINO RESPONDENTS IN THE PRESENT ANALYSES

The Latino elderly sample utilized in this chapter was drawn from the larger study, "Growing Older in New York City in the 1990s," commissioned by the Center for Policy on Aging of the New York Community Trust (see Chapter 1). Although for sampling purposes potential Latino respondents were identified using a dictionary of Spanish surnames, only older respondents who answered affirmatively to the question, "Are you of Hispanic origin or descent?" were designated as being of Latino ethnicity for the purpose of analysis. Interviews were conducted by Louis Harris and Associates in either English or Spanish (as preferred by the respondent). From this base sample, 337 respondents who identified themselves as of Hispanic origin or descent were selected for the sample used in these analyses.

Using information provided on nativity and country of origin, the Latino sample was further subdivided into four Latino origin groups: Puerto Ricans comprising the largest group (57%); followed next by Dominicans (14%) and Cubans (7%). The remaining 22% of the sample had immigrated from a variety of countries in Central and South

America and the Caribbean and were classified for analytical purposes as other Latino origin, in as much as there were too few from any single country to be classified into a separate category.

WHO ARE THE LATINO ELDERLY OF NEW YORK CITY?

Age

Latino elderly persons ranged in age from 65 to 97 years of age. On average, minority elderly respondents, both Latino and African American, are slightly younger (73.6 and 73.5 years, respectively) than their White peers (74.5 years). Latino elderly are also less likely to be among the old-old, that is, over 75 year of age, compared to non-Hispanic White elderly New Yorkers. Country of origin was not significantly related to the age of Latino elderly respondents (see Table 6.1).

Gender and Marital Status

Like all elderly populations, women outnumber men, and nearly two thirds of the Latino elderly cohort are women. In line with the preponderance of women, the largest group of elderly Latinos were widowed (39%), followed closely by those who were still married (34%), while about one-fifth were either divorced or separated, and 6% had never married. There were no significant differences in terms of country of origin with regard to gender or marital status (see Table 6.1).

Acculturation

In studying the lives and needs of older Latinos, the role of acculturation and place of origin are major points of interest. In the present analyses, two measures of acculturation were employed: length of residence in New York City and language usually spoken at home with family and friends (i.e., Spanish only, Spanish and English, or English only). These measures have often been used in other studies (e.g., Keefe & Padilla, 1987), and research has suggested that persons with longer residency and those speaking only English at home tend to have incorporated the mores, values, and attitudes of the majority culture to a greater degree than more recently arriving and non-English speaking immigrants.

With regard to length of New York City residency, older Latinos reported that they had been in the city for 39.9 years on average, with the largest proportion reporting residencies of between 41 and 60 years (see Table 6.1). Smaller proportions report living in New York either a relatively short time (i.e., 21 years or less) or all or most of their lives (i.e., 61 years or more). Given the differing immigration patterns, length of residency varied significantly according to country of origin. Older Puerto Ricans reported the longest average residency (46.7 years), while Dominicans were the most recent arrivals, having been city residents for only 26.5 years on average, with Cubans and older Latinos of other origins falling in between.

Although there were differences in time in the city, the vast majority of older Latinos, nearly three-quarters, reported speaking only Spanish at home with family and friends. About one in ten reported speaking only English at home, while about one-sixth spoke both Spanish and English. Differences in language spoken at home parallel those regarding length of residency (see Table 6.1). Puerto Rican elderly, the group with the longest city tenures, were the most likely to speak at least some English at home, while Dominicans, the most recent arrivals, were the least likely to use English in their households. Cubans and Latino elderly of other origins reported intermediate levels of English language use. However, regardless of country of origin, the majority of Latino elderly in New York City speak only Spanish at home, and it is likely that for many elderly Latinos, lack of fluency in English serves as a major barrier to full participation in the opportunity structure of New York City, particularly with respect to the use of available health and social services (see Table 6.1).

Health Status

In line with other studies of Latino elderly, older Latinos in New York City tend to report poorer health than the elderly population in general. Over half reported their health as fair (41%) or poor (15%). Of the remainder, most (37%) reported their health as good, and only 7% felt they were in excellent health (see Table 6.1). In addition, elderly Latinos evidenced a higher level of functional impairment than their White or African American peers (Berkman & Gurland, 1993). In light of the fact that Latino elderly tend to be somewhat younger on average than their New York City peers, the larger proportion evaluating their health as fair or poor is particularly significant. Puerto Rican

TABLE 6.1 Major Demographic Characteristics of New York City Latino Respondents by Place of Origin (Percent)

(n)	Total (337)	Puerto Rican (192)	Dominican (47)	Cuban (25)	Other Origin (73)
Age group:					
65 to 69 years	21.1	22.4	25.5	20.0	15.1
70 to 74 years	23.4	25.5	21.3	28.0	17.8
75 to 84 years	42.1	39.1	44.7	36.0	50.7
85 years or more	13.4	13.0	8.5	16.0	16.4
Gender:					
Males	37.4	34.4	44.7	28.0	43.8
Females	62.6	65.6	55.3	72.0	56.2
Marital status:					
Married	33.8	31.3	44.7	40.0	31.5
Widowed	38.6	42.7	31.9	32.0	34.2
Divorced/ separated	20.2	19.8	14.9	24.0	23.3
Never married	6.2	5.2	6.4	4.0	9.6
Refused/not sure	1.2	1.0	2.1	0.0	1.4
Perceived health:					
Excellent	7.4	6.3	10.6	4.0	9.6
Good	36.5	35.9	36.2	44.0	35.6
Fair	40.7	43.2	38.3	44.0	34.2
Poor	14.8	14.6	14.9	8.0	17.8
Refused/not sure	0.6	0.0	0.0	0.0	2.7
Length of residence***:					
20 years or less	14.2	3.1	34.0	16.0	30.1
21 to 30 years	21.1	10.9	34.0	40.0	32.9
31 to 40 years	19.0	21.4	10.6	32.0	13.7
41 to 60 years	27.9	40.1	12.8	12.0	11.0
61 years or more	14.2	21.4	2.1	0.0	8.2
Refused/not sure	3.6	3.1	6.4	0.0	4.1
Language at home*:					
Spanish only	72.0	64.9	87.2	80.0	78.1
Spanish and English	17.0	20.9	10.6	12.0	12.3
English only	11.0	14.1	2.1	8.0	9.6

Note: Totals equal 100%.
* = $p < .05$; ** = $p < .01$, *** $p < .001$/Chi-square tests of significance.

elderly respondents were the most likely to report fair or poor health, followed next by Dominicans, and lastly Cubans and those of other origins.

THE SOCIOECONOMIC STATUS OF OLDER LATINOS

Education

In addition to potential language barriers, Latino elderly suffer from lower educational attainment than is the case with other older people in New York City. Three-fifths of Latino elderly reported educational attainments of 8th grade or less, one-quarter attended high school, with half receiving diplomas, while less than 5% of the Latino elderly cohort reported any postsecondary education (see Table 6.2). Place of origin was related to educational attainment, with elderly Dominicans, the most recent immigrants, having the fewest years of education on average, only 5.8 years. This compares to average education levels of 6.4 and 6.2 years among Puerto Ricans and Cubans, respectively, and 8.0 years in the case of older Latinos of other origins. As expected, higher educational levels were associated with higher levels of acculturation (i.e., longer tenures in New York and speaking English at home).

Socioeconomic Status

Of the many factors that impact quality of life in old age, none is probably more fundamental than adequacy of income. Findings regarding the economic status of elderly Latinos in New York City, whether in terms of social class, occupational history, income, extent of poverty, or perceived economic well-being reveal a consistent picture of low socioeconomic status and inadequate financial resources. For older Latinos, as for all elderly persons, financial position in old age is the result of a lifetime of choices and opportunities in occupation and education that determine in large measure available retirement income, particularly with regard to Social Security and pensions. Latino elderly in the present cohort reported low average levels of education and severely limited employment opportunities. Constrained by their English language skills and facing discrimination in the workplace, most older Latinos worked in low skilled or service occupations that rarely offered pension benefits. As a result, two-thirds of elderly

Latinos were found to be in the lowest socioeconomic strata as measured by Hollingshead's (1957) Two-Factor Index of Social Position,
which is based on occupational and educational attainment, and there
were no significant differences in social class among the four Latino
origin groups (see Table 6.2).

1989 Income Levels

Although over two-thirds of older Latinos in New York had worked
during their adult years, the vast majority (95%) are currently retired,
and of those who had not been employed, almost all were women who
had stayed at home to care for their families. And congruent with their
limited educational and occupational histories during their working
years, most older Latinos currently suffer from grossly inadequate
incomes in old age. Approximately 40% reported annual incomes of
$6000 or less, with an additional 19% reporting incomes of between
$6001 and $8500 per year. Thus, three of five older Latinos in New
York City reported incomes of less than $8500 per year, and virtually
none (2%) reported incomes over $25,000 per year (see Table 6.2). The
median income for the group as a whole was $7251, while the aver-
age income was only $7239[1], reflecting the overwhelming concentra-
tion of elderly Latinos in the lower income brackets. However, level
of income differed sharply by national origin: Puerto Rican and Cuban
elderly had the highest median incomes ($7251 in each group), while
Dominicans and older Latinos of other origins had the lowest median
incomes, only $3000 for each group.   The impact of acculturation on
economic well-being was illustrated by the relationship between
length of city residency and current income. Latino elderly individuals in the city for less than 30 years reported average incomes of
between $3503 and $5088, as compared with average incomes of $6589
for persons with 41 to 60 years residence and $9390 for those who had
lived in the city 61 years or more. It is clear from these findings that
Latino immigrants who arrive later in life face severe challenges in
terms of financial resources as they grow older in New York City.

---

1. In the "Growing Older in New York City the 1990s" report (Vol II), the average income for elderly Latinos was reported as $7480 vs. the $7239 reported here.
The slight difference in average incomes reported is the result of weighting the
entire sample in the first report to make it representative of the elderly population in New York. However, this analysis is based on unweighted data to take
advantage of the full number of older Latinos in the sample.

TABLE 6.2 Socioeconomic Indicators Among Older Latino New Yorkers by Place of Origin (Percent)

(n)	Total (337)	Puerto Rican (192)	Dominican (47)	Cuban (25)	Other origin (73)
Level of Education***:					
8th grade or less	58.8	57.3	68.1	60.0	56.2
Some high school	11.0	14.1	4.3	8.0	8.2
High school graduate	13.6	17.7	4.3	12.0	9.6
Some college	3.3	2.1	0.0	12.0	5.5
College graduate	0.9	0.5	0.0	0.0	2.7
Postgraduate	0.9	0.0	0.0	0.0	4.1
Refused/not sure	11.6	8.3	23.4	8.0	13.7
Hollingshead Socioeconomic Status group:					
High (I)	10.4	6.8	21.3	8.0	13.7
Medium high (II)	4.2	4.2	0.0	8.0	5.5
Medium (III)	5.9	4.7	4.3	8.0	9.6
Medium low (IV)	35.3	38.5	31.9	32.0	30.1
Low (V)	44.2	45.8	42.6	44.0	41.1
1989 Income ($):					
6000 or less	38.9	33.9	48.9	28.0	49.3
6001 to 8500	19.0	21.4	14.9	28.0	12.3
8501 to 10,000	8.3	8.3	0.0	12.0	12.3
10,001 to 12,500	3.6	5.2	0.0	0.0	2.7
12,501 to 15,000	3.9	5.7	2.1	0.0	1.4
15,001 to 25,000	4.5	4.2	2.1	12.0	4.1
25,001 to 35,000	0.9	0.5	2.1	4.0	0.0
35,001 to 50,000	0.9	0.5	0.0	4.0	1.4
50,001 or More	0.0	0.0	0.0	0.0	0.0
Refused/not sure	20.2	20.3	29.7	12.0	16.4
Poverty level*:					
At or below poverty	56.9	50.3	81.8	45.5	63.9
101% to 150% poverty	28.3	32.7	9.1	31.8	26.2
Over 150% poverty	14.9	17.0	9.1	22.7	9.8

Note: Totals equal 100%.
Note: Mean income based on midpoints of income categories.
* = $p < .05$; ** = $p < .01$, *** $p < .001$/Chi-square tests of significance.

Income and Poverty Status

But perhaps most telling with regard to the paucity of financial resources available to older Latinos in New York City is the rate of poverty among them. Over half (57%) reported 1989 incomes at or below the poverty level, while another 28% were in near poverty (i.e., 101% to 150% of poverty level income) (see Table 6.2). Thus, virtually all Latino elderly persons (85%) reported poverty or near poverty incomes, and the rate of poverty among New York's Latino elderly population is double that found among older Latinos nationwide (23%).

The incidence of poverty was significantly related to both country of origin and acculturation. Dominican elderly individuals, the latest arrivals, were the most likely to report incomes at or below poverty, while Puerto Ricans and Cubans were the least likely to be impoverished, although close to half of these two groups also reported poverty level incomes. The incidence of poverty decreased with longer New York City residency, and older Latinos who spoke English at home were also less likely to be found among those with poverty level incomes. Poverty was also found to be especially pervasive among older Latinos living alone; nine of 10 reported poverty or near poverty incomes.

Primary Source of Income

Social Security is the major source of income for most elderly Latinos. However, both nationally and in New York City, older Latinos have lower rates of Social Security participation than African Americans and Whites, and the participation rate was significantly different among the four Latino origin groups. Older Puerto Ricans were the most likely (91%) to report Social Security income, the result of their life-long United States citizenship, followed by older Dominicans (79%), older Cubans (72%) and those of other Latino origins (62%). The second most frequently reported income source was Supplemental Security Income, and the precarious financial situation of many older Latinos is further illustrated by the fact that for one of five respondents, Supplemental Security Income is their primary income source. Again, there were significant differences among the four Latino origin groups regarding the receipt of Supplemental Security Income; Dominicans and older Latinos of other origins being far more likely to receive it (52% to 53%), compared with 44% of Cuban elderly and less than one third (30%) of older Puerto Ricans. Pensions, an important secondary source of income for many older people, were rarely reported by the older Latinos. Only 29% received any income from pensions, and although the likelihood of receiving pensions did not differ significantly by Latino origin, there was a trend toward greater pension coverage among Puerto Ricans, while pensions were virtually absent among Dominicans.

Given the pervasively low levels of income reported by older Latinos in New York City, it is not surprising that four of five expressed difficulty in managing on their current incomes. As expected, the more acculturated Latinos (i.e., those with longer residency and speaking English at home) were less likely to report economic hardship, and economic difficulty was most prevalent among recent arrivals.

Perhaps most sobering in the economic sphere are the findings regarding the underutilization of needs-based entitlements specifically aimed at mitigating the effects of severe economic want. Among elderly Latinos with poverty level incomes, only about half reported enrollment in the Supplemental Security Income (54%), and the likelihood of receiving it differed significantly by Latino origin among those in poverty. Over two-thirds of older Cubans and Latinos of other origins in poverty were enrolled (70% and 69%, respectively), compared with 56% of elderly Dominicans and only 44% of older Puerto Ricans in poverty. The food stamp program also appears to be underutilized by older Latinos in poverty; only 41% were receiving food stamps, and this did not differ significantly among the four Latino origin groups. Medicaid coverage was somewhat higher, with 74% of older Latinos with the requisite poverty level incomes reporting Medicaid coverage, and again, there were no significant differences by Latino origin in this regard. It would appear that health is an area in which government assistance is sanctioned, while needs-based economic assistance poses more barriers for many impoverished older Latinos. It should be noted that in Puerto Rico government-supported medical care is the norm, so that for many older Puerto Ricans the use of Medicaid is congruent with their preimmigration experience.

LIVING ARRANGEMENTS AMONG ELDERLY LATINOS

The living arrangements of older people have important implications for the availability of help during times of need. Having someone else in the household enhances the chance of assistance at time of illness or crisis and may minimize feelings of isolation and loneliness. It has often been assumed that minority elderly persons, particularly recent immigrants, are in a advantageous position with respect to having other people in the household to turn to (Himes, Hogan, & Eggebeen, 1996). However, contrary to common assumptions, not all Latino elderly live with others, either a spouse or with children in an extended family household. In fact, over one-third of the Latino elderly in the present sample live alone, and the proportion living alone in New York City has risen significantly in the last 20 years from approximately 25% in 1970 to 37% in 1990. And the proportion of older Latinos living alone in New York is considerably higher than national figures; 16% of those 60 and older in 1990 (Himes et al., 1996).

The remaining two thirds of Latino elderly are currently equally divided between those living with a spouse (32%), and those living with others, mainly children, but not a spouse (31%). Living arrangements were not related to country of origin, but the extent of acculturation and gender affected with whom older Latinos lived. Older Latino males were more likely to live with a spouse than were females. Among older Latina women, living with family or living alone were the more prevalent arrangements (38% of women live with others but not a spouse, 39% live alone, while only 23% are living with a spouse). Although living arrangements were not related to national origin, they did vary significantly by length of residency in the city, particularly with respect to living alone and living with family other than spouse. Thus, as length of residency increased, the proportion of live alones also increased, while the proportion living in an extended family household was greatest among the most recent arrivals and decreased with great length of residency. These findings suggest the interplay of immigration, economic, and acculturation factors in influencing the type of household in which older Latinos reside. Interestingly enough, among the increasing proportion of persons living alone in the Latino community, women are just about as likely to live alone as men (39% and 34%, respectively), suggesting a possible shift in cultural values regarding dependency and independence, as well as the appropriateness of living alone in the case of older Latinas in New York City. The decrease in extended-family households among older Latinos in the last two decades may also reflect the shortage of large, affordable apartments in the New York metropolitan area, as well as the desire of both older and younger Latinos to emulate their mainstream American peers by establishing nuclear family households as they become increasingly acculturated.

Summary

The foregoing section presented a profile of older Latinos in New York City with regard to their personal characteristics, household composition, economic well-being, and work and retirement. This profile revealed important differences between older Puerto Ricans, Dominicans, Cubans, and older Latinos of other origins, especially in terms of acculturation (i.e., length of residency and language use) and economic resources. Puerto Rican elderly are among the most acculturated in terms of length of residency and language use, yet low levels of education and poor occupational opportunities result in continued economic challenges for these older New Yorkers. Dominican elderly are among the most recent Latino arrivals to New York and are the least acculturated in terms of length of residency and language use. They seem to have compensated for these disadvantages somewhat by relying on extended families and multigenerational households to maximize economic resources. Cuban older New Yorkers are also relatively recent arrivals to the city, but their generally higher levels of educational and occupational achievement have given them a small measure of economic security in old age. For older Latinos of other origins, there is a somewhat mixed picture, with varying levels of acculturation and education, however, most of these individuals suffer from a lack of economic resources as well.

THE INFORMAL SUPPORT NETWORK OF OLDER LATINOS IN NEW YORK CITY

As noted in chapter 2, because of the interdependent nature of human beings, support from other members of the social network is crucial both in terms of functional capacity, and more importantly, survival (Clark & Anderson, 1967). However, the acceptance of this concept of interdependence varies from culture to culture and from society to society, depending on their history and current state of economic development (Cantor & Brennan, 1993c). Within Latino cultures, while independence is highly valued (Rodriguez, 1987), the interdependence of family members has been traditionally accepted and viewed as a strength of the Latino culture (Torres-Gil, 1990).

However, it should be noted that the strength of the Latino family is not uniform, nor can it be assumed that it is unchanging. As pressures of acculturation and assimilation increase, Latinos are having fewer children, and the traditionally strong bonds of these families are being eroded (Torres-Gil, 1990). Furthermore, younger Latinos themselves face problems of unemployment, poverty, drug and alcohol abuse, and AIDS, and may not be in a position to render assistance to older family members. Because many policy makers have viewed the family in Latino communities as substitute providers for community-based programs, and justified Latino underutilization of services because of strong Latino families (Rodriguez, 1987; Torres-Gil, 1990), it is crucial to examine the current extent and configuration of the informal networks of older Latinos in New York City and the amounts and the types of assistance that such networks provide.

Informal social support networks of older people are comprised of six major components, each of which may play an important role in the provision of instrumental assistance and socialization opportunities. Of these six components, four are members of the kin network (i.e., spouse, child, sibling, and other relatives) and two are nonkin significant others (i.e., friend-confidants and neighbors). Findings from the 1990 Growing Older in New York City in the 1990s revealed distinctly different patterns in the informal networks of Latino, African American, and White older New Yorkers with respect to these six components (Cantor & Brennan, 1993c).

Overview of the Informal Networks of Older Latinos

Networks of Latino elderly were more kin-centered and less broad-based than was the case among older Whites and African Americans. Thus, elderly Latinos had the most children on average, the most children living nearby, and the most frequent face-to-face contact with children. In addition, many older Latinos reported the presence of a spouse. As a group, Latinos had larger networks of siblings and other relatives in New York City than did their White and African American counterparts. But in accordance with the emphasis on kin as the mainstay of their social networks, Latino elderly were the least likely of the three groups to report having a nonrelated friend-confidant or to know neighbors well. Thus, if family members are either unable or unwilling to provide the necessary assistance, the elderly Latinos have fewer compensatory options, such as friends and neighbors, than do older African Americans and Whites. Furthermore, their difficulties with the English language make turning to community-based agencies even more problematic for elderly Latinos (Cantor & Brennan, 1993c).

Given this general overview of the informal networks of older Latinos and how they compare with the networks of their White and African American peers, it is now important to examine the extent to which older Latinos possess each of the six aforementioned components of the informal system and whether the presence of and interactions with these members of the informal network differ among Latinos of Puerto Rican, Dominican, Cuban, or other national origin. Furthermore, it is also necessary to examine the extent to which the nature and patterns of informal care are affected by the level of acculturation, as well as by personal characteristics such as class.

SPOUSE

We first look at the spouse, who when present, provides the cornerstone of the informal support network. Not only are spouses in closest proximity, but they are the most likely to provide immediate instrumental assistance as well as emotional intimacy. One-third (34%) of older Latinos report the presence of a spouse (see Table 6.3), as compared with approximately one half of White and one quarter of Black older New Yorkers. Among the remainder who were without a spouse, 39% were widowed, 20% were divorced or separated, and 6% had never married. There were no significant differences among the four Latino origin groups in the likelihood of having a spouse, though Dominican elderly were slightly more likely to report the presence of a spouse (45%), followed next by Cubans (40%), compared to only about 30% of Puerto Rican and older Latinos of other origins.

CHILDREN

Children follow the spouse as the next most crucial component in the social support systems of older persons. Older persons who are childless or who have children unable or unwilling to provide needed assistance are forced to turn to more distant relatives, friends or neighbors, or community agencies to obtain needed support. While in 1990 there was no significant difference in the likelihood of having a child between Latino, African American, and White older New Yorkers, Latinos had significantly more children on average than did these other two groups (Cantor & Brennan, 1993c). Nearly four of five (79%) older Latinos in New York reported they had at least one living child (including both biological children and other children raised), and

TABLE 6.3 Social Network Components Among Older Latinos in New York City by Place of Origin (Percent)

(*n*)	Total (337)	Puerto Rican (192)	Dominican (47)	Cuban (25)	Other origin (73)
Component:					
Spouse	33.8	31.3	44.7	40.0	31.5
Child**	78.6	81.3	83.0	52.0	78.1
*Mean***	*(2.8)*	*(2.6)*	*(3.8)*	*(1.5)*	*(3.1)*
Sibling–living	73.0	69.3	83.0	72.0	76.7
*Mean number in NYC**	*(1.5)*	*(1.4)*	*(2.6)*	*(1.1)*	*(1.2)*
Other NYC relative**	47.5	43.2	74.5	44.0	42.5
*Mean number in NYC***	*(3.5)*	*(3.5)*	*(5.7)*	*(2.6)*	*(2.2)*
Confidant	39.8	39.6	36.2	48.0	39.7
Mean	*(0.6)*	*(0.6)*	*(0.5)*	*(0.7)*	*(0.6)*
Friend/confidant	27.3	29.2	17.0	36.0	26.0
Mean	*(0.4)*	*(0.4)*	*(0.2)*	*(0.4)*	*(0.4)*
Neighbor known well	47.2	47.9	44.7	44.0	47.9
Mean	*(1.6)*	*(1.7)*	*(1.6)*	*(0.9)*	*(1.5)*
No components	3.0	3.1	2.1	4.0	2.7

$* = p < .05; ** = p < .01.$
NYC, New York City.

among those with children, the average number of such children was 3.6. Interestingly enough, the proportion of older Latinos in New York City with children is somewhat lower than that reported nationally among Latino elderly (89%), as compared with only 79% among New York's Latino elderly population (Commonwealth Fund, 1989b).

There were significant differences in both the likelihood of having a child and the number of reported children among the four Latino origin groups. Cuban elderly were the least likely to have a child (52%), compared with approximately four fifths of Latinos in the other groups (Dominicans, 83%; Puerto Ricans, 81%; other Latino origin, 78%). Cuban elderly also reported the fewest children on average (2.9), as compared with 4.6 in the case of elderly Dominicans, followed by

Latinos of other origins (4.0) and Puerto Ricans (3.2). Thus, while Cuban elderly are the least likely to have children and have fewer such children to turn to, the elderly Dominicans are both the most likely to have a child, and have the largest number of children in their informal networks on average. Older Puerto Ricans and those of other Latino origins fall between these two extremes (see Table 6.3).

PROFILE OF THE CHILDREN OF THE LATINO ELDERLY

Gerontological research on the informal support system has consistently stressed the role of children as perhaps the most important source of ongoing care and assistance for older people, particularly in situations where a spouse is not present. An examination of the role of alternative resources as a potential barrier to the use of community-based services in the case of the Latino elderly population would not be possible without a clear understanding of the number of available children, their geographic proximity and frequency of contact, and the amount of help they provide to parents and receive from their parents in return.

Age and Gender of Children

The vast majority of the children of Latino elderly parents (86%) were either young adults (22 to 40 years old) (36%) or middle aged (41 to 60 years old) (50%). Only 2% were 21 years of age or less, and 6% were 61 or more years of age and approaching late life themselves. This pattern of age distribution characterized the children of older Puerto Ricans, Dominicans, and those of other Latino origins, but was less true in the case of children of Cuban elderly parents. Among them, the proportion of children who were themselves in late adulthood is surprisingly high. Nearly one of five children of Cuban elderly (19%) were 61 years of age or more, a factor that could limit their ability to provide necessary assistance to parents due to their own problems of health or disability. The gender of the children of Latino elderly was almost equally divided between males (50%) and females (49%). As was the case with age, this even split between males and females was true for all origin groups except for Cubans. Among the children of Cuban elderly, there was a slightly higher proportion of males (57%) than females (43%). The somewhat different age and gender distribution of the children of Cubans compared to their Latino peers may be related to the immigration history of this group, with more sons and more highly educated and financially well-off children fleeing the Castro regime and bringing their older parents along with them.

Geographic Location of Children

The ability of the children of older persons to provide assistance both during times of crisis and with ongoing activities of daily living is strongly related to the geographic proximity of the child to the elderly parent. Like the vast majority of older persons in the United States, nationally most Latino elderly have at least one child in fairly close proximity (Commonwealth Fund, 1989b). Moreover, in New York City, Latino elderly were found to have even greater numbers of children in close proximity than was the case for elderly African Americans and Whites (Cantor & Brennan, 1993c).

One third (33%) of the children of older Latinos live in the same immediate neighborhood as their parents (13% with their parents, 7% in the same building, and 13% within walking distance), while approximately another fifth (21%) live within the five boroughs of New York City. Still another 15% reside in the metropolitan area and could probably reach parents in a relatively short time during a crisis. However, nearly one-third (27%) of the children of Latino elderly parents live beyond the metropolitan area, making the provision of hands-on assistance to an older parent more problematic.

The close knit nature of the Dominican community, the most recent Latino arrivals, is suggested by the greater likelihood of the children of Dominican elderly to live in the immediate vicinity (i.e., same apartment or building or within walking distance) as compared to the children of their Latino peers; 41% of the children of Dominicans compared with 36% of the children of Latinos of other origins, and 30% in the case of both the children of Puerto Ricans and Cubans. In contrast, Cuban elderly reported the highest proportion of children living beyond the metropolitan area (38%), followed next by Latino of other origins (32% of children), while only about one quarter of the children of Dominican and Puerto Rican elderly live far away from their parents (26% and 25%, respectively).

Face-to-Face Contact with Children

Findings on the frequency of contact between elderly parents and their children in both the 1970 "Elderly of the Inner City" and the 1990

"Growing Older In New York" studies belied the myth that older people had been abandoned by their children: older people in New York City with children were in frequent face-to-face or telephone contact with most of their children on a regular basis (Cantor & Brennan, 1993c). Furthermore, given the close geographic proximity of most children of Latino elderly, Latino older New Yorkers were found to have even higher levels of face-to-face contact with their children than their African American and White counterparts.

Frequency of contact can be categorized at three levels: (a) very frequent (daily or weekly contact); (b) moderately frequent (i.e., monthly or several times per year); and (c) infrequent (i.e., once a year or less or no contact at all). Well over one half (58%) of the children of Latino elderly were seen by parents very frequently (either daily or weekly), while another one-fifth (22%) maintained regular albeit less frequent contact (12% seeing parents at least monthly and 11% several times a year). Infrequent contact was reported for the remaining one fifth of children (19%), with 15% being seen once a year or less and 4% never seen at all.

However, there were differences in the visitation patterns among the children of the four Latino origin groups. Dominicans with the greatest numbers of children and the most children living in close proximity, were the most likely to report very frequent contact with children when compared to their Latino peers: two thirds (67%) of Dominican children were seen either daily or weekly, and another 16% have moderately frequent face-to-face contact with parents monthly or at least several times per year. Cubans, although the least likely to have children and with fewer children on average, were the next most likely to see children either very frequently (60%) or fairly frequently (15%). However, among Cubans a substantial proportion of children (39%) live beyond the New York metropolitan area, and most of these children are seen infrequently or not at all. The greater geographic dispersion and less frequent visitation among the children of Cuban elderly compared to the other Latino origin groups is likely a reflection of the political circumstances in Cuba that led to immigration and the larger number of children who may have remained behind, whether or not out of choice.

Among Puerto Ricans, the largest group of Latino elderly in New York City and the group with the longest average residency (one measure of acculturation), a somewhat smaller proportion of children (55%) are in very frequent face-to-face contact, while another substantial group (28%) sees their parents moderately frequently (i.e., either monthly or several times per year). Among Puerto Rican elderly only a small proportion of children are seen infrequently or not at all (15%), very similar to their Dominican counterparts (17% of children seen infrequently or never).

Finally, among Latinos of other origins, although over one-half (55%) are seen very frequently (i.e., daily or weekly), there is a dichotomy in the frequency of face-to-face contact, similar to the situation among Cuban elderly and their children. Thus, 32% of these children live outside the metropolitan area and may have remained in the homeland, and therefore, one-quarter (25%) are seen infrequently or never seen at all.

Telephone Contact With Children

When face-to-face contact with an elderly parent cannot be maintained due to geographic, financial, or time constraints, regular, on-going contact may be maintained through the use of the telephone. Among the three major ethnic groups of elderly in New York City, the children of Latinos were second only to those of Whites in the frequency of telephone contact with their older parents (Cantor & Brennan, 1993c).

As was the case with face-to-face contact, well over half (59%) of the children of Latino elderly are in at least weekly telephone contact with their parents, with 27% speaking to parents on a daily basis and 32% speaking to parents at least once per week. An additional 13% of the children of Latino elderly are in monthly contact, while 10% speak to their parents several times per year. However, the proportion of children who never have telephone contact with their Latino parents (11%) is somewhat greater than the proportion who never have face-to-face contact (4%).

The pattern of telephone contact between older parents and their children among the four Latino origin groups closely resembles patterns of face-to-face contact. The children of Dominican elderly had the highest frequency of phone contact, with two thirds (68%) in phone contact on at least a weekly basis, compared with 57% of the children of Puerto Ricans, 56% of the children other Latino origins, and 54% of Cuban children. Cuban elderly reported the greatest proportion of children who were never spoken to on the phone (27%), compared to only 12% of the children of Dominicans, 10% of the children of Puerto Ricans, and 9% of the children of older Latinos of other origins.

Closeness to Children

Overall, older Latinos feel very close to 81% of their children and feel somewhat close to another 11%. Elderly Latinos reported feeling not too close (4%) or "not close at all" (3%) to only a very small proportion of their children. While a high level of positive feeling toward children was evidenced in all four Latino origin groups, Dominican elderly reported the greatest proportion of children whom they feel very close to, followed next by Puerto Ricans and older Latinos of other origins, and lastly by Cubans (Dominicans reported being close to 91% of their children; Puerto Ricans and other Latinos, 80%; and Cuban elderly, 70%). In contrast, Cuban elderly reported the greatest proportion of children with whom they did not feel close (16%), compared with only 4% to 7% of the children of Latinos in the other origin groups. These findings suggest that the close proximity and frequent contact between Dominican elderly parents and their children are reflected by closer affectional bonds. Among Cubans, whose children are more likely to be dispersed and in relatively infrequent contact, the impact of the past political tensions and resultant embargo between the United States and Cuba may have resulted in weakened emotional bonds between some older parents and children.

To further ascertain the extent of affective bonds between elderly parents and their children, respondents were asked whether, in general, they would like to see their children more often, as much as at present, or less often than now. The majority (55%) reported they are satisfied with the current level of contact, while 41% said they would like to see their children even more often despite the high levels of reported contact. Very few older Latinos (1%) said they would like to see their children less often than at present. Reflecting the overwhelming desire of most older parents to have contacts with children, there were no significant differences in the proportion desiring to see children more often among the four Latino origin groups.

Grandchildren and Great-Grandchildren

Grandchildren and great-grandchildren may provide one of the most emotionally satisfying experiences for an older person. As life expectancy increases, families of three and even four generation are becoming more common. Furthermore, as grandchildren grow older they may serve an important role in providing needed instrumental assistance to their aging grandparent, and just as valuable, emotional support that may benefit the grandchild as much as the older person.

However, the involvement of grandparents in the lives of their grandchildren and great-grandchildren may arise from more practical, and sometimes tragic, circumstances. With the steady increase in the numbers of working women and single-parent families and the loss of available parents due to incarceration, drug and alcohol abuse, and AIDS, many grandparents, particularly those in poor or minority communities, are increasingly called on to provide regular, on-going care to their grandchildren and great-grandchildren.

Among older Latinos with children (80% of total), nearly nine of ten (89%) also had a grandchild and over half (55%) reported a great-grandchild. These older Latinos had, on average, 10.5 grandchildren and 4.7 great-grandchildren. Among the four Latino origin groups, Cuban elderly with children were the least likely to have a grandchild, only 69%, compared with close to 90% in the case of older Puerto Ricans, Dominicans, and older Latinos of other origins. Cubans also had the smallest average number of grandchildren (3.5), while Dominicans reported the most on average (11.7), followed closely by Latinos of other origins (10.9) and Puerto Ricans (10.7).

With regard to great-grandchildren, the situation is somewhat different. Latino elderly parents of other origins were the most likely to report the presence of great-grandchildren (63%), followed next by Puerto Ricans (54%), then Cubans (44%), and Dominicans (37%). Among Latino elderly great-grantparents there was no statistically significant difference among Latino origin groups in the average number of great-grandchildren, which was 4.7 overall.

Regular Care of Grandchildren and Great-Grandchildren

Respondents with grandchildren and great-grandchildren were asked if they were engaged in the regular, on-going care of these children, as opposed to the relatively intermittent care provided through baby-sitting. Only about 12% of Latino grandparents were involved in the regular care of a grandchild, and there was no statistically significant difference in the proportions caring for a grandchild among the four Latino origin groups. However, there was a trend toward a greater likelihood of providing grandchild care in the case of Dominican elderly grandparents as older Dominicans were twice as likely to be involved in the care of a grandchild than was the case for Puerto Ricans, Cubans, and Latinos of other origins. Among elderly Latinos who cared for a grandchild, over three-quarters provided care because the parents were working (76%), while 10% indicated it was because the parents were unable to provide care (e.g., illness, incarceration), and 3% reported it was for some other reason. Caring for a grandchild was provided mostly because parents were working in all four Latino groups, although Puerto Ricans (14%) and Dominicans (13%) were the most likely to report that they provided care to grandchildren because the parents were unable to do so.

Despite the relatively large numbers of older Latinos caring for grandchildren on a regular basis, the vast majority of older Latinos and those of Dominican, Cuban, or other national origin are not mainly responsible for raising these children. However, in the case of Puerto Ricans who provide regular grandchild care, over one-third (36%) reported that they are the person mainly responsible for raising the child, and 7% reported that they share responsibility. Given the generally poor health status of older Puerto Ricans, the added responsibility of raising small children may prove to be a costly burden to the older person's own limited health and economic resources.

INTERGENERATIONAL ASSISTANCE BETWEEN
OLDER LATINOS AND THEIR CHILDREN

Perhaps the most interesting aspect of intergenerational relations, and most germane to our interest in examining the alternative resources and cultural barriers hypotheses regarding the utilization of formal services, is the extent of reciprocal assistance provided by children to parents and by parents to children. It is important to examine not only the nature and amount of such assistance, but also the evaluations of older Latinos regarding the availability and adequacy of instrumental and emotional support received from the informal network because the sufficiency of assistance is fundamental in understanding the role of informal supports in old age.

With this in mind, respondents were first asked to provide information on the types of intergenerational assistance that were exchanged both from older people to their children, and from children to elderly parents. Given the somewhat different proximity of children and frequency of child interaction among the four Latino origin groups, it was of considerable interest to examine whether these differences would be manifested in the types and amount of assistance rendered between older Latinos in New York City and their children. Types of assistance between parents and children were grouped into three main categories of social support: instrumental support, informational support, and gifts or monetary support.

Parental Assistance to Children

We consider first the assistance provided by older Latino parents to their children. In the area of instrumental support, the most frequently reported assistance given was help during times of illness (58%). Babysitting, in addition to the regular care of grandchildren reported previously, was the next most frequent type of assistance (28%), followed closely by shopping or running errands (25%). Latino elderly parents were involved in the actual running of the household or making home repairs relatively infrequently; 17% of parents helped children with housekeeping, while 12% rendered assistance in the form of home repairs.

There were significant differences by Latino origin in only two areas of instrumental assistance from parent to child. Dominican elderly were the most likely to be involved in babysitting (39%), compared with 30% of elderly parents of other Latino origins, and less than one-quarter of Puerto Rican and Cuban elderly parents (24% and 23%, respectively). Dominicans were also the most likely to report helping their children with housekeeping (33%), followed by 23% of Cuban elderly parents, 19% of parents of other Latino origins, and only 12% of Puerto Rican elderly parents. The greater likelihood of Dominican elderly to assist their children in the areas of babysitting and housekeeping is likely a reflection of several factors, including the higher incidence of multigenerational households in this group and the close-knit nature of the Dominican community, the newest group of New York's Latino immigrants.

Far fewer Latino elderly parents were involved in giving advice than was the case in either providing instrumental or financial assistance to children. Thus, there were no instances in which more than 31% of parents reported providing advice or information. The most frequent type of advice or information provided was with respect to running the home or raising children (31%), followed by advice concerning a job or business (22%), and help with large purchase decisions (19%). This lower level of assistance in the area of providing advice or information in the case of Latinos was equally true among White and African American older New Yorkers (Cantor & Brennan, 1993c). But, particularly in the case of older Latinos, these findings suggest an erosion of the traditional role of the elder in Latino society as a source of knowledge and wisdom.

The only significant difference among Latino origin groups was in the area of providing advice on jobs or business. Older Latinos of other origins were the most likely to provide this type of assistance (30%), while Puerto Rican parents were the least likely (17%) to provide advice on finances or jobs, with the other two groups falling in between (23% among Cubans and 26% among Dominicans). The somewhat lower involvement of Puerto Rican elderly in giving advice, particularly with regard to jobs and business matters, may be a reflection of the longer residency of Puerto Ricans as a group in New York City. It is likely that Puerto Rican children have had greater exposure to mainstream culture and the job market and are therefore less inclined to seek out or even welcome advice from parents, particularly in financial matters. Thus in the case of older Puerto Ricans and their children, the effects of acculturation may work toward minimizing the importance of advice giving, both on the part of parent and children. It should be noted that the proportion of elderly parents receiving advice from children was also low, ranging from 30% to 33%, depending on the issue.

With regard to financial support either in the form of gifts or money to one's children, Latino elderly were found to be less likely than either African American or White older parents to render this type of assistance, likely the result of their poorer economic circumstances (Cantor & Brennan, 1993c). However, two-thirds (67%) of older Latino parents reported giving gifts to their children, and nearly one-quarter (24%) helped their children out with money. The only significant Latino group difference in this domain was with regard to gift giving; Cuban elderly were the most likely to give gifts to children (85%), followed by 69% of Puerto Rican parents, 64% of Dominican parents, and 58% of parents of other Latino origins. Again, it is likely these differences reflect the variation in economic resources among these groups.

Child Assistance to Elderly Parents

The nature of assistance provided by children to their elderly parents closely parallels that provided by parents to children, but the levels of child to parent assistance are considerably higher. In addition, in only one area—receiving monetary help—did the level of assistance vary significantly by the Latino origin of the parent. As was the case with parental assistance to children, children were the most active in providing help to their parents in the areas of instrumental support and financial assistance. Giving advice or information was mentioned far less frequently in the provision of support from children to their parents.

With regard to instrumental support, the most frequently reported type of assistance was help during times of illness or other health crisis. Nearly four of five parents (79%) received such help from children, which, it should be noted, is greater than the proportion of parents who helped children during times of illness (58%). Closely following help during illness, was child assistance with shopping and running errands (66% of Latino parents received such help), driving or escorting older parents to the doctor or other places (57%), and performing home repairs (54%). As was the case with help during illness, the proportion of children providing help in each of these remaining categories far exceeds the proportion of older Latino parents who provide similar types of assistance to their offspring.

Interestingly, a smaller proportion of elderly Latinos received assistance from children with housekeeping (34%) or in cooking meals but not keeping house (28%). There were no significant differences among the four Latino origin groups in the proportion receiving instrumental assistance from children in these areas.

With regard to information and advice provided by children, respondents were asked if they received this type of support in two areas: money matters and making a decision on a large purchase. In both cases no more than one-third of older Latino parents received such advice from children (33% in the case of money matters and 29% in large purchase decisions). The likelihood of receiving information and advice from children did not differ significantly by place of Latino origin, although Latino elderly of other origins were slightly more likely than those in the other three groups to be the recipients of advice from children.

It is particularly in the area of financial assistance, whether in the form of gifts or money, that the flow of assistance from children to parents far outstrips the assistance parents receive from children. In the final domain of financial support, the most frequently reported type of assistance from children was in the form of gifts. Over 80% of older Latinos received gifts from their children, while slightly less than half (42%) received monetary assistance. Among elderly New Yorkers in general, Latinos were found to be the most likely to receive monetary help from children (Cantor & Brennan, 1993c), and it was in this area that significant differences emerged between the Latino origin groups.

Well over half (59%) of Dominican parents reported receiving money from their children, followed by 51% of Latino elderly parents of other origins. This compares with 36% of Puerto Rican parents and 31% of Cuban parents who reported receiving monetary help from their children. The greater likelihood of Dominican parents and those of other Latino origins to receive money from children undoubtedly reflects the more adverse economic conditions in these two groups. As reported previously, Dominicans and Latinos of other origins had the lowest median incomes ($3000/year) compared with their Puerto Rican and Cuban peers (median, $7251 per year). Our research on older New Yorkers over the past 20 years has consistently shown that increasing need on the part of the parent is reflected by increasing amounts of assistance provided by children, and the greater financial assistance provided to older Latinos with the lowest incomes is an illustration of this selection process in action.

Comparison of Patterns of Help From Parents to Children and Children to Parents

Reciprocity between generations is a topic of particular interest in the area of intergenerational support. Such reciprocity can be considered from a life-cycle perspective, with parents expected to provide the bulk of care and resources while children are growing up, while later in the life cycle, the now adult children provide in return most of the care to their aging parents. However, in appraising the adequacy of social care, it is also appropriate to examine the issue of reciprocity at a single point in time, in this case, old age. In the current study, 10 similar types of assistance were asked about regarding assistance from both parents and children, thereby allowing an examination of the extent to which the flow of assistance was balanced between generations. The findings regarding the flow of intergenerational assistance in the case of Latino elderly in New York City revealed some definite patterns of help reciprocity, heavily influenced by the respective needs and resources available to the two generations of parents and children.

First, the level of help provided by children to parents was considerably greater than that given by older parents to children. This finding is illustrated by the proportion in each group providing assistance in the 10 areas inquired about. Children of Latino elderly were more likely to provide help in all of the items regarding instrumental and financial assistance, while in the area of giving advice, the proportions of parents and children providing such assistance is relatively minimal and at approximately the same low levels. Thus, close to 80% of elderly parents reported receiving help from children during an illness or crisis, compared to 58% of parents who helped children in this situation. Similar differences in the level of help were also evident with respect to shopping, running errands, home repairs, and housekeeping. Most significant is the fact that 84% of parents received gifts and 42% received monetary help from children, while only two thirds of parents gave their children gifts and about one-quarter provided monetary assistance to children.

Second, on average, children helped in a greater number of ways (five), compared to the average number of types of assistance provided by older Latinos to their children (three).

Finally, the number of ways children and parents helped each other were compared on a case-by-case basis to obtain an overall measure of parent-child help reciprocity and collapsed into three categories: parents help in more ways; parent and children help equally (reciprocity); and children help in more ways. Among older parents in New York City, Latinos were found to be the most likely to receive more help from children than they themselves provided in comparison with either African American or White elderly parents, and were the least likely of the three ethnic groups to be either in situations of equal help reciprocity or providing more help to children than they received in turn (Cantor & Brennan, 1993c).

Among Latinos elderly parents received more help from children than they provided in return in close to three quarters (71%) of the cases, while in only 12% of the cases was there equal parent-child help reciprocity. And in 17% of the cases, parents provided more help to their children than they themselves received. Thus, even though the Latino community in New York City is far from financially well off, the balance of need is probably even greater on the part of elderly Latino parents as compared with their children and is reflected in the greater flow of assistance from children to parents than as compared with parent to child help.

SIBLINGS AND OTHER RELATIVES OF LATINO OLDER NEW YORKERS

Presence of Siblings in New York City

The vast majority of Latino elderly respondents (73%) reported having a living sibling, but many of these siblings do not live in New York City or the immediate vicinity. Thus, only about two of five Latino elderly (40%) reported having one or more siblings in New York City. Although the likelihood of having a living sibling was not significantly different among the four origin groups, Dominican elderly were somewhat more likely to report having a sibling (83%) and had a significantly greater number of siblings living in New York City. Thus, in the case of Dominican elderly, the average number of siblings was 2.6, as compared with averages of 1.1 to 1.4 siblings living in New York among Puerto Ricans, Cubans, and Latinos of other origins (see Table 6.3).

Contact With Siblings

Not only does geographic distance act as a deterrent to contact with siblings, but age, illness, frailty, and lack of money in certain instances can limit frequent interaction. As a result, among older Latinos with siblings, only about one-third (35%) saw a sibling frequently (i.e., at least one or more times per month), 15% saw a sibling several times a year, while the largest proportion, nearly one-half (48%), saw their siblings infrequently, either once a year or less (33%) of never (16%). However, the frequency of face-to-face contact with siblings varied significantly by Latino origin. Older Dominicans (44%) and Puerto Ricans (41%) with siblings were the most likely to see a sibling with some frequency (at least one or more times per month), compared with 28% in the case of elderly Cubans and 21% of older Latinos of other origins. Cubans were the most likely to report they never saw a sibling (33%), as compared with 8% to 20% of Latinos in the other three origin groups. The large proportion of Cuban elderly who never see a sibling is probably due, at least in part, to the political situation that exists between Cuba and the United States, making visiting difficult between Cubans in New York and those siblings who may have remained behind in Cuba.

Although telephone contact may act as a substitute for face-to-face visits, bridging barriers of geographic distance and poor health, the high cost of telephoning, particularly overseas calls, is a limiting factor in the extent of phone contact between older Latinos and their siblings. Therefore, it is not surprising that a substantial proportion of elderly Latinos with siblings (43%) have only infrequent telephone contact with their brothers and sisters, at most several times per year or less frequently. Among those with more frequent phone contact, 37% are in weekly phone contact, while 19% speak to their siblings at least monthly. The frequency of phone contact with siblings did not differ significantly by Latino origin, although Dominicans, the group with the greatest average number of siblings in the city, were the most likely to speak to a sibling at least weekly (51%), followed next by Puerto Ricans (39%), while only about one-quarter or less of Cubans and those of other Latino origins were in such frequent telephone contact with their siblings.

Given the fact that only 40% of older Latinos reported a sibling in New York City, coupled with the high cost of overseas phone calls, it appears that the potential for both emotional and instrumental assistance from siblings is somewhat limited in the case of many Latino elderly persons, with the exception perhaps of older Dominicans, and to a lesser extent, elderly Puerto Ricans.

Other Relatives in New York City

The final component of the kinship network is other, more distant relatives, such as nieces and nephews, aunts, uncles, and cousins, all of whom may play a part in the provision of social support to older family members. Respondents were asked about the number of these relatives who live in New York City, and how many of these relatives they see or hear from on a regular basis. While Latino, African American, and White elderly respondents were equally likely to report the presence of other relatives in New York City, on average, the Latinos reported significantly more of these other relatives (Cantor & Brennan, 1993c).

Older Latinos in New York were almost equally divided between those who reported the presence of other, more distant relatives in New York City (48%), and those who had no other relatives in their social network (52%). Both the likelihood of having other relatives in New York, as well as the average number of these relatives varied significantly by Latino origin. Dominican elderly were far more likely to have at least one other relative in New York City and to have a greater number of such relatives on average than was the case among Puerto Rican, Cuban, and Latino elderly of other origins: 75% of Dominicans reported having other relatives in New York City, as compared with 44% in the case of Cubans, and 43% in the case of older Puerto Ricans and Latinos of other origins. Furthermore, elderly Dominicans reported an average of 5.7 other relatives, as compared with an average of 3.5 in the case of elderly Puerto Ricans, while the average number of other relatives was 2.6 among elderly Cubans and (2.2) among elderly Latinos of other origins (see Table 6.3).

In addition to the kin components so central to the social network of older people, friends and neighbors, when present, may also play a role in providing the necessary instrumental and emotional support. Friends and neighbors are particularly important in the arena of emotional support, as well as being potential sources of short-term instrumental assistance in times of crisis. Furthermore, friends and neighbors often serve as important pathways to community services, providing both information and assistance in making contacts with formal health and social service providers. As noted previously, elderly Latinos, regardless of country of origin, are less likely to report the presence of friends or neighbors known well in their social networks compared with White and African American older New Yorkers

CONFIDANTS AND FRIENDS OF OLDER LATINOS

Research in gerontology has demonstrated the importance of confidants in the social networks of older people, that is, a person with whom one feels close and can share a sense of intimacy. While confidants may provide instrumental support to older people, the emotional support that they provide may be of crucial importance in maintaining mental health and a positive sense of well-being (Cantor & Brennan, 1993c). With this in mind, respondents were asked, "Is there anyone that you feel very close to—such as a friend, relative, or neighbor? This would be someone you share confidences, feelings, or problems with." For each person identified, respondents were asked to indicate the relationship of the person to themselves, their relative age, geographic proximity, and frequency of face-to-face and telephone contact. Among older New Yorkers, Latino elderly were the least likely to report a confidant and had fewer confidants on average, compared to African Americans and Whites (Cantor & Brennan, 1993c).

Only two of five (40%) elderly Latinos in New York reported the presence of a confidant, and the average number of confidants was 0.6 (see Table 6.3). Both the likelihood of having a confidant and the average number of confidants were not significantly different among the four Latino origin groups. However, elderly Cubans were slightly more likely to report a confidant (48%), followed by 40% of both Puerto Ricans and Latinos of other origins and 36% of Dominicans (see Table 6.3).

Even given the infrequency of reporting a confidant, among older Latinos who reported a confidant the majority were kin (i.e., spouse, child, siblings, or other relatives). Less than half (45%) of reported confidants were non-related friends (hereafter referred to as friend/confidants). Among the four Latino origin groups, Puerto Rican elderly individuals reported the highest proportion of friend/confidants (51%), followed by Cubans (42%) and those of other Latino origins (41%). Less than one third (29%) of the confidants of Dominican elderly persons were not family members.

Friends

Although kin members form the crux of the social network of many older people, particularly elderly Latinos, the presence of nonkin members in the social networks of the elderly has important implications for their continued well-being. Within Latino communities, nonkin members of the social network often assume important responsibilities, being part of the *compadrazgo* system of intimates that often provides assistance to the older persons in lieu of formal agencies (Rodriguez, 1987). Furthermore, elderly without families may rely on friends and neighbors as surrogate kin, while when family is present, friends may provide important opportunities for emotional support, socialization, or act as conduits of information on available services and entitlements. As such, friends often complement the role of family in the social networks of older persons (Cantor & Little, 1985).

Among the elderly population of New York City, Latinos were found to be not only the least likely to report a confidant, but also the least likely to report a nonrelated confidant or friend compared with older Whites and African-Americans (Cantor & Brennan, 1993c). While 40% of older Latinos report the presence of a confidant, only 27% reported the presence of a friend, and the average number of such persons was only 0.4 (see Table 6.3). There was no significant relation between Latino origin and either the likelihood of having a friend or the average numbers of such persons. However, in keeping with the relatively strong emphasis on kin in the social networks of Dominican elderly, it is worth noting that Dominicans were the least likely to report the presence of a friend in their social networks (17%), while Cuban elderly were the most likely to mention a friend (36%). The greater likelihood of having a friend among Cuban elderly may be due to their somewhat looser ties to the kin members of their networks, when compared with older Latinos from the other origin groups (see Table 6.3).

Characteristics of Friends

Information on the relative age, location, and frequency of face-to-face and telephone contact was collected for each person named as a confidant by respondents, and therefore was available for the 134 friends identified by Latino respondents.

With regard to the relative age of friends, the majority (60%) were younger than the respondent, one-quarter (25%) were the same age, and 12% were older than the respondent. The finding that most friendships among older Latinos were with persons younger than themselves was true for all four Latino origin groups. The tendency for older people to have friendships with persons younger than themselves was also noted among White elderly as well as older Latinos, suggesting that age as such is not a barrier to the formation of friendship in later years.

The relatively limited life space of older people is underscored by the location of friends. Over four of five (82%) of the friends of Latino elderly were found to live in close proximity to the respondent, either in the same building (47%) or within walking distance (35%). Thus, the distinction between friends and neighbors rests in the degree of closeness rather than geographic location, and the boundaries between friends and neighbors may, in fact, be overlapping. Of the remaining friends of elderly Latinos, most (12%) were at least within city limits. There was no substantial difference in the location of friends among the four Latino origin groups.

Given the close geographic proximity of friends, it is not surprising that virtually all (88%) were in face-to-face contact with respondents on a regular basis, either daily (52%) or at least weekly (33%). Only 8% of friends were seen on a monthly basis, and 6% were seen only occasionally, at several times per year. Less than 2% (1.5%) were seen once per year or less. Again, there was very little difference among Latino origin groups in the frequency of face-to-face contact with friends.

Not only did face-to-face contact between older Latinos and friends occur frequently, but the level of telephone contact was also quite high. Two thirds of the friends of Latino elderly individuals are in phone contact at least daily or weekly (27% and 40%, respectively). Of the remaining friends of Latinos, 9% were in at least monthly contact, and only 1% were in phone contact several times per year. An additional 9% of friends were never in phone contact with Latino respondents. However, given the close proximity of friends, this may merely be an indication that these persons are seen face-to-face so often that phone contact is unnecessary. As was the case with face-to-face contact, the frequency of telephone contact with friends was relatively stable across the four Latino origin groups.

In summary, the presence of a close friendship network can be of considerable significance to older people providing emotional sustenance and compensatory support if family members are unavailable or unable to provide help. But for most of the current elderly Latino cohort, friends appears to play a less important role in social networks than is the case with either African American or White older New Yorkers. Thus, only a relatively small proportion of Latino elderly reported the presence of one or more friends in their social networks (27% in the case of Latinos as compared with 39% among Whites and 47% among African Americans), and such friends rarely number more than one. However, those Latino elderly with friends had close relationships with these significant others. Most friends lived in close proximity, and the level of interaction between the older friends and their friends was substantial, second only to that reported by elderly African Americans (Cantor & Brennan, 1993c). Among future cohorts of elderly Latinos, the picture with regard to the importance of non-related friend-confidants may change, but at present, the kin-centered nature of most older Latino's social networks does not seem conducive to relationships with nonrelated confidants or friends.

THE ROLE OF NEIGHBORS IN THE LIVES OF ELDERLY LATINOS

Neighbors comprise an additional nonkin element in the social networks of older people that may be called on to provide emotional and instrumental assistance in the absence of family members. And even for those elderly with strong family networks, neighbors may provide additional complimentary assistance and socialization to that provided by the family (Litwak & Szelenji, 1969). Thus, in addition to the role of friends in the networks of older people, it is important to examine the role that neighbors play in the lives of older people, particularly in dense urban areas like New York City.

In a situation similar to that involving friends, Latino elderly were found to be the least likely to report knowing at least one neighbor well as compared with older African Americans and Whites (Cantor & Brennan, 1993c). Only about half (47%) of older Latinos reported knowing one or more neighbors well, as compared with 59% among African Americans and 65% in the case of Whites. The average number of neighbors known well by Latino elderly was 1.6 (see Table 6.3). There were no significant differences in the likelihood of knowing at least one neighbor well among the four Latino origin groups, although Puerto Ricans (48%) and those of other Latino origins (48%) were somewhat more likely to know a neighbor well, followed by Dominicans (45%) and Cubans (44%). The average number of neighbors known well also did not vary significantly by Latino origin.

Flow of Assistance Between Older Latinos and their Neighbors

To examine the types of helping exchanges occurring between older New Yorkers and their neighbors, respondents who knew at least one neighbor well were asked the amount of help that is exchanged with their neighbors, as well as the types of activities that they and their neighbors do for one and other. Over four-fifths (82%) of older Latinos who knew neighbors indicated they and their neighbors help each other a lot (37%) or at least in emergencies (45%). Only 16% knowing neighbors well reported that they did not provide or receive any assistance from their neighbors. There were no significant differences among Latino origin groups in the amount of help each exchanged with neighbors. However, Cuban elderly were somewhat more likely than the other groups to report helping neighbors only in emergencies.

In addition to the amount of neighbor help, respondents were asked to identify the types of activities they did with or for their neighbors. The importance of neighbors in providing opportunities for socialization is underscored by the finding that visiting with neighbors was the most frequently reported activity (82%). However, the availability of neighbors to provide instrumental assistance at times of crisis was underscored by the finding that helping neighbors during times of illness was the second most frequently reported type of activity (60%). Other types of instrumental assistance were reported by substantial proportions of older Latinos with neighbors known well, such as picking up mail (44%), shopping (42%), and escorting to the doctor or clinic (31%). Only a small proportion (12%) were involved in providing financial support to neighbors in the form of monetary assistance. The types of activities shared with neighbors did not vary significantly by Latino origin.

ELDERLY LATINOS WITH TRUNCATED OR
NON-EXISTENT INFORMAL SUPPORTS

While the overwhelming majority of older Latinos in New York City
reported having two or more of the six informal support elements previously described (i.e., spouse, child, sibling, other relative, friend, and
neighbor), regardless of Latino origin, there is a small group of approximately 13% of Latino elderly persons who have no informal support
components (3%) or have a meager or truncated network containing
only one component (10%). Thus, there are a substantial number of
Latino elderly people in New York City dependent either on the formal system or their own resources in times of need or crisis. Given the
population of New York City's Latino elderly 65 years and older
reported in the 1990 census (108,700), somewhere in the neighborhood
of 14,000 Latino elderly individuals in New York may be without a
viable social support system.

Although there were no statistically significant differences
among elderly Latinos by country or origin in the likelihood of having an absent or truncated social support network, again there was
a trend for Cubans to be more likely to report these limited networks,
with almost one of five elderly Cubans having no or only one network component. In contrast, elderly Dominicans were the least
likely (6%) to be without informal supports or have only one support element present.

These findings suggest that Dominicans, the most recent immigrants, have tended to migrate as families or hometown groups, with
many young and old family members coming to the United States
either together of in a limited time frame. On the other hand, Cuban
migration, heavily rooted in political conflict, probably reflects familial differences in attitudes and migration patterns. Whether the somewhat more truncated nature of the informal system among the Cuban
elderly cohort is particular to New York City, and therefore, different
from other concentrations of Cuban immigrants, such as in Miami, is
not known.

EXTENT AND SIZE OF INFORMAL NETWORKS OF
ELDERLY LATINOS—A SUMMARY

When describing informal networks, it is common to characterize
them according to several dimensions, including the breadth or number of components in the network, the number of individual network

members, and the nature of interaction between the elderly and persons in their networks. Looking first at the breadth of informal networks among elderly Latinos, most respondents (71%) reported networks containing three or more of the six possible components. Thus, the average number of components in the case of elderly Latinos (3.2) is comparable with the average number of network components among elderly African Americans in New York City (3.2 components). However, older Whites had broader networks than did their minority peers: White elderly respondents reported significantly more network components on average (3.5), than did older African Americans and Latinos. It is likely that the difference in the average number of network components between majority and minority elderly groups lies in the greater likelihood of White elderly to have a spouse present (47%), as compared with 39% in the case of Latinos and 26% of African Americans (Cantor & Brennan, 1993c).

Country of origin was not significantly related to the average number of network components among elderly Latinos. But Latino elderly networks are heavily skewed toward close kin components and additionally are less likely to include a friend or neighbor than in the case of African American and White older New Yorkers. Thus, the breadth of the social support networks among Latino elderly individuals is generally limited to kin components, and to a much lesser extent, friends or neighbors (see Table 6.3).

With respect to the size of Latino social networks (i.e., the number of persons in the network), these networks range in size from one person to 21 persons or more. Older Latinos reported an average network size of 10.4 individuals, which is very close to the average number of persons in the networks of older Whites. African American elderly networks are the largest, on average, containing 11.8 persons.

Among elderly Latinos, there were again no statistically significant differences in network size among the four Latino origin groups, but there was a trend for Latinos of other and Cuban origin to report a smaller average number of network members (7 and 9 persons, respectively), compared to 11 persons on average among Puerto Ricans and an average of 13 persons among older Dominicans.

The Effect of Acculturation on the Breadth and Size of Informal Networks Among Older Latinos

As we have seen in the previous discussion, country of origin does not appear to be an important factor with regard to either the extent (i.e., number of components) or size (i.e., number of persons) in the informal social networks of elderly Latinos in New York. There is, however, a trend toward Cubans having smaller networks, in contrast to older Dominicans who tend to have the most extensive networks. However, it is possible that other factors, particularly level of acculturation and personal characteristics, may be more relevant than country of origin in affecting both the breadth and the size of the informal networks of older Latinos. To examine the relative importance of these other factors in addition to country of origin, both the number of network components and the size of the network were examined using multiple regression, with the following predictor variables entered hierarchically in the following order: country of origin; length of New York City residency; language spoken at home; and the personal characteristics of age, gender, education (a proxy for class), and living arrangements (dummy coded as live alone and live with others but not a spouse, and using live with spouse as the reference group) (see Table 6.4).

With regard to the number of components in the network among Latino elderly persons, neither country of origin nor level of acculturation emerged as significant predictors. Living arrangements and age, however, were significant predictors in the number of network components. Those living alone and those living with others (but not a spouse) have fewer network components compared to elderly Latinos who lived with a spouse. Furthermore, as the age of the respondent increased, the number of network components decreased (see Table 6.4). These findings that living alone or with others but not a spouse and increased age significantly predicted fewer support elements suggests that the presence or absence of a spouse was the key factor in the breadth of informal networks among older Latinos. But equally important from a support perspective, is the finding that elderly persons living alone are more likely to have more limited informal networks with fewer support elements to call on in time of need. For persons working with elderly Latinos, the nature of their living arrangement and age are important clues to the breadth of their informal networks and have greater relevance than degree of acculturation or country of origin.

The regression analysis on the total number of persons in the network (i.e., network size) explained only a small proportion of the variance (cumulative $R^2 = .03$ as compared with $R^2 = .26$ in the regression on the breadth of the network) (see Table 6.4). But consistent with the repeated findings regarding the larger networks among elderly

TABLE 6.4 Multiple Regressions on the Number of Components and Size of Social Network (Number of Persons) Among New York City's Elderly Latinos ($n = 337$)

	beta	r	% R^2 change
Number of components[a]			
1. Place of origin			
— Puerto Rican	-.05	-.05	.00
— Dominican	.07	.12*	.01
— Cuban	-.05	-.04	.00
2. Acculturation			
— Length of NYC residence	.11	.01	.00
— Language spoken at home	.01	.04	.00
3. Personal characteristics			
— Age	-.11*	-.19**	.04
— Gender (female)	.07	-.05	.00
— Education	-.03	.00	.00
— Live alone	-.53**	-.32**	.09
— Live with others (not spouse)	-.41**	-.14**	.11
Size of network[b]			
1. Place of origin			
— Puerto Rican	.09	.04	.00
— Dominican	.14*	.07	.01
— Cuban	.03	-.02	.00
2. Acculturation			
— Length of NYC residence	.04	.04	.00
— Language spoken at home	-.05	-.00	.00
3. Personal characteristics			
— Age	-.06	-.06	.00
— Gender (female)	.08	.06	.00
— Education	.08	.06	.01
— Live alone	.04	.05	.00
— Live with others (not spouse)	-.02	-.04	.00

[a] Multiple $R = .51$/Cumulative $R^2 = .26$.
[b] Multiple $R = .17$/Cumulative $R^2 = .03$.
* = $p < .05$, ** = $p < .01$.
NYC, New York City.

Dominicans, Dominican origin was the only significant predictor of having more persons in the informal network. Again, level of acculturation was not a significant predictor of network size, nor did personal characteristics (i.e., age, gender, education, or living arrangements) emerge as significant predictors.

ADEQUACY AND AVAILABILITY OF INFORMAL
SOCIAL SUPPORT AMONG OLDER LATINOS

As we have seen, most older Latinos in New York City are involved in viable social networks with a high degree of interaction and support exchanges. In general, members of these networks tend to be kin and most live in close proximity, but nonkin members, when present, are also highly involved. A small proportion of elderly Latinos (3%) are without informal networks and have no one to turn to for needed assistance, while another 10% have only a truncated informal network containing only one support element and have at most one or two persons in their networks.

Objective information on informal networks with respect to size, extent, and degree of interaction is revealing and provides a valuable indicator regarding the likelihood that the informal system will provide assistance when needed. However, equally important in determining the viability of informal social supports are the perceptions of older people themselves as to the availability and adequacy of the support that they receive from informal sources. Respondents were therefore asked to evaluate social support in two areas—tasks of daily living or instrumental support and emotional support. The first question, which pertained to availability read, "If you needed some extra help (with tasks of daily living or emotional support), do you have someone who could help you most of the time, some of the time, only occasionally, or not at all?" The second question concerned adequacy of support and asked, "During the past year, could you have used a lot more, some more, a little more (emotional support or instrumental assistance), or did you get all the help/support you needed?"

Instrumental Assistance

For older people, help with tasks of daily living (i.e., shopping, housekeeping, cooking, transportation) can often mean the difference between remaining in the community, moving in with children, or institutionalization. Having someone to count on for assistance with instrumental tasks of daily living can have a profound impact on elderly persons in terms of quality of life and their own personal sense of well-being. Over three-quarters (77%) of older Latinos in New York City reported they had someone to count on for instrumental help either most of the time (61%) or some of the time (16%). Eight percent (8%) of older Latinos reported that instrumental help was available only occasionally, while 13% said that no help with instrumental tasks was available. Perceptions regarding the availability of instrumental assistance did not differ significantly among the four Latino origin groups. But as might be expected, elderly Dominicans with their relatively extensive family networks, were the most likely (85%) to report that instrumental assistance was available most or some of the time. In contrast, Cubans were the most likely to report the absence of instrumental assistance when needed (28% of elderly Cubans reported the absence of such help, compared with 15% of Latinos of other origins, 12% of Puerto Ricans, and only 6% of older Dominicans).

With regard to the adequacy of instrumental support, the vast majority of Latino elderly reported that they were satisfied with the amount of assistance they received, 63% reporting they received all the help they needed, and 15% reporting they could have used only a little more help. However, about one of five older Latinos could have used either some more (13%) or a lot more help (8%) with tasks of daily living, indicating a substantial pocket of unmet need in help with instrumental activities. While there were no significant Latino group differences in perceptions of the adequacy of instrumental support, a paradoxical trend emerged. While elderly Cubans were the least likely to report the availability of someone to assist with instrumental tasks, they were the most likely of the four groups to report that they were satisfied with the amount of help received (88%), compared with 82% of Dominicans, 79% of Puerto Ricans, and 66% of those of other Latino origins, who said they received all the help they needed or only needed a little more help.

Emotional Support

Emotional support as typified by having someone to talk things over with or assist in making critical decisions has long been considered a critical function of the informal support system. When elderly Latinos were asked if there was someone they could count on to provide emotional support, four-fifths reported such a person was available either most of the time (64%) or some of the time (19%). Eight percent (8%) of older Latinos reported that emotional support was available only occasionally, while 7% reported that no such emotional support was available. As in the case of instrumental support, group differences in the reported availability of emotional support were not significant. But again, Cubans were somewhat less likely to report the availability of emotional support (68% of older Cubans reported emotional support was available at least some of the time, compared with 89% of Dominicans, 84% of Puerto Ricans, and 79% of those of other Latino origins).

With regard to the adequacy of emotional support, again about four-fifths (80%) reported they received all the emotional support they needed (67%) or could have used a little more support (13%). Fourteen percent (14%) of elderly Latinos said they could have used some more emotional support, but only 4% said they could have used a lot more emotional support. However, with respect to perceptions of adequacy of emotional support, statistically significant differences emerged among the four groups of older Latinos. Cubans were significantly less likely to indicate a need for more emotional support than those in the other three groups, with only 8% of Cubans desiring some or a lot more emotional support, compared with approximately 18% to 19% of older Dominicans, Puerto Ricans, and Latinos of other origins. The fact that Cubans felt the least need for more emotional support is particularly interesting in as much as they, as a group, were also the least likely to report having someone available to supply emotional support. It is impossible to tell whether not needing help or not having someone to help came first in the case of the Cuban elderly group, but throughout the findings there is a suggestion of a lower level of dependency on kin with respect to Cuban elderly, than was found among elderly Dominicans and Puerto Ricans.

Despite the fact that older Latinos reported the largest social networks, which were particularly well endowed with children living nearby and in frequent contact, Latino elderly were similar in their level of need for additional assistance (about one-fifth) in comparison to African American and White elderly. This finding is partially explained by the fact that elderly Latinos tend to have poorer health, greater frailty, and lower levels of income as compared with their counterparts, resulting in greater levels of need for assistance. However, this discrepancy may also be a reflection of greater expectations for assistance from family members, especially children, which typifies Hispanic and other more traditional cultures.

USE OF FORMAL SERVICES AMONG
ELDERLY LATINOS IN NEW YORK CITY

The continuing national debate on the topic of long-term care is illustrative of the increasing importance of public policy decisions concerning older Americans. Indeed, as the aging of the population continues to unfold and with the imminent entry of the baby-boom cohort into the ranks of senior citizens, the need is likely to grow for more extensive social services in support of older individuals. As noted previously, social care is conceived as an interlocking system of both informal and formal providers of assistance to older people, directed toward strengthening the capacity for independent living in the community through opportunities for socialization, help with tasks of daily living, and help with personal care in times of crisis (Cantor, 1989; Cantor & Brennan, 1993c). As noted in chapter 2, whether support is obtained from informal sources or community agencies depends on the nature of the situation, the attitudes held by the elderly persons and their families on the appropriate providers of such services, the level of service need, and the availability of providers in both the formal and informal systems (Cantor, 1989).

Findings on the informal social networks of older Latinos in New York City have demonstrated that most are involved in extensive social networks, composed primarily of family members, and characterized by a high level of interaction and provision of mutual support. Thus, Latino elderly are well situated in terms of social care with regard to the informal network. At the same time, elderly Latinos were found to have the lowest level of formal service utilization compared with older African American and White New Yorkers,(Cantor & Brennan, 1993c). This lower rate of utilization of formal services coupled with the heavy reliance on family systems could potentially place elderly Latinos at considerable disadvantage with respect to the provision of adequate social care.

The underutilization of social and health services by the Latino population has been well documented in numerous studies both in New York, and nationally (Commonwealth Fund, 1989b; National Council of La Raza, 1992; Rodriguez, 1987; Rodriguez & Mahard O'Donnell, 1992; Torres-Gil, 1990). Two theories have been postulated to explain the underutilization of community services by Latinos: the alternative resource theory and the barrier theory. The alternative resource theory suggests that Latinos do not use formal services because they are able to obtain any needed assistance from members of their informal networks (Rodriguez, 1987; Rodriguez & Mahard O'Donnell, 1992). Thus, the close social networks of Latinos act as a substitute for services from community-based agencies.

The barrier theory, in contrast, postulates that the underutilization of services by Latinos results from sociocultural obstacles in procuring services at both the individual and institutional level (Rodriguez, 1987; Rodriguez & Mahard O'Donnell, 1992). Institutional barriers include lack of culturally sensitive services and non-Spanish speaking staff (Rodriguez, 1987; Rogler, Malgady, Constantino, & Blumenthal, 1987; Torres-Gil, 1990). Individual barriers include language ability, knowledge of available services, and attitudes and willingness to turn to formal agencies. In fact, data from Growing Older in New York in the 1990s revealed that elderly Latinos have a greater preference for turning to family members rather than formal service providers in situations requiring assistance, when compared with older Whites and African Americans (Cantor & Brennan, 1993c).

UTILIZATION OF FORMAL SERVICES

Given the clear preference for assistance from family or significant others in times of need, to what extent do the elderly Latinos use community services, and what types of formal services are they most likely to be involved? As noted earlier in the case study of older Jews, to gather relevant information, respondents were presented with a list of special groups or agencies in New York City which help older people when in difficulty and asked to indicate which, if any, of these agencies they had turned to in the past year. It should be noted that the question was worded to exclude mere contact with an agency and to elicit responses concerning the more positive concept of turning to an agency in times of need. The list of agencies represented a broad constellation of available services ranging from basic entitlements (Social Security, Medicare, and Medicaid offices) to long-term care agencies (home care, visiting nurse, nursing home, Veterans Administration), local government services (Department for the Aging, Department of Social Services, Police, Housing Authority), religious leaders (minister, priest, rabbi, or spiritualist), and senior centers. (Note: the item on senior centers appeared in a separate section of the questionnaire and pertained to use during the past month, as opposed to the past year in the case of the other services).

Extent and Types of Formal Services Used by Elderly Latinos

In line with the preference for family for needed assistance, only 43% of the Latino elderly population in New York City turned to one or more community agencies during the previous year, a significantly lower proportion than found among Whites and African Americans (58% and 57%, respectively) (Cantor & Brennan, 1993c). Given the relatively minimal utilization of formal services among Latinos, the level of utilization of any particular service was low, with no more than 13% of older Latinos turning to any single agency. The services most frequently turned to by older Latinos in New York were the Social Security office (13%), Medicare office (12%), and Medicaid office (8%) (see Table 6.5). Long-term care services were the next group most frequently utilized. Twelve percent (12%) of older Latinos had turned to home care services in the past year, while 4% utilized visiting nurse services, and 3% turned to the Veterans Administration or Veterans Administration Hospital. No older Latinos reported the use of nursing home services in the past year. Local government agencies were turned to even less frequently, with only 8% of older Latinos reporting involvement with the Department of Social Service, 6% turning to the city Housing Authority, and only 4% turning to either the Department for the Aging or the police.

Attendance at a senior center was reported by 9% of older Latinos in New York City, a significantly lower proportion than in the case of White and African American elderly respondents (19% and 14%, respectively) (Cantor & Brennan, 1993c). Finally, 5% reported turning to a religious institution (i.e., priest, minister, rabbi, spiritualist) for assistance in the previous year (see Table 6.5). The likelihood of using any specific service did not differ significantly among elderly Puerto Ricans, Dominicans, Cubans, or older Latinos of other origins.

Number of Formal Services Used

As noted previously, only 43% of older Latinos in New York reported turning to formal community agencies for assistance, and the average number of services utilized was comparably low, only 0.9 for the group as a whole. Approximately half of older Latinos who turned to a formal agency used only one type of service, while an additional quarter used two services. A very small group, only about one of 10 older Latinos in New York (11%) were heavy formal service users and

TABLE 6.5 Types of Formal Services Used by Elderly Latino New Yorkers in Past Year by Place of Origin (Percent)

	Total (337)	Puerto Rican (192)	Dominican (47)	Cuban (25)	Other origin (73)
(*n*)					
Type of service:					
Entitlement offices					
Social Security	13.1	14.1	10.6	12.0	12.3
Medicare	11.9	9.9	6.4	20.0	17.8
Medicaid	8.0	7.3	2.1	8.0	13.7
Long-term care services					
Home care (all types)	12.2	13.6	12.8	8.0	9.7
Visiting nurse	4.2	4.2	2.1	0.0	6.8
V.A./V.A. hospital	3.0	4.7	2.1	0.0	0.0
Nursing home	0.0	0.0	0.0	0.0	0.0
Government agencies					
Dept. Social Services	7.7	6.3	6.4	20.0	8.2
NYC housing authority	6.2	6.8	4.3	4.0	6.8
Dept. for the Aging	3.9	4.7	2.1	0.0	4.1
Police	3.6	3.1	2.1	0.0	6.8
Socialization/recreation					
Senior center (past month)	8.9	10.9	2.1	12.0	6.8
Religious					
Priest/minister/rabbi	5.3	2.6	6.4	12.0	9.6
Spiritualist	0.3	0.0	0.0	0.0	1.4

Note: Independent items, total does not equal 100%.
* = $p < .05$, ** = $p < .01$.
NYC, New York City; VA, Veterans Administration.

reported turning to three or more agencies in the past year. Interestingly enough, although White and African American older New Yorkers were significantly more likely than older Latinos to turn to the formal sector for help, the average number of services used by Whites and African-Americans (1.2 in the case of both groups) was not significantly higher than the average number of services used by older Latinos (0.9) (Cantor & Brennan, 1993c). There were no significant differences in the average number of services used among the four Latino origin groups. However, there was a noticeable trend for Dominican elderly to be somewhat less likely to use one or more formal service (36%), followed by those of other origins (40%) and 44% of older Puerto Ricans. Elderly Cubans were the most likely to use at least one formal service (56%). The slightly higher proportion of Cubans using formal services may be partially explained by their higher income levels, their somewhat greater facility with the English language, and their lower level of dependency on kin for needed assistance.

ADDITIONAL SERVICES NEEDED BY OLDER LATINOS

One cannot assume that the low level of service utilization indicates that older Latinos do not require the assistance of the formal system. Older Latinos may have needs that outstrip the capacities of their informal caregivers and helpers or may not seek out community-based services due to their cultural beliefs about independence and the appropriateness of accepting social services (Rodriguez, 1987, Torres-Gil, 1990). For other older Latinos, lack of information about available services or difficulty in locating and traveling to service providers may limit access to these agencies (Torres-Gil, 1990).

Consequently, in any analysis of the role of the formal system in the lives of older Latinos, it is important to learn about unmet needs as well as patterns of service utilization. Following the questions pertaining to formal agencies turned to during the previous year, respondents were presented with a list of 10 commonly needed services and asked if they had needed help in any of these areas during the past year. An opportunity was given to indicate any other needed service as well. The service needs presented can be grouped into five main domains: tasks with daily living (i.e., help with housekeeping, meals brought to one's home, home repairs, or an escort/ride); health care (i.e., someone to care for you after a hospital stay or visiting nurse); socialization (someone to call or visit regularly); entitlement advocacy; and personal or job counseling.

Despite the relatively low rate of turning to formal agencies for assistance among older Latinos (43%), there appears to be considerable unmet need in the elderly Latino community. Almost one half (46%) of Latino elderly in New York identified one or more areas in

TABLE 6.6 Types of Formal Services Needed by Elderly Latino New Yorkers in Past Year by Place of Origin (Percent)

(n)	Total (337)	Puerto Rican (192)	Dominican (47)	Cuban (25)	Other origin (73)
Type of Service:					
Tasks of daily living					
Escort/ride	31.2	33.9	29.8	20.0	28.8
Housekeeping/ personal care	25.8	28.6	23.4	28.0	19.2
Home repairs	11.9	12.5	8.5	8.0	13.7
Meals at home	4.7	5.2	2.1	8.0	4.1
Health services					
Visiting nurse	8.6	8.3	10.6	8.0	8.2
Posthospital care	7.1	7.8	8.5	0.0	6.8
Counseling					
Personal counseling	1.2	1.0	0.0	0.0	2.7
Help finding job	0.3	0.5	0.0	0.0	0.0
Socialization					
Someone to call or visit	9.5	12.0	4.3	12.0	5.5
Advocacy					
Help getting entitlements	13.9	11.5	12.8	16.0	20.5

Note: Independent Items, total does not equal 100%.
$* = p < .05$, $** = p < .01$.

which they could have used assistance during the past year. Among older Latinos the greatest area of needed assistance identified was with tasks of daily living. Nearly one-third (31%) of older Latinos indicated they needed assistance with transportation (i.e., escort or ride), while over one-quarter (26%) reported needing help with housekeeping and personal care (see Table 6.6). The need for help with home repairs was reported by 12% of older Latinos, while 5% said they needed help with meals brought to them at home. Assistance with tasks of daily living was the greatest type of reported need among elderly Latinos, despite their close and highly interactive family networks and the relatively high likelihood of living in multigenerational households or extended families.

After help with tasks of daily living, the most frequently reported need among older Latinos was for someone to help them obtain needed entitlements (14%). This finding suggests that, indeed, institutional barriers may be limiting older Latinos from accessing community-based services. The next most frequently reported type of service need was in the area of opportunities for socialization, with 10% saying that they needed someone to call or visit regularly (see Table 6.6). The fact that older Latinos were less likely than both African American or White elderly respondents to either attend a senior center or to have a friend-confidant is probably another manifestation of the need for socialization opportunities among Latino elderly individuals outside of their kin networks.

Assistance with health care followed next, with 9% reporting the need for a visiting nurse, and 7% indicating that they needed help following a hospital stay. Personal (1%) and job (0.3%) counseling were rarely reported service needs. The likelihood of needing any of these 10 types of services did not vary significantly among the four Latino origin groups (see Table 6.6).

Number of Services Needed

Of those reporting service needs, the majority reported a need for only one or two services, and the average number of needs identified was 1.1 for the group as a whole. There were no significant differences in the number of services needed among the four Latino origin groups. However, there was again a trend for the Cuban elderly group to be the most likely not to express any needs for service (60%), followed by 55% in the case of Latino elderly of other origins and 53% in the case of both older Puerto Ricans and Dominicans.

In conclusion, although there is a sizable proportion of Latino elderly who verbalized unmet need (46%), a majority did not indicate any need for service. For many older Latinos, either the informal support system provides the necessary assistance or a variety of individual cultural and institutional barriers may prevent them from considering assistance from formal service providers in times of need (with the exception, perhaps, of economic assistance). Furthermore, assistance in dealing with bureaucracies was an important expressed need for all older New Yorkers, regardless of ethnic background (Cantor & Brennan, 1993c). Frustration with red tape, excessive paper work and complicated forms, and the need for great familiarity with the city to reach the proper office would all seem to be particularly daunting obstacles in the case of Latino elderly, many of whom are fairly recent arrivals with a limited proficiency in English. The importance of pathways to formal services seems to be particularly relevant to older Latinos who are newer arrivals with cultural and language barriers to the formal system.

BARRIERS TO SERVICE UTILIZATION AMONG ELDERLY LATINOS

Most literature on service utilization among minority elderly persons, including the findings just discussed, suggest that elderly Latinos are generally low utilizers of community services (Cantor & Mayer, 1978; Rodriguez, 1987; Rodriguez & Mahard O'Donnell, 1992). Despite their poorer economic position and greater reported health problems, the Latino elderly population in New York City was the least likely of the three major ethnic groups (i.e., Latino, African American, and White) studied in "Growing Older in New York City in the 1990s" to report the use of a series of community services and, with the exception of Medicaid, the least likely to use needs-based entitlements such as Supplemental Security Income and food stamps. Furthermore, as noted in chapter 3, when presented with a series of common situations requiring help, Latino elderly were far more likely to choose a child or other relatives rather than a friend, neighbor, or community agency as potential sources of assistance.

The reasons for low service utilization among elderly Latinos has been the subject of considerable speculation on the part of practitioners and researchers alike. Some studies suggest that the strength of the informal social support system provides an alternative resource structure, except in situations of high distress (Rodriguez, 1987). Thus Rodriguez (1987) notes, ". . . given the low acculturation of the Hispanic elderly and the familial character of Hispanic life we would expect an even stronger relation between social network integration and reliance on alternatives to professional services." On the other hand, others have hypothesized that cultural attitudes and institutional barriers act to mitigate against the use of formal services (Rodriguez, 1987; Wallace, Campbell, & Lew-Ting, 1994). In "Growing Older in New York City in the 1990s", specific data concerning institutional barriers was not gathered with regard to the use of formal services presented in the questionnaire. However, a major need expressed by all respondents, Latinos as well as Whites and African Americans, was for assistance and advocacy in negotiating the bureaucratic system to obtain needed entitlements and services. The strength of this expressed need would suggest that institutional barriers are a serious problem for all elderly regardless of ethnicity and are particularly daunting for older more recent immigrants and those with any limitations in English, such as in the case of many Latinos.

However, it is possible with the available data to further illuminate the relative importance of cultural barriers as opposed to alternative resources as explanations for the low use of services by Latino elderly population in New York City. Using a hierarchical regression model, predictor variables that are representative of both alternative resources and cultural barriers were included, as well as factors that previous research has suggested may play a role in the utilization of formal services. The explanatory model chosen includes four domains: informal supports, cultural barriers, personal characteristics of the respondent, and level of need. The factors included in this hierarchical regression model were entered in a four-stage analysis, which allowed the examination of the importance of the individual domains as well as their combined effects, particularly with respect to alternative resources and cultural barriers. The dependent variable regressed on the four domains was the number of formal services used in the past year.

The first stage of analysis considered the impact of the nature and extent of the informal system on the number of services used to test the hypothesis of alternative resources. The second stage examined the effects of acculturation (the proxy for cultural barriers), while the third stage analyzed the combined effects of alternative resources and cultural barriers. In the final and fourth stage, personal characteristics (including age, gender, country of origin, and living arrangements) and level of need (as measured by the number of expressed service needs, level of functional ability, and depression) were added to control for these other factors that may be related to service utilization (see Table 6.7 for the order of predictor variables and regression analysis results).

Looking first at the impact of the six variables measuring various facets of the extent and strength of the informal system, two factors, the level of interaction with members of the informal network and the extent to which respondents are involved in helping relationships with neighbors, were significant predictors of service utilization among older Latinos. If little or no interaction occurs with informal network members on a regular basis, there is a significantly greater likelihood of formal service use, while higher levels of interaction are associated with less frequent use of community services. This finding suggests that the informal support system does operate to provide alternative resources in many situations of older Latinos well embedded in their informal networks. However, an interesting finding was that neither the size of the informal network nor perceptions of satisfaction with informal assistance received during the past year emerged as significant predictors of formal service use, although such perceptions may be influenced by the frequency of interaction between elderly Latinos and members of their informal networks.

However, the second variable that significantly predicted service utilization in the alternative resources domain was the measure of helping involvement with neighbors, either frequently, only in emergencies, or not at all. Older Latinos who were involved in helping exchanges with neighbors were significantly more likely to avail themselves of community services than those whose involvement was limited to family-centered networks. Furthermore, the level of neighbor involvement retains its significance, even in the final analysis stage when all four domains are considered in the regression model. Thus, our current findings, in line with past research, suggest that neighbors often serve as pathways to the broader community, providing not only additional social support, but information about available services beyond the scope of the narrow family network.

In the second stage of analysis the impact of cultural barriers and attitudes about the appropriateness of using nonfamily sources of assistance was measured in the current study under the broad rubric of acculturation. It was hypothesized that elderly Latinos who have lived in New York City for a longer period of time and have greater facility with English (assessed in terms of speaking English at home) would use formal services more frequently than their more recently arriving and non-English speaking peers. However, these cultural barriers, as such, failed to significantly predict the level of formal service utilization. But having an existing connection to the formal system through the use of needs-based entitlements (i.e., Medicaid, Supplemental Security Income, or food stamps) did significantly predict greater use of the formal service system. Thus, once a pathway has been established, there is a greater likelihood that despite any lingering cultural barriers, older Latinos in need will utilize community services.

When alternative resource and cultural barrier domains were considered together in the third stage of analysis, the level of overall infor-

TABLE 6.7 Multiple Regression Analyses on the Number of Formal Services Used by Latino Elderly New Yorkers (n = 337)

	Analysis stage							
	One		Two		Three		Four	
Variable Domain	b	(R^2)	b	(R^2)	b	(R^2)	b	(R^2)
A. Alternative resources								
1. Social network size	.00	(.00)			-.00	(.00)	.02	(.00)
2. Network interaction	-.15**	(.01)			-.11	(.01)	-.07	(.01)
3. Instrumental support satisfaction	-.03	(.00)			-.03	(.00)	.01	(.00)
4. Emotional support satisfaction	-.01	(.00)			-.02	(.00)	.06	(.00)
5. Number of ways children help	.03	(.00)			.03	(.00)	.01	(.00)
6. Neighbor involvement help	.20**	(.04)			.20**	(.04)	.18**	(.04)
B. Cultural barriers								
1. Length of NYC residence			.10	(.01)	.07	(.00)	-.01	(.00)
2. Language spoken at home (English)			.08	(.00)	.07	(.00)	.11	(.00)
3. Connection to formal needs-based entitlements			.16**	(.02)	.14*	(.02)	.16**	(.02)
C. Personal characteristics								
1. Age							.06	(.01)
2. Gender (female)							-.15**	(.01)
3. Education level							-.01	(.00)

TABLE 6.7 (continued)

	Analysis stage							
	One		Two		Three		Four	
Variable Domain	b	(R^2)	b	(R^2)	b	(R^2)	b	(R^2)
4. Living arrangements								
-Alone							.03	(.00)
-With spouse							.04	(.00)
5. Place of origin								
-Puerto Rican							-.04	(.00)
-Dominican							-.08	(.01)
-Cuban							.01	(.00)
6. Income adequacy							.07	(.00)
D. Extent of Need								
1. Perceived number of needs							.31**	(.11)
2. Activity limitations							-.13	(.00)
3. Depression							.29**	(.05)
Multiple R =	.22		.17		.27		.51	
R^2 =	.05		.03		.07		.26	

* = $p < .05$, ** = $p < .01$

mal network interaction diminished in importance, and only two variables significantly predicted the level of service utilization; involvement with neighbors and a connection to the formal system. Thus,
Latino elderly who know and are involved with neighbors and have
some degree of connectedness to the formal system continue to be
more frequent users of community services, regardless of their level
of interaction with informal network members.

Finally, with the addition of personal characteristics and need factor domains in the fourth stage, five factors emerged as significant predictors of service use among elderly Latinos: involvement with
neighbors; gender (i.e., males used services more often than did
females); connection to the formal system; and most importantly, the
level of need in terms of number of perceived needs and depression,
both of which predicted greater service use. Thus, neither alternative
resources nor cultural barrier theories provided sufficient explanations, in and of themselves, for the low level of service utilization
among older Latinos. Rather, older Latinos with greater numbers of
needs, particularly those stemming from frailty and depression, are
more likely to be frequent users of community services, particularly
if they possess well-established pathways to the broader community
network, either through involvement with their neighbors or by a connection to the needs-based entitlement system.

As is the case with extant research on community service utilization among older adults, once an older person has a level of need
beyond the capacity of the immediate family, the likelihood of turning to community agencies for help increases. But perhaps most
important in these findings regarding the Latino elderly community
is the significant role played by pathways to formal services. If Latinos
know neighbors and are involved with them in helping relationships,
or have any connection to the formal system through needs-based
entitlement programs, there appears to be a greater utilization of community services. Furthermore, experience with one community agency
can help to mitigate against cultural barriers regarding the use of formal service providers, particularly if the experience has been positive.

Consequently, both alternative resources and cultural barriers
affect service utilization among Latino elderly. As the findings in this
chapter suggest, the family plays a major role in the lives of elderly
Latinos, and it is the family who provides the bulk of day-to-day assistance to older Latinos at times of need. Older Latinos without family
with whom they can interact on a regular basis are clearly disadvantaged. But as need for assistance increases and becomes more com-

plex, involving frailty, depression, and other challenges to independent living, the capacities of the family may be overreached, and both
older Latinos and their families will need pathways to the broader
community and the services that it offers. It is at this point that neighbors, friends, clergy, and community leaders play a most important
role as pathways to needed services, offering knowledge, support,
even direct intervention, and assistance in linking the older person in
need with the appropriate community agency. Such pathways also
serve to minimize cultural and institutional barriers to formal services,
as well as to provide alternatives to sole dependency on family
resources.

Interventions that connect Latino family networks with the community at large may be crucial in the delivery of needed assistance
both for older Latinos and younger members of their families. The factors affecting the level of service utilization among Latino elderly are
complex, and are clearly affected by both alternative resources and
barriers to services. But, in addition and even more relevant for the
future, may be the development of theory and practice modalities
involving not only the activation of pathways to services but also the
evolution and support of these avenues to the resources of the larger
community.

CONCLUSION AND IMPLICATIONS

The analyses of the lifestyles and needs of the elderly Latinos presented in this chapter allows us to draw some conclusions regarding
the nature of growing older and Latino in New York City. Some of the
questions raised by the findings can only be answered by further
research, but there are clearly some implicit recommendations concerning the needs of the Latino elderly population and ways to
enhance their later years and participation in the larger community.
Based on the major findings presented above, this concluding section
highlights implications of use to policy makers and practitioners as
well as suggested avenues of research to be pursued in the future.

In recognition of the diversity found among all groups of elderly
persons, throughout this chapter we have chosen to disaggregate the
Latino elderly population of New York City according to their place
of origin. Such an approach allows us to ascertain the similarities and
differences among older Latinos who have diverse backgrounds and
immigration histories. Furthermore, where appropriate, we have
stressed the impact of acculturation on behavior, attitudes, and the

resources available in old age. Guiding this approach is the belief that older Latinos are not a homogenous entity, and that to discuss the situations of Latino elderly without appreciating their differences as well as their similarities is to do them a great disservice. However, as suggested by the findings, there are some important fundamental commonalities in many aspects of the lives of elderly Latinos that outweigh the differences.

Most, regardless of origin and even level of acculturation, are severely economically disadvantaged and struggle in old age on very limited incomes, generally at or near the poverty level. Many report their health as poor or at best fair, and their functional ability is more limited than other groups of elderly, as measured by their level of impairment in carrying out tasks of daily living, compared with their White and African American peers (Berkman & Gurland, 1993). Furthermore, there is a pervasive underutilization of community services, be they entitlements such as Supplemental Security Income or food stamps or other programs such as senior centers or in-home long-term care services. At the same time, there is considerable unmet service need among older Latinos, regardless of place of origin or level of acculturation.

Balanced against these deficits is the strong Latino family-centered informal support system, and most older Latinos are well integrated into such networks, receiving considerable assistance from younger members of the kin system. Although immigration patterns and the level of acculturation have an impact on the extent and composition of these networks (for example, at present favoring older Dominicans and limiting to some extent the size and composition of the networks of older Cubans), the family remains the central focus and principal source of assistance for virtually all older Latinos in New York City. This strong family orientation and dependency on kin may partially limit involvement with nonrelated persons, such as friends and neighbors, as well as community agencies. The robust family networks of older Latinos continue to counterbalance and to some extent mitigate the deficits found in other aspects of their lives. However, the question must be raised as to how long this situation will continue. Is there any evidence of erosion or change in the role of family that will affect current and future cohorts of older Latinos? And most importantly, how can the larger society address the difficulties faced by far too many elderly Latinos with respect to inadequate incomes, poor health status, and the underutilization of community resources? Because these issues are generic to the vast majority of elderly Latinos, cutting across place of origin and level of acculturation, the program and policy implications noted below tend to address the Latino elderly population as a group. However, although the focus of the implications concerning older Latinos may be global, it is imperative to remember that all older Latinos are not alike, and that there are differences in immigration history, length of residency in New York City, and facility with the English language, as well as personal and family characteristics that require consideration whether one works with older individuals or groups of Latino elderly.

Living Arrangements

During the past 20 years there has been a steady increase in the proportion of Latino elderly living alone; from 26% in 1970 to 37% in 1990. Although older Latinos are less likely to live alone than African American and White elderly, poverty is more pervasive among Latinos, and elderly persons living alone do not have the resources of shared households. Furthermore, not having the benefit of anyone else in the dwelling unit can act to reduce the immediacy and availability of family support at times of illness or crisis. It is therefore likely that many live alones may be at risk without assistance from the community, and the increasing numbers of Latino elderly living alone bears close attention to insure that their social and health needs are being met. Clearly, living alone is not synonymous with abandonment by family, but among those without family or with weak kin networks, the role of community outreach will be particularly critical. Considering the low incomes reported by so many older Latinos living alone (nine of 10 are in poverty or near poverty), this group deserves particular attention to prevent loneliness and isolation, as well as insuring that assistance will be available at times of illness or crisis.

Additionally, findings suggest that the longer Latino elderly have been in the country, the less likely they are to live in extended family households and the more apt they are to live alone or with only with a spouse. Thus, among Latino elderly who have been in New York since early adulthood (i.e., for the last 40 years or most of their lives), the proportion living alone in old age increases to between 44% and 50%. This finding may be related to a combination of several economic and acculturation factors such as the relatively greater income of elderly Latinos with longer residency in the city permitting independent living and the more widespread acceptance on the part of both younger and older Latino family members to the norms of intimacy at a distance, so characteristic of majority elderly persons and their families in most industrialized countries. But the increase in the number of older Latinos living alone may also reflect the inability to find housing suitable for large combined households or tensions between generations regarding the desirability of shared housing. Whatever the reasons, in the future it is likely there will be fewer older Latinos living in extended family households, and there will be a need for both younger and older generations to adjust their patterns of providing assistance to the realities of separate domiciles.

Family and Long-Term Care

In line with changing family structure, increasing proportions of working women, and changes in lifestyles resulting from upward mobility on the part of many younger Latinos, it is likely that when frailty occurs, older Latinos will find themselves needing assistance from persons outside the immediate family. Thus, for Latino elderly as well as their White and African American peers, a comprehensive long-term care system needs to be in place, including the funding to cover a variety of in-home services. Such a system would undoubtedly continue to incorporate assistance from children, but the nature of the help provided by Latino family members will probably change, with more community intervention required.

The role of the family as the sole providers of long-term care to older Latinos is particularly problematic in light of the poor health and inadequate financial resources faced by many Latinos in old age. It is interesting that in the current study almost one-half of Latino elderly identified one or more areas in which they could have used more assistance during the previous year, and that in-home assistance with tasks of daily living was the greatest type of reported need, despite their close interactive family networks. Furthermore, even at the present time, there is a small though sizable minority of older Latinos who indicate that assistance from family is either unavailable or inadequate, suggesting the need for further examination of the operation of the continuum of care in the Latino community and casting doubt on the stereotype that within Latino communities the family is able to care for its own. The desire on the part of Latino families to provide assistance to their older members has certainly not been eroded, but circumstances now and in the future would seem to preclude total reliance on family care. Thus, the availability of supportive community services will be essential if families are to continue caring for their elderly members, even if on a more limited basis. To insure that long-term care providers work in partnership with younger Latinos in the care of chronically ill older family members, long-term care agency staff must be sensitized to the values and cultural expectations of the Latino communities in which they work, and ideally should be able to communicate in Spanish, the language used by most older Latinos.

Health Care

This study has noted that many older Latinos report their health as poor or at most fair, and that as a group, that elderly Latinos have a higher level of functional impairment compared with other elderly persons in New York City (Berkman & Gurland, 1993). Given this poorer health status, which is related to their lower socioeconomic class during their earlier years, it is likely that as a group, older Latinos may require extensive health and long-term care services at an earlier age than their majority peers, that is, in their early sixties rather than their middle to late seventies and eighties. Therefore, projections by gerontologists regarding the extension of relatively good health farther along the age continuum with severe frailty occurring for a brief time near the end of life may not apply to Latino and other minority elderly persons, with lifetimes of economic deprivation and health problems. The age at which severe disability occurs in older minority populations is certainly an important subject for further study and will have a major impact on the level of community services required by older Latinos as they become more frail and dependent. It is likely that such dependency will occur when adult children are in early middle-age at the height of the economic and time demands placed on them by their own families, so that the concept of the sandwich generation will continue to be applicable to the children of Latino elderly, even as it has been shown to be no longer applicable to their majority White counterparts.

With respect to health, there is also a case to be made for the availability of preventive health care not presently covered under Medicare if older Latinos are to postpone severe frailty and disability. Universal coverage and an adequate package of benefits for all children and adults under a national health care program could have a positive impact on the physical well-being of future Latino elderly cohorts. However, the current cohort is burdened by a legacy of poor health that requires the marshaling of resources, whether in the form of preventative, acute, or long-term care. Furthermore, Latino families can in no way play their role in providing assistance to older members without adequate health and social services in place in the community.

Economic Security

Perhaps the most serious challenge facing Latino elderly is their marginal economic position and the meager financial resources that they possess. Such poor economic conditions not only preclude a decent quality of life in old age, but exacerbate all the other problems previously discussed, particularly poor health and difficulty in obtaining needed services. Although three-quarters of older Latinos in poverty are covered by Medicaid, only slightly over half (54%) have Supplemental Security Income and even fewer (41%) receive food stamps. In the case of Supplemental Security Income, it is unlikely that assets are a barrier, but current regulations regarding persons living with family members (i.e., reduced benefits or even ineligibility) must certainly have a negative impact on participation on the part of many Latino elderly persons. Careful attention should be paid to such regulations, and they clearly must be modified so as not to penalize older persons living in multigenerational households. But above all, what is most needed are major outreach efforts to inform older Latinos and their families of available benefits and to enroll them in the various programs to which they are entitled.

Future Latino elderly cohorts will continue to suffer from high rates of poverty unless educational, training, and occupational opportunities are made available to younger Latinos, allowing them to enter old age with more advantageous employment histories, which translate into higher levels of Social Security benefits and adequate pensions on retirement. The high rates of unemployment and underemployment among Latinos in New York City do not bode well for the improvement in the economic circumstances of future cohorts of older Latinos. And little improvement relative to the current cohort of elderly Latinos can be expected without massive training and employment opportunities targeted at minority communities.

Utilization of Community Services

The final issue for consideration, and one that comprises a core element of the present chapter, is the underutilization of community services by the Latino elderly population. All elderly in New York City indicated a preference for turning to kin in times of need, and mainly use the formal system sporadically according to need, after informal resources have been found wanting or exhausted. But older Latinos, in addition to this general resistance toward community services, face strong cultural mores that may act as barriers to the use of formal services. Furthermore, older Latinos possess strong family networks, and there is evidence of considerable sharing of both economic and social resources, particularly among the more recent arrivals. Thus, the hypotheses that alternative resources and cultural barriers are responsible for the underutilization of community services are frequently postulated. Utilizing a hierarchical regression model to test the relative importance of cultural barriers as opposed to alternative resources, our findings suggest that while both alternative resources in the form of strong family networks and cultural barriers have an impact on service utilization, neither provide sufficient explanations, in and of themselves, for the low level of formal service utilization among Latinos in New York City. Rather, older Latinos with greater numbers of needs, particularly those stemming from frailty and depression, are more likely to be frequent users of community services, particularly if they possess well-established pathways to the broader community network, either through involvement with neighbors and friends or through a connection to the needs-based entitlement system. It would seem that as long as the family can supply the necessary assistance, particularly everyday help with tasks of daily living, there is little incentive to turn to the outside community. But as need for assistance increases and becomes more complex, the capacities of the family may be overreached, and both Latino elderly and their families will need pathways to the broader community and the services it offers.

It is at this point that neighbors, friends, clergy, and community leaders, such as block organizers or even auxiliary police play a most important role as pathways to needed services, offering knowledge, support, and even direct intervention and assistance in linking the older person in need with the appropriate community agency. Such pathways also serve to minimize cultural and institutional barriers to formal services, as well as to provide alternatives to sole dependency on family resources.

Although our study had no test of institutional barriers, as such, it is clear that given the language limitations of the Latino elderly community and their experience with large scale bureaucracies, many older Latinos in need have difficulty accessing services. It is of significance that help in negotiating the bureaucracy to obtain needed entitlements was one of the most frequently mentioned types of assistance needed by Latinos, as well as their minority and majority peers. Thus, to be useful, pathways clearly involve more than merely providing information, but must also include strong advocacy and even direct intervention to assume that services needed are, in fact, realized. It would appear that there is a need for serious study of how agencies reach out to older Latinos and how pathways are developed between family centered elderly in need and the resources form the broader community.

There are also ways in which the formal sector may act to break down some of the barriers to the use of community services among Latino elderly. Because older Latinos often experience difficulties with the English language, it is essential that not only Spanish-speaking staff be available, but that forms and informational material about programs and activities for elderly persons also be printed in Spanish. Additionally, any announcements affecting services and benefits for older Latinos should certainly appear in Spanish language newspapers or Spanish television and radio. Elderly Latinos should also have available persons to serve as translators when they have dealings with providers and bureaucracies that do not have Spanish-speaking staff. While family members, especially children and grandchildren, are the obvious sources of such assistance, the growing number of older Latinos living alone suggests that many may not have someone nearby or available to provide translation assistance. Additionally, future cohorts of older Latinos may desire to improve their English language skills, and instruction in English should be made available at schools, churches, or senior centers for those who want it.

Finally, the formal system could be made more accessible if there were single points of entry into the community-based service network. Findings from the present chapter have shown that older Latinos who have previously been connected with the entitlement system are higher users of other formal services, suggesting that the agencies themselves can work to link those in need to the appropriate service provider. New York City's elderly population tends to be neighborhood based, obtaining needed services within a 10-block radius of their homes, and this is especially true for older Latinos. Thus, the point of entry to the formal system should be located in the neighborhood as well, such as senior centers, churches, or health centers. Because senior centers have been established in many neighborhoods of the city, they would be an obvious choice as the point of entry to the system. However, Latinos are the least likely of the city's elderly population to attend senior centers, so outreach efforts would be needed to attract participation in senior centers on the part of elderly Latinos. Greater participation in senior centers might also serve to broaden their social networks beyond family members, which in turn may aid in the formation of pathways to the larger community.

Thus, barriers to the use of community services include lack of knowledge about available services, the ability to locate and access the system, advocacy in dealing with entrenched bureaucracies, and the multiplicity of applications and eligibility requirements for various programs, as well as the often articulated need for bilingual staff and sensitivity to Latino culture and its values. It is clearly no accident that the factors that predict service utilization begin with need and are affected by the availability of alternative resources from the family to provide adequate care, but in addition require some connecting mechanism or pathway between the informal and formal service systems.

If one considers only the large proportion of Latino elderly persons with poverty level incomes who are currently not enrolled in Medicaid, food stamps, or Supplemental Security Income regardless of place of origin, the need for outreach and concerted efforts to establish connecting pathways between older Latinos and the broader community is painfully apparent. These pathways are crucial not only with regard to those services that are specifically concerned with aging such as long-term care, but also for the broad constellation of available health, mental health, and nutrition programs that would greatly improve the quality of life for many Latinos who are growing older in New York City.

7

Growing Older and African American in New York City in the 1990s

INTRODUCTION

The increasing numbers of minority elderly have brought about dramatic shifts in the racial and ethnic profile of Americans over the age of 65, and older African Americans comprise one of the fastest growing segments of this population. In New York City, the number of African Americans over the age of 65 increased by 30% in the period from 1980 to 1990 and now accounts for approximately 17% of the city's elderly population (Hanreider, 1992b). Given the continued projected increase in the proportion of minorities in the city's population, African Americans can be expected to comprise an even larger proportion of New York's elderly population in the future. Thus, knowledge about the life styles of African American elderly will become increasingly important for policy makers, planners, and those involved in service delivery to the older population.

Although among the earliest arrivals to the Americas, the historic experience of African Americans in this country has been characterized not by assimilation and increasing opportunities, but rather by economic and racial exploitation, first in the form of slavery and, following emancipation, manifested by segregationist Jim Crow laws and other forms of racial prejudice. Today's cohort of Black older New Yorkers was in young to middle adulthood during the struggles for racial equality in the 1950s and 1960s. And while the current status of

201

many in the African American community would indicate that much remains to be done to mitigate the effects of poverty and racism, the appearance of a substantial group of older Black New Yorkers with moderate retirement incomes in the present cohort argues that the end of legal segregation and the implementation of affirmative action have not been without benefit. The question remains, however, if future cohorts of African American elderly will enjoy some measure of economic security in retirement, given the current political climate regarding affirmative action and the chronic unemployment and underemployment among minority youth.

Research on older Black Americans, including the findings presented later in this chapter, illustrate three recurrent themes when examining this older population; diversity, vulnerability, and family and community strengths. These themes arise from the aforementioned historical and social context of the current cohort of elderly African Americans. As is true of all elderly, there is considerable heterogeneity within the older African American population in terms of economic resources, interactions with kin and friends and neighbors, and reliance on the formal community-based service system. And one major goal of this chapter is to better understand how the economic diversity among the current generation of older African Americans affects their quality of life and the provision of both formal and informal social care. But the diversity of elderly Blacks does not arise solely from economic differences, although poverty certainly plays a role. For example, older Blacks are just as likely as older Whites to live alone, but are more likely to live in multiperson households without a spouse and are more likely to undergo changes in household composition, usually due to death of a spouse (Hays, Fillenbaum, Gold, Shanley, & Blazer, 1995). Blacks are also more likely to live in multigenerational households than their White peers, which may be in part a way of pooling economic resources under conditions of persistent poverty (Mutran, 1985).

The second theme present in today's cohort of older African Americans is one of vulnerability. Despite the many positive changes for Blacks Americans in terms of civil rights and affirmative action in the past four decades, it has been difficult to overcome centuries of poverty and racism. For example, according to Jackson and colleagues (Jackson, Taylor, & Chatters, 1993), the limited opportunity structure that results from racial discrimination at earlier stages of life often translates into a truncated range of retirement options and a paucity of economic resources in old age. Furthermore, Gibson (1993) notes that because of this disadvantage in the workplace, the current cohort of older African Americans are more likely than other elderly persons to have worked at low status jobs, which tend to result in sporadic work patterns and low earnings and rarely carry retirement benefits. Therefore, a second major goal of this chapter was to examine how past access to the opportunity structure in terms of education and occupation during earlier adulthood is reflected in the present quality of life of African Americans who are growing older in New York City in the 1990s.

However, disenfranchisement from the opportunity structure of American society has had wider repercussions than retirement incomes and pension benefits, as evidenced by the well-documented effect of poverty on access to medical care and health over the lifespan. Blacks have not yet achieved equality to non-Hispanic Whites in terms of either health or life expectancy (Crimmins, Hayward, & Saito, 1996). As noted by Crimmins and colleagues, there is an earlier onset of disability among older Blacks as a function of lower socioeconomic status and level of education, resulting in increased difficulties for both the individuals and their families, who are often called on to provide caregiving. And among the cohort of older African Americans who form the basis of findings in the present chapter, activity limitation scores (an index of functional ability) did not decrease among older Blacks with high levels of education as they did for older Whites and Latinos (Berkman & Gurland, 1993).

The third major theme that emerges when examining the current cohort of older Blacks in the United States is one of family and community strengths, despite and in some sense resulting from the vulnerabilities sketched above. Centuries of racial discrimination and prejudice, as well as common cultural traditions, for example, the role of Black churches, serve as a strong bonds in the African American community (Smith, 1993). However, as is true of all elderly persons regardless of ethnicity, the family remains the primary and preferred source of social support both in emergencies and in the more day-to-day forms of assistance that may be required for independent living. But current demographic trends in the Black community, including the rise of female-headed households, lower rates of marriage, and decreased fertility may strain the family's ability to provide care for its older members (Taylor & Chatters, 1991). However, an illustration of the strength of the African American family is found in the reports that more distant kin, such as siblings, nieces and nephews, grandchildren, and even nonrelated individuals such as friends and neighbors provide important instrumental forms of support to older Blacks, as well as assist in managing help received from formal providers (Connell & Gibson, 1997; Luckey, 1994; Miner, 1995). Historically, the Black church has served as the focus of activity in the African American community, providing direct social care to its member as well as providing important avenues for community organization and social opportunities (Levin, Taylor, & Chatters, 1994).

ANALYSIS SAMPLE

The older African American sample employed in this chapter, as noted in chapter 1, was drawn from the larger study, "Growing Older in New York City in the 1990s" (Dumpson et al., 1993). From this base sample, 388 non-Hispanic Blacks were selected to serve as the sample for the analyses presented in this chapter. An important finding from "Growing Older in New York City in the 1990s" was the emergence of a small but substantial group of moderate income African American elderly that was not apparent in the 1970 study of older New Yorkers (Cantor & Brennan, 1993a). This finding led us to focus on income in the present within-group analyses of elderly African Americans because of its implications.

First, one of the major goals of the civil rights movement of the 1950s and 1960s was to eliminate institutional impediments facing racial minorities in obtaining an education and the middle-income jobs that would move them into the mainstream of American life. Over the last decade, our society has revisited the affirmative action programs born of the civil rights movement. The emergence of this group of moderate-income Black elderly in the 1990 New York City sample allows one of the first glimpses of how better equality in education and occupation during one's working years affects one's quality-of-life during retirement. In other words, does this group of older African Americans with moderate retirement incomes exhibit concurrent benefits from the historic changes to the opportunity structure during their lifetimes? In part, this would provide support for the hypothesis that the status and roles of older African Americans exhibit continuity with status and roles at earlier stages of the lifespan (Jackson, Chatters, & Taylor, 1993).

Second, our earlier findings based on cross-ethnic comparisons with the 1990 "Growing Older" sample and other research has suggested that social class, as opposed to ethnicity, is a more important determinant of intergenerational patterns of assistance (Cantor, Brennan, & Sainz, 1994; Mutran; 1985). Thus, we were also interested in whether the informal networks of low-income Black elderly persons would differ from those of moderate-income Blacks. Specifically, would the extent and configuration of the informal network and patterns of assistance vary as a function of income levels among elderly African Americans in New York City? If so, this would replicate our findings that among Black, White, and Latino elderly groups, the provision of social care was more strongly influenced by class rather than ethnic or cultural differences (Cantor et. al, 1994). Of futher interest was whether differences in income level would reveal variations in patterns of formal service among African American older adults.

To better address this question, a group of White elderly with the same median incomes as the moderate-income Black elderly group was included in our analyses for comparison purposes. Thus, in instances where the low-income Blacks and moderate-income Blacks were similar to each other and different from the moderate-income Whites, we postulated that culture rather than economics was the determining factor. In contrast, when moderate-income Blacks more closely resembled moderate-income Whites instead of their lower income Black peers, economics was presumed to play a more important role than cultural factors. Additionally, income was included as an independent variable in our analysis concerning predictors of formal service utilization among older Black New Yorkers to determine if this factor would independently predict levels of utilization in a multivariate model.

The topics covered in this chapter are far ranging—from personal and economic characteristics of African American elderly New Yorkers, to the importance of family, friends, and neighbors in their lives, and to the role of community-services and need for additional help. The key findings presented in this chapter will expand the knowledge base regarding social care among the African American elderly population and provide a foundation for policy implications that affect the lives of both older and younger members of the Black community across the United States.

WHO ARE THE AFRICAN AMERICAN
ELDERLY OF NEW YORK CITY?[1]

Profile of the African American Elderly

As was previously noted, one of the most significant shifts in the income picture of older New Yorkers over the past 20 years has been the relative position of today's African American elderly compared with previous cohorts. Although White elderly income in the current cohort of older New Yorkers still surpasses that of their African American peers, for the first time a sizable proportion of elderly African Americans—20%—have retirement incomes in the moderate range of $10,000 to $25,000 per year (compared with one third of Whites and 12% of Latinos). Many of these elderly had worked in occupations typically found in the public sector or as unionized employees, holding positions that provided benefits in terms of both job security and retirement pensions (see below). As a result, this group of African American older New Yorkers reported relative economic security in old age. To better understand the factors contributing to their relative economic security, older African Americans with retirement incomes of $10,000 and above were compared with their lower income counterparts on a variety of demographic and economic indicators. The profile that emerged tells us a great deal about income security in old age.

Income Comparison Samples

The sample of elderly African Americans was divided into two groups. The low-income Black group (n = 218) reported poverty or near poverty incomes (i.e., to 150% of poverty). The moderate-income group (n = 83) were those with reported incomes over 150% of poverty. Median 1989 household income for the low-income group was only $7251, but was $20,001 for the moderate-income group. A group of

---

1. In the discussion of demographic and economic characteristics presented below between-group comparisons of African American elderly and their White and Latino counterparts are based on weighted data from "Growing Older In New York City in the 1990s" (Cantor & Brennan, 1993a). Within-group comparisons of African Americans based on income status use unweighted data to maximize sample size for statistical power.

moderate-income White elderly (n = 430) having the same median income as the moderate-income Black elderly sample was used for comparison purposes (see below for discussion of economic factors).

Age

Older African Americans in the study sample ranged in age from 60 to 94 years. Low-income Black elderly were significantly older on average compared to both moderate-income Black and moderate-income White elderly. Low-income Blacks had an average age of 77 years, and nearly two thirds (63%) were age 75 or older. Among moderate-income Blacks and Whites, the average age was approximately 75 years, and only half were over the age of 75 (48% and 51%, respectively) (see Table 7.1).

Gender

Generally, women tend to outnumber men in elderly populations, and this is especially true in the case of the African American elderly of New York City, among whom two-thirds are women. Thus, older African American women outnumber men by a ratio of two to one. While women outnumber men among older Latino and White New Yorkers, this difference is less pronounced, with the ratio of elderly women to men being about three to two. Low-income older Blacks were overwhelmingly female (approximately three-quarters of this group were women [73%]), while among the moderate-income Black and moderate-income White elderly groups, the proportions of males and females are nearly the same.

Current Marital Status

Given the relatively greater prevalence of women among the African American elderly population of New York City and the greater likelihood of older women to be widowed, it is not surprising that older African Americans were the least likely to be currently married (26%) and the most likely to be widowed (45%) compared to either White or Latino elderly. African American elderly, as was the case with their Latino peers, were also more likely to be divorced or separated (19%) relative to older Whites (7%), but were equally likely as Whites to never have married (9%). The marital status of the current cohort of

TABLE 7.1 Characteristics of Low Income Black, Moderate Income Black, and Moderate Income White Elderly Groups (Percents)

		Low Income Blacks (n = 218)	Moderate Income Blacks (n = 83)	Moderate Income Whites (n = 430)
Age (years)*:	65 to 69	18.3	27.7	25.3
	70 to 74	18.8	24.1	23.3
	75 to 84	46.3	39.8	42.6
	85 or more	16.5	8.4	8.8
Average age (sd)***:		77.1 (7.1)	74.4 (6.6)	75.2 (6.5)
Gender***:	Male	26.6	55.4	48.1
	Female	73.4	44.6	51.9
Marital Status***:	Married	15.6	48.2	55.8
	Widowed	56.4	34.9	30.9
	Divorced	8.7	4.8	4.2
	Separated	11.9	4.8	1.4
	Never married	7.3	7.2	7.7
Education***:	8th Grade or less	42.6	24.6	16.9
	Some high school	25.4	28.3	16.3
	High school graduate	24.5	30.9	30.4
	Some college	4.4	7.4	15.6
	College graduate	1.5	4.9	7.9
	Postgraduate	1.5	3.7	12.9
Average years education (sd)***:		9.2 (3.2)	10.7 (3.2)	12.3 (3.7)
Perceived health***:	Excellent	9.3	16.9	22.0
	Good	38.4	47.0	43.9
	Fair	34.3	32.5	27.8
	Poor	18.1	3.6	6.3

* $p < .05$, ** $p < .01$, *** $p < .001$.
sd, standard deviation.

older African Americans has shown little change in comparison to the 1970 "Elderly in the Inner City of New York" findings (Cantor, 1979a). As expected, there were significant gender differences in marital status among African American elderly. Older African American women were twice as likely to be widowed compared with their male counterparts (61% and 29%, respectively), while nearly half (48%) of African American elderly men were currently married compared with only 15% of older women. There was little difference between elderly African American women and men in the proportions who were divorced or separated or had never married. The differences in current marital status between African American elderly men and women is a reflection of the greater longevity of older women compared with men, along with the tendency for men to marry women younger than themselves. Given their relative age and gender differentials, it is not surprising that low-income Blacks were the least likely to be currently married (16%) and the most likely to be widowed (56%) of the three groups. Among the moderate-income Black and moderate-income White elderly groups, approximately half were married, and only about one third were widowed (see Table 7.1).

Education

On average, older African Americans reported 9.6 years of education, less than that of White elderly (11.7 years), but greater than the average education of older Latinos (7.4 years). Among elderly African Americans, over one third (35%) reported education levels of 8th Grade or less, about half had attended high school (51%), with half of them earning diplomas. About 10% of older African Americans had attended some college, but only 4% had earned college degrees.

Elderly African American males reported significantly higher educational attainment than their female counterparts, on average 10.1 years as compared with 9.2 in the case of older women. However, despite having lower educational attainments than their White peers, some progress has been made as the proportion of African American elderly New Yorkers with 8 years or less of education has decreased substantially over the past 20 years from two-thirds in 1970 to about one-third at present.

As noted previously, one's economic circumstances in old age often result from a lifetime of educational and occupational choices and opportunities, and these factors explain to a large extent the income disparities among older African Americans in New York City.

Elderly African Americans with moderate incomes reported 1.5 additional years of education on average as compared with their lower income peers (10.7 and 9.2 years, respectively). As these differences in average years of education would indicate, low-income Black elderly persons were the most likely to report education levels of 8th grade or less (43%), as compared with one quarter (25%) of moderate-income Blacks and 17% of moderate-income Whites. Moderate-income Whites were the most likely of the comparison groups to have received a college degree (21%), followed by moderate-income Black older New Yorkers (9%), but only a very small proportion of low-income Blacks held college degrees (3%) (see Table 7.1).

Health Status

When asked to compare their health to other people their age, over half (52%) of older African Americans considered their health to be good (39%) or excellent (13%). In comparison to the other ethnic groups, African Americans were less likely (52%) than Whites (59%) but more likely than Latinos (44%) to rate their health as good or excellent. About one third (31%) of the African American elderly in New York City rated their health as being fair, while 14% considered their health to be poor. The proportion rating their health as poor was similar to that found among elderly Latinos (16%), but was almost twice as high as found among older Whites (9%).

Moderate-income elderly Whites reported the highest levels of perceived physical health, followed closely by moderate-income elderly Black, about two thirds reported their health as being good or excellent. However, among low-income Black elderly persons, less than half (45%) reported good or excellent health, and this group was the most likely to report poor health, nearly one of five (18%), as compared to approximately 5% of their moderate income peers (see Table 7.1).

Nativity, Origin, and Language Spoken at Home

Older African Americans were more likely to have been born on the United States mainland than either their White (69%) or Latino (10%) counterparts, and there has been little change in the nativity of elderly African American elderly since 1970. In contrast to the Northeastern origin of most native born elderly White elderly, most native born African American came from the South, most often from South

Carolina, North Carolina, and Georgia. Of the remainder, about one third (31%) were from the Northeast, primarily New York State. Most older African Americans not born on the mainland were of Caribbean origin, primarily from Jamaica, Haiti, or the U.S. Virgin Islands. Most older African American are long-term residents of New York City— one third (31%) have lived in the city for all or most of their lives (i.e., 60 years or more), and the average length of city residency was 49.5 years, fewer years on average than older Whites (60.8 years) but greater than that found among older Latinos (39.0 years). As a reflection of the high proportion of native born African Americans, virtually all older African Americans (96%) reported speaking only English at home, and African American elderly were more likely to speak only English at home compared to either older Whites or Latinos (81% and 11%, respectively).

Living Arrangements Among Elderly African Americans

The presence of others in the households of elderly individuals is of great importance with regard to the availability of help during times of illness or other crisis or in the provision of more ongoing forms of assistance and support. Other persons in the household also help to mitigate feelings of loneliness and isolation among the elderly persons. It is too often assumed that minority elderly have an advantage over their White counterparts in terms of having other persons in the household who may serve as potential sources of assistance (Himes, Hogan, & Eggebeen, 1996).

However, contrary to common misconceptions, many of New York's older African Americans do not live in extended family households. Two of five (42%) live alone, and 26% live with spouse. Only 33% of older African Americans live with others. Since 1970, the proportion of African American elderly living alone has risen from 33% 20 years ago to 42% at the present time. In fact, in New York City today older African Americans are just as likely to live alone as their White peers (42% and 40%, respectively).

With regard to the presence of others in the household, elderly African Americans were the least likely (26%) of the three ethnic groups to be living with a spouse compared to older Whites (47%) or Latinos (36%), reflecting differences in current marital status among the three groups. However, approximately one-third of both African American and Latino elderly (33% and 30%, respectively) live in households with others, mainly children, but without a spouse, and minority elderly were twice as likely as Whites (15%) to live in such households.

There are clear gender differences among elderly African Americans with regard to living arrangements. As is the case with most elderly populations, African American males were significantly more likely than females to be living in a household with a spouse (46% and 14%, respectively), reflecting the greater likelihood of elderly men to be married as compared with women. In contrast, half (49%) of older African American women reported living alone as compared with approximately one-third (32%) of older men, while over one-third of older women (37%) were living in households with others, mainly children but without a spouse, as compared with 23% of elderly African American men. However, reflecting the importance of shared resources in the face of poverty, the vast majority of older African American women have not moved in with children because they can no longer live independently in the community. In fact, four of five older African American women living with others without a spouse report heading the households in which they reside.

Moreover, half of low-income Black elderly respondents reported living alone (49%), as compared with only about one third in the case of moderate-income Black and moderate-income White elderly (29% and 35%, respectively). However, African Americans, regardless of income, were the most likely to live with others (usually children), but without a spouse (36% among low-income Black and 23% among moderate-income Black), as compared with only about one of 10 (11%) of moderate-income Whites.

THE ECONOMIC WELL-BEING OF OLDER AFRICAN AMERICANS

Socioeconomic Status

Adequacy of income is one of the primary determinants of quality of life in old age, and historically many older African Americans have faced economic deprivation throughout most of their lives. Discrimination in the workplace has often relegated African Americans to low-paying jobs in the service sector, with dire consequences for financial security in old age due to low lifetime earnings and the absence of retirement pensions. Legislation promoting equal opportunities in the workplace may have come too late for many African Americans in the current elderly cohort. Nearly four of five (78%) who worked as adults did so in skilled or unskilled occupations, while only 13%

had administrative, clerical, or sales positions, and 9% held high status occupations such as managers, professionals, or executives. Thus, given the limited occupational and educational opportunities among this group, it is not surprising that almost 80% of elderly African Americans were classified in the lowest two socioeconomic strata on Hollingshead's (1957) Index of Social Position, which is based on occupational status and level of education. About one-fifth (22%) of older African Americans were classified as middle socioeconomic status or higher, illustrative of the emerging middle-class among the African American population. However, this proportion is only half the proportion of middle-class elderly found among elderly Whites New Yorkers.

This differential in terms of education is reflected in the lifetime occupations of these two groups. Moderate-income African American elderly individuals were nearly three times as likely as their lower income peers to have held high status occupations as managers, professionals, proprietors, semiprofessionals, or administrative positions (14% and 5%, respectively) and were more than twice as likely to have held clerical or sales positions (18%) compared with their low income counterparts (7%). Interestingly enough, there was virtually no difference in the proportion of each group who had performed skilled or unskilled labor (about one third of each group) or those who had been housewives (approximately 27%). Furthermore, lower income African American elderly were much more likely to have never worked (26%) as compared with moderate income Blacks (7%).

1989 Income Levels

Elderly African Americans in New York City tend to suffer from inadequate incomes, despite the fact that four of five worked during their adult years. (Virtually all of those who never worked were women who remained home to care for their families.) The impact of racism and its resultant lifetime of limited employment opportunities and minimal pension coverage is reflected in the fact that nearly half (46%) of older African American New Yorkers reported 1989 incomes of $8500 or less, and the median income was only $7251 per year, the same as found among elderly Latinos and substantially less than the median income for older Whites ($13,751).

Although the majority of older New Yorkers have incomes concentrated in the moderate or lower ranges, as expected, income varied as a function of ethnicity. African American and Latino elderly were far more likely than White elderly to report annual incomes of $10,000 or less. Approximately one half of older African Americans reported such low incomes, with one quarter having incomes of $6000 or less per year. Very few elderly African Americans had incomes in the upper ranges—only 6%, and the vast majority of these were in the $25,000 to $35,000 category; less than 1% of older African Americans reported incomes of $50,000 per year or greater.

However, as already noted, one of the most significant shifts in the overall income picture of older New Yorkers over the past 20 years has been the emergence of a small but significant group of moderate retirement income older African Americans with 1989 incomes ranging from $10,000 to $25,000. Thus in 1990 20% of African American elderly reported such moderate level incomes as compared with one third of Whites and only 12% of older Latinos. Many of them were public sector or unionized employees, holding positions that provided benefits in terms of both job security and retirement pensions. Who these moderate income African American elderly are will be examined further at the close of this section on economic security for the clues that they offer to financial well-being in old age.

Poverty Among African American Elderly New Yorkers

Given the sizable numbers of older African Americans reporting low incomes, it is not surprising that one-third (35%) of African American elderly reported 1989 incomes at or below poverty, a poverty rate comparable to the national rate of 34% among all older African Americans. However, an additional one-third of New York's older African Americans had near poverty incomes (i.e., 101% to 150% of poverty). Thus, two-thirds of the African American elderly population in New York City are living in poverty or near poverty, as compared with nearly 85% of the Latino elderly population and 43% of the White elderly population who are at or near poverty. Among elderly African Americans, single persons were nearly twice as likely (39%) to be in poverty as married ones (24%). In as much as older African American women as a group were more likely to be without a spouse, African American elderly women were far more likely to be living in poverty (46%) as compared to men (18%).

Given the high rates of poverty among African American elderly persons in New York City, it was of interest to examine the extent of the utilization of needs-based entitlements (i.e., Supplemental Security

Income, Medicaid, and food stamps) among elderly persons with poverty incomes, in as much as these programs were designed to mitigate some of the effects of severe economic want. Among older African Americans with poverty level incomes, only 53% were covered by Medicaid and 50% received Supplemental Security Income, while only about one-third (32%) were enrolled in the food stamp program. When compared with other older New Yorkers, older African Americans in poverty reported an intermediate level of use of these programs; elderly Latinos were the most likely to use these entitlements, and elderly Whites were the least likely to do so. Although eligibility for these programs is determined by assets as well as income, clearly there is an underutilization of these needs-based entitlements by African American elderly in poverty (as well as by their White and Latino peers), indicating the need for continued outreach programs to enroll eligible elderly individuals in programs. Although there have been attempts by various groups, including the state of New York, to attract enrollment in the Supplemental Security Income, such outreach has had only limited success. Thus, why eligible persons do not utilize these needs-based entitlements and the best methods for breaking down organizational, attitudinal, and knowledge barriers to these programs certainly warrants further investigation in the future if such needs-based entitlements are to have a serious impact on the poverty status of many older African Americans.

Sources of Income

For elderly African Americans, as well as their older peers both in the city and across the nation, Social Security is the most frequently reported source of retirement income. Social Security is received by nine of 10 older African Americans in New York City, with two thirds (67%) reporting Social Security as their primary income source. As a reflection of the employment advances among this African American elderly cohort, pensions were the next most frequently reported income source (42%), and 13% relied on pensions as their principal source of income (the same proportion of White elderly named pensions as their primary source of income). However, as a reflection of the precarious financial position of large numbers of older African Americans, Supplemental Security Income was the third most frequently mentioned principal source of income among this group (9%). Although almost two-thirds of elderly Whites reported receiving income from interests and dividends, only 19% of elderly African

American received income from savings of investments, while among elderly Latinos 13% received such additional income.

Higher status occupations tend to have better retirement benefits in terms of pensions and savings plans, and these benefits may determine to a large extent the economic security of an older person once they leave the work force. This disparity appears to explain the differences in levels of income among older African Americans in New York City, as revealed by comparing sources of income. While both moderate and low income African American elderly were about equally likely to receive Social Security (93% and 89%, respectively), there were sharp differences in terms of retirement pensions and investment income. African American elderly with moderate incomes were over three times as likely to receive pensions (77%) compared with their lower income peers (25%), and over one third (35%) reported income from interests and dividends, as compared with only 17% of their lower income counterparts. Finally, as a reflection of the increased likelihood for persons in higher status occupations to delay retirement, moderate income elderly African Americans were much more likely to report income from wages and salaries (15%) as compared to only 3% of their low income peers.

Perceptions of Income Adequacy

Although objective measures of economic well-being such as class, income, and poverty level are important in understanding the quality of life of older people, equally revealing are the perceptions of the elderly persons themselves on their ability to manage on their incomes. Given the finding that approximately two-thirds of older African Americans in New York City report poverty or near poverty incomes, it was not unexpected that virtually the same proportion (65%) mentioned that they either could not make ends meet or just managed to get by on their current income. About one-fifth (22%) reported that they had enough money to get by with a little extra, but only one of 10 (9%) reported that money was no problem at all. However, the somewhat improved economic situation of African American elderly in 1990 compared to previous cohorts is illustrated by the finding that in 1970, 82% of older African Americans reported difficulty managing on their incomes, as compared with 65% in the current cohort. Similarly, decreases in perceptions of difficulty managing on one's income were observed among White and Latino older New Yorkers. Among older Whites, the proportions reporting difficulty managing with current income decreased from 73% to 50% in the period from 1970 to 1990, while among elderly Latinos, the proportions were 82% and 66%, respectively. Thus, while some progress has been made in improving the economic circumstances of both African American and other older New Yorkers in the past two decades, much remains to be accomplished, and efforts must be made to insure that the gains experienced by this cohort do not evaporate in the future. But it is sobering to note as well that even among middle-income older African Americans, a serious long-term illness could well jeopardize any economic security that they may presently enjoy.

Summary

Older African Americans with moderate incomes are disproportionately male; over half were men as compared with only about one-quarter of their lower income peers. As a result, moderate-income elderly African Americans are much more likely to be currently married (48%) than widowed (35%), while the opposite is true for their lower income counterparts, among whom only 16% are currently married while 56% have been widowed. As a reflection of the relation between income and health in later life, those with moderate incomes were much more likely to report that their health was either excellent or good (64%) compared with less than half (48%) of those reporting low incomes.

African Americans are just as likely as Whites to live alone, and the increased propensity of older African Americans to live with others is more than offset by the fact that they, particularly the women, are far less likely to have a spouse in the household. Furthermore, many of those living with others in extended families do so for economic reasons, and a relatively high proportion of African American women who do live with others serve as head of the households in which they and their children reside. Thus, although there may be others in the household with them, for many such African American women, the level of responsibility they carry for children and grandchildren probably far exceeds the help that they receive in return.

It appears that differences in educational and occupational attainments explain to a large degree how a sizable group of these elderly have attained some measure of economic security in old age. While this finding on the existence of a sizable proportion of middle-income elderly African Americans is encouraging, two caveats are in order. First, although income level among this group of older African

Americans points to a more favorable economic picture, given the history of pooling resources in the African American community, many of these elderly may be involved in supporting dependent family members who suffer from problems endemic to inner-city neighborhoods, such as alcohol and substance abuse, unemployment, incarceration, or AIDS. Indeed, findings on the social networks of older African Americans presented below reveal that a substantial number of grandparents are involved in the regular care of a grandchild because the parents are unable to provide the needed support. Second, because many of the jobs held by this group of older African Americans were either in the public sector or unionized positions, the continued improvement of the financial circumstances of this group are in jeopardy, given the fiscal pressures to downsize government employment and the move to a service economy.

THE INFORMAL SOCIAL NETWORKS OF
NEW YORK CITY'S AFRICAN AMERICAN ELDERLY

The profile of older African Americans presented thus far illustrates many of the problems faced by the African American community that stem from centuries of poverty and racism in the United States. As discussed previously, many African American elderly have had limited opportunities in their lifetimes for educational and occupational advancement, seriously affecting their ability to manage financially in their later years and diminishing their quality of life (Jackson, Taylor, & Chatters, 1993). As a strategy for dealing with poverty and racism, historically, there has been a considerable flow of resources from more fortunate members of the African American community to individuals in need, with diminished regard to kinship ties, per se In part, this strategy has given rise to extended family households where members pool their resources, and greater emphasis has been placed on relationships with nonfamily members such as friends and neighbors (Jayakody, 1993; Stack, 1974). Indeed, many of these nonrelated members of the social network serve as fictive kin, and are considered to be as close as family despite the absence of blood ties. As will be seen in the examination of the social networks of the African American elderly population of New York City, such close friends and neighbors continue to play an important role in the provision of emotional and instrumental support.

However, the relatively greater involvement between Black elderly individuals and nonkin does not mitigate the importance of family in the lives of African Americans of all ages. The soundness of the Black family has been source of contraversy in past decades. However, research has found that Black families are well integrated, not female-dominated, and crucial to the survival and prosperity of its members (Markides & Mindel, 1987). If anything, Black families may be "more extensive and cohesive than among the White population" (Mutran, 1985; Staples as cited in Markides & Mindel, 1987). Although this assertion has not received universal endorsement, at a minimum, empirical evidence has found a considerable reciprocal exchange of assistance between Black parents and children, equal to if not exceeding that observed in White populations (Chatters & Taylor, 1993; Markides & Mindel, 1987; Mutran, 1985).

The parent–child bond appears to be a critical linchpin for the provision of social care in the Black community. The older African American may not only be a recipient of assistance, but research has found them to be more likely than White counterparts to continue to provide both emotional and instrumental support until a greater age. Futhermore, the flow of assistance is often greater from parent to child than from child to parent, and this flow of assistance may extend to grandchildren as well (Chatters & Taylor, 1993; Markides & Mindel, 1987). However, children are important sources of assistance to the older Black parent. Not only do children provide considerable assistance to parents, particularly with advancing age, but also seem to activate more distant elements of the Black extended family network in providing social care in times of need. In addition, children may provide linkages to formal support elements, such as churches or other support for their older Black parents (Chatters & Taylor, 1993).

The strength of Black families in caring for their members can be considered both as an alternative and as a compliment to public and private formal social services. To the extent services are not available, which may be due to lack of financial resources, awareness of availability, or access, informal supports may provide the most viable alternative in meeting the needs of elderly Blacks. However, research has found that older Blacks who receive high levels of formal assistance, tend to concurrently receive a great deal of help from informal networks, such that the two types of support complement one another (Markides & Mindel, 1987).

In the following section, we will describe the informal networks of older African American New Yorkers, as well as examine the extent to which income level, as well as race may be related to both the presence of network elements (i.e., spouse, child, sibling, other relatives, friends, and neighbors), and the interaction of such elements with the older person. Therefore, the three comparison groups described earlier, namely, low-income Blacks, moderate-income Blacks, and moderate-income Whites, will provide the foundation for an examination of the presence and extent of interaction between older people and the members of their informal social networks.

THE FAMILY LIFE OF ELDERLY AFRICAN AMERICANS

Spouse

A spouse, when present, serves as the cornerstone of the informal social network, potentially providing both emotional intimacy and instrumental support. Given the findings on age, gender, and marital status among low-income Black, moderate-income Black, and moderate-income White older New Yorkers, it is not surprising that low-income Black elderly persons were the least likely to report the presence of a spouse (16%), as compared with approximately half of moderate-income Black and moderate-income White elderly New Yorkers (48% and 56%, respectively). Thus, low-income Blacks are at a disadvantage compared to their moderate income African American and White counterparts in terms of this important component of informal support. Not only is a spouse the most likely network member to be available during times of crisis, he or she is also the most likely to provide assistance with ongoing activities of daily living, often needed by older and frailer individuals to avoid institutionalization (see Table 7.2).

Children

Other than spouses, children comprise the most crucial social support component in the networks of older people. Elderly without children or those whose children are unavailable or unwilling to provide needed assistance are considerably disadvantaged and must turn instead to more distant relatives, friends and neighbors, or the larger community for help during times of crisis or in situations requiring more ongoing assistance. As is true for their White and Latino counterparts, about three quarters (76%) of elderly African Americans have at least one living child (including both biological children and other children raised), and the average number of children reported by older African American parents was 2.9.

TABLE 7.2 Presence of Social Network Components Among Low Income Black, Moderate Income Black, and Moderate Income White Elderly Groups (Percent)

	Low Income Blacks (n = 218)	Moderate Income Blacks (n = 83)	Moderate Income Whites (n = 430)
Spouse**:	15.6	48.2	55.8
Child—			
At least one living*:	71.6	83.1	79.1
Average number (sd)**:	2.1 (2.3)	2.4 (2.3)	1.8 (1.4)
Sibling in New York City**:	57.3	63.9	75.1
Other relative in New York City:	53.2	62.7	50.0
Confidant (any):	66.1	71.1	64.2
Friend-confidant:	44.5	55.4	41.6
Neighbor known well:	62.4	66.3	67.2
Average network size (sd):	12.9 (21.8)	10.3 (7.6)	11.2 (17.7)
Number of Support Elements*f**: One	9.8	2.4	3.0
Two	22.0	16.9	12.9
Three	29.9	16.9	29.0
Four	25.7	32.5	26.6
Five	11.7	25.3	22.7
Six	0.9	6.0	5.8

* $p < .05$, ** $p < .01$, *** $p < .001$.
sd, standard deviation.

Findings on the relation between income level and the presence of living children are similar to those regarding a spouse. Low-income Black elderly New Yorkers were significantly less likely to report the presence of at least one living child (72%). And again, the proportions of moderate-income Blacks and moderate-income Whites reporting at least one living child were very similar; 83% among the moderate-income Blacks and 79% among moderate-income Whites. However,

African American elderly reported significantly more children, on average, as compared with moderate-income White elderly, regardless of income. Low-income Black and moderate-income Black elderly parents reported 2.1 and 2.4 children, respectively, on average as compared with 1.8 children among the moderate-income White group (see Table 7.2). While the presence and number of children is an important measure of the potential for the provision of instrumental and emotional support, it is also important to consider the characteristics of these children to better understand the functionality of children as support elements among their parents.

Age and Gender of Children

African American older New Yorkers were more likely to report a small, but substantial proportion of minor children; 5% of the children of low-income Black elderly parents and 7% of the children of moderate-income Blacks were under 21 years of age, as compared with only 1% of the children of moderate-income White elderly parents. Low-income Blacks were also the most likely to report children over the age of 60 years (5%) as compared to 2% among moderate-income Black and 3% of moderate-income White older parents. This finding would suggest that even though Black elderly parents report the greatest number of children on average, approximately one of 10 may either be too young or too old to be a reliable source of assistance in times of need (10% and 9% of the children of low-income Black and moderate-income Black elderly parents, respectively) relative to moderate-income White elderly parents (4% of children). Among all three groups, children were almost equally divided between males and females, although low-income Black elderly parents reported the greatest proportion of female children (56%), as compared with 49% among moderate-income Black and 47% among moderate-income White elderly New Yorkers.

Geographic Proximity

Over half (53%) of the children of African American elderly parents live within relatively close proximity (17% live in the same household as their parent and another 3% live in the same building; 9% are in the immediate neighborhood within walking distance; while another quarter (24%) live beyond walking distance but within the five boroughs of New York City). Fifteen percent (15%) of the children of older African Americans live beyond the city limits but within the New York metropolitan area and could get to their parents within 1 to 2 hours. However, nearly one-third (30%) of the children of African American elderly live beyond the metropolitan area and would need to travel long distances in order to be with their older parents.

Children of moderate-income White elderly are somewhat more geographically dispersed compared to children of elderly African Americans regardless of income. The children of Black elderly parents are more likely to be within walking distance of their parents; 29% of the children of low-income Blacks and 24% of the children of moderate-income Blacks as compared with 18% of the children of moderate-income White elderly. Children of low-income Black elderly parents are also more likely to live beyond walking distance but within the five boroughs of New York City (25%), as compared to the children of both moderate-income Black and moderate-income White elderly (20% and 20%, respectively). Children of both moderate-income Black and moderate-income White elderly parents are the most likely to live in suburbs surrounding the city (18% and 18%, respectively, or to live beyond the metropolitan area (39% and 42%, respectively) as compared with 13% of the children of low-income Black elderly parents who reside in suburban areas and 31% who live beyond the metropolitan area. In addition, low-income Black elderly parents were significantly more likely to report at least one child in the New York metropolitan area (89%) as compared with 80% of among moderate-income Black and 77% among moderate-income White older parents. Thus, low-income Black elderly parents are at somewhat of an advantage in terms of having a child living close enough so that they could be with their parent in approximately 1 hour or less.

Degree of Face-to-Face Contact Between Children and Older Parents

Given their close geographic proximity, it is not surprising that the children of African American elderly are in frequent face-to-face contact with their older parents. One-half (49%) of the children of older African Americans are in face-to-face contact with parents on a weekly basis (26% see parents daily while 23% see parents at least weekly). About one-third of the children of older African Americans see parents either monthly or several times per year (12% on a monthly basis while 18% see parents several times per year).

Infrequent or nonexistent face-to-face contact was reported for slightly under one fifth of the children of African American elderly (16% saw parents once per year or less, while 2% were reported to never have face-to-face contact with their parents).

Given their closer geographic location, it is not surprising that the children of low-income Black elderly are more likely to have face-to-face contact with parents on both a daily (28%) and weekly (22%) basis, approximately half of these children see their parents at least once per week. Among moderate-income African American and White elderly alike, only about 40% of children see their parents this frequently. Children of moderate-income Black and White older New Yorkers were the most likely to see parents on a monthly basis (18% and 25%, respectively) or several times per year (about one-quarter of children in both groups). In contrast, only about one-quarter of the children of low-income Black elderly see their parents only occasionally, that is, monthly or several times per year. Thus, it follows that low-income Black elderly parents were the most likely to be in at least weekly face-to-face contact with a child (74%), compared to 62% in the case of both moderate-income Black and moderate-income White older New Yorkers.

Telephone Contact Between Children and Elderly Parents

Although some children cannot see parents frequently due to career and family responsibilities as well as geographic distance, ongoing contact can be maintained through the use of the telephone. Given the frequent face-to-face contact between older African Americans and their children, there is in addition considerable ongoing telephone contact. As was the case with face-to-face contact, about half (53%) of the children of African American elderly speak to their parents on the phone on at least a weekly basis (22% daily and 31% at least weekly), while another 10% are in moderately frequent telephone contact with parents every month. Only about one-quarter of the children of older African Americans are in infrequent phone contact with their parents (12% several times per year, 4% once per year or less, and 12% never are in phone contact).

Children of moderate income elderly, who tend to be more dispersed, were the most likely to phone older parents either daily or weekly regardless of ethnicity (74% of the children of elderly Whites and 61% of children of elderly Blacks). This compares to only half of the children of low-income elderly Blacks who phone their parents either daily or weekly. Moreover, low-income Black elderly parents were the most likely to report never being in phone contact with a child (16% of children), compared to 7% or fewer of children in the case of both moderate-income Black and moderate-income White elderly parents.

Degree of Closeness to Children and Desire to See Children More Often

Although all elderly parents reported feeling very close to the majority of their children, the proportion of close children was higher among moderate-income Black and White elderly (81% of children in both groups) as compared with 72% of children of low-income elderly Blacks. A further indication of the strength of this intergenerational bond between parents and children is in the proportion of older parents who desire to see children more often. Moderate-income Black elderly parents were the most likely to report being satisfied with the current level of contact (67%), followed by low-income Black parents (60%), as compared with about half (47%) of moderate-income White older parents. Given their somewhat greater dispersal, it follows that moderate-income White elderly parents expressed the greatest desire to see children more often (50%), as compared to about one-third of both low- and moderate-income Black elderly parents.

Presence of Grandchildren and Great-Grandchildren

Two-thirds (67%) of older African Americans parents also report having grandchildren, and one-third (34%) have great-grand-children as well. The average number of grandchildren and great-grandchildren was 6.1 and 4.4, respectively. Among those with children, moderate-income Black elderly parents were the most likely to report the presence of one or more grandchildren (93%), compared to low-income Black and moderate-income White older New Yorkers (86% and 86%, respectively). Furthermore, elderly African Americans, regardless of income level, reported significantly more grandchildren on average as compared with older Whites. Low-income Black elderly parents reported the greatest number of grandchildren on average, 5.8, followed next by moderate-income Blacks (4.8 grandchildren on average). Among older White parents, the average number of grandchildren was only 3.5.

With respect to great-grandchildren, elderly low-income Black grandparents were the most likely to report great-grandchildren (63%) and reported the greatest average numbers of these offspring (2.9), compared to either moderate-income Black or moderate-income White grandparents. Moderate-income Black elderly grandparents were significantly more likely than moderate-income White grandparents to report the presence of a great-grandchild (47% and 20%, respectively), and also reported greater numbers of great-grandchildren on average (1.9 and 0.7, respectively). Thus, older African Americans of both low and moderate income levels were more likely to report the presence of great-grandchildren as compared with Whites.

Care of Grandchildren and Great-Grandchildren

Grandchildren and great-grandchildren can provide emotionally enriching experiences for many grandparents and are themselves potential sources of instrumental support to their grandparents as they enter adolescence. However, across the country, grandmothers and even grandfathers are increasingly being called on to provide both intermittent and ongoing care for grandchildren and great-grandchildren due to the rising number of working mothers as well as the impact of drug and alcohol abuse, AIDS, and incarceration all too common in minority communities.

Care of grandchildren and great-grandchildren can occur in two time frames; the intermittent care represented by babysitting while parents are out and the more long-range and taxing care of grandchildren on a regular basis (i.e., daily or several times per week). Thirty-six percent of African American grandparents reported babysitting for grandchildren (or great-grandchildren). In contrast, 19% of these grandparents reported the regular, ongoing care of a grandchild. The proportion of Black grandparents caring for grandchildren was far greater than that found among their White and Latino peers (8% and 15%, respectively).

Although not statistically significant, there was a trend for African American grandparents to be more involved in the ongoing care of a grandchild or great-grandchild (14% among low-income Black and 21% among moderate-income Black grandparents). And again, while not significant, there was a trend for African American grandparents involved in the day-to-day care of a grandchild to be the person mainly responsible for care (22% and 39% of low-income Black and moderate-income Black grandparents, respectively), while only 4% of moderate-income White elderly grandparents who regularly care for a grandchild were the person primarily responsible for care.

The reasons for caring for grandchildren, as noted earlier, may range from the child's parent being at work to the parent being unavailable. As a reflection of the disproportionate incidence of social problems among minority and low-income communities, low-income Blacks and moderate-income Blacks were the most likely to report that they cared for a grandchild or great-grandchild because the child's parent was unable to do so (29% and 39%, respectively), as compared with only 4% of moderate-income White elderly grandparents regularly caring for a grandchild. Moderate-income White grandparents providing grandchild care were most likely to be doing so because the parent was working (74%), as compared with 61% and 46% of their low-income Black and moderate-income Black counterparts, respectively.

Thus, substantial numbers of older African American grandparents in New York City are involved in the regular care of grandchildren and great-grandchildren, and although in the majority this care is provided because parents are working and child care options are limited, a substantial minority of older African American grandparents have assumed responsibility for their grandchildren because of the inability of the child's parents to provide the necessary care. While caring for grandchildren may be an enriching experience, for many such care involves burdens in terms of time, energy, finances, and emotional strain. It is likely that the need for grandparents as surrogate parents will continue to grow in minority communities given the current level of public support for child care, drug rehabilitation and treatment, and the care and support of persons with AIDS and their families.

Flow of Assistance From Older Parents to Children

Elderly parents were asked to indicate the types of assistance they provided to children and the types of assistance they received in return in four major domains; instrumental assistance with tasks of daily living, emotional support, information and advice, and financial assistance. With regard to elderly parental assistance to children, it should be noted that moderate-income elderly, both Black and White, were more likely to provide help to children (94% and 95% of parents, respectively), as compared with 87% of low-income Black elderly parents, who tend to be older, in poorer health, and under more severe economic constraints.

Although the moderate-income Black and moderate-income White elderly parents were slightly more likely to report providing crisis intervention such as providing help during times of illness (59% and 62%, respectively) as compared to low-income Black elderly parents (56%), these differences were not significant. In terms of instrumental assistance, moderate-income Whites were the most likely to report babysitting for grandchildren (43%), as compared to less than one-third of both low-income Black and moderate-income Black elderly parents (30% and 32%, respectively). However, as noted previously, it was the elderly African Americans, regardless of income, who were the most likely to be involved in the ongoing care of grandchildren (14% among low-income Blacks and 21% among moderate-income Blacks) compared to moderate-income White elderly grandparents (8%). In addition, the relatively lower proportion of Black grandparents reporting babysitting for grandchildren probably reflects the greater tendency for them to be living in multigenerational households. For these elderly grandparents, babysitting may not have the same meaning as for grandparents living separately from children and grandchildren.

Moderate-income elderly parents were significantly more likely to report shopping and running errands for children regardless of ethnicity. Among moderate-income Black and moderate-income White parents, nearly one-third reported providing such assistance (28% and 29%, respectively) as compared with 14% of low-income Black older parents. However, when it came to help with housekeeping, the situation was reversed, with 17% of low-income Black elderly parents reporting the provision of this type of assistance as compared to approximately one of 10 moderate-income parents (9% in the case of moderate-income Black parents and 10% of moderate-income White parents). This finding is at least in part a reflection of the fact that low-income Black elderly parents are the most likely to live in extended-family households, where the provision of this type of help is part of the daily routine. There was no significant difference in the proportion of elderly helping with home repairs, ranging from 15% to 22%.

In terms of information and advice, African American elderly parents were significantly more likely to provide advice on the home and raising children (36% among both low-income Black and moderate-income Black older parents), as compared with 23% of moderate-income White elderly parents. Again, this finding is likely a reflection of the greater incidence of living with children (and grandchildren) among Black elderly as compared with their White peers. But it may also be a reflection of the greater integration of elderly African Americans in family life, regardless of whether they share a place of residence. In contrast, when it comes to giving advice on jobs or business matters, moderate-income elderly were the significantly more likely to assist children in this area. Moderate-income Black elderly parents were the most likely to report helping children in this domain (39%), followed by 29% of moderate-income Whites, and about one quarter (26%) of low-income Black elderly parents. But the differences in the proportion of low-income Black, moderate-income Black, and moderate-income White elderly parents reporting giving advice to children concerning large purchases (21%, 27%, and 27%, respectively), were not significant.

In terms of financial assistance, moderate-income elderly parents were more likely to provide financial assistance in the form of gifts or money as compared with low-income Black older parents. While the majority of elderly parents in all groups reported giving gifts to children, the proportion was much higher among moderate-income Black (90%) and moderate-income White (93%) older parents, as compared to their low-income Black peers (62%). A similar pattern was observed in the more direct form of financial assistance of giving money; moderate-income White were the most likely to provide such help (55%) closely followed by moderate-income Black elderly parents (51%), while less than one third of low-income Black parents (30%) reported giving money to children. Findings about the relative proportions of older parents providing financial help to children clearly reflect the differences in economic resources among the low-income Black, moderate-income Black, and moderate-income White older New Yorkers with children.

Flow of Assistance From Children to Older Parents

With regard to the proportion of older parents who receive help from children, there were no significant differences between low-income Black, moderate-income Black, and moderate-income White older New Yorkers (92%, 94%, and 96%, respectively); approximately nine of 10 receive some form of child assistance. As was the case with parent to child assistance, financial help was the most frequently reported type of assistance provided by children to older parents, with significant between-group differences. Moderate-income elderly parents, both African American and White, were the most likely to receive gifts from children (87% and 92%, respectively), as compared with 81% of low-income Black older parents. However, it was the low-income Black elderly parents who were the most likely to report direct monetary help from children (45%), followed by one-third (33%) of moderate-income Black elderly parents, while only 13% of moderate-income White elderly parents reported receiving money from children.

The next most frequently reported type of help provided by children to older parents was assistance during an illness or other crisis, and the proportion of parents reporting receiving such help did not differ significantly between low-income Black, moderate-income Black, and moderate-income White elderly parents (78%, 67%, and 67%, respectively). But when it comes to instrumental assistance with activities of daily living, low-income elderly Blacks were the most likely to report receiving this type of help in three of the five areas examined. Over two-thirds (70%) of low-income Black parents reported children helped them with shopping and running errands, as compared with 54% of moderate-income Black and 46% of moderate-income White older parents. The Black elderly group was far more likely to receive instrumental assistance with household tasks from children compared to older Whites. Nearly two-fifths of low-income Black elderly parents reported receiving help with housekeeping or preparing meals (39% and 39%, respectively), followed by one-third of moderate-income Black parents (30% and 32%, respectively), while only approximately 15% of moderate-income White elderly parents reported receiving this type of assistance from children. Although low-income Black elderly parents were somewhat more likely than their moderate-income counterparts to receive help with home repairs or transportation, these differences were not statistically significant.

There were also no significant differences among low-income Blacks, moderate-income Blacks, and moderate-income Whites in the proportion of older parents reporting the provision of advice on financial matters by their children (33%, 26%, and 24%, respectively), or who received advice on large purchase decisions (38%, 38%, and 29%, respectively). Although differences in the proportions of older New Yorkers receiving advice from children in either area were not significant, overall, there was a trend for Black parents to report receiving more advice from children compared to their moderate-income White counterparts. Perhaps most interesting is the finding that among all three groups, giving advice was reported far less frequently than all other types of assistance, regardless of whether assistance was from parent to children or from children to parent.

Siblings

Although some siblings may drift apart through lack of emotional closeness or geographic distance, for many elderly, sisters and brothers comprise an important source of both emotional and, to a lesser extent, instrumental support. This is true, in part, because siblings constitute one of an older person's longest-standing relationships going back to the family of origin. Almost two-thirds (62%) of older African Americans reported the presence of at least one living sibling, and 40% reported having a brother or sister living in New York City. Moderate-income White elderly were the significantly more likely to report having a sibling (75%), as compared to Black older New Yorkers regardless of income level; 64% of moderate-income elderly Blacks and 57% of low-income elderly Blacks (see Table 7.2). However, among those with a New York City brother or sister, Black elderly reported significantly more siblings on average (low-income Black = 1.9; moderate-income Black = 2.1 siblings), as compared with 1.6 siblings on average among moderate-income White older New Yorkers.

Frequency of Contact With Siblings

African American elderly were somewhat less likely (33%) to have regular (i.e., at least monthly) face-to-face contact with siblings as compared to either older White or Latino New Yorkers (41% and 40%, respectively). Neither race nor income level appears to influence the amount of contact with siblings; the proportions of elderly having face-to-face contact with a brother or sister at least weekly were 29% among low-income Blacks and 30% among moderate-income Blacks, as compared with 24% of moderate-income Whites. Low-income elderly Blacks, were the most likely to report only infrequent contact with a sibling (once per year or less often [33%]), compared to both moderate-income Black (19%) and moderate-income White (24%) elderly. However, differences in the level of face-to-face contact with a sibling were not significant. With regard to contact by telephone, moderate-income White elderly were the most likely to talk to a sibling on the phone at least weekly (51%), followed by low-income elderly Blacks (45%) and moderate-income Blacks (41%), but again, these differences were not significant.

Other Relatives in New York City

Overall, slightly more than one-half (54%) of African American elderly reported the presence of other relatives (e.g., cousins, aunts, uncles) in New York City. While differences in the presence of other New York City relatives were not significant, moderate-income Black elderly were more likely to report having such a relative (63%) as compared with 53% of low-income Black and 50% of moderate-income White older New Yorkers. There were also no significant differences in the average number of other relatives overall, nor in the average number of other relatives with whom the elderly are in frequent contact, which ranged from three among low-income Blacks, to approximately four among moderate-income elderly of both races.

THE ROLE OF NONKIN IN THE SOCIAL NETWORKS OF OLDER AFRICAN AMERICANS

Confidants and Friends

As mentioned earlier, in the face of poverty and racial discrimination African Americans have often extended their definitions of family beyond kinship bonds to nonrelated significant others in their social networks. In addition, gerontological research has suggested the importance of older people having a confidant, that is, someone with whom they feel very close and share a sense of intimacy. Such persons have been found to provide important emotional and even instrumental support and may be even more important than family members in ensuring positive mental health and a sense of well being (Cantor, 1979a). The vast majority of older New Yorkers have one or more persons whom they designated as a confidant, and among African American elderly New Yorkers, the proportion was nearly three-quarters (71%). There were no significant differences in the proportions of low-income Black, moderate-income Black, and moderate-income White elderly New Yorkers reporting the presence of a confidant (66%, 71%, and 64%, respectively) (see Table 7.2) or in the average number of confidants reported which ranged from 1 to 1.5.

Confidant's Relationship to Older Person

Because both moderate-income Black and moderate-income White elderly were more likely than low-income Blacks to be currently married, it is not surprising that they were the most likely to name a spouse as confidant (6% and 9%, respectively), while only 1% of low-income Black elderly named a spouse as confidant. The confidants of moderate-income White elderly were the most likely to be members of the kin network (55% of confidants) as compared to 47% of the confidants of low-income Black and 46% of the confidants of moderate-income Blacks. Reflecting the historic importance of strong nonkin ties in the African American community mentioned above, older African Americans, were more likely to name nonrelated persons as confidants (53%) than family members (45%), further illustrating the importance of these nonrelated significant others in the African American community. The proportion of confidants who were nonrelated were 51% and 52% of low-income Blacks and moderate-income Blacks, respectively, as compared with 44% of the confidants of moderate-income Whites. We turn now to the presence and interaction with these nonkin confidants (hereafter called friends).

Presence of Friends

The proportions of low-income Black, moderate-income Black, and moderate-income White older New Yorkers reporting at least one or more friends was not significantly different; 55% among moderate-income Black, 45% among low-income Blacks, and 42% among moderate-income White older New Yorkers (see Table 7.2). There were not significant differences in the average number of friends among the three groups overall. However, among those reporting a friend, moderate-income White elderly reported significantly more friends on average (2.1), as compared to 1.6 and 1.5 friends on average among low-income Black and moderate-income Black elderly, respectively.

Characteristics of Friends

Regardless of race or ethnicity, friends of New York City's elderly population were not necessarily age peers, thus only a small proportion of the friends of low-income Black, moderate-income Black, and moderate-income White elderly were the same age as the respondent; while approximately three-fifths of friends named were younger. However, friends of moderate-income Blacks were the most likely to be the same age as the respondent (28% of friends) compared to about one of five friends of both low-income Blacks and moderate-income Whites. Friends of elderly African Americans, regardless of income level, tended to be in closer geographic proximity in comparison to those of moderate-income Whites. Twenty-eight percent of the friends of moderate-income White elderly resided either in the suburbs outside of New York City or beyond the metropolitan area, as compared to 17% of the friends of low-income older Blacks and 12% of the friends of moderate-income elderly Blacks. Given their closer proximity, friends of low-income Blacks and moderate-income Blacks were somewhat more likely to be in face-to-face contact with the respondent at least weekly (77% and 71% of friends, respectively), as compared with 68% of the friends moderate-income Whites. However, friends of low-income Black elderly were reported to be in the most frequent telephone contact (81% in at least weekly contact), as compared with 72% in the case of the friends of moderate-income Black and 63% of the friends of moderate-income White older New Yorkers.

Neighbors Known Well

Because of their close proximity to an older person, neighbors can serve an important role in the social support systems of older people, particularly in an emergency. Approximately two-thirds of low-income Black, moderate-income Black, and moderate-income White older New Yorkers reported knowing at least one or more neighbors well (62%, 66%, and 67%, respectively) (see Table 7.2). And there were also no significant differences in the average number of neighbors known well both among the elderly groups overall and among those knowing neighbors. The average number of neighbors known well ranged from four in the case of low-income Black and moderate-income Black elderly to three among moderate-income White older New Yorkers.

Amount of Help Exchanged With Neighbors

Although most elderly receive considerable social support from their children, those without children or who have children who are either unable or unwilling to provide assistance must often turn to more distant relatives or neighbors and friends to receive needed assistance. However, knowing neighbors well may not, in and of itself, ensure that a supportive relationship exists between an older person and the neighbor. Therefore, respondents were asked to provide information on the amount of help exchanged between themselves and their neighbors, as well as the types of activities they and their neighbors shared.

Among African American elderly knowing one or more neighbors well, about one-third (35%) reported that they and their neighbors help each other a lot, while half (48%) said they and their neighbors helped each other at least in emergencies. Only 17% reported not helping neighbors at all. The level of neighbor help exchanged did not differ significantly among the three groups. Approximately one-third of low-income Black, moderate-income Black, and moderate-income White elderly with neighbors known well reported exchanging a lot of help, but about one-half indicated that help with neighbors was exchanged only in emergencies. The most frequently reported type of assistance between elderly and their neighbors was in the arena of emotional support. Approximately four-fifths of those knowing neighbors well in all three groups reported providing emotional support, and there were no significant differences in this regard. Visiting was closely followed by crisis intervention in the form of help during times of illness (approximately 70%), and again there were no significant differences among the three comparison groups.

Instrumental and financial assistance between elderly and their neighbors were reported less frequently, but in these domains significant differences emerged. In the instrumental arena, moderate income elderly regardless of race, were significantly more likely to report that they and their neighbors picked-up mail for each other, 66% in the case of moderate-income Blacks and 68% in the case of moderate-income Whites knowing neighbors well. Only 40% of low-income Blacks knowing neighbors reported exchanging this type of assistance. However, when it comes to financial help, African American older New Yorkers, regardless of income, were more likely to report they lent money to neighbors or vice versa; 40% of moderate-income Blacks and 29% of low-income Blacks knowing neighbors, as compared to only 13% of their moderate-income White elderly peers.

Social Network Size and Number of Support Elements

The size of the social network (i.e., number of persons) did not differ significantly between the three comparison groups, ranging between 10 and 13 persons, on average (see Table 7.2). However, another consideration of the viability of the informal network to assist an older person in times of need concerns the presence or absence of each of the six network elements noted earlier, namely, spouse, children, siblings, other relatives, friends, and neighbors. Largely due to their lesser likelihood to report either a living spouse or child, low-income Black elderly respondents were significantly more likely to report fewer network elements as compared with their moderate-income Black and moderate-income White counterparts. One of 10 low-income Black elderly New Yorkers reported only a single support element, compared to 3% or less among the moderate-income groups, indicating a small but substantial proportion of older New Yorkers are vulnerable not only economically, but also in terms of social supports. In contrast, in addition to their economic advantages, moderate income elderly are the most likely to report five or six support elements (31% among moderate-income Blacks and 28% among moderate-income Whites). In comparison, only 12% of low-income Black older New Yorkers report such broad-based social networks.

ADEQUACY OF AVAILABLE SOCIAL SUPPORT AS
PERCEIVED BY AFRICAN AMERICAN ELDERLY

The foregoing section detailing the social support systems of older African Americans in New York City has revealed that many have rich social networks and have a high degree of interaction with both kin and nonkin network members. But perhaps even more important are the perceptions of the elderly individuals themselves concerning the viability of their informal social support systems. Therefore, respondents were asked to evaluate both the availability and adequacy of instrumental and emotional support they had received during the year prior to the interview.

Instrumental Support

Assistance with tasks of daily living such as housekeeping, cooking, and transportation can often mean the difference between an older person's continued independent living in the community and moving in with family or even institutionalization. When asked about the availability of instrumental help during the past year, two-thirds (68%) of African American elderly reported someone was available either most of the time or some of the time. However, the availability of instrumental help when needed was in question for a sizable minority; one-third (32%) reported that assistance with tasks of daily living was available either only occasionally or not at all.

Although not statistically significant, there was a trend for low-income Black elderly to report that help with activities of daily living was less available than was the case among either moderate-income Black or moderate-income White older New Yorkers. Low-income Blacks were the least likely (48%) to report that instrumental help was available most of the time, compared with moderate-income Blacks or Whites (59% and 55%, respectively). Conversely, low-income Black elderly were more likely to report that instrumental help was only intermittently available (29%) (some of the time-19%; only occasionally-10%). Among moderate-income elderly Blacks, 18% reported that instrumental help was only available intermittently, with 23% of moderate-income elderly Whites indicating intermittent availability. Interestingly, the proportions of low-income Black, moderate-income Black, and moderate-income White elderly indicating that instrumental help was not available at all was virtually identical among the three groups (20%, 19%, and 19%, respectively).

With respect to the adequacy of the instrumental support received the responses were even more positive, about three-quarters (78%) of African Americans indicated that they had received all the help they needed or could have used only a little more help. But again, a not insubstantial group (22%) reported that they could have used either some more or a lot more help with tasks of daily living during the past year. In line with the trend in group differences regarding the availability of instrumental assistance, low-income elderly Blacks were the least likely to report that they had received all of the instrumental help they needed in the past year (59%), followed by moderate-income Blacks (68%), and moderate-income White (75%). Among low-income Blacks, 11% indicated the need for a lot more help, 14% indicated that they needed some more help, and 15% reported needing a little more instrumental assistance. Among moderate-income Blacks, only 1% indicated needing a lot more help, 12% reported needing some more help, and 17% reported needing a little more assistance. Moderate-income elderly Whites were the least likely to report that they needed additional help with tasks of daily living (5%-a lot more, 9%-some more, and 9%-a little more help). Thus, although most African American elderly appear satisfied with the amount of instrumental support they received in the past year, approximately one of five indicated the need for more assistance with the everyday activities of daily living.

Emotional Support

Having someone to talk to and help in making critical decisions has long been considered an important function of the informal social support system of older people. African American elderly in New York City are even more positive about the availability of someone to provide this type of emotional sustenance than they were concerning instrumental assistance; four of five (82%) older African Americans indicated that they had someone to turn to for emotional support either most or some of the time. However, as was the case with instrumental assistance, a small but significant minority (18%) indicated that emotional support was available only occasionally or not at all.

Low-income elderly Blacks also appear to be in a disadvantaged position in terms of the receipt of emotional support from their informal networks as compared to their moderate-income Black and moderate-income White peers. Low-income Black older New Yorkers were the least likely to indicate that emotional support was available most of the time (59%), as compared with 70% of moderate-income Blacks and three quarters (75%) of moderate-income Whites. Nearly one-third (29%) of low-income elderly Blacks reported that emotional support was available only some of the time (20%) or only occasionally (9%). While among both moderate-income elderly Blacks and Whites, such intermittent emotional support was less likely to be reported (some of the time-22%; only occasionally-15%). There were only slight differences in the proportions of low-income Black, moderate-income Black, and moderate-income White older New Yorkers reporting that emotional support was not available at all (10%, 6%, and 8%, respectively).

Responses concerning the adequacy of the emotional support received followed the same pattern. Again, 80% of older African Americans reported that they had received all of the emotional support they needed, or could have used only a little more emotional support. But one-fifth of African American elderly reported that they could have used anywhere from some more to a lot more emotional support in the past year. The disadvantage of low-income elderly Blacks in terms of the functionality of their informal support systems relative to their moderate-income Black and moderate-income White counterparts was also evident in responses concerning the adequacy of emotional support in the past year. Only two-thirds (66%) of low-income elderly Blacks reported receiving all of the emotional support they needed, significantly less than among moderate-income Black (78%) and moderate-income White (78%) older New Yorkers. Among low-income Blacks; 12% indicated needing a little more, 11% indicated needing some more, and nearly one of 10 reported needing a lot more emotional support in the past year. Eleven percent of moderate-income elderly Blacks needed a little more emotional support, while about 9% needed either some or a lot more emotional support. Among moderate-income elderly Whites, 8% indicated needing a lot more emotional support, while 6% reported needing both some more or a little more emotional assistance.

Summary of the Availability and Adequacy of Instrumental and Emotional Support

For the vast majority of elderly African Americans in New York City, the informal social support system appears to meet their needs for instrumental assistance with tasks of daily living as well as the emotional support so crucial for psychological well being and quality of life. However, for about one of five older African Americans in New York City, informal social supports are either unavailable or inadequate for meeting their needs for instrumental help and emotional sustenance. Such findings call into question the notion that minority communities, in this case Blacks, are always able to care for their own and brings into sharp relief the importance of formal community-based services for many elderly African Americans, even those with viable kin, friend, and neighbor networks.

Summary of the Social Networks of Elderly African Americans

In discussions of the need for formal support to help minority elderly remain independent in their communities, the conventional wisdom has held that they, including elderly African Americans, are well endowed with rich and interactive informal support networks that will substitute for formal providers. However, in light of the present findings, that argument appears to be overstated. Economic realities, not race or ethnicity, play a strong role in the ability of the informal system to provide help to older persons in times of need. Low-income elderly Blacks are vulnerable; they tend to be older and in poorer health than their peers, and they are the most likely to be without a spouse or living children and the most likely to live alone. Children of low-income Black elderly parents are the most likely to live nearby and have frequent contact with their parents, and these children provide high levels of instrumental and direct monetary help to parents compared to the children of moderate-income elderly parents.

However, it is also the low-income elderly Blacks who appear to be in greatest need of assistance, and the high levels of assistance provided by children may only reflect the high cost of obtaining outside formal assistance with housekeeping and personal care. And while the children of low-income Black elderly parents appear to be rising to meet this challenge, it is also likely that these caregiving burdens are only adding to the strains felt by many individuals in minority communities resulting from poverty, crime, and other social ills. Furthermore, there is nothing in our findings to indicate that other, more distant members of the informal system compensate for the lack of spouse and children among low-income elderly Blacks relative to their moderate-income Black and moderate-income White counterparts.

Moderate-income elderly Blacks, in contrast, are just as likely as moderate-income elderly Whites to have either a spouse or child, and patterns of intergenerational assistance between parents and children are remarkably similar between these two groups. But one must keep in mind that while similarities exist between elderly African Americans and elderly Whites with moderate incomes, it does not imply that these two groups are equivalent because of the history of poverty and racism faced by Blacks in the United States. The finding that moderate-income elderly Blacks were more likely to be involved in the ongoing care of grandchildren than their White peers suggests that problems within the African American community, for example, substance abuse and the spread of AIDS, do not respect economic boundaries. Thus, findings from this analysis should not be taken to mean that all is well among moderate-income elderly Blacks.

In conclusion, planners and policy makers should be more aware of the needs of minority elderly particularly those in poverty or near poverty. It cannot be assumed that they do not require assistance from the formal system to remain independent in the community. As we have seen among low-income elderly Blacks, who comprise the majority of the Black elderly population in New York City, many are lacking the informal support elements that are the most likely to provide care in times of need. And although a great deal of instrumental assistance is provided by the children of low-income elderly Blacks, this cannot substitute for assistance from formal providers, particularly in situations in which specific skills or technical expertise are required. Therefore, we reiterate that for elderly individuals to remain independent in the community, which is extremely cost-effective compared with institutionalization, partnerships must be formed between the informal and formal providers of assistance to our elderly citizens.

THE USE OF COMMUNITY-BASED SERVICES AMONG ELDERLY AFRICAN AMERICANS

THE EXTENT OF FORMAL SERVICE UTILIZATION AMONG AFRICAN AMERICAN ELDERLY

Although there is a marked preference for assistance from informal sources on the part of older African Americans in New York City, this does not degrade the importance of formal organizations. Approximately one quarter of elderly African Americans have no living children, while 2% reported that they were without an informal support system. And, for about one of five elderly African Americans, the instrumental and emotional support supplied by informal sources is either not available or inadequate to meet their needs for assistance; for such older people community agencies may be essential. Furthermore, there are situations when the requisite skills and knowledge required to meet an older person's need for assistance are beyond the scope of the care provided by informal helpers, even when such persons are available to provide support.

In terms of the utilization of formal services by older Blacks, the evidence is mixed. While findings have indicated relatively low levels of community-based formal supports among older Blacks, there is evidence that when such formal supports are utilized it is not done to the exclusion of informal assistance, but rather, as a compliment to this form of help (Luckey, 1994; Markides & Mindel, 1987; Miner, 1995; Spence, 1991). And it must be noted that a considerable community resource for older African Americans both at present as well as historically has been the Black church, serving as a lens to the conditions and stressors that have affected this community related to racial differences and ensuing poverty (Levin, Taylor, & Chatters, 1994). As noted by Levin and colleagues, the higher rates of religious participation by Blacks compared to their peers may reflect the central community-organizing role of the Black church, particularly in the form of social supports and problem-solving resources.

But while the vital family, friend and neighbor, and church-related social supports of the Black community may serve as a tremendous resource, they may also serve to limit other available resources. The current political climate has seen the strengths of minority families and communities used as an argument for the vitiation of entitlement programs affecting both the poor and the elderly population. Such an approach results in a reduction of benefits to a segment of the population that already may suffer poor quality of life by advancing the idea that minority communities will take care of their own (Gratton & Wilson, 1988; Himes et al., 1996). However, one should keep in mind the diversities and vulnerabilities among older Blacks that affect the uniform provision of informal help to elderly discussed in the previous section, which make formal community-based services all the more vital in maintaining independence and quality of life.

To ascertain the level and types of formal services used, respondents were presented with a list of "special groups or agencies in New York City which help older people with any difficulties" and asked which, if any, they had turned to in the previous year. This list contained a broad spectrum of community agencies including basic entitlement offices (Medicare, Social Security, Medicaid), the hospital emergency room, a variety of long-term care agencies (home care, visiting nurse, nursing home, Veterans Administration), local government agencies (Department for the Aging, Department of Social Services, police, Housing Authority), senior centers, and religious leaders. Among older African Americans in New York City, 57% had turned to one or more of these community agencies in the past year, similar to the extent of formal utilization among older Whites (56%), but more prevalent than the rate of utilization among older Latinos (43%). The average number of services used by older African Americans was 1.2, indicating that most who turned to the formal system had utilized one, or at most, two community services. There was no significant difference in the proportion of low-income Black, moderate-income Black, and moderate-income White elderly respondents who reported turning to the formal system in the past year (60%, 53%, and 51%, respectively). However, low-income elderly Blacks used significantly more services on average (1.4), as compared to an average of 1.1 services in the case of both moderate-income Blacks and Whites.

The most frequently turned to agency among African Americans were the basic entitlement offices of Social Security (24%) and Medicare (13%) and the hospital emergency room (22%), followed by senior centers (14%) and religious leaders (13%). The importance of church in the lives of older Blacks was suggested by the finding that turning to ministers for assistance was most prevalent among African American older New Yorkers. In the area of long-term care, 10% of elderly African Americans reported turning to the Veterans Administration, followed by homecare (8%) and visiting nurse (6%). Local government agencies such as police, Department for the Aging, and the Housing Authority were utilized by 10% or less among the African American elderly in New York City.

Effects of Income Status on Types of Services Used by Black Older New Yorkers

Overall, there was a tendency for significant differences among low-income Black, moderate-income Black and moderate-income White elderly persons in the types of services utilized to be organized around income level, however, the influence of both need for service and cultural factors emerged in these analyses as well. Low-income elderly Blacks tended to be the most likely to use a number of providers, as might be expected, Medicaid and the Department of Social Services (9% and 11%, respectively), and the New York City Housing Authority (10%), reflecting the greater likelihood for this group to live in public housing (see Table 7.3).

In terms of the in-home services of visiting nurse and homecare, low-income elderly Blacks were also the most likely to report having turned to one of these providers in the past year (15% and 12%, respectively), again reflecting the greater age and frailty of this group. Only about 5% of moderate-income Blacks and moderate-income Whites reported using visiting nurse services in the past year (see Table 7.3). However, moderate-income White older New Yorkers closely followed low-income Blacks in use of homecare (9% and 15%, respectively), while only 4% of moderate-income Black older New Yorkers had used homecare services. The finding of greater use of homecare services by low-income Black and moderate-income White elderly persons as compared to moderate-income Black older New Yorkers again highlights the greater willingness of these groups to consider support from formal providers in this area.

The greatest proportion of elderly turning to the Veterans Administration (VA) or a VA hospital was among moderate-income Blacks (13%), as compared to 6% of low-income Black and 4% of moderate-income White older New Yorkers. This finding may reflect that between World War II and the onset of equal employment legislation, the military served as an avenue to economic security for many African Americans, providing important training as well as a decent income and benefits that were not available due to discrimination in the civilian sector. This finding would indicate that many of these Black Americans maintained their economic security into their retirement years and are continuing to benefit from their status as veterans.

TABLE 7.3 Type of Formal Community-Based Services Used Among Low Income Black, Moderate Income Black, and Moderate Income White Elderly Groups (Percents[a])

Type of service	Low Income Blacks ($n = 218$)	Moderate Income Blacks ($n = 83$)	Moderate Income Whites ($n = 430$)
Entitlements			
Social Security	21.8	20.5	15.3
Medicare	12.6	12.0	18.5
Medicaid***	8.5	1.2	1.2
Dept. of Social Services***	11.1	1.2	4.5
In-home services			
Homecare (all types)**	15.2	3.6	9.2
Visiting nurse service**	11.5	4.8	5.4
Health services			
Nursing home	0.5	0.0	1.9
Veterans Administration/			
V.A. Hospital**	6.0	13.4	4.0
Emergency room	26.5	15.7	21.3
Inpatient hospital	20.7	10.8	17.6
Local community services			
Senior center	15.8	15.9	16.9
NYC Dept. for the Aging	2.8	3.6	4.0
NYC Housing Authority***	10.1	3.6	1.9
Police Department	6.5	7.2	9.9
Rabbi/minister/priest*	13.8	16.9	8.9

[a] Independent items, totals *do not* equal 100%.
* $p < .05$, ** $p < .01$, *** $p < .001$, Chi-Square tests of significance.
NYC, New York City.

Given the historic role of the Black church in the African American community, it was not surprising that regardless of income level, Black older New Yorkers were significantly more likely than their moderate-income White peers to report turning to a religious leader, such as a minister, priest, or rabbi. Moderate-income Black older New Yorkers were the most likely to turn to a religious leader (17%), closely followed by 14% of low-income elderly Blacks. Among moderate-income White older New Yorkers, 9% had turned to a religious leader in the past year.

Factors Associated With the Use of Formal Services Among Elderly African Americans

To better understand the utilization of the formal, community-based system among African American older New Yorkers, multivariate multiple regression analysis was performed to determine the relative importance of a series of predictive factors on the number of formal services used in the past year. Predictive factors were organized in three major domains based on earlier analyses with this data set on formal service utilization (see Brennan & Cantor, 1993; Cantor & Brennan, 1993c; Cantor, et al., 1994). These domains were: (a) predisposing characteristics (i.e., age, gender, Hollingshead's Index of Social Position for socioeconomic status, and live alone); (b) personal resources (i.e., connection to the welfare system, size of informal social network, number of ways children help, presence of confidant, care for grandchild, neighbor involvement, and evaluations of informal support sufficiency); and (c) need factors (i.e., number of additional services needed [see following section], health, functional ability, and income adequacy) (see Table 7.4). Among elderly African Americans, as is also true for their White and Latino counterparts, subjective need for services was the single most important factor in predicting service utilization. However, pathways to services such as being connected to the welfare system and being involved with neighbors who could help direct or escort an older person to needed services were next in importance, closely followed by gender, with older African American females being more likely to use services than their male peers. Interestingly enough, characteristics of the informal system did not emerge as significant predictors of formal service use, perhaps because of the generally high level of involvement of children and other informal components in the lives of New York's older African Americans. Thus, for elderly African Americans, need is clearly the overriding factor in determining whether formal, community-based services are utilized. But once such need is recognized, pathways to the formal system become important in linking the older person in need to the appropriate community agency. This relationship of need and pathways in the use of formal services was also true for White and Latino older New Yorkers.

TABLE 7.4 Multiple Regression on Number of Services Used by Black Older New Yorkers [ab]

Predictor	beta	Zero-order r	%R^2 Change
Predisposing			
Age	-.07	.03	.00
Female gender	.12*	.17**	.03
Socioeconomic status	.04	-.05	-.00
Lives alone	.08	.14**	.01
Resources			
Connection to welfare (SSI, Medicaid, food stamps)	.13*	.20**	.02
Size of functional[a] informal network	-.01	-.03	.00
Number of ways children help	-.01	.04	.00
Level of neighbor assistance	.10*	.07	.01
Has functional[a] confidant	.04	.02	.00
Regularly cares for grandchild	.05	.04	.00
Instrumental support-availability	.00	-.04	.00
Instrumental support-adequacy	-.01	-.11**	.01
Emotional support-availability	-.04	-.06	.00
Emotional support-adequacy	-.03	-.11**	.00
Need for service			
Number of service needs	.40**	.41**	.14
Townsend index of functional ability	.02	.23**	.00
Self-perceived health status	.02	.10	.00
Perceived income adequacy	.07	-.06	.00

Multiple R = .48
Cumulative Adjusted R^2 = .19

[a] A functional informal network member is one seen at least monthly or spoken to on phone at least weekly.
[b] n = 301.
$p < .05$, ** $p - .01$, *** $p < .001$.

Additional Assistance Needed by
Elderly African Americans

The fact that 43% of older African Americans did not turn to a community agency does not necessarily mean that these older people did not need help from the formal system. Many may have needs that are beyond the capacities of their informal helpers, but because of psychological barriers or lack of knowledge about available services, they did not utilize formal services in the past year. Therefore, following the question on agencies utilized during the previous year, a companion question concerning services they may have needed in the past year was posed. A series of 11 commonly needed services were presented and respondents were given the opportunity to suggest other types of services not on the list. The services inquired about were grouped into five main areas of social care; tasks of daily living, assistance with health care, socialization, entitlement advocacy, and personal or job counseling.

Two of five older African Americans (42%) indicated that they needed additional assistance from the formal system during the previous year, and the average number of services needed was 1.0. The extent of additional assistance needed by older African Americans was similar to that of elderly Latinos, but there was a trend for elderly Whites, who tend to be older on average, to be more likely to indicate the need for additional assistance. This finding was also true when comparing low-income Black, moderate-income Black, and moderate-income White elderly in terms of the proportion needing assistance. One half (50%) of low-income Black older New Yorkers indicated the need for additional assistance as compared with one third (34%) of moderate-income elderly Blacks. However, moderate-income elderly Whites were as equally, if not slightly more, likely than low-income elderly Blacks to report needing additional assistance. But while the extent of need for additional help was similar in comparing low-income older Blacks and moderate-income elderly Whites, low-income Black older New Yorkers reported a significantly greater number of service needs on average (1.4), as compared with either moderate-income White (1.2) and particularly moderate-income Black (0.7) older New Yorkers. This finding is particularly important in light of the fact that low-income elderly Blacks are the most financially deprived and the most likely to suffer from poor health in comparison to their peers. Furthermore, low-income elderly Blacks are the least likely of the three comparison groups to report either the presence of a spouse or a living child (see Table 7.2), factors that all help to explain their greater perceived need for help from formal community-based providers.

Among elderly African Americans, the most frequently reported types of need involved task of daily living, such as an escort or ride to places like the doctor (24%), help with housekeeping and personal care (19%), and home repairs (16%). Assistance with long-term care was mentioned by about one of 10 elderly African Americans, with 9% indicating the need for homecare services and 7% mentioning the visiting nurse. Socialization needs were reported by 9%, who indicated that they needed someone to call or visit regularly. And finally, 9% of older African Americans reported needing someone to help them negotiate the bureaucracy to obtain needed entitlements. Thus, a sizable minority of elderly African Americans expressed difficulty in securing income and health entitlements, which was also true for their White and Latino elderly peers.

The disadvantaged position of low-income Black older New Yorkers relative to their moderate-income Black and moderate-income White peers was further illustrated when considering service needs by income level (see Table 7.5). When there were significant differences, most often it was the low-income elderly Blacks who reported the greatest levels of need. This was true for needed help with activities of daily living such as homemaker or personal care (29%), escort or ride to the doctor/clinic (33%), and home-delivered meals (7%), as well as health-related assistance such as visiting nurse services (15%) or help after a hospital stay (14%). Low-income elderly Blacks were also the most likely to report socialization needs; 14% indicated that they needed someone to regularly call or visit. Moderate-income White older New Yorkers were similar to low-income elderly Blacks in terms of needing help with homemaker/personal care (25%), an escort or ride to the doctor (24%), and help after a hospital stay (9%). However, only with respect to needing help with home repairs was the greatest level of need found among moderate-income White older New Yorkers (33%), which reflects their greater likelihood to be home owners. Overall, moderate-income elderly Blacks indicated the lowest levels of need for additional services relative to these other groups.

CONCLUSIONS AND IMPLICATIONS

Throughout this examination of the life styles and needs of older African Americans as revealed in the study "Growing Older in New

TABLE 7.5 Types of Formal Community-Based Services Needed Among Low Income Black, Moderate Income Black, and Moderate Income White Elderly Groups (Percents[a])

Type of need	Low Income Blacks (*n* = 218)	Moderate Income Blacks (*n* = 83)	Moderate Income Whites (*n* =430)
Activities of daily living			
Homemaker/personal care**	28.6	10.8	25.1
Home repairs***	14.4	15.7	33.4
Escort or ride to doctor**	33.2	18.1	24.1
Home-delivered meals*	6.9	1.2	3.5
Health care			
Assistance after hospital stay*	13.8	6.0	8.7
Visiting nurse service***	15.2	3.6	5.2
Socialization			
Someone to call or visit regularly**	14.3	4.8	8.5
Personal/job assistance			
Help finding a job	0.5	1.2	1.2
Personal/family counseling	1.4	1.2	3.3
Advocacy			
Help with entitlements	13.4	6.0	8.5

[a] Independent items, totals *do not* equal 100%.
* $p < .05$, ** $p < .01$, *** $p < .001$, Chi-Square tests of significance.

York City in the 1990s" there are several major themes that help to integrate the findings.

The first pertains to the heterogeneity of the older African American population of New York City and the importance of recognizing differences as well as similarities in policy planning and program implementation. To illustrate, older African Americans in New York live in several different kinds of living arrangements, each of which affects the availability of having someone to assist at times of need. Contrary to popular stereotypes, the extended family is not necessarily the dominant form of living arrangement among elderly African Americans, although one-third live in such multigenerational households. But two of five elderly African Americans (42%) live alone, a proportion similar to that found among elderly White New Yorkers, the most numerous group in the city. And approximately one quarter of elderly African Americans live in their own households with a spouse. However, reflecting differences in current marital status, older African Americans are the least likely of the three major ethnic groups to be living with a spouse. Gender makes a tremendous difference with respect to living arrangements, as well as poverty and income security. Older African American women are far less likely than men to be found living with a spouse, and it is elderly African American women who are most likely to be either living alone or living in multigenerational households, which by and large they head. Thus, older African American women are more frequently found carrying primary responsibility not only for their own economic and social well-being, but for that of the generations that follow as well.

There is also considerable diversity in occupations, income, and pension coverage among older African Americans, ranging form the third who live on poverty level incomes, to another third who have near poverty incomes (i.e., 101% to 150% of poverty), to the 22% who are part of the emerging middle class in the African American community. This latter group reports higher levels of education and were mainly involved in highly skilled blue-collar occupations, in public sector professional and administrative jobs (at all levels of government), or in business and professions such as teaching, nursing, and social work. As a result, this small but significant group of older African Americans are more economically secure in old age and frequently have pensions to supplement Social Security as well as some income from interest and dividends to help cushion retirement. Thus, the overall income picture of older African Americans in New York City has improved significantly since 1970.

Differences between the characteristics of elderly New York African Americans in poverty and those in the rising middle class along a variety of socioeconomic variables clearly illustrate how the opportunity structure of earlier years affects the nature and quality of life in old age. However, given the current shift in the country and particularly in the New York City area away from highly skilled factory and blue-collar jobs toward service occupations, coupled with the current attempts to downsize government and the excessive rate of unemployment and underemployment among young African American males, future cohorts of older African Americans may be in a far less favorable position in the decades ahead, and the trend toward an increasing middle class among older African Americans may be slowed or even brought to a halt. It is clearly important in policy determinations to recognize the interrelationship between the early and later parts of the life cycle, for what happens to African Americans in young and middle adulthood directly determines the quality of life that they can expect in old age.

Given the diversity in the elderly African American population in New York City, any approach to programming must recognize the differences as well as the historic and cultural similarities among older African Americans. In the future it will be important to tailor programmatic interventions to meet differing needs of differing segments of this population. Where emphasis on the amelioration of the effects of poverty and methods for stretching income may be paramount for the largest group of older African American New Yorkers, among the more economically secure middle-class retirees, programs emphasizing educational, recreational, and travel opportunities may be more important. And perhaps most challenging will be how to utilize the talents and abilities of this better educated, more economically secure group of elderly African Americans to help meet the pressing needs of the broader African American community, particularly its children.

The second theme is one of vulnerability. The African American elderly population in New York tend to suffer from inadequate incomes, despite the fact that most had worked during their adult years. Although there has been some improvement in the socioeconomic and income levels of some African American elderly New Yorkers since 1970, the vast majority still live very much on the economic margin. The median income of elderly African Americans was only $7251 in 1989, considerably below the median of $13,751 for elderly Whites. Furthermore, nearly half of older African Americans had incomes below $8000 per year, and one-quarter had incomes of $6000 or less. Thus, two-thirds of elderly African Americans and 85% of older Latinos in New York City are living in poverty or near poverty as compared with 43% among elderly Whites. African American women are particularly vulnerable with regard to poverty, as are single persons in general. Furthermore, the needs-based entitlements aimed at helping to mitigate the effects of poverty are considerably underutilized among New York's elderly population, particularly among older African Americans and Whites. Thus, only about half of elderly African Americans in poverty used Medicaid or Supplemental Security Income, while only one-third were enrolled in the food stamp program. Given the low wage structure during adult working years experienced by most African Americans, is not likely that excessive assets are the cause of nonenrollment. Rather, we must look to organizational, informational, and attitudinal barriers as well as inadequate outreach as possible reasons for underutilization. Given the picture of economic need among so many older African American New Yorkers, concentrated efforts to encourage participation in the entire variety of entitlement programs offered in New York City and by the state is a crucial necessity in the period ahead.

In addition to vulnerability in the income arena, many older African American New Yorkers suffer from vulnerability in health and social domains as well. Increasingly, older African Americans are being called on to carry heavy family responsibilities involving the care of grandchildren, great-grandchildren, and sick kin as well. In such cases, incomes must be pooled between generations, and the pressures of assuming parenting roles at the very point in the life cycle where health may be failing has tremendous consequences for young and old alike. Clearly, further planning and supportive programming for such elderly African Americans, the group of older New Yorkers most affected, is required if the impact of substance abuse, AIDS, and incarceration so prevalent in minority communities of the city are to be in any sense mitigated for the older generation and the children for whom they are so responsible.

The third theme—that of family and community strengths—is related to vulnerability as well. Again and again, research (including this chapter) illustrates the strength of the African American family, its high degree of solidarity and close interaction between members, and its ability to pool resources in the face of need. The African American family is an inclusive one in the broadest sense, and includes fictive kin, friends, and neighbors who together with family face the difficulties of poverty and living in an urban environment. Fortunately, most older African Americans have lived in New York City all or most of their adult lives, and their roots in church and community are deep. But there is a tendency to assume that such families can care for their own with a minimum of outside help from the formal system. Findings in this chapter attest to the fact that most older African Americans feel that they can access the instrumental and emotional support they need from informal sources. But at least one in five among the current cohort of elderly African Americans report they do not have anyone they can count on for such assistance, and that the support received during the previous year was inadequate. Thus already there are not insignificant numbers of older African Americans who are in need of the services provided by community agencies.

But perhaps as important is the assistance needed by elderly African Americans and all elderly New Yorkers in negotiating the large-scale bureaucracies to obtain needed entitlements and services. The need for advocacy and assistance in dealing with the formal sector and obtaining services has been persistently voiced since the first large-scale study of New York's elderly population in 1970 ("The Elderly in the Inner City of New York"). Involved in these requests for assistance are several factors affecting both private not-for-profit agencies and public agencies alike. Significant factors requiring attention include the need for simplification of forms and applications, a single entry point in the neighborhood for both information and enrollment in the plethora of entitlement programs currently operating in New York City and the state of New York, and the need for on-the-spot assistance in completing applications, garnering needed documentation, and advocacy in moving through the system. In the minority communities particularly there is a need to develop pathways to service, namely, people in the community such as neighbors, church leaders, school social workers, health practitioners, and so forth, who can act as gatekeepers and direct persons to the services that they need. The cry for assistance in obtaining needed services echoes throughout the elderly population of New York City, but it is particularly crucial for the minority elderly persons, African Americans and others, who are the most needy and the most likely to be outside of the system.

PART III

The Future of Social Care: Implications for Policy and Practice

8

The Elderly and the Informal Social Care System of the Twenty-first Century

The focus of this book has been to examine how social care contributes to successful aging and the maintenance of the independent status of older people in the densely populated urban environment of New York City. Recognizing the increasing diversity among the elderly population of New York and the country at large, we have concentrated on the experiences of three distinct groups: elderly Jews, Latinos and African Americans. In many respects, Jewish elderly, a prototype for future aging cohorts, constitute a segment of the White population of New York, with strong cultural and religious ties that have historically set them apart and still provide a strong sense of community. The elderly African Americans and Hispanics represent the major ethnic and racial minorities of older adults and provide the opportunity to study the effects of ethnicity and social class in the provision of social care. Each of these groups has been examined separately because we believe that culture, ethnicity, and class are major structural factors that influence both how social care is provided, as well as attitudes toward the relative importance of informal and formal care. In this examination, we have stressed the socioeconomic, cultural and ethnic factors which distinguish African American, Latino and Jewish elderly persons of New York City as we approach the twenty-first century. At the end of each case study, implications for social care have been suggested based on the unique experiences of each of these three groups of older New Yorkers.

In the final two chapters we turn to the future and examine the trends that are likely to affect both the nature and the amount of social care provided to elderly in the decades ahead. To achieve this goal, it is necessary to examine separately the three major components of the Social Care Model that have served as the organizing framework for this book: the elderly, their families, and the system of formal community-based services (see chapter 2, Figure 2.1). In this chapter, we will address the projections regarding the demographic profile of the elderly of the future in terms of their numbers, racial and ethnic composition, extent of frailty and disability, and the changing role of their families and other primary informal caregivers. Where appropriate, findings from the case studies presented earlier will be used for illustration. In the final chapter, we will turn to the formal system of social care, its weaknesses and strengths, and the relative role of the individual and government in assisting older people and their families. In conclusion, we will suggest a number of policy and practice implications that cut across all levels of the Social Care Model to ensure that the social care of the elderly population will be adequate and promote an acceptable quality of life in the twenty-first century.

If there is to be adequate assistance available to meet both current and future needs of older adults, there must be a synergism among the individual parts of the social care system as well as a recognition of the differing strengths each brings to the situation. In gerontological research, policy, and practice, great emphasis has been placed on informal providers of social care in terms of who they are, what they do, and what are their needs. But in the future it is likely, given current demographic and societal trends, that formal providers of social care will play an increasingly important role. Thus, the formal sector deserves more attention, particularly in the articulation of its functions in relation to informal helpers.

As noted throughout this book, the concept of social care is a broad one that ranges from opportunities for socialization and self-actualization, to the provision of interactive assistance between generations in everyday tasks, to the more intensive assistance associated with caregiving of frail elderly individuals. Whether provided by the informal or formal system, social care has as its goal the enhancement of independent functioning and personal self-actualization. Adequate social care is deeply involved in all three components of "successful aging" as conceptualized by Rowe and Kahn (1998): low risk of disease and related disability, high levels of cognitive and physical functioning, and active engagement with life. Although each component is significant in its own right, it is their combination that most fully represents successful aging. In a similar vein, it is the availability of a full range of informal and formal support elements that best represents social care for the elderly. As a complement to both preventive and acute health care, social care emphasizes the potential for individuals to avoid disease and its deleterious effects. Furthermore, the reciprocal nature of informal social care, whether between family, friends or neighbors, acts to expand the opportunities for older people to maintain high levels of engagement. Finally, to the extent that older people are provided opportunities for creativity and intellectual expression through senior centers and volunteer or educational activities, they will be able to enhance the high levels of cognitive functioning envisioned as essential to successful aging (Rowe & Kahn, 1998). Thus, as adequate health care is essential to minimize disease and disability, adequate social care is essential to the positive engagement and maintenance of high levels of cognitive and physical functioning that constitute successful aging.

One note of caution before we look at the implications regarding the future of social care for the elderly community. In gerontological research, policy and practice, the terms *caregiving* and *caregivers* have too often been loosely applied to the multifarious types of assistance provided by the informal system. This is both inaccurate and misleading. In fact, there are several levels of assistance involved in the continuum of care provided by both informal and formal systems. These levels are distinguished by the degree of functional ability of the elderly person in any given situation, and are influenced by the cultural norms of the elderly and their families. The bulk of assistance needed by, and provided to, older people is of the ordinary type of ongoing and intermittent assistance helpful in carrying out the day-to-day tasks of living. Such assistance is provided within the family/significant others network as members help each other as needed and may be both intra- and intergenerational. These activities are not caregiving, per se, and are usually not accompanied by excessive burden or strain on the part of those providing the assistance. As illustrated in our three case studies, this level of exchange occurs both within more traditional extended family households, as well as between related nuclear households that comprise the kinship networks in modern industrialized nations.

At the other end of the continuum, and highly associated with considerable physical and cognitive frailty, are the more long-range and intensive types of assistance, which are valid manifestations of the concept of caregiving. These types of assistance include activities of daily living (ADL's) and instrumental activities of personal care (IADL's) required on a constant or nearly continual basis. Some elderly individuals clearly fall somewhere between these two extremes, requiring both garden-variety types of assistance, as well as low levels of ongoing help, usually involving housekeeping or transportation. Furthermore, the boundaries between day-to-day assistance and true caregiving are fluid as functional capacities ebb and flow over the last years of life. However, as will be discussed, in the years ahead only a small proportion of older people at any one time are projected to require the level of assistance that constitutes caregiving. But it is within this level that caregiving burden is most associated and the crossover between informal and formal services is most likely to occur (Harel & Noelker, 1995). Thus, implications for the future of social care tend to be grouped into those applying to the vast majority of elderly persons with high to moderate levels of functional ability, and those applying to the frail elderly individuals who require caregiving more intensive and long-term in nature.

What are some of the current trends that could alter or modify the social care system as we know it and the way social care will be provided in the future? And in the future, what roles will culture, ethnicity, and class play in the maintenance of adequate levels of social care that constitute such a vital element of successful aging?

THE ELDERLY IN THE TWENTY-FIRST CENTURY

A central theme in this book has been the notion of diversity with regard to ethnicity, culture, and class, as well as age and gender, and how these structural factors affect the need for assistance and the provision of social care. Population aging is typically discussed in global terms. But, as illustrated by the three case studies in this volume, is important to reiterate that the same patterns and projections may not apply equally to all groups in the older population, or to all segments within a particular subgroup of elderly persons. However, there are some overarching trends in the demography of aging that will affect all groups of older people in the United States in the coming decades, regardless of ethnic or cultural backgrounds or socioeconomic class.

Increase in the Proportion of Older People in the Total Population

First and perhaps most important in projecting the social care needs of the future is the dramatic increase in the number and proportion of persons 65 years and older that has occurred from 1900 to the present, and the continued projected increase into the twenty-first century. In 1900, persons 65 years or more comprised 4% of the total U.S. population. By 1970, when The Elderly in the Inner City of New York survey was conducted, the elderly population had increased to 9.8% of the total U.S. population, roughly 20 million persons. Twenty years later, at the time of the second, follow-up study, Growing Older in New York in the 1990's, the proportion of elderly people had risen to 12.6 % of the total population, or about 32 million persons. This steady growth in the numbers and proportions of elderly persons is projected to continue for the foreseeable future. By 2020 it is projected that 17.5 % of the total population will be 65 years and over (i.e., 51 million), while by 2040 older people will comprise 22.9 % of the population or approximately 67 million persons. Furthermore, adjusting old-age mortality rates for gains in health and life expectancy has indicated that the future size of the older population could be even larger than currently projected (Day, 1985; National Institute on Aging, 1995; Rivlin & Weiner 1988; Siegel & Taeuber, 1986; Taeuber 1989; Levna, 1993; U.S. Bureau of the Census, 1990, 1995).

Several factors have contributed to this dramatic increase of older persons, most notably increasing life expectancy. In the United States, life expectancy at birth has risen from 49 years at the turn of the century to 76 years at present, while life expectancy at age 65 has increased to 17 years, 5 years longer than in 1900 (Rowe & Kahn, 1998). Women continue to live about 7 years longer than men, although the gender gap is narrowing. And there are important racial and ethnic differences in life expectancy as well. White women live on average 6 years longer than African American women, while White men live about 8 years longer than Black men. Furthermore, given the poorer health and lower incomes of Hispanic and other racial and ethnic minorities, it is likely that a similar pattern of differential life expectancy applies to these groups of elderly persons as well, although exact longevity estimates currently are not available (Cantor, 1991).

Coupled with increased life expectancy has been a declining birth rate in the twentieth century (Moody, 1998). However, one exception to the long-term declining birth rate is important to note: the sudden surge in births after World War II that produced the baby-boom generation now coming of age. The tremendous increase in the number of elderly persons and of the oldest-old projected in the next 50 years stems both from the large cohorts born during the postwar years soon to reach late adulthood, and the increased survivorship at all ages due to medical advances, especially among the oldest-old (Angel & Hogan, 1991).

The Growth of the Oldest-Old in the Aging Population

The fastest growing segment of the aging population includes persons 85 years and over (i.e., the old-old), who are most at risk of frailty and concomitant disability (Kassner & Bectal, 1998; Rivlin & Weiner, 1988). The current 85 and older population is expected to more than quadruple from 4 million in the year 2000 to 18 million in 2050, as the baby-boom generation joins the ranks of the oldest-old (Kassner & Bectal, 1998; Soldo & Manton, 1985a). Given their higher incidence of disability, it is within this segment of the elderly population that the greatest need for extensive, hands-on long-term care from both informal and formal providers can be expected.

The Increase in the Proportion of Minority Elderly

Although currently 85% of the American elderly population is comprised of non-Hispanic Whites, the minority population is growing at an even faster pace than the older population in general (Taeuber & Smith, 1988). By the middle of the twenty-first century, only about 69% of the elderly population will be non-Hispanic White, and the extent of ethnic diversity will be even more striking than at present. Some specific projections highlight this important change in the aging population of the next century. There will be a dramatic rise in the number of elderly Blacks, which will nearly triple to 7.8 million by 2030, with proportions increasing to 10% by 2010 and 17% by 2030 (Angel & Hogan, 1991). The Hispanic older population is also growing rapidly and will double from the current 6% of the older population to 13% by 2030 . At present, there are approximately 1 million older Latinos, which will rise to 2.5 million by 2010, and to 5.6 million by 2030. Minority elderly persons from other races (i.e., Asian, Native American, Eskimo and Aleut) have also increased considerably from 81,000 in 1960 to 603,000 in 1990, and are projected to reach 1.5 million in 2010 and double again by 2030. For these minority elderly persons, the projected rise is from 7% in 1990 to 16.1% by 2030. Thus, while non-Hispanic Whites will constitute the majority of the elderly population in the years ahead, Blacks, Hispanics, and other minorities will make up an increasingly important component of the aging population (Angel & Hogan, 1991; Taeuber, 1990; U.S. Bureau of the Census, 1985, 1992).

Although the current Black and Hispanic elderly populations are tilted toward the young-old (65 to 74 years), this picture is expected to change somewhat in the twenty-first century, when minority elderly populations, as in the case of Whites, will see large increases in the oldest-old. For example, the number of Blacks over 85 increased from 67,000 in 1960 to 251,000 in 1990 and is expected to further rise to 1.8 million by 2050. Among Hispanics the number of oldest-old nearly doubled between 1980 and 1990 (49,000 to 95,000 persons) and will also grow rapidly, numbering more than 1.5 million by 2050 (Angel & Hogan, 1991). Growth among the old-old is projected for other minorities as well.

In general the most dramatic growth in the old-old in the minority populations is projected to occur between 2020 and 2050. Whereas fewer than one-in-ten minority elderly persons are currently 85 or older, the proportion will increase to one-in-five by 2050 (Angel & Hogan, 1991). Thus among both majority and minority elderly we can expect to have increasing numbers of the old-old, when disability is more concentrated and social care demands are most extensive. To illustrate, among the three groups examined in this volume, elderly Jews with the highest proportion of persons 85 or over (17.3%), were more likely to utilize in-home and visiting nurse services, and were also more likely to express a need for additional home care services than was true for elderly African Americans and Hispanics who were approximately one half as likely to be 85 years old or more. But as illustrated in these case studies, there are cultural and ethnic norms that affect service utilization in addition to level of disability.

It is clear that the need to consider race, ethnicity, and culture will be even more important in the planning and delivery of formal services to the elderly population in the years ahead. In the past, research on aging has too often been a study of elderly Whites and the diversity of the aging population has been ignored. Given the growing prominence of minority elderly in the older population, both at present and in the future, a change of emphasis is critical to both understanding of the aging of America and to sound public policy planning for the twenty-first century.

PROJECTIONS OF DISABILITY AMONG THE OLDER POPULATION

The increasing numbers of elderly persons alone does not accurately portray the need for social care in the future, though it does provide a broad indication of the potential boundaries of social care needs. An equally important consideration is the level of disability in the older population and the extent to which disability may be increasing or decreasing. Nowhere is the heterogeneity of aging more evident than with respect to health and disability status. Wide variations in the prevalence and type of disability are found even among the old-old. Furthermore, most elderly persons are not frail or in poor health, although many suffer from one or more chronic illness. Of persons 65 to 74 years in 1994, 89% had no reported disabilities. Although the proportion of elderly without disability declines with age, among those 75 to 84 years of age, approximately three-quarters still report no serious functional limitations. And even among the oldest-old, 40% are fully functional (Rowe & Kahn, 1998).

As noted earlier, the prevalence of severe functional disability requiring extensive caregiving is mainly concentrated among persons in their late seventies and eighties. According to age-specific estimates computed in 1994, 5.5% of persons aged 75 to 84 and 7.2% of those 85 and older are severely functionally impaired, which is characterized by the inability to perform one or more of the personal activities of daily living[1], such as bathing or eating. However, in terms of the instrumental activities of daily living, such as preparing meals or doing housework, which are important for maintaining one's independent status[2], the proportion who are unable to perform one or more of these activities rises to 25% among those 75 to 84 and 57% among persons aged 85 years and older. These estimates include both

---

1. ADL (for activities of daily living) includes requiring help with the following tasks, eating, getting into/out of bed, moving about outdoors, dressing, bathing, and using toilet;

2. IADL (for instrumental activities of daily living) include household work, laundry, meal preparation, moving about outdoors, walking, money management and using a telephone.

community-dwelling and institutionalized elderly persons (Manton, Corder, & Stallard, 1997).

Contrary to popular assumptions, chronic disease and disability do not necessarily lead to permanent degeneration in the older population. Evidence from the 1984 Longitudinal Study on Aging and the 1982-84 National Long-Term Care Survey indicate that the potential for recovery of function is far greater than commonly expected. About one of five elderly persons improved in functional capacity over a 24-month period (Kovar, 1988; Manton, Conder & Stallard, 1993, 1997). Additionally, any true representation of the extent of disability among the elderly must take into account the substantial amount of comorbidity that often exists, with older persons frequently having multiple acute conditions and chronic diseases. Failure to account for this phenomenon may lead us to underestimate the extent of social care needed by the elderly population at any point in time (Manton & Soldo, 1985) .

However, there has been a decline in the prevalence of chronic disability among the aged beginning in 1982 and continuing at a slightly accelerated pace until 1996, the latest year for which data are available. Based on these changes in prevalence rates, it is estimated that despite the increase of numbers of elderly during this period, the total number of severely chronically disabled elderly persons of all ages declined somewhat. Thus, at present, there are 1.4 million fewer disabled older people than would be had the status of the elderly population not improved since 1982 (Rowe & Kahn, 1998). These declines in disability have been attributed to medical advances that have reduced morbidities that affect the elderly, namely , heart disease, high blood pressure, and some forms of cancer. Lower rates of disability can also be ascribed to improved life-style factors, such as exercise and diet, which directly influence physical fitness and risk of disease (Rowe & Kahn, 1998). Higher educational and income levels of successive cohorts of elderly, particularly among Whites, which have been linked to better physical functioning, coupled with biomedical advances, suggest that rates of chronic disability may continue to decline into the twenty-first century (Harel & Noelker, 1995).

Disability Among Minority Elderly

Unfortunately, there is a dearth of ethnic-specific projections of disability among minority elderly persons. However, research has repeatedly demonstrated strong relationships between measures of socio-economic status and health. Better educated Americans have lower mortality rates than poorer educated Americans at all ages. This gap also reflects racial and income differences (National Institute on Aging, 1995).

The relationship between socioeconomic class and health status was highlighted in Growing Older In New York City in the 1990s. Elderly Hispanics, who were the most likely to report incomes at or below poverty, reported the poorest health and the highest levels of functional disability, despite the fact that they were younger, on average, then both their White and African American peers. Elderly Blacks were also found to have poorer health and more disability than Whites, even after controlling for gender and income. The two most significant factors in predicting higher levels of disability for older New Yorkers as a whole were income and level of education. Furthermore, the study findings also suggest that functional impairment has a consistent bearing on an older person's need for formal services (Berkman & Gurland, 1993).

The interaction of class and health status is further illustrated in the case study on the African American elderly. Middle-class Blacks are more similar to middle-class Whites in self-reported health status than to their lower income Black counterparts. Given the documented differential in income and education between majority and minority elderly currently and in the foreseeable future, one can only conjecture that although rates of disability may decline among minority elderly persons to some extent, it is probably elderly Whites who will benefit most from the medical advances and life-style factors related to decreases in disability. As a result, levels of disability and the resultant need for long-term supportive services may be even more acute for the substantial numbers of minority elderly persons who enter old age with poorer health, diminished economic resources, and weaker educational backgrounds (Kassner & Bectal, 1998).

Another factor affecting social care with respect to minority elderly persons is the point in the age continuum when disability is most likely to occur. It is postulated that medical advances and technology, coupled with better life-style habits, will enable older people to live longer in relatively good health, with severe disability occurring only at the very end of life, that is, the "squaring of the morbidity curve" as predicted by Frees (1988, 1984). However, this may not be equally true in the case of minority elderly individuals who enter old age in poorer health and with higher levels of co-morbidity. Thus the onset of disability may be earlier in their case, the functional limitations more severe, and the duration of the disability span a greater proportion of old age.

SOCIAL CHARACTERISTICS AFFECTING THE NEED FOR ASSISTANCE

Health, disability, and life expectancy set the parameters of the need for assistance in old age. But in addition there are social factors, particularly gender, income, marital status, living arrangements, and family structure that greatly influence both who will need assistance and who will care for those in need. Although differences in life expectancy between women and men are narrowing, they are unlikely to converge in the near future. Thus, gender-related differences in marital and social care patterns are likely to continue in the decades ahead (Cantor, 1991; Longino, Soldo, & Manton, 1990; Soldo & Manton, 1985b; Taeuber, 1989).

Gender differences in marital patterns are reflected both in living arrangements and who is likely to provide social care. Because men are currently more likely to be married and live with a spouse, functionally disabled men are usually cared for by their wives (Cantor, 1991; Soldo & Manton, 1985b). Women, on the other hand, are more likely to be living alone, or, if severely disabled, living with children. Thus, women are more dependent than men on children, other relatives, and formal service providers for social care (Cantor, 1991). Ethnicity further confounds the picture of widowhood. The chance of living longer without a spouse is true for all groups of elderly women. But in New York City, for example, the likelihood of an older Black woman being widowed is far greater than among Whites and Hispanics (Cantor & Brennan, 1993a).

In summary, based on what is known about disability and the demand for care, all signs point to social care needs increasing exponentially, particularly with respect to the most difficult types of assistance required by the functionally and cognitively impaired elderly. Underscoring the potential care needs in the future are the projections that by the year 2000 the number of chronically disabled community-based elderly persons will grow by 31% to 7.6 million people. Furthermore, there is the growing incidence and prevalence of disability among younger people resulting from, among other causes, the spread of AIDS and increased drug addiction, which will have an impact on the resources available for the provision of long-term care, both informal and formal, for the elderly population now and in the future (Cantor, 1991; Manton, 1988, 1989; Branch & Ku, 1989; Smith & Longino, 1995).

FAMILIES AND OTHER INFORMAL SUPPORTS OF ELDERLY PERSONS: WILL THEY BE THERE IN THE FUTURE?

We turn now to the second major component of the Social Care Model—the family and significant others of the informal network. The family continues to be the mainstay of such assistance, both in terms of routine day-to-day assistance as well as the extended and involved caregiving associated with chronic disability.

THE CHANGING STRUCTURE OF THE AMERICAN FAMILY

Families have always been important in the care of elderly family members and they are no less important today. But the structure of the family and the nature of its involvement has changed over time as has the role of women, the primary caregivers of the elderly. These changes will have a critical impact on how older people will be cared for in the future. Just as there has been a widespread myth about the abandonment of the elderly by the family in industrialized societies, there has also been a tendency to idealize the place of the three generational family in American history. Hareven (1992) notes that, in fact, there never was a time when the mythical extended family of yore was the dominant family form in the United States or even Europe. Historically in America the predominant form of residence has been one in which the older generations maintained separate households, although there tended to be proximity of residence on the same land in the rural areas, or in the same neighborhood in urban areas. The prevalence of residential separation between generations was modified in the face of severe mental or physical frailty. In such cases, the parent was either taken into the household of one child, or frequently one child continued to reside with the parent(s) and became the parent keeper. Thus, Hareven (1992) notes that "intimacy at a distance," the preferred mode of generational relations in contemporary American society, has been persistent since the early settlement and reaches back into the European past."

In the study, "Growing Older in New York City", from which the present case studies are drawn, the vast majority of elderly (84%) were living in their own residences, which was clearly the norm (Cantor & Brennan, 1993a). The case studies presented earlier highlight this shift toward older people living apart from other members of the kin network. Among Jewish elderly, who appear to be prototypical of the White elderly of the future, virtually no one lived with others than a spouse, and only 5% had moved in with children, principally due to frailty. In the case of the elderly African Americans and Latinos, where poverty has made shared housing a necessity, a larger proportion (approximately one-third and one-fifth, respectively) were living in such households. Among elderly Blacks, many of these shared households are headed by an older women who may be involved in caring for grandchildren or even great-grandchildren.

But even among the minority elderly population of New York City, most live in their own households, either alone or with a spouse. Most significant has been the increase during the last 20 years in the numbers of Black and Hispanic older New Yorkers who live alone. Among elderly Blacks, the proportion of living alone, rose from 33% in 1970 to 42% in 1990, and among elderly Hispanics from 26% to 34%. Furthermore, with a view to the future, the living arrangements of middle-income older Blacks in our case study are more similar to middle-class elderly Whites than low-income Blacks. Currently, Hispanic elderly, particularly recent immigrants, represent a more transitional stage. As noted in the case study, the likelihood of elderly Latinos living in an extended family household was greater among more recent immigrants and decreased with greater length of residency. But even among Hispanics, the proportion living alone or only with spouse is on the rise, and it is likely that this trend will continue in the future.

Thus, the first and perhaps most crucial factor affecting the family and social care in the future is that the vast majority of older people will be found living in their own households, either alone or with spouses or partners. Although most elderly persons, including the widowed and the frail, prefer independent living, the proliferation of separate living arrangements makes the provision of adequate social care more difficult due to a scarcity of available assistance within the household. And when the household contains two older persons (i.e., spouse or partners), the possibility of both being frail and in need of assistance becomes more likely over time. For those without a spouse, particularly older women, the burden of care will fall even more heavily on children or community agencies.

CHANGES IN KINSHIP ROLES AND
SOCIAL CARE OF ELDERLY

Although the family has always been the mainstay of care for its older members, industrialization and geographic dispersion of families has resulted in some shifts in how this responsibility is manifested. In the nineteenth and into the early twentieth centuries, the period of greatest United States immigration, families clustered together, and the interdependence and mutual assistance among extended kin, as well as within a particular family unit, was more strongly emphasized. Kin were almost exclusively the source of assistance in coping with critical life situations (e.g., unemployment, illness, poverty). Furthermore, obligations incurred to one's relatives were even more complex than in contemporary society, and individual interdependency with kin was a manifestation of family culture (Hareven, 1992). Such an approach was intensified during the Great Depression and, as noted in the Jewish and Hispanic case studies, was particularly associated with immigrant groups. At the same time, the notion of self-help via the kinship system has historically characterized the Black community as a positive response to poverty and discrimination.

In the United States, World War II and the post-war economic recovery marked a turning point in the concept and patterning of familial responsibility. With opportunities like the G. I. Bill, the proliferation of automobiles, and the explosive growth of suburbs, children began moving out of the neighborhood of parents and extended kin. Thus, the geographic dispersion of families emerged as a feature of modern life. In many situations parents supported their children's aspirations for upward mobility even if, as noted in the Jewish case study, children were less available to assist parents or other relatives on a day-to-day basis. As Hareven (1992) notes, the younger generation began to make the transition from an extended kin orientation to a more individualistic approach, with boundaries between family and extended kin more firmly drawn. Furthermore, the advent of public programs providing income and medical support for the older population, such as Social Security and Medicare, helped to make the elderly more independent and minimize the need for assistance from children and extended kin. The result has been a noticeable shift in attitudes regarding kin as the only appropriate source of support for elderly. Additionally, the prevalence of separate residences as the norm for the elderly has affected the ability of the kin system to provide hands-on assistance and long-term care. Thus, in concert with the increasing separation of the households of young and old, has been the modification of the kinship structure and its built-in mechanisms for shared provision of support.

OTHER CHANGES AFFECTING THE PROVISION OF SOCIAL CARE FROM FAMILIES

The American family is also undergoing other structural transformations that will affect its ability to care for elderly members. The U.S. Census Bureau defines a family as a group of two or more persons related by birth, marriage or adoption (Himes, 1992). However, throughout this book we have used the term family in its broadest sense to include the various constellations of related and nonrelated individuals who live together and function as family to each other, both instrumentally and emotionally. Only such a broad definition captures how care of elderly people occurs in a family sense (Cantor, 1991).

In light of the increasing likelihood of elderly persons in the United States to live in their own households and the decreased dependency on extended kin, several other structural changes in the family are worth noting. First, families today are becoming increasingly verticalized, leading to the "bean pole family," with greater numbers of relationships that cross generational lines, along with fewer siblings and other age peers within a single generation (Bengtson & Dannefer, 1987; Hagested, 1986; Bengtson, Rosentha, & Borton, 1990). In addition, kin networks are increasingly becoming top heavy, with more older family members than young. For the first time in history, the average married couple has more parents than children (Preston, 1984). Furthermore, due to lengthening life expectancy and lower birth rates, shifts are occurring in the time spent in various family roles. For example, middle-generation women in the future will probably spend, on average, more years with elderly parents than with minor children (Watkins, Menkin, & Bongaarts, 1987). Changes in the timing of child-bearing, the increasing incidence of divorce, reconstructed or step-families, and single-parent families are also affecting and complicating family structures (Riley, 1983; Uhlenberg & Myers, 1996).

In the future there will be an increased probability that an older person will be living with a spouse and will also have a surviving child (Himes, 1992). As noted previously, along with increased longevity is the greater likelihood that an older person will require caregiving assistance later in life (Verbrugge, 1984, 1989). At the same time, the very people most responsible for providing care, spouses and children, will be either old themselves or approaching old age and may be suffering from age-related impairments. It will, therefore, not be unusual to find children in their middle sixties or even in their seventies caring for parents in their eighties or nineties.

Two other structural trends are worth underscoring as they affect social care for the elderly populace. First is the increase in the proportion of adults remaining childless. Second is the increase in late childbearing. Thus, parents in the future will have fewer children to draw on for assistance (Korbin, 1983). Furthermore, those children may be involved in parent care at the same time that they are providing financial assistance to their own children (e.g., college or graduate school education, buying a home). Moreover, the blight of AIDS and high rates of incarceration prevalent in minority communities, if unchecked, will result in fewer available children to assist minority elderly parents.

PRIMARY CAREGIVERS OF THE FRAIL AND DISABLED ELDERLY

Changes in family structure and increased longevity that affect the ability of the informal system to provide the direct hands-on care required by functionally or cognitively impaired elderly has both human and policy implications. In principle, various combinations of informal and formal help could be utilized. Previous research, including the case studies presented in this volume, indicate that most elderly individuals have a network of kin and nonkin who provide various levels of assistance both on a routine basis and at times of illness and functional disability (Boaz & Hu, 1997; Cantor & Brennan, 1993c; Doty, Jackson, & Crown, 1998; Stone & Kemper, 1989). With declining functional capacity, one member of this network most usually becomes the primary informal caregiver of the older person. But other network members may serve as secondary helpers, providing more limited or specialized assistance or substituting for the primary caregiver when necessary. Still others may serve as reserve helpers, becoming active in emergencies when the primary caregiver is unavailable, unable to provide care due to extenuating circumstances, or is in need of respite.

In addition, informal caregiving is sometimes supplemented by formal care under the aegis of Medicare or Medicaid. However, such assistance is limited by eligibility regulations and income limitations in the case of Medicaid. Finally, caregiving assistance can be paid for out-of-pocket by the older person or the family. An analysis of payment sources for formal help in the 1982 and 1989 National Long-Term Care Surveys revealed that older people or their kin paid, in whole or part, for approximately 50% to 60% of the long-term services used by disabled elderly (Liu & Manton, 1994). However, the high cost of private care means that only certain groups of elderly have the option of obtaining paid assistance. Research has shown that about 90% of dependent community-dwelling elderly individuals receive care from kin, friends, and neighbors, about one-quarter use a combination of both informal and formal care, while only 9% rely solely on formal providers (National Alliance for Caregiving, 1997; Stone, Cafferata, & Sangl, 1987). The relative balance of informal and formal care in the case of impaired older persons is further illustrated by findings on the number of hours spent in caregiving from the 1989 National Long-term Care Survey and its companion the Informal Caregivers Survey. The average weekly hours of care for disabled elders from all sources was 38.4. On a weekly basis, the average time provided by informal primary caregivers was 28.7 hours, decreasing to 5.7 hours among secondary informal caregivers, and 4.0 hours in the case of paid help (Doty et al., 1998). Thus, the overwhelming importance of the primary caregiver as the mainstay of informal care is clear, and it is therefore not surprising that most research on caring for disabled older persons focuses on primary caregivers.

The vast majority of research points to the spouse (or partner) and children as the primary caregivers of the elderly. Although friends are important members of the social networks of older people, their role is mainly secondary as providers of emotional support, companionship, and short-term assistance. However, when family is not present or unavailable, friends may assume the role of primary caregivers. But our research suggests that they are more likely to be involved in short-term care rather than the extended care required by severely incapacitated elderly persons (Cantor & Johnson, 1978). At present, nearly one-in-four caregivers are wives and 13% are husbands, while 29% are adult daughters or daughters-in-law, and 9% are sons or sons-in law. The remaining 26% are siblings, other relatives, grandchildren, or friends and neighbors (National Alliance for Caregiving, 1997; Stone, Cafferata, & Sangl, 1987).

Spouse or Partners as Caregivers

Both in the gerontological and popular literature, one gets the impression that children, particularly daughters, are most likely to be the informal caregivers of disabled elderly. But this is only partially true. In fact, research indicates that in most cases the caregiver will be a spouse, if one is available (Cantor, 1991; Horowitz, 1985; National Alliance for Caregiving, 1997). Increasingly, older people are living with domestic partners of either the same or opposite sex. Therefore, the discussion concerning spouse applies equally to such partners. Additionally, such relationships will be even more important among the future cohorts of the aged. Thus, it is important to remember that although we employ the term spouse, we are using it in its broadest connotations.

Research suggests that ". . . spouses are a singularly important group who often carry a substantial part of the support function, probably suffer from more strain, and about whom relatively little is known" (Cantor, 1983). Findings from the 1984 National Long-Term Care Survey and the National Long-Term Care Demonstration Project illustrate the emerging importance of spouse in the care of elderly persons (Stephens & Christianson, 1986; Stone & Kemper, 1989). In both studies, spouses were the major actors when they were available. Again, in the 1989 Long-Term Care Survey, the importance of a spouse is further supported: 41% of primary caregivers were husbands or wives (Doty et al., 1998). In all three studies cited above, the spouse, if available, was more likely to be the primary caregiver, with children operating in supportive roles as secondary caregivers.

It is important to stress that caregiving spouses are not always women; husbands also serve as primary caregivers for disabled wives. For example, Soldo and associates note that in the 1982 National Long-Term Care Survey nearly all disabled married women lived with a spouse, and that 85% of these women were dependent on their husbands for personal care (Soldo, Wolf, & Agree, 1990). Furthermore, husbands constitute 36% of spousal caregivers and provide long hours of consistent care to wives, sometimes with limited assistance from others (Chang & White-Means, 1991; Harris, 1998; Stone et al., 1987).

However, the likelihood of older person's being married and having a spouse to assist them is not uniform across all groups of elderly. As discussed previously, older men are more likely than older women to have a spouse or partner. In addition, there are class and ethnic differences in the likelihood of having a spouse, as reflected in the three case studies presented earlier. Among African American elderly, only 20% were married and living with a spouse as compared with 40 % of Latino elderly. While among the prototypical older Jewish elderly, 51% still had a spouse residing with them. Particularly interesting is the role of socio-economic class in the likelihood of still living with a spouse. Older Jews, the most affluent of the three groups, were more likely to still be married. But among Black older New Yorkers, moderate-income elderly persons were also significantly more likely to be married (48%) as compared to low-income elderly Blacks (16%). Furthermore, the difference in martial status between moderate income Blacks and Whites (48 % and 56 %, respectively) is relatively small. From the trends already evident in the present case studies of the elderly population of New York City, it can be argued that in the future, differentials with respect to having a spouse among ethnic groups will be less sharp, and that gender and class will be the predominant factors in explaining any continued differences.

But what of the role of spouse caregivers in the future? Given the projected increase in longevity among men as well as women, it is likely that couples, with one or both partners disabled, caring for each other will become far more common in the twenty-first century. Cantor (1991) summarized the future of spouses as providers of care:

> Although incoming cohorts of elderly will probably include more "never married," as well as larger numbers of unrelated persons living as family, there is no evidence to suggest that the principle of hierarchical compensatory selection of primary caregiver will be altered in the future. Thus, where a spouse exists we can expect such a wife or husband to serve as principal caregiver. With more men expected to live to older ages in the decades ahead, it is likely that spouse as caregiver will be even more important in the future and that elderly couples will play a more significant role in family life (whether such couples are composed of original partners or result from remarriage or co-residence). However, a word of caution about the caregiving capacities of such old-old couples. As a concomitant of increased age, and greater prevalence of morbidity, many of the older spouse may themselves be impaired and unable to provide extensive assistance with the activities of daily living without help from either children or the formal sector. Thus, although there may be more couples, the pool of

active spouse caregivers may not increase proportionally, and children may find themselves responsible for two frail or disabled parents attempting to care for each other."

Adult Children as Providers of Care

Although spouses have a role in providing care to disabled elderly partners, the largest burden falls on children. Adult children, mostly daughters and daughters-in-law, are the principal caregivers of older widowed women, the largest single component of the disabled elderly population. Daughters are also the main caregivers of older men without spouses and couples where both partners are functionally frail or disabled, and are secondary caregivers when spouses are still alive and able (Abel, 1991; Brody, 1990; Horowitz, 1985). In all, it is estimated that at a minimum, 7% of all adults in the United States (about 13.3 million) are children or spouses of disabled elderly individuals and potentially involved in caregiving decisions. According to an analysis of the 1984 Long-Term Care Survey, the vast majority of these potential caregivers, about 85% (11.4 million) are adult children, mostly between the ages of 45 and 65.(Stone et al., 1987; Stone & Kemper 1989).

Considering only those persons actively involved in caregiving, about 2.7 million adult children provide hands-on assistance to their parents. (Cantor, 1991; Stone & Kemper, 1989). But even in roles as secondary caregivers, adult children are a vital source of backup and respite to the spousal caregiver and also provide crucial socialization, emotional sustenance, and financial assistance. In addition, children often serve as financial managers and intermediaries to obtain services from the formal system (Cantor 1991; Cantor, Brook, & Mellor, 1986; Chappell, 1985, 1990; Horowitz, 1985). Further illustrative of the crucial role played by adult children in the care of disabled elders are findings from the National Long-Term Channeling Demonstration project. In a sample of primary caregivers only, about one-half were children, one-quarter were spouses, and the remainder were other relatives, friends, and neighbors (Stephens & Christianson, 1986).

Although daughters are more likely than sons to carry the major responsibility for the care of impaired parents, sons also are involved in family caregiving. Studies that have made the distinction between primary and secondary caregivers report that sons comprise from 10% to 12% of primary caregivers and 52% of secondary caregivers. The limited research on the role of sons in the caregiving process suggests that sons are likely to provide intermittent assistance with occasional tasks, but are less involved in the more routine household tasks or in providing hands-on assistance to parents, relative to daughters (Dwyer & Coward, 1991; Harris, 1998; Horowitz, 1985). There is also evidence that as parents become more functionally disabled, sons relinquish the caregiving role (Chang & White-Means, 1991). However, Harris (1998) notes that, "...demographic and social trends such as the growing elderly population, smaller average family size (resulting in fewer siblings available for elder care), greater sibling mobility, and changing gender roles point to the probability that a growing number of sons will become caregivers to their elderly parents." Additionally, one must consider the increasing prevalence of women in the labor force, necessitating the sharing of family responsibilities between husbands and wives with respect to both child and parent care.

Competing Responsibilities in Caring for the Elderly

Two competing responsibilities, child care and employment, are often cited as limiting factors with respect to family caregivers, particularly adult children. Approximately 20 years ago when Elaine Brody coined the phrase "the sandwich generation" to refer to the dual responsibilities of caregiving daughters with respect to young children and parents, such competing demands were more relevant. Today, with the increasing age at which disability is likely to occur, adult children involved in parent care are primarily middle-age or even elderly themselves. To illustrate, in the 1984 Long-Term Care Survey sample, almost two thirds of the daughters were either middle-aged or older persons, and more likely to be grandmothers than mothers of young children. Such adult children are more likely to be involved in providing financial assistance to their children with tuition, down payments on first homes, or giving gifts to grandchildren, rather than being beset by child care responsibilities. This is not to minimize the potential for stress in families contending with conflicting financial demands between children and elderly parents. But the trend for elder caregiving at a later age will at least mitigate the tension between care of young children and frail or disabled parents. However, for some groups of elderly the conflict between child rearing and parental care has, in fact, increased. Currently, poor inner-city communities are beset by increases in parental poverty, joblessness, single parenthood, AIDS, and incarceration. As a result, among Black and other minority groups, many grandmothers and grandfathers are increasingly carrying full responsibility for raising their grandchildren, caring for their own adult children, and often caring for older parents as well (Burton & DeVries, 1992). In the case study of the elderly African Americans in New York City, approximately 16% of the respondents reported being solely responsible for the care of grandchildren. The 1990 U.S. Census confirmed these new caregiving responsibilities as a national demographic trend when it found that between 1980 and 1990 the number of children living exclusively with grandparents increased to almost one million (Joglin & Brovard, 1995).

Far more pervasive and serious as a barrier to family care of impaired elderly member is the impact of employment on caregiving. Because paid work has traditionally been dominated by men, it is easy to assume that employment would most likely have a negative impact on the availability of husband and son caregivers. However, given the changing patterns of female employment and attitudes regarding the role of women as principally responsible for the needs of family members (Stohs, 1994), conflicts between work and elder caregiving apply equally to women at the present time. Considering that both in the past and at present women have been the principal caregivers of older people, the employment conflicts with caregiving may be a much more pressing problem for women than men.

To what extent does employment affect the ability of spouses and adult children, particularly employed women, to provide needed care for functionally impaired elderly individuals? To begin, it is important to gauge the extent to which employed Americans are also involved in caring for disabled elderly persons. Based on analyses of the 1984 Long-Term Care Survey, Stone and Kemper (1989) estimate that at least one half of the spouses and adult children of disabled elderly are working full time—over 7.4 million persons. The current importance of women in the work force is illustrated by the fact that 42% of daughters and wives of the disabled population are employed, and 69% of sons and husbands work full time. Furthermore, among employed caregivers 1.5 million (2 % of the total work force) are actively involved in providing help with the activities of daily living, and nearly 40% of active caregivers hold primary responsibility for care. As might be expected, women working full time are four times as likely to be the primary caregivers as men (Cantor, 1991; Stone & Kemper, 1989).

Findings from a recent national study of caregivers further underscore the extent of employed workers' involvement in dual work and caregiving responsibility (National Alliance for Caregiving, 1997). In the representative sample, approximately two thirds of caregivers had both work and caregiving responsibilities; slightly over one-half worked full time, while another 12% worked part time. The proportion working either full time or part time remained at about two-thirds among Black, Latino and White caregivers. However, among Asian American caregivers, the proportion working full- or part-time rose to 77%. The importance of employment among both men and women caregivers was evidenced by the fact that only 10% gave up work because of elder care responsibilities, and only 7% reduced work to part-time or took a less demanding job. But the competing pressures of caregiving and employment were evidenced by the finding that about 50% of employed caregivers had to make work schedule adjustments, including arriving later, taking time off during the day, leaving early, or taking a leave of absence. As one would expect, employment causes greater conflict among principal caregivers and in cases where the recipient requires more involved care. Thus, the proportion of employed caregivers leaving the job or forced to make work adjustments decreased to only 3% to 7% when recipients required minimum or moderate care, but rose to 45% among persons caring for extremely functionally or cognitively impaired elderly persons (National Alliance for Caregiving, 1997). Possibilities for ameliorating this conflict will be discussed in the next chapter, which focuses on the formal system.

The past decades have seen a steady rise in the rates of work force participation among women. As noted previously, caregiving has increasingly become the responsibility of women in their middle and later years. Therefore, the recent labor force participation of middle-aged and older women is particularly germane to this discussion. As of 1993, 77% of women 35 to 44 years old and 74% of women aged 45 to 54 were employed. However, labor force participation declined to 57% among women 56 to 59 years of age, 37 % among women aged 60 to 64, and to 8% among women 65 years and over (Met Life, as cited in Doty, Jackson, & Crown, 1998). The decline in employment in the later years probably reflects retirement decisions, as older women tend to follow husbands out of the labor force, and as couples have greater economic resources to support early retirement.

Doty and colleagues employed data from the 1989 National Long-Term Care Survey and its companion, The Informal Caregivers Survey, to examine in detail issues concerning female primary caregivers of disabled elders. Among female primary caregivers, 41% were working age (i.e., 18 to 64 years), and 52% of these were working full- or part-time. This differential between the proportions employed and not working reflects the fact that many of the female caregivers were wives and relatives over 65 years of age. A comparison of the employment rate between the female primary caregivers and similarly aged women in the United States in 1989 indicated that the caregivers were only slightly less likely to be employed than other women their age. However, the largest differential in employment rate between female primary caregivers and their age peers occurred among women 45 to 54 years old, where employment rates were 56% and 79%, respectively (Doty et al., 1998).

Replicating findings from the National Caregivers Survey (National Alliance for Caregiving, 1997), over one-half of the employed female primary caregivers in the National Long-Term Care Survey reported making work accommodations to manage conflicts with care, mainly by rearranging their work schedules (Doty et al., 1998). Most employed female primary caregivers worked 35 hours a week or more, and only a minority of these indicated working fewer hours because of elder care. In contrast, nearly one half of those working part-time indicated working fewer hours because of caregiving responsibilities.

The impact of employment on the ability of primary caregivers to meet the needs of the elderly they care for is of at least equal importance as the effects of caregiving on labor force participation. To study this question, Doty and colleagues (1998) compared the number of hours and sources of care received by elderly recipients of employed and nonemployed female primary caregivers. The major findings were as follows:

- Employed female primary caregivers continue to provide substantial amounts of care, on average, 18 hours per week for the group as a whole; 16 hours per week among women working full time; and 21 hours per week for those working part time. As the disability severity of the care recipient increased, the employed female primary caregivers provide more hours of assistance, on average, between 32 and 39 hours per week.
- There was no significant difference in the total hours of care provided between employed and nonemployed female primary caregivers; however, the source of care did differ. Employed female primary caregivers provide fewer hours of care themselves, compensating for time constraints of employment by accessing other sources of help, including paid formal and secondary informal helpers. However, women who

were employed more than half-time experienced greater difficulty providing or securing the total hours needed by the elderly care recipient.

- At higher levels of disability , that is those requiring assistance with three or four personal core activities (ADLs)—commonly the indicator for nursing home placement—female employed primary caregivers experienced severe limitations in the amount of time they could provide personally, and were confronted with the choice between reducing hours of work, accessing more paid care, or institutional placement. In many cases, the cost of required paid help becomes prohibitive.
- The living arrangement of the care recipient is a major factor in the balancing conflicts between employment and elder care. If the older care recipient lives in the same house as the caregiver, the trade off between reducing work hours and requiring paid assistance is somewhat mitigated. In such cases, spouses are more likely to provide back-up assistance.
- Income is therefore an important determinant in decision making regarding provision of care. If an employed female primary caregiver has a high enough salary and is willing to spend more money on formal paid help, it may be possible for the parent to remain in their own home. Otherwise the female employed primary caregivers can only continue to work without a reduction in hours by bringing the care recipient into their home or placing him or her in an alternate living arrangement or institution (Doty, Jackson & Crown, 1998).

Clearly, some of these same decisions are faced by caregivers who do not work. But the additional factor of employment, whether in the case of women or men caregivers, adds a further complication to the often difficult decisions involved in caring for older parents. The findings reported by Doty and colleagues (1998) suggest that employment does not result in wives, daughters and daughters-in-law abandoning their caregiving responsibilities or severely limiting the amount of assistance provided to elderly family member. But the fact that care recipients of employed primary caregivers receive relatively more assistance from outside the family, than in cases where primary caregivers are not employed, has important implications for the future as more and more women are in the labor force. These findings illustrate the current shift in focus from the family as sole provider of care to shared responsibility between informal and formal systems as exemplified by the case study on Jewish older New Yorkers.

It is important to note that the conflict between work and caregiving puts tremendous strain not only on the caregivers, but on employers as well. An examination of the financial loss to U.S. businesses due to decreased productivity by employees caring for disabled older family members conservatively concluded the aggregate costs at about $11.5 billion per year (Met Life Mature Market Group, 1997). Included in this hidden cost of caregiving were the cost of replacing workers forced to leave jobs, absenteeism, the need to adjust work schedules, work interruptions due to phone calls and other responses to elder care crises, and supervisory costs in providing information and emotional support. Although the majority of the caregivers surveyed reported sympathetic attitudes from supervisors, it is likely that in the decades ahead this problem will become even more acute. And if there is an increase in the retirement age under Social Security, the situation will only be exacerbated and will require a range of public, private, intrafamilial, and work place solutions. And as Cantor (1991) notes, ". . . the work trajectory of women, many of whom enter the growth periods of their careers later, may be different from men. And older women in the future may be even less willing or able to follow men out of the labor market than at present. Thus, working until the middle seventies may be far more common in the future, for both men and women, a phenomenon which could restrict the availability of adult children as primary providers of 'hands-on' care."

Bearing out the greater likelihood of people working beyond retirement age in the future are the results of a recent study of retirement attitudes and plans among baby-boomers. Of a cross-section of more than 2000 persons born between 1941 and 1964, the majority indicated that they expect to work either full- or part-time after retirement (Lewis, 1998). Such attitudes undoubtedly reflect a combination of factors, including increased longevity, improved health status, higher expectations regarding standard-of-living, and concerns about the viability and adequacy of Social Security and pensions to provide for one's needs during an ever lengthening period of retirement.

SPOUSE AND ADULT CHILDREN AS CAREGIVERS IN THE FUTURE

The foregoing suggests both strengths and weaknesses in the ability of families to care for impaired elderly members requiring long-term care. For the vast majority of elderly persons who are well or have only moderate functional impairments, family, friends, and neighbors will continue to provide the bedrock of care, involving mainly routine, sporadic assistance, or occasionally more intensive care required in an acute episode. But some will find themselves in long-term social care dependency, namely, the majority of those over 85, a smaller proportion of middle-old individuals, and even fewer of the young old. To what extent will the family and particularly adult children be able to adequately respond to these needs? As has been discussed, there are important demographic, social, and structural trends that will crucially affect and serve to limit the ability of the family and significant others to provide the necessary care.

One final comment about a still unknown factor that may radically affect the role of family members as providers of social care: attitudes about the appropriate role of family and community in the care of frail elderly persons. A key finding of The Elderly in the Inner City of New York (Cantor, 1975a,b) and replicated by other research, including Growing Older in New York in the 1990s (Cantor & Brennan, 1993c) was the reluctance of older people to consider utilizing formal services, except as a last resort. But there is evidence that attitudes about appropriate sources of assistance may be changing. The elderly currently entering the aged cohorts will be better educated, have greater resources to purchase formal assistance, and in all likelihood will feel differently about the use of services such as home care and adult day care. The case study of the elderly Jews clearly suggests that such a change is already occurring among some segments of the White elderly population. Thus, changes in attitudes among the elderly and their children about appropriate sources of social care, as well as additional mechanisms for financing formal help, could radically alter the picture of family caregiving in the future.

Potential limitations to the pool of available primary caregivers , whether spouse or children, does not mean to suggest that families in the future will be any less responsive to the needs of their older members. Assistance to older people is based both on deep psychological needs as well as long-established social norms, and there is no evidence that the willingness of families to care for frail elderly members is diminished by the social, structural, and attitudinal trends enumerated above. But it is clear that the nature of the family role will, in all likelihood, undergo substantial transformation, and that formal providers of community services will have an expanded role to play. This may be manifested by providing respite to families, or assuming responsibility for more of the direct care previously supplied by family and other informal supports. Such an enlarged role is already evident in the United States and other developed countries. Thus, the way we solve the problems associated with the care of increasing numbers of frail elderly people will, undoubtedly, be a major public policy issue in the coming century. With this in mind, we turn now to an examination of the final element in the social care model, namely, the formal system and the role it will play in the care of frail elderly persons in the United States in the future.

9

The Future of Formal
Community-Based Social Care

In all countries where it exists at present, the formal or community-based support system provides services that supplement, complement, and in some instances substitute for informal care. Given the heterogeneity of the elderly population and hence their needs, formal services take a variety of forms. As is the case with informal care, there is a relationship between the dependency needs of elderly persons and the extent and nature of services provided. However, the extent of formal services is also a reflection of macro-level factors, including the proportion of elderly in the population, the current economic picture, and the dominant value system regarding the appropriate role of individuals and society in providing care for dependent people of all ages (Cantor, 1989).

THE CURRENT PROVISION OF FORMAL SOCIAL CARE

As was done when discussing informal assistance, we turn to the age-dependency continuum in discussing formal services and the form they take at the present time. Formal services are utilized by all three groups of elderly: the generally well young, the moderately impaired older, and the very frail oldest-old. The nature and extent of the formal services required varies between these three groups. In the case of the young elderly, formal services mainly involve opportunities for socialization and personal development, as well as contributions to the community through volunteerism.

Probably the most widespread example of formal services for this group are the senior centers and nutrition programs across the country.

Such programs operate under the aegis of the local Area Agencies on Aging, as mandated under The Older Americans Act (1965, amended 1973). In addition to providing a hot meal and socialization opportunities, centers often offer heath promotion and exercise programs essential to the maintenance of good health in old age. Senior centers may also provide information and referral services for entitlement and other programs. Area Agencies on Aging, in addition to coordinating senior services, also provide information and referral services and offer a vehicle for planning and advocacy on aging issues at all levels of government that are important to elderly persons of all ages and abilities. Opportunities for volunteer service are also important to the well elderly. Thus organizations such as the Retired Senior Volunteer Program (R.S.V.P), Foster Grandparents, the Peace Corps, and the myriad of voluntary agencies, hospitals, and schools that welcome older people as volunteers provide outlets for seniors to contribute to their communities with a minimum of governmental involvement. Finally, in the arena of personal development, public and private educational institutions offer older people opportunities to study, sometimes with reduced tuition. Not as widespread at present are employment programs and counseling for older adults, but it is likely that such services will play an increasingly important roll as the baby-boomers enter the aged cohorts.

Moderately frail elderly persons take part in some of the programs discussed above, but in addition, receive limited help from formal organizations with tasks of daily living such as housekeeping, chores, transportation, and shopping. For those with emerging frailty or desiring living environments more in line with their lifestyles and needs, religious and not-for-profit voluntary agencies have increasingly turned to the sponsorship of alternative living arrangements, such as senior-housing and assisted living or continuing care communities. The increased popularity of such housing alternatives has also encouraged private real estate development in this area, but usually targeted at the higher income elderly. In-home services such as visiting nurses, home health aids, or homemakers are important for older people with acute episodes of illness and frequently follow hospitalization. On a short-term basis, these services are usually covered by Medicare or Medicaid for those with sufficiently low incomes. There are also both for-profit and voluntary home care agencies that provide private, for-pay home care.

For impaired older adults of any age to remain in the community, a wide range of long-term care services are needed by these elderly and their families. In some communities, services available for disabled older persons and their families consist of home health care, including visiting nurse, home health aids, and to a limited extent, physical therapists, homemaker and personal care services, adult day care, hospice, meals-on-wheels, telephone reassurance, and protective services, including assistance in abuse situations. In the case of families caring for impaired elderly, particularly those suffering from Alzheimer's disease and other cognitive disorders, family support groups, assessment and case management services are sponsored by community agencies and some mediating structures (e.g., religious congregations) in many parts of the country. And finally, when there are no other options, nursing homes are available and often advisable for severely impaired elders who may be without family, have no family nearby, or whose family can no longer carry the burden of care.

At present the most glaring deficiency in the formal system for impaired elderly is in the area of long-term care, particularly in-home services. Despite the preference of the elderly (and their families) to remain at home as long as possible, only 25% of the disabled elderly in the community receive any formal in-home services (U.S. Department of Health and Human Services, 1982). Because of the relatively limited funding for long-term care by all levels of government, there is a paucity of publicly sponsored in-home services, and private paid care is too expensive for most older Americans (Cantor, 1989). The demand for these services is clearly illustrated in the three case studies presented. Among all three groups—Jewish, African American and Hispanic elderly—home care was among the most highly utilized services and was the single most often-mentioned service with respect to the need for additional help in the previous year. The relationship between advancing age and the need for in-home assistance is further illustrated in the case study of the Jewish elderly. Older on average and presenting greater levels of frailty than their peers, older Jews were also far more likely to have utilized the visiting nurse and home care services during the past year than older New Yorkers in general. In part, this difference can also be attributed to their greater willingness to use the formal system, but advanced age and frailty are the primary triggers for publicly and privately sponsored formal services.

Although not in every community nor in sufficient quantity to meet the level of need, it is clear from the above description of the wide range of services that presently exist that we have considerable knowledge and organizational experience with the formal services that can make life richer for the elderly and enable them to remain in the community as long as possible. For the well elderly and those who are moderately impaired, formal services can help them to continue to actively participate in the community and socialize with peers. For the impaired older person, formal services may act as a backup or provide needed respite when the family is an active caregiver. In the absence of a functional informal network, formal community agencies may act as a substitute for family and assume surrogate responsibilities through the provision of in-home or institutional care (Cantor, 1989).

As we have seen in the case studies, not all elderly require the services of the formal sector, and not all use available services, except those associated with the basic entitlements, such as Social Security and Medicare. The informal system continues to be the major provider of assistance to the elderly in the community, and will undoubtedly carry this role in the future. Some of the reluctance to turn to the formal sector is attitudinal, some is due to lack of knowledge about available services, and some is due to the difficulty in accessing a system that is fragmented and often very bureaucratic. But when serious difficulties arise, whether health or income related, the formal system becomes involved, and its assistance is often crucial in allowing older people to continue to reside in the community, or if necessary, offer them required institutional care. But what of formal services in the future? Will they be available in sufficient quantity and quality to meet the needs of a growing elderly population, one that is better educated and potentially more willing to turn to the community for assistance in times of need? As noted previously, because of the increased numbers of disabled elderly occurring later in the life cycle and the pressures on families, particularly employed women, to continue to provide the long-term care of severely incapacitated elderly, the importance of formal services as a crucial part of the social care system is not in question. But very much at stake at the current time are questions regarding the relative responsibility of individuals/ families and society in assuring the availability of needed services, how such services should be financed, and the appropriate role and level of government involved in the provision of formal services. How these important policy issues are resolved will greatly affect the well-being of the current and future elderly cohorts.

HISTORICAL ROOTS OF THE CURRENT DEBATE
ON FORMAL SERVICES TO THE ELDERLY

To help bring into focus the current debate on the provision of formal income, health, or other services, whether under the Social Security, Medicare, or the Older Americans Act, it is helpful to trace the origin of such legislation and the value system on which they are based. Since the founding of the country there has been a strong value attached to the work ethic and the belief that the private sector would provide all citizens with the opportunity to realize the fruits of society (Morris & Hanson, 1997). However, with the advent of the Great Depression in the 1930s and the evidence that in an industrial society some people could fall through the cracks, despite their diligence and efforts, there began to be a greater recognition and acceptance of the notion that the government and the local community had a responsibility at least to provide a safety net for persons in need, whether from industrial displacement or agricultural ruin as happened in the Oklahoma Dust Bowl. Thus, social welfare was originally designed to insure against deficiencies in a market economy, and assistance was reserved for the needy, who through no fault of their own, were victims of the deficiencies in this economic system. As a result, employment-oriented legislation aimed at improving the economy of the country was enacted, which brought about programs such as unemployment insurance, farm subsidies, the W.P.A (Works Progress Administration), and the C.C.C (Civilian Conservation Corps). for the young. These and other New Deal programs of the 1930s also represented a ". . . complete reversal, shifting traditional responsibilities from locality or state to the national government" (Morris & Hanson, 1997).

Against this background, elderly persons, mainly out of the labor market, were seen as a particularly needy and worthy group, requiring some form of long-term income support from government. The passage of the Social Security Act of 1935 was the first major recognition of the need for assistance for an entire segment of the population, the elderly and disabled (Hudson, 1998a). In the intervening years, a series of laws aimed at securing both the economic and health status of older people were passed, most importantly Medicare for all who are elderly and disabled, and Medicaid and Supplemental Security Income for the poor. Furthermore, it was deemed appropriate to assist all older people, regardless of income, to have a more meaningful old age with the passage of the Older Americans Act (OAA). OAA programs were aimed not only at providing hot lunches through nutrition programs, but also at providing opportunities for socialization at senior centers and assistance in securing entitlements. Subsequent additions to the OAA provided for a variety of other programs, including legal services for poor elderly, extending limited home care to middle-income elderly (the poor had coverage under Medicaid), and opportunities for volunteerism under the Foster Grandparents Program. From this base has grown in many, but not all, communities the melange of services currently available to enhance the life of the elderly. Some students of the New Deal suggest that older people were chosen as the centerpiece of so much liberal legislation because of their need and humanitarian feelings (Achenbaum, 1986). However, others such as Graebner (1980) suggest that Social Security and other aging services were based on the need to remove elderly persons from the work place, thereby opening opportunities for younger workers. Whatever the motivation, legislation such as the Social Security Act and Medicare have been institutionalized into the mainstream of American society.

Hudson (1998a) notes that as long as the elderly were seen as a set-apart, needy group requiring assistance from the government, the idea of special services for older people was supported by society at-large, resulting in the tremendous expansion of community services in the 1970s and 1980s. It is noteworthy that older people were perceived by both government and society as a monolithically needy group; hence questions of means testing and the separation of the poor from those better-off was not a major issue in this period of legislative and service expansion. Services were designed to be equally available to all, except in the case of specific programs aimed at the poor (e.g., Supplemental Security Income, Medicaid, and Food Stamps). Government involvement in the social care of older people was viewed as entirely compatible with the underlying notion of individual responsibility in a market-based economy. In other Western countries, services for older adults were already available as part of universal health and welfare programs, such as the National Health System in the United Kingdom, rather than the more segmented approach implemented in this country for the elderly.

Hudson (1998a) argues that only when aging became institutionalized in this country, because of the large number of elderly, their improved economic situation and their growing political power, did an increased willingness emerge among more market-oriented politicians and segments of the population to raise the issue of divesting government, particularly the federal branch, from responsibility for even the elderly. This change in attitude has fueled increasing pressure for the privatization of both Social Security and Medicare, as well as the reduction of the budget for programs under the OAA. Hudson (1998b) notes that ". . . a guiding tenet of contemporary conservatism lies in locating private solutions to public problems. In this it differs from liberalism, which has long promoted public interventions as the remedy for the array of social problems it has seen throughout American society. Although differing from earlier conservatives, who denied even sub-optimal conditions as problems, today's conservatives recognize as problems both selected social conditions and most public interventions, proposing for both market-based private sector solutions."

Thus, at present we find ourselves in a very difficult period with respect to formal services for the elderly. Liberal forces and community agencies serving the elderly are on the defensive regarding the continued role of government in assisting older people. In addition, the positive results of earlier legislation (e.g., Social Security, OAA) are being used as arguments against further government support and expansion of aging services. This is occurring despite the projected growth of the older population in the future, particularly the oldest and frailest segment for whom catastrophic illness brings with it financial disaster for even middle-class elderly individuals and their families. Given the lower Social Security and pension benefits historically accrued by older women, the issue of paying for long-term care is particularly critical for older women, who constitute the majority of the oldest-old, and their families.

THE FUTURE OF LONG-TERM CARE

Although the current debate regarding the relative responsibility and fiscal role of government and the individual is centered around Social Security and Medicare, an additional and even more critical public policy issue looms in the future—the provision of long-term care. The issue of providing long-term care will serve, to a large extent, as a measure of our willingness as a society to continue assuming at least some responsibility for the oldest and frailest in the population. Binstock (1998) notes that congruent with the recent emphasis on personal responsibility ". . . governments and many for-profit corporations have cut back on benefits that they used to provide and consequently individuals will need to cope with the vicissitudes of the market much more than they have had to in the last half of the twentieth century. In addition, public policy actions have shifted some of the government fiscal burden for health and welfare programs to the private sector, also increasing the scope of responsibility that individuals must take on for their well-being." As a result Binstock notes, ". . . although the prospects of expanded governmental financing for long term care seemed good in the early 1990s, the issue has disappeared from the public agenda." Yet as noted earlier, the demand for long-term care can only be expected to grow more sharply as the number of elderly persons expands, as longevity continues to increase, and as the growing presence of women in the work place renders the care of elderly disabled by family even more uncertain.

While the public tends to equate long-term care with nursing homes, an effective long-term care system also involves a continuum of community-based services. These formal services may range from case management to a variety of in-home services, rehabilitation specialists, and adult day care. In addition, long-term care is also manifested in various forms of supportive housing, such as assisted living and continuing-care communities. Although nursing homes serve less than one quarter of disabled elderly persons, at present they dominate long-term care financing. To illustrate, it is estimated that in 1987, about 33 billion dollars was spent on nursing home care for elderly individuals, with only about 8.6 billion spent for in-home care, estimated to cover twice as many people (Rivlin & Weiner, 1988). Because a solution to long-term care directly affects not only the elderly but also their families, it will certainly become a major public policy issue in the future.

THE CURRENT PROVISION OF LONG-TERM
CARE TO OLDER AMERICANS

Almost universally, the care of the elderly, whether for short-term assistance or long-term care, is largely provided by relatives and other members of the informal system (see for example, Cantor & Brennan, 1993c). Although most older people are not disabled, in 1984, 21% of the 33 million adults over the age of 65 had some level of severe disability. Of these, almost three-quarters lived at home, and most received unpaid care from informal providers (Rivlin & Weiner, 1988; Weiner & Stevenson, 1997).

At present, both the public and private sectors play a role in financing long-term care, and the current method is makeshift and inadequate. Rivlin and Weiner (1988) note that, ". . . neither the public nor the private sector has developed ways of pooling the risks of long-term care or spreading the costs over time." Both sectors are simply coping with the rising costs as best they can, and the resultant fragmented and inadequate system satisfies no one. Strikingly, only a small portion of long-term care is reimbursed by any form of private insurance because most policies do not cover long-term care. Currently Medicare pays for time-limited home care after an acute hospitalization. Thus, the bulk of long -term care payments come from the means-tested Medicaid program and out-of-pocket spending by the elderly and their families. According to Weiner and Stevenson (1997), ". . . in 1993 Medicaid paid for 35% of long-term care for the elderly, older people and their families paid for 42%, with Medicare paying 19%, while private insurance paid for less than 1%." As a result, Rivlin and Weiner (1988) conclude that, "Incomes are strained, life savings used up. The burden falls heavily on persons unlucky enough to need extensive long-term care and on their families. The pain and anxiety inherent in becoming disabled and in caring for a disabled relative are compounded by worries over how to pay for care without turning to welfare."

Other problems with the current fragmented system include rising public costs and the tendency to create a two-tiered system of long-term care. This two-tiered system has arisen because persons often receive better care in private facilities paid for out-of-pocket, as compared with institutions that are primarily dependent on Medicaid patients. Finally, because financing is more limited for home care, such services are in more limited supply, despite the desire of the elderly and their families to be cared for at home.

OPTIONS FOR THE FINANCING OF LONG-TERM CARE

Despite the extensive emotional and financial burden currently borne by older people requiring long-term care and their families, a growing public perception that the elderly are more affluent has resulted in increased pressure for shifting more responsibility for long-term care to them and their children. Thus, among states that share the costs of Medicaid with the federal government, there are increasing attempts to recoup any Medicaid moneys spent on nursing home care, by attaching the home or other assets following the death of the older person. In addition, as is the case of Social Security and Medicare programs, there are demands for market-oriented, private sector solutions to long-term care. To what extent, then, is it realistic to further shift the cost of long-term care to families, particularly middle- and working-class, and will the market effectively respond to the rising demands for long-term care as the baby-boomers reach old age?

In considering appropriate methods of financing long-term care in the future, it is important to realize that on any given day only approximately one-quarter of older people are patients in a nursing home and only between one-third and one-half of those over 65 will ever spend time in such a facility (Manton et al., 1997; Weiner & Stevenson, 1997). The fact that relatively few people spend long periods of time in nursing homes involving large expenses suggests that long-term care is particularly well suited for insurance and risk-pooling. The idea of many people contributing to a fund to cover the extraordinary expenses of the few lies at the heart of current approaches, such as private health and long-term care insurance and Medicare.

Rivlin and Weiner (1988) as well as other policy analysts (e.g., Binstock, 1998) have carefully examined the potential of public and private long-term insurance as sources of financing for long-term care for the elderly currently and in the future. The consensus is that the elderly alone, even with financial help from families, cannot carry the full responsibility themselves. Therefore, some combination of public and supplemental private efforts will be required to assure that disabled elderly individuals will receive the assistance they need without resulting in impoverishment of either them or their families.

PRIVATE SECTOR OPTIONS

Private insurance is widely utilized to spread the risk of infrequent but potentially devastating costs associated with fire, theft, automobile accidents, and hospitalization. At present, a large proportion of elderly people currently buy Medicare supplemental insurance. The private long-term care insurance market is growing, but only about 5% of older people have any type of long-term care (Weiner & Stevenson, 1997). In addition most analysts point to some serious problems with the current policies and practices of selling long-term care insurance. Perhaps most serious are the high costs of premiums and inflation protection charges rendering such policies unaffordable for most older people. In 1991, a high-option policy (i.e., adequate nursing home and in-home care with inflation protection) cost from $1785 to $3768 per year if purchased at age 65, rising to between $3941 to $5635 if first purchased at age 75 (Consumers Reports, 1991). Clearly such policies are out of the reach of most elderly persons.

In addition to high premiums, exclusions for preexisting conditions prevent many from obtaining long-term care insurance. Furthermore, the waiting period before benefits are triggered can run from 90 to 120 days, effectively placing deductibles at $9000 for a $100 per day nursing home coverage (Binstock, 1998). Thus, even with private long-term care insurance, elderly persons and their families can still sustain large out-of-pocket costs. It should be noted that these same general limitations apply to other private sector options, such as individual medical accounts and continuing care retirement communities, which seem useful only for the high end of the elderly market. Rivlin and Weiner (1988) concluded that,

> ". . . although private sector financing mechanisms for long-term care could grow substantially, private sector approaches are unlikely to be affordable by a majority of elderly, to finance more than a modest proportion of total nursing home and home care expenditures, or to have more than a small effect on medical expenditures and the number of people who spend down to Medicaid eligibility. For example, by 2016-20 optimistic estimates are that private long term care insurance may be affordable by 25% to 45% of the elderly, may account for 7% to 12% of total nursing home expenditures, and may reduce Medicaid expenditures and the number of home patients by 1% to 5%."

Binstock (1998) summarizes the problem with dependency on the private sector and particularly private long-term care insurance by noting that despite the projected increased incomes and assets status of the baby-boomers, the dynamics of cost inflation in the long-term care market suggest that, under present conditions, the financial burden of paying for long-term care will not abate for most middle-class families.

PUBLIC SECTOR OPTIONS

Given that the private sector alone cannot adequately insure the financing of long-term care for many elderly persons, the question remains, what is the appropriate role for the public with respect to long-term care? Three different approaches have been proposed. The first would decrease the tax burden of society by increasing family financial responsibility for Medicaid nursing home patients and retaining a welfare-based strategy making it more difficult to obtain benefits. This would, of course penalize middle-class families who spend down to Medicaid eligibility and diminish the potential for adequate long-term care for working-class and poverty level elderly, particularly minorities. The second solution involves incrementally expanding the public role through programs such as providing either tax incentives or cash supports to families caring for disabled elderly members, expanding public spending on home care while retaining eligibility requirements, case management and cost sharing to keep down expenses, and lastly liberalizing Medicaid to make it more accessible, though retaining its essential character as a public charity (Rivlin & Weiner, 1988). All of these programs have some merit, but they would still leave a fragmented system that would not remove the burden of long-term care from all but the most abject of the poor.

The last strategy, the most preferred by advocates for older Americans would be to cover the costs of long-term care under a general social insurance program like Medicare. Such an approach implicitly recognizes that long-term care is a normal risk of old age, and that society as well individuals have a role in assuring that disabled elderly persons receive needed services in the face of catastrophic illness. The inclusion of long-term care in the Medicare program would provide universal coverage, and everyone would contribute to public long-term care insurance and share its risks and benefits. Like other provisions of Medicare, such insurance should involve substantial cost sharing, and have specific eligibility requirements to limit costs and control services. Further, private sector financing need not be eliminated but could become supplemental to provide greater financial protection and services, similar to the role currently played by Medicare supplemental health insurance policies. But careful attention should be given to guaranteeing that basic long-term care costs are covered through the public-pooled risk insurance, so as to preclude a two-tiered system. Germany and Japan have recently instituted long-term care insurance programs paid for through payroll deductions. In

Germany, benefits accrue to individuals and can be used to secure services either public or private. While in Japan, a comprehensive and integrated institutional and community-based system of long-term care is envisioned, which will be available as needed under its insurance system. In conclusion, we share with Binstock (1998) and others the hope that the baby-bloomers, ". . . may perhaps precipitate a grass roots movement that will successfully insure the placing of expanded public funding for long-term care on the public policy agenda."

MICRO-LEVEL IMPLICATIONS FOR IMPROVED FORMAL SERVICES FOR OLDER PEOPLE

Clearly the most pressing macro-level policy decisions affecting the elderly concern the maintenance of Social Security as a basic retirement income for all, Medicare as a viable health insurance system, and a solution for the long-term care needs of frail and disabled elderly that is universal and equitable, and does not pauperize elderly individuals or their families.

But in addition to these broad policy questions, there are several important micro-level implications from the data presented in this book that have the potential for making the formal sector of the social care system of older Americans more user friendly and less fragmented. We have noted that there are a number of challenges faced by the formal service system to meet both current and future needs. It is anticipated that the need for community services will grow, not only as a result of increased numbers of elderly, particularly the oldest-old, but because of poverty, lack of both acute and long-term health care, and the devastating social problems that intrude on the lives of the elderly and their families, especially in poor and minority communities. In many cases, formal community-based services can help alleviate these problems. Yet the utilization of formal services, particularly the basic entitlements of Supplemental Security Income (S.S.I.), Medicaid, and Food Stamps is not high, even among the poorest elderly and recent immigrants. It is startling that in the 1990 study of older persons in New York City, 57% of Hispanics and 25% of African-American elderly have incomes at or below the poverty level (Cantor & Brennan, 1993a). Even among Jewish elderly, the most affluent of the three groups, 10% are in poverty and another one-fifth have near poverty incomes. Furthermore, the 1990 data indicate a serious gap between those in poverty and the utilization of means-based programs aimed at ameliorating low incomes, such as S.S.I., Medicaid and Food Stamps.

The picture with respect to other formal services is not much more promising. Aside from the Social Security and Medicaid offices, the emergency rooms of hospitals, and to a lesser extent senior centers, the utilization of formal services is low (Cantor & Brennan, 1993c). Some of this may result from a lack of need, but it is important to know more about the attitudinal and organizational barriers to service utilization. Structural barriers to use of services, such as lack of accessibility, inability to negotiate the bureaucracy, and lack of knowledge about service availability are clearly part of the picture, and the elderly of New York City in both the 1970 and 1990 studies clearly noted these obstacles. But sociocultural barriers such as language, attitudes about seeking help outside the family, and fears concerning involvement with government agencies are also apparent and too often overlooked. Thus major outreach efforts to older persons, whether for entitlement programs, senior centers, adult day care or elder abuse assistance, require careful attention to the particular characteristics of the community involved, including language, cultural mores regarding help-seeking behavior, and the organization and leadership structure of the community. The case study of the Latino elderly speaks to the importance of involving neighbors and other significant community leaders (both informal and formal) as potential pathways to services. These individuals are capable of providing information, support, and even direct intervention and assistance, thereby linking older persons and their families to the appropriate community resource (Brennan & Cantor, 1993). Furthermore, it is clearly not enough to label the older person as the *client*. In contrast, the urgency of perceiving elderly persons as part of a family and neighborhood system is critical if we are to reach many of them with our service message, particularly those with less education, and racial and ethnic minorities.

Another important issue in making services more accessible and easier to use is the nature of the organizational bureaucracy involved in the provision of entitlement, health, and social services to older people. The need for advocacy and assistance in dealing with the formal sector has been persistently voiced by the elderly of New York City in the last two decades (Cantor & Brennan, 1993c). The elderly of all socioeconomic strata have mentioned the difficulties involved in negotiating the system, but these problems are exacerbated in the case of minority elderly with lower than average education. Are the eligibility requirements and necessary steps to obtain services understandable and comprehensible to the average older person? A most recent example of this type of problem is the confusion concerning the coming changes in Medicare under The Balanced Budget Act of 1997, particularly the Medical Saving Accounts provisions. Are eligibility requirements fair, or do they penalize particular groups of elderly such as recent immigrants, those living in multigenerational households (the current situation with Supplemental Security Income), or grandparents caring for grandchildren? Do they require the stripping of all assets before services are provided? Often such questions are both philosophical and organizational, but the way they are addressed can have far-reaching consequences for the well-being of the older population.

Perhaps most serious is the fragmented nature of formal services in communities across the country, including the multiplicity of funding streams, application forms, eligibility requirements, and the need to make separate visits to each office or agency to obtain assistance. For years professionals and researchers in the field of aging have been calling for the creation of a single entry point to services in a community or neighborhood. Our research (Cantor, 1975a; Cantor & Brennan, 1993b) has shown that in the case of elderly persons a neighborhood is comprised of a 10-block radius, and that most older people shop, bank and carry out their daily affairs within this life space. Thus, the decentralization of service entry points is extremely important to ease of utilization. In many places, senior centers or nutrition programs would seem to be a logical choice as a focal point, capable of appealing to a broad cross-section of elderly individuals, including the well and the frail, and the young and the old alike. In other communities, libraries or Offices for the Aging may be more appropriate. Of course, establishing a single point of entry is much simpler when setting up a new program as a demonstration. But it is far more difficult to achieve a single entry point when coordination among a group of extant agencies with different funding sources is required (Cantor & Little, 1985). Many senior centers already attempt to function as entry points to community services, but are typically lacking funds for social workers or other staff required to help elderly persons and their families access the formal system. It is important to reiterate that in all three case studies, older people with any connection to the formal system were higher users of other formal services, underscoring the importance of providing an easily accessible and language friendly entry point to the formal sector.

However, to achieve meaningful accessibility, service coordination must go on simultaneously at the individual, community, and state levels. What is needed is a systems coordination, both within the social care system and the health care system, and within a reasonable cost frame. To date, no country has discovered answers to this ongoing problem. A holistic approach involving systems-wide coordination is essential, even if the delivery of services is not located in a single agency or service system, particularly for the frail elderly requiring long-term care (Cantor & Little, 1985).

Finally, we must recognize that the elderly population is changing and will change even more when the baby-boomers join the aging cohorts. The elderly of the future as illustrated by the case study of Jewish elderly and reflected in the growing middle-class found among African Americans in our study, will be better educated, more comfortable financially, more likely to live independently, and have improved health for a longer time. Elderly persons of the future are also expected to carry into old age the many cultural and recreational interests that characterized them earlier in life. To what extent will community services reflect this changing elder population, most of whom will live as much as 20 years after retirement? As noted in the Jewish case study, for the younger elderly, many with greater personal resources, challenges to the productive use of time will be pertinent to successful aging. In a society that tends to equate productivity with gainful employment, we will need to rethink the meaning of productivity in the case of older people and expand our conception to include a variety of activities, including volunteering in communities agencies, schools, libraries, museums, and hospitals, and providing opportunities to study and develop new skills and careers. These are only a few of the many possibilities to engage the upcoming elderly and insure that their talents and abilities are utilized for society's benefit. Particularly important will be intergenerational opportunities to assure that older people are part of the mainstream of neighborhoods and communities; interactions that are crucial to minimize potential differences or conflicts between generations in the allocation of scarce resources. Will our current institutions be flexible enough to respond to such challenges? For example, senior centers will have to rethink programs to encompass not only the older more frail elderly whom they currently mainly serve, but the more vigorous elderly as well. This may involve more diversified programming, including more emphasis on educational activities and opportunities to share new interests (e.g., computers and the internet). Centers can also serve as conduits to volunteer opportunities in concert with other community agencies. Some senior centers already have such broad programming, but they are still too few in number.

Thus, the formal service system for older people in the future requires multiple foci to meet multiple types of populations. First and foremost, our findings suggest the necessity of insuring that the basic services required by elderly persons in need, whether due to poverty, frailty, recent immigration, or ethnic or minority status, continue to be in place. For such groups, on-going emphasis on income maintenance, health care, housing and public safety will be essential. But at the same time there is a need to reach out to the younger, better educated, more affluent elderly who have many skills of value to the community. They will require opportunities for volunteering, as well as assistance in connecting their interests and skills with emerging community needs. In periods of scarce resources, the assistance of older volunteers can make a tremendous difference in the continuation and expansion of community organizations. Clearly, priorities must be set in program planning and delivery. But the major challenge to the formal service system in the future is the degree to which it can flexibly and cost-effectively meet the needs of the diverse groups that comprise the elderly population.

CONCLUSION

In concluding our discussion of future implications for the social care system of the elderly in the United States, we return to the social care model, including both the informal and formal systems, which provide together, in an interactive manner, the assistance required by older people to age successfully. We have suggested dynamic changes in both the composition of the elderly population and in the social care system that will be required to support this growing population in the future. Some of the demographic trends are relatively clear, others regarding morbidity and disability are still emerging. However, central to any picture of an aging America is the interdependence of generations and the role of one generation in caring for the other. Thus, the family, broadly defined, will continue to play a central role in the welfare of its older members. But the environment in which families function is also changing rapidly, including greater geographic dispersion and the crucial entrance of large numbers of women into the workforce. The nature of family care is already reflecting these changes, and it is unlikely that the family, however well-meaning, can continue to carry the full responsibility for social care alone, without community supports. Most significant will be the emerging role of the formal system in providing assistance with long-term care: developing social, educational, and recreational resources, and in ensuring that the elderly of the future have meaningful opportunities to contribute their knowledge and skills to the broader community. Particularly important will be intergenerational opportunities so that the wisdom of one generation is passed to the next, and so that young people have the opportunity to see older people as strong, functioning members of our aging society (Cantor, 1989, 1991; Cantor & Little, 1985).

Such a vision will require new responses to the provision of social care on the part of both the informal and formal systems, as well as assistance from mediating structures in the social care model, such as clergy, store keepers, and neighborhood organizations. During the 1960s and 1970s, the United States witnessed the development of a panoply of formal services; these services laid the foundation for community-based formal care. In the 1980s and 1990s, attention has shifted to informal care as research documented the presence of a viable informal system that coexisted with the formal system and, in fact, provided most of the basic care for older people (Cantor, 1985, 1989, 1991). Although some policy makers now view the family system as capable of assuming an even greater role in caring for elderly members, most experts agree that the family alone cannot sustain the total responsibility for care without assistance from the formal system. At present, the formal system provides basic income maintenance and health care and shares with families the cost of social care, especially in terms of long-term care of the physically and cognitively impaired (Cantor, 1985, 1991; Cantor & Little, 1985). Furthermore, there is evidence that in the future elderly persons and their families may be more receptive to assistance from the formal sector, particularly in the arena of instrumental home care, while continuing to provide overall case management and supervision, as well as crucial affective and socialization support (Cantor, 1985; Cantor & Brennan, 1993c). Some argue that any expansion of formal services, particularly in the home, will result in increased demand and costs beyond the capacity of our society to bear. However, a survey of experience in providing care to frail elderly and their caregivers suggests that the provision of a range of community interventions aimed at supporting families, such as respite care, adult day care, in-home assistance, and transportation does not reduce the involvement of families but encourages the continuation of their efforts (Mathematica Policy Research, 1986).

Cantor (1989) has summarized the challenges ahead with respect to social care for the elderly, as follows:

> As we move into the next century, the growing numbers of elderly, coupled with increases in working women and changing family structures will require new responses to social care on the part of families and communities. Most important will be a more integrated approach to the provision of social care in which the several components of the system (i.e. informal, mediating and formal) will contribute according to their capacity. What is required is the establishment of a partnership between family and community including the expansion of community respite interventions and the sharing of financial costs involved in providing social-health care. The family (in its broadest sense) will remain important in the future but it cannot continue to act alone. This does not relieve the family of the basic responsibility of managing the care of older relatives but recognizing that, in many cases, the direct day-to-day in-home assistance may have to be provided by specially trained and carefully supervised home care workers under the aegis of community agencies.

The model of social care presented in this book has stressed repeatedly that both the informal and formal subsystems have and will continue to have interlocking responsibilities for the welfare of older people. Thus, the capacity of both as partners in assisting elderly individuals to live out a meaningful life must be considered and nurtured in the structuring of social care interventions, whether on an individual or macro-level. Such a partnership would insure that whether family or community components assume responsibility in any given situation would be a function of a variety of determinants. These factors include the preferences of the elderly and their families, the impact on the total family system, the level of specialized services required, and the availability of assistance in the immediate family and environment. Such an approach places a premium on the interface of informal and formal providers of social care to maximize available resources for the benefit of older people and their families (Cantor, 1989). There must be a note of caution in any discussion of partnership between the informal and formal systems, particularly in the light of the current interest among some segments in our society in downsizing government and increasing the emphasis on personal responsibility. This greater stress on dependence on the private sector and volunteerism coincides somewhat too conveniently with calls for a reduction in the role of government in the name of fiscal austerity and "tax reform". Given such a climate, it is important to insure that interest in interface and integration between informal and formal components is not a rationale for further reduction or elimination of formal social services. We must also guard against further undermining our sense of social responsibility toward the elderly, most particularly the poor and racial or ethnic minorities who are often most in need of public assistance. An informal support network that lacks a foundation of widespread community-based formal services will find it impossible to meet the social care needs of a burgeoning elderly population as we enter the twenty-first century.

References

Abel, E. K. (1991). *Who cares for the elderly: Public policy and experience of adult daughters.* Philadelphia: Temple University Press.

Achenbaum, A. (1986). *Social Security: Visions and revisions.* New York: Cambridge University Press.

Adams, J. (1980). Service arrangements preferred by minority elderly: A cross-cultural study. *The Gerontologist, 3,* 39–57.

Angel, J. L., & Hogan, D. P. (1991). The demography of minority aging populations. In *Minority elders: Longevity, economics, and health: Building a public policy base.* Washington, DC: The Gerontological Society of America. 1–14

Antonucci, T. C. (1985). Personal characteristics, social support and social behavior. In R. H. Binstock (Ed.), *Handbook of aging and the social sciences,* 2nd ed. (pp. 94–128). New York: Van Nostrand Rheinhold.

Antonucci, T. C. (1990). Social supports and social relationships. In R. H. Binstock and L. K. George (Eds.), *Handbook of aging and the social sciences,* 3rd ed. (pp. 201–226). New York: Academic Press.

Antonucci, T. C., & Akiyama, H. (1987). Social networks in adult life and a preliminary examination of the Convoy Model. *Journal of Gerontology, 12,* 519–527.

Bengtson, V. (1986). Sociological Perspectives in Aging. In M. Bergen (Ed.), *Perspective on aging: The 1996 Sandoz Lectires in gerontology.* New York: Academic Press.

Bengtson, V. L., Burgess, E. D., & Parrott, T. M. (1997). Theory, explanation and a third generation of theoretical development. *The Gerontologist, 52B,* 572–588.

Bengtson, V. L., & Dannefer, D. (1987). Families, work and aging: Implications of disordered cohort flow for the 21st century. In R. Ward & S. S. Tobin (Eds.), *Health in aging: Sociological issues and policy directions.* New York: Springer.

Bengtson, V. L., & DeTerre, E. (1980). Aging and family relations. *Marriage and Family Review, 3,* 51–76.

Bengtson, V. L., Rosenthal, C., & Burton, L. (1990). Families and aging: Diversity and heterogeneity. In R. H. Binstock & L. K. George (Eds.), *Handbook of aging and the social sciences, 3rd ed.* New York: Academic Press.

Bengtson, V. L., & Treas, J. (1980). The changing family context of mental health and aging. In R. B. Sloane & J. J. Birren (Eds.), *Handbook of mental health and aging* (pp. 400–428). Englewood Cliffs, NJ: Prentice-Hall.

Berger, P., & Neuhaus, R. (1977). *To empower people.* Washington, DC: American Enterprise Institute.

Berkman, C., & Gurland, B. (1993). The impact of health problems on the quality of life of older New Yorkers. *Growing older in New York City in the 1990s: A study of changing lifestyles, quality of life, and quality of care,* Vol. III. New York: The New York Center for Policy on Aging, the New York Community Trust.

Binstock, R. H. (1998). Personal responsibility and privatization in public policies on aging. *The Public Policy and Aging Report, 9 (2),* 6–9.

Blenkner, M. (1969). The normal dependencies of aging. In R. Kalish (Ed.), *The dependencies of old people* (pp. 27–37). Ann Arbor, MI: University of Michigan-Wayne State University: Institute of Gerontology.

Boaz, R. F., & Hu, J. (1997). Determining the amount of help used by disabled elderly persons at home: The role of coping resources. *Journals of Gerontology: Social Sciences, 52B,* S317–S324.

Branch, L. G., & Keku, L. (1989). Transition probabilities for the elderly over a decade: Uses in long-term care financing. *Journal of Aging and Health, 1,* 370–408.

Brennan, M. (1995). *The context of integrity development in later life.* Unpublished doctoral dissertation, Fordham University, Bronx, NY.

Brennan, M., & Cantor, M. H. (1993). *The effect of need, pathways, and informal resources in predicting formal service utilization among White, African-American, and Latino older New Yorkers.* Paper presented at the Meeting of the Gerontological Society of America, New Orleans, LA.

Brody, E. M. (1966). The aging family. *The Gerontologist, 23,* 51–56.

Brody, E. M. (1978). The aging of the family. *Annals of the American Academy of Political and Social Sciences, 438,* 13–27.

Brody, E. M. (1981). Women in the middle and family help to older people. *The Gerontologist, 21,* 471–480.

Brody, E. M. (1985). Parent care as a normative family stress. *The Gerontologist, 21,* 19–29.

Brody, E. M. (1990). *Women in the middle.* New York: Springer.

Brody, E. M., & Brody, S. J. (1981). New directions in health and social supports for the aging. In M. A. Lewis (Ed.), *The aging: Medical and social supports in the decade of the 80s* (pp. 35–48). New York: Fordham University Third Age Center.

Burton, L., & DeVries, C. (1992). Challenges and rewards: African American grandparents as surrogate parents. *Generations, 17,* (3), 17–24.

Cantor, M. H. (1975a). Life space and the social support system of the inner city elderly of New York. *The Gerontologist, 15,* 23–27.

Cantor, M. H. (1975b). *The formal and informal social support system of older New*

Yorkers. Paper presented at the International Congress of Gerontology, Jerusalem, Israel.

Cantor, M. H. (1977). *Neighbors and friends: An overlooked resource in the informal system*. Paper presented at the Meeting of The Gerontological Society of America, San Francisco, CA.

Cantor, M. H. (1979a). The informal support system of New York's inner city elderly: Is ethnicity a factor? In D. E. Gelfand & A. J. Kutzik (Eds.), *Ethnicity and aging: Theory, research, and policy* (pp. 153–174). New York: Springer.

Cantor, M. H. (1979b). Neighbors and friends: An overlooked resource in the informal support system. *Research on Aging, 1,* 434–463.

Cantor, M. H. (1980). The informal support system, its relevance in the lives of the elderly. In E. Borgotta & M. McCluskey (Eds.), *Aging and society* (pp. 111–145). Beverly Hills, CA: Sage.

Cantor, M. H. (1981a). The extent and intensity of the informal support system among New York's inner city elderly. In *Strengthening social supports for the aging*. New York: Community Service Society.

Cantor, M. H. (1981b). *Social care for the aged in the United States: Issues and challenges*. Paper presented at the International Congress of Gerontology, Hamburg.

Cantor, M. H. (1983). Strain among caregivers: A study of experience in the United States. *The Gerontologist, 23,* 597–624.

Cantor, M. H. (1985). *The interface between informal and formal supports: A systems approach to social care for the elderly*. Paper presented at the International Congress of Gerontology, New York, NY.

Cantor, M. H. (1989). Social care: Family and community support systems. *Annals of the American Academy of Political and Social Sciences, 503,* 99–112.

Cantor, M. H. (1991). Family and community: Changing roles in an aging society: Donald P. Kent Award Lecture. *The Gerontologist, 31,* 337–346.

Cantor, M. H. (1992). Families and caregiving in an aging society. *Generations, 17,* 69–70.

Cantor, M. H. (1994). Family caregiving and social care. In M. H. Cantor (Ed.), *Family caregiving: Agenda for the future* (pp. 1–8). San Francisco, CA: American Society on Aging.

Cantor, M. H., & Brennan, M. (1993a). The elderly of New York City: A demographic and economic profile. *Growing older in New York City in the 1990s: A study of changing lifestyles, quality of life, and quality of care,* Vol. II. New York: The New York Center for Policy on Aging, the New York Community Trust.

Cantor, M. H., & Brennan, M. (1993b). New York City as a place of residence for older people: Life space, environment, and impact of crime. *Growing older in New York City in the 1990s: A study of changing lifestyles, quality of life, and quality of care,* Vol. IV. New York: The New York Center for Policy on Aging, the New York Community Trust.

Cantor, M. H., & Brennan, M. (1993c). Family and community support systems of older New Yorkers. *Growing older in New York City in the 1990s: A study of changing lifestyles, quality of life, and quality of care,* Vol. V. New York: The New York Center for Policy on Aging, the New York Community Trust.

Cantor, M. H., Brennan, M., & Sainz, A. (1994). The importance of ethnicity in the social support systems of older New Yorkers: A longitudinal perspective (1970 to 1990). *Journal of Gerontological Social Work, 22,* 95–128.

Cantor, M. H., Brook, K. H., & Mellor, M. J. (1986). *Growing old in suburbia: The experience of the Jewish elderly of Mt. Vernon.* New York: Brookdale Research Institute of the Third Age Center, Fordham University.

Cantor, M. H., & Mayer, M. J. (1978). Factors in differential utilization of services by urban elderly. *Journal of Gerontological Social Work, 1*(1), 42–61.

Cantor, M. H., & Hirshorn, B. (1989). Intergenerational transfers within the family context: Motivating factors and their implications for caregiving. *Women and Health, 14,* 39–51

Cantor, M. H., & Johnson, J. (1978). *The informal support system of the familyless elderly: Who takes over?* Paper presented at the symposium, "Informal Supports: Implications of Research for Policy and Practice," at the 31st Annual Meeting of The Gerontological Society of America, November, 1978, Dallas, TX.

Cantor, M. H., & Little, V. (1985). Aging and social care. In R. H. Binstock & E. Shanas (Eds.), *Handbook of aging and the social sciences* (2nd ed., pp. 745–772). New York: Van Nostrand Reinhold Co.

Chang, G. F., & White-Means, S. I. (1991). The men who care: An analysis of male primary caregivers who care for frail elderly at home. *Journal of Applied Gerontology, 10,* 343–358.

Chappel, N. L. (1985). Social support and the receipt of home care services. *The Gerontologist, 25,* 47–54.

Chappel, N. L. (1990). Aging and social care. In R. H. Binstock and L. K. George (Eds.), *Handbook of Aging and the Social Sciences* (pp. 338–454). San Diego, CA: Academic Press.

Chatters, L. M., Taylor, R. J. & Jackson, J. S. (1986). Aged black's choices for an informal help network. *Journal of Gerontology, 41,* 94–100.

Chatters, L. M., & Taylor, R. J. (1993). Intergenerational support: The provision of assistance to parents by adult children. In J. S. Jackson, L. M. Chatters, & R. J. Taylor (Eds.), *Aging in Black America* (pp. 69–83). Newbury Park, CA: Sage.

Clark, M., & Anderson, B. G. (1967). *Culture and aging.* Springfield, IL: Charles C. Thomas.

Climo, J. J. (1985). *Ambivalence in the elderly parent-adult child relationship: The Murray Avenue Jews.* Paper presented at the Meeting of the Anthropological Association, Washinton, D.C.

Climo, J. J. (1987). Elderly parents and adult children in the aging revolution. *The Reconstructionist, 53,* 9–13.

Cohen, R., & Rosen, S. (1992). *Organizational affiliations of American Jews: A research report.* New York: American Jewish Committee, S.

Commonwealth Fund. (1989a). *A survey of elderly Hispanics: Final report.* Baltimore: The Commonwealth Fund, Commission on Elderly People Living Alone.

Commonwealth Fund. (1989b). *Poverty and poor health among elderly Hispanic Americans.* Baltimore: The Commonwealth Fund, Commission on Elderly People Living Alone.

Connell, C. M., & Gibson, G. D. (1997). Racial, ethnic, and cultural differences in dementia caregiving: Review and analysis. *The Gerontologist, 37,* 355–364.

Connelly, J. R. (1980). An expanded outline and resource for teaching a course on the Native American Elderly. In G. Sherman (Ed.), *Curriculum guidelines in minority aging, Part IV.* Washington, DC: National Center on Black Aging.

Connidas, I. A., & Davis, L. (1990). Confidants and companions in later life: The place of family and friends. *The Journal of Gerontology, 45,* 141–149.

Connidas, I. A., & Davis, L. (1992). Confidants and companions: Choices in later life. *The Journal of Gerontology, 47,* S115–S122.

Consumer Reports. (1991). An empty promise to the elderly? *Consumer Reports, 56 (6),* 425–442.

Crimmins, E. M., Hayward, M. D., & Saito, Y. (1996). Differentials in active life expectancy in the older population of the United States. *Journals of Gerontology: Social Sciences, 51B,* S111–S120.

Cuban American National Council Inc. (1989). *The elusive decade of Hispanics.* Miami, FL: The Cuban American Policy Center.

Day, A. T. (1985). Who cares? Demographic trends challenge family care for the elderly. *Population Trends and Public Policy, no. 9.* Washington, DC: Population Reference Bureau.

Dobrof, R., & Litwak, E. (1977). *The maintenance of family ties of long-term care patients: Theory and guidance of practice.* Washington, DC: U. S. Government Printing Office/National Institute of Mental Health.

Dono, J. E., Falbe, C. L., Kail, B., Litwak, E., & Sherman, G. (1979). Primary groups in old age: Structure and function. *Research on Aging, 1,* 403–433.

Doty, P., Jackson, M. E., & Crown, W. (1998). The impact of female caregivers' employment status on patterns of formal and informal eldercare. *The Gerontologist, 38,* 331–341.

Dowd, J. J. (1978). Aging as exchange: A preface to theory. *The Gerontologist, 3,* 584–594.

Dowd, J. J. (1980). *Stratification among the aged.* Monterey, CA: Brooks-Cole Publishing Co.

DuKippo, F. (1980). *The elder American Indian.* San Diego, CA: The University Center on Aging, San Diego State University.

Dumpson, J. R., Dobrof, R., Cantor, M. H., Gurland, B., Berkman, C., &

Brennan, M. (1993). *Growing older in New York City in the 1990s: A study of changing lifestyles, quality of life, and quality of care,* Vol. I. New York: New York Center for Policy on Aging, the New York Community Trust.

Dwyer, J. W., & Coward, R. T. (1991). A multivariate comparison of the involvement of adult sons versus daughters in the care of impaired parents. *Journal of Gerontology, 46,* S258–S269.

Fries, J. F. (1980). Aging, natural death, and the compression of morbidity. *New England Journal of Medicine, 303,* 130.

Fries, J. F. (1989). The compression of morbidity: Near or far? *Milbank Quarterly, 67,* 208.

Gelfand, D. E., & Barreci, C. M. (1987). *Ethnic dimensions of aging.* New York: Springer.

Gelfand, D. E., & Kutzik, A. J. (1979). *Ethnicity and aging: Theory, research and policy.* New York: Springer.

Georges, E. (1990). Pathways to political participation of recent immigrants: Dominicans in New York City. In H. Romo (Ed.), *New directions for Latino public policy research.* Austin, TX: The Center for Mexican American Studies, University of Texas at Austin.

Gibson, R. C. (1993). The Black American retirement experience. In J. S. Jackson, L. M. Chatters, & R. J. Taylor (Eds.), *Aging in Black America* (pp. 277–297). Newbury Park, CA: Sage.

Glicksman, A., & Koropeckyj-Cox, T. (1994). Jewish aged in the United States: Sociodemographic and socioeconomic characteristics. In Z. Harel, D. Biegel, & D. Guttman (Eds.), *Jewish aged in the United States* (pp. 23–45). New York: Springer.

Goldstein (1993). *Profile of American Jewry: Insights from the 1990 national Jewish population survey.* New York: Center for Jewish Studies, City University of New York.

Graebner, W. (1980). *A history of retirement.* New Haven, CT: Yale University Press.

Gratton, B., & Wilson, V. (1988). Family support systems and the minority elderly: A cautionary analysis. *Journal of Gerontological Social Work, 13,* 81–93.

Greeley, A. M. (1974). *Ethnicity in the United States: A preliminary reconnaissance.* New York: Wiley.

Gurian, B. S., & Cantor, M. H. (1978). Mental health and community support systems for the elderly. In G. Usdin & C. Hofling (Eds.), *Aging: The process and the people* (pp. 184–205). New York: Brunner-Mazel.

Gurland, B. G., Dean, L., Gurland, R., & Cook, D. (1978). Personal time dependency in the elderly of New York: Findings from the U. S. - U. K. Cross-National Geriatric Community Study. In *Dependency in the elderly of New York City* (pp. 9–45). New York: Community Council of Greater New York.

Hagestad, G. O. (1986). The aging society as a content for family life. *Daedalus, 115,* 119–139.

Hanreider, B. D. (1992a). *The older population in New York City: Changes in size and age, 1980 to 1990.* New York: City of New York, Department for the Aging.

Hanreider, B. D. (1992b). *The older population in New York City: Changes in race, Hispanic origin and age, 1980 to 1990.* New York: City of New York, Department for the Aging.

Harel, Z. (1986). Ethnicity and aging: Implications for service organizations. In L. Hayes, R. A. Kalish, & D. Guttman (Eds.), *European-American elderly: A guide for practitioners.* New York: Springer.

Harel, Z., Biegel, D., & Guttman, D. (Eds.) (1994). *Jewish aged in the United States and Israel.* New York: Springer.

Harel, Z., & Noelker, L. S. (1995). Service vulnerability and long-term care. In Z. Harel & R. E. Dunkle (Eds.), *Matching people with services in long-term care* (pp. 5–21). New York: Springer.

Harel, Z., & Kart, C. (1994). Jewish aged: Diverse ethnic and national origins. In Z. Harel, D. Biegel, & D. Guttman (Eds.), *Jewish aged in the United States* (pp. 5–21). New York: Springer.

Hareven, T. K. (Ed.) (1978). *Transitions: The family and the life course in historical perspective.* New York: Academic Press.

Hareven, T. K. (1992). Family and generational relations in the later years: A historical perspective. *Generations, 17,* (3) 7–16.

Harris, P. B. (1998). Listening to caregiving sons: Misunderstood realities. *The Gerontologist, 38,* 342–352.

Hayes, G. I., Kalish, R. A., & Guttman, D. (1986). *European-American elderly: A guide for practitioners.* New York: Springer.

Hays, J. C., Fillenbaum, G. G., Gold, D. T., Shanley, M. C., & Blazer, D. (1995). Black-White and urban-rural differences in stability of household composition among elderly persons. *Journal of Gerontology: Social Sciences, 50B,* S301–S311.

Herz, F. M., & Rosen, E. J. (1982). Jewish families. In M. McGoldrick, J. K. Pearce, & J. Giordano (Eds.), *Ethnicity and family therapy* (1st ed., pp. 207–223). New York: Guilford Press.

Himes, C. L. (1992). Social demography of contemporary families. *Generations, 17,* (3) 13–16.

Himes, C. L., Hogan, D. P., & Eggebeen, D. J. (1996). Living arrangements of minority elders. *Journal of Gerontology: Social Sciences, 51B,* S42–S48.

Hollingshead, A. B. (1957). *Two Factor Index of Social Position.* New Haven, CT: Yale Station.

Horowitz, A. H. (1985). Family caregiving to the frail elderly. In C. E. Eisdorfer, M. P. Lawton, & G. Maddox (Eds.), *Annual Review of Gerontology and Geriatrics, Vol. V* (pp. 194–246). New York: Springer.

Horowitz, A. H., & Dobrof, R. (1982). *The role of families in providing long-term care to the frail and chronically ill elderly living in the community.* Final report submitted to the Health Care Financing Administration (HCFA). New York: Brookdale Center on Aging of Hunter College, City University of New York.

Horowitz, A. H., & Shindelman, L. (1982). Reciprocity and affection: Past influences on current caregiving. *Journal of Gerontological Social Work, 5,* 5–20.

Horowitz, B. (1993). *United Jewish Appeal - Federation of Jewish Philanthropies 1991 New York Jewish population study.* New York: United Jewish Appeal -Federation of Jewish Philanthropies.

Hudson, R. B. (1998a). Privatizing old-age benefits: Re-emergent ideology encounters organized interest. In J. Gonyea (Ed.), *Restructuring Social Security and Medicare: Understanding privatization and risk* (pp. 11–19). Washington, DC: The Gerontological Society of America.

Hudson, R. B. (1998b). Public vs. private: Successes and failures. *The Public Policy and Aging Report, 9,* (2), 1–4.

Ingersoll-Dayton, B., & Antonucci, T. C. (1989). Reciprocal and non-reciprocal social support: Contrasting sides of intimate relationships. *Journal of Gerontology: Social Sciences, 43,* 65–73.

Jackson, J. S. (1980). *Minorities and aging.* Belmont, CA: Wadsworth.

Jackson, J. J. (1985). Race, national origin, ethnicity and aging. In R. H. Binstock & E. Shanas (Eds.), *Handbook of aging and the social sciences* (2nd ed., pp. 264–304) New York: Van Nostrand Reinhold.

Jackson, J. S., Taylor, R. L.. &. Chatters, L. M., (1993). Roles and resources of the Black elderly. In J. S. Jackson, L. M. Chatters, & R. J. Taylor (Eds.), *Aging in Black America* (pp. 1–18). Newbury Park, CA: Sage.

Jayakody, R. (1993). Neighborhoods and neighbor relations. In J. S. Jackson, L. M. Chatters, & R. J. Taylor (Eds.), *Aging in Black America* (pp. 21–37). Newbury Park, CA: Sage.

Johnson, C. L. (1985). Dyadic family relations and social support. *The Gerontologist, 23,* 372–383.

Johnson, C. L., & Catalano, D. (1983). A longitudinal study of family supports to impaired elderly. *The Gerontologist, 23,* 612–618.

Kahana, E., & Kahana, B. (1984). Jews. In E. Palmore (Ed.), *Handbook of the aged in the United States.* Westport, CT: Greenwood Press.

Kahn, R. L. (1994). Social support: Content, causes and consequences. In R. Abeles, H. Gift, & M. Ory (Eds.), *Aging and quality of life.* New York: Springer.

Kahn, R. L., & Antonucci, T. C. (1980). Convoys over the life course: Attachment roles and social supports. In P. B. Baltes & O. G. Brim (Eds.), *Life Span Development and Behavior* (pp. 253–286). New York: Academic Press.

Kahn, R. L., & Antonucci, T. C. (1984). *Supports of the elderly: Family, friends, professionals.* Final Report to the National Institute on Aging. Washington, DC: U. S. Government Printing Office.

Kassner, E., & Bectal, R. (1998). *Midlife and older Americans with disabilities: A chartbook.* Washington, DC: Public Policy Institute, AARP.

Keefe, S. E., & Padilla, A. M. (1987). *Chicano ethnicity.* Albuquerque, NM: University of New Mexico Press.

Kendig, H. L. (Ed.) (1986). *Ageing and families: A support network perspective.* Sydney, Australia: Allen-Unwin.

Kendig, H. L., & Rowland, D. T. (1983). Family support of the Australian aged: A comparison with the United States. *The Gerontologist, 23,* 643–649.

Klaff, V. Z. (1987). *Residence as a variable in Jewish community life.* Paper presented at the Meeting of the Association of Jewish Studies, Boston, MA.

Kobrin, F. E. (1983). Fall in household size and rise of the individual. In M. Gordon (Ed.), *The American family in social-historical perspective.* New York: St. Martin's Press.

Kosmin, B. A., Goldstein, S., Waksberg, J., Lerer, N., Keysar, A., & Scheckner, J. (1991). *Highlights of the Council of Jewish Federations 1990 National Jewish Population Survey.* New York: Council of Jewish Federations.

Kovar, A. (1988). Family caregiving to the frail elderly. In C. Eisdorfer (Ed.), *Annual Review of Gerontology and Geriatrics, Vol. 5.* New York: Springer.

Levin, J. S., Taylor, R. J., & Chatters, L. M. (1994). Race and gender differences in religiosity among older adults: Findings from four national surveys. *Journal of Gerontology: Social Sciences, 49,* S137–S145.

Lewis, R. (1998). Boomers may spend their retirement working. *AARP Bulletin, 39 (7),* 8.

Litwak, E. (1965). Extended kin relations in an industrial democratic society. In E. Shanas & G. Streib (Eds.), *Social structures and the family: Generational relations* (pp.290–326). Englewood Cliffs, NJ: Prentice-Hall.

Litwak, E. (1978). Agency and family linkages in providing services. In D. Thursz & J. Vigilante (Eds.), *Reaching people: The structure of neighborhood services, Vol. III. Social Service Delivery Systems: An International Annual* (pp. 59–95). Beverly Hills, CA: Sage.

Litwak, E. (1985). *Helping older people. The complimentary roles of informal networks and social systems.* New York: The Guilford Press.

Litwak, E., & Messeri, P. (1989). Organizational theory, social supports and mortality rates: A theoretical convergence. *American Sociological Review, 54,* 49–67

Litwak, E., & Meyer, H. (1966). A balance theory of coordination between bureaucratic organizations and community primary groups. *Administrative Sciences Quarterly, 112,* 31–56.

Litwak, E., & Szekebyi, I. (1969). Primary group structures and their functions: Kin, neighbors, and friends. *American Sociological Review, 34,* 54–64.

Liu, K., & Manton, K. G. (1994). Changes in home care use by disabled elderly persons: (1982–1989). *CRS Report for Congress.* Washington, DC: Congressional Research Service, Library of Congress.

Longino, C., Soldo, B. J., & Manton, K. G. (1990). Demography of aging in the United States. In K. Ferraro (Ed.), *Gerontology: Issues and perspectives.* New York: Springer.

Lopata, H. (1975). Support systems and elderly urbanites: Chicago of the 1970s. *The Gerontologist, 15,* 35–41.

Luckey, I. (1994). African American elders: The support network of generational kin. *Families in Society: The Journal of Contemporary Human Services, 75*, 82–89.

Maldonado, D., Jr. (1990). The Hispanic elderly: Vulnerability in old age. In *Aging and old age in diverse populations: Research papers presented at minority affairs initiative empowerment conferences.* Washington, DC: American Association of Retired Persons.

Manton, K. G. (1988). Planning long-term care for the heterogeneous older populations. *Annual Review of Gerontology and Geriatrics, Vol 8.* New York: Springer.

Manton, K. G. (1989). Disability policy: Restoring socioeconomic independence. *The Milbank Quarterly, 67* (2).

Manton, K. G., Corder, L. S., & Stallard, E. (1993). Estimates of change in chronic disability and institutional incidence and prevalence rates in U. S. populations from the 1982, 1984, and 1989 National Long-Term Care Survey. *Journal of Gerontology, Social Sciences, 49*, S153–S166.

Manton, K. G., Corder, L., & Stallard, E. (1997). Chronic disability trends in elderly United States populations. *Proceedings of the National Academy of Sciences, 94*, 2593–2598.

Manton, K. G., & Liu, K. (1984). *The future growth of the long-term care population: Projections based on the 1977 National Nursing Home Survey and the 1982 Long-term Care Survey.* Paper presented at the Third National Leadership Conference on Long-term Care Issues. Washington, D.C.

Manton, K. G., & Soldo, B. J. (1985). Dynamic health changes in the oldest old: New perspectives and evidence. *Milbank Quarterly, 63(2)*, 206–285.

Markides, K. S. (1983). Minority aging. In M. W. Riley, B. B. Hess & K. Bond (Eds.), *Aging in society-selected reviews and recent research* (pp. 115–137). Hillsdale, N.J.: Lawrence Erlbaum Associates.

Markides, K. S., Boldt, J, & Pray, L. A. . (1986). Source of helping and intergenerational solidarity: A three-generations study of Mexican-Americans. *Journal of Gerontology, 41*, 506–511.

Markides, K. S., Liang, J., & Jackson, J. S. (1990). Race, ethnicity, and aging, conceptual and methodological issues. In R. Binstock, & L. K. George (Eds.), *Handbook of aging and the Social Sciences* (3rd ed.). San Diego: Academic Press.

Markides, K. S., & Mindel, C. H. (1987). *Aging and ethnicity.* Newbury Park, CA: Sage.

Mathematica Policy Research Inc. (1986). *The evaluation of the National Long-term Care Demonstration Project: Final report.* Princeton, NJ: Author.

McCullock, J. B. (1990). The relationship of intergenerational reciprocity of and to the morale of older parents: Equity and exchange theory comparisons. *The Journal of Gerontology, 45*, 150–153.

Messeri, P., Silverstein, M., & Litwak, E. (1993). Choosing optimal support groups: A review and reformulation. *Journal of Health and Social Behavior, 34*, 122–137.

Met Life Mature Market Group & National Alliance for Caregiving (1997). *The Met Life Study of Employer Costs for Working Caregivers* (pp. 1–7). Westport, CT: Met Life Mature Market Group.

Miner, S. (1995). Racial differences in family support and formal service utilization among older persons: A nonrecursive model. *Journal of Gerontology: Social Sciences, 50B,* S143–S153.

Moody, H. R. (1998). *Aging concepts and controversies.* Thousand Oaks, CA: Pine Forge Press.

Morris, R., & Hanson, J. E. (1997). A decade-long drift to public conservatism. Redefining the federal roles in social welfare, anticipating the future and preparing for it. In *National government and social welfare.* Westport, CT: Auburn House.

Mutran, E. (1985). Intergenerational support among Blacks and Whites: Response to cultural or socioeconomic differences. *Journal of Gerontology, 40,* 382–389.

Myerhoff, B. (1978). *Number our days.* New York: C. P. Dutton.

The National Alliance for Caregiving (1997). *A National Survey of Caregivers Conducted by ICR Survey Research Group* (pp. 1–24). Bethesda, MD: The National Alliance for Caregiving.

National Council of La Raza. (1992). *State of Hispanic America 1991: An overview.* Washington, DC: National Council of La Raza.

National Institute on Aging. (1995). *Aging trends and forecasts.* Washington, DC: Population Reference Bureau, Author.

Peters, G. R., Hoyt, D. R., Babchuk, N., Kaiser, M., & Iijima, Y. (1987). Primary support systems of the aged. *Research on Aging, 9,* 392–416.

Preston, S. (1984). Children and the elderly: Divergent paths for American dependents. *Demography, 19,* 549–565.

Reinhardt, J. P. (1996). The importance of friendship and family support in adaptation to chronic vision impairment. *Journal of Gerontology: Psychological Sciences, 51B,* P268–278.

Riley, M. W. (1983). The family in an aging society: A matrix of latent relationships. *Journal of Family Issues, 4,* 439–454.

Rivlin, A. M., & Weiner, J. M. (1988). *Caring for the disabled elderly: Who will pay?* Washington, DC: The Brookings Institute.

Roberto, K. A. (1989). Exchanges and equity in friendships. In R. C. Adams & R. Blieszner (Eds.), *Older adult friendships: Structure and process* (pp. 147–165). Newbury Park, CA: Sage.

Rodriguez, O. (1987). *Hispanics and human services: Help-seeking in the inner city.* Bronx, NY: Hispanic Research Center, Fordham University.

Rodriguez, O., & Mahard O'Donnell, R. (1992). Help-seeking and the use of mental health services by the Hispanic elderly. In D. K. Padgett (Ed.), *Handbook on ethnicity, aging, and mental health.* Westport, CT: Greenwood Press.

Rogg, E. M., & Cooney, R. S. (1980). *Adaptation and adjustment of Cubans: West*

New York, New Jersey. Bronx, NY: Hispanic Research Center, Fordham University.

Rogler, L. H., Malgady, R. G., Costantino, G., & Blumenthal, R. (1987). What do culturally sensitive mental health services mean? The case of Hispanics. *American Psychologist, 42,* 565–570.

Romo, H. (1990). Public policy research on contemporary Latino issues. In H. Romo (Ed.), *New directions for Latino public policy and research.* Austin, TX: The Center for Mexican American Studies, University of Texas at Austin.

Rook, K. S. (1987). Reciprocity of social exchange and social satisfaction among older women. *Journal of Personality and Social Psychology, 52,* 145–154.

Rook, K. S. (1989). Strains in older adults' friendships. In R. C. Adams & R. Blieszner (Eds.), *Older adult friendships: Structure and process* (pp. 166–194). Newbury Park, CA: Sage.

Rook, K. S. (1996). Compensatory processes in the social networks of older adults. In G. Pierce, B. Sarason, & I. G. Sarason (Eds.), *The handbook of social support and family relationships* (pp.219–248). New York: Plenum Press.

Rosen, E. J., & Weltman, S. F. (1996). Jewish families: An overview. In M. McGoldrick, J. Giordano, & J. K. Pearce (Eds.), *Ethnicity and family therapy* (2nd ed., pp. 611–629). New York: Guilford Press.

Rosenmayr, L. (1977). The family as a source of help for the elderly. In E. Shanas & M. Sussman (Eds.), *Family, bureaucracy and the elderly* (pp. 132–157). Durham, NC: Duke University Press.

Rosenthal, C. (1984). *Intergenenerational solidarity in later life: Ethnic contrast in Jewish and Anglo families.* Paper presented at the 37th Annual Meeting of The Gerontological Society of America, San Antonio, TX.

Rowe, J. W., & Kahn, R. L. (1998). *Successful aging.* New York: Pantheon Books.

Rubinstein, R. L. (1994). The Aging in the Jewish community: Community, cultural and life-course factors. In Z. Harel, D. Biegel, & D. Guttaman (Eds.), *Jewish aged in the United States and Israel.* (pp. 61–79). New York: Springer Publishing Co.

Sanua, V. D. (1981). Psychopathology and social deviance among Jews. *Journal of Jewish Community Service* LVIII, (1), 12–23.

Shanas, E. (1967). Family help patterns and social class in three countries. *Journal of Marriage and the Family, 29,* 257–266.

Shanas, E. (1979a). Social myth as hypothesis: The case of the family relations of older people. *The Gerontologist, 19,* 3–9.

Shanas, E. (1979b). The family as a social support system in old age. *The Gerontologist, 19,* 169–174.

Shanas, E., Towsend, P, Widderburn, D., Friis, H., Milhoj, P., & Stehouver J. (Eds.) (1968). *Old people in three industrial societies.* New York: Atherton Press.

Siegel, J, & Taeuber, C. M. (1986). Demographic dimensions of an aging population. In A. Pifer and D. L. Bronte (Eds.), *Our aging society: Paradox and promise.* New York: Norton.

Smith, J. M. (1993). Function and supportive roles of church and religion. In J. S. Jackson, L. M. Chatters, & R. J. Taylor (Eds.), *Aging in Black America.* Newbury Park, CA: Sage.

Smith, M. H., & Longino, C. F. (1995). People using long-term care services. In Z. Harel & R. E. Dunkle (Eds.), *Matching people with services in long-term care* (pp. 45–48). New York: Springer.

Soldo, B. J., & Manton, K. G. (1985a). Demographic challenges for socioeconomic planning. *Socio-Economic Planning Sciences, 19,* 227–247.

Soldo, B. J., & Manton, K. G. (1985b). Health status and service needs of the oldest old. *The Milbank Quarterly, 63,* 286–319.

Soldo, B. J., Wolf, D, & Agree, E. M. (1990). Family households and care arrangements of frail older women: A structural analysis. *The Journal of Gerontology, 45,* 238–249.

Spence, S. A. (1991). Social support for the black elderly: Is there a link between informal and formal assistance? *Journal of Sociology and Social Welfare, 18,* 149–158.

Stack, C. (1974). *All our kin: Strategies for survival in the black community.* New York: Harper & Row.

Stephens, S., & Christianson, J. (1986). *Informal care of the elderly.* Lexington, MA: D.C. Heath & Co.

Stohs, J. H. (1994). Alternative ethics in employed women's' household labor. *Journal of Family Issues, 15,* 550–561.

Stoller, E. P., & Pugliesi, R. L. (1988). Informal networks of community-based elderly: Changes in composition over time. *Research on Aging, 10,* 499–516.

Stone, R. I., Cafferata, G. L., & Sangl, J. (1987). Caregivers of the frail elderly: A national profile. *The Gerontologist, 27,* 616–625.

Stone, R. I., & Kemper, P. (1989). Spouses and children of disabled elders: How large a constituency for long-term care reform? *The Milbank Quarterly, 67,* 485–506.

Sussman, M. B. (1965). Relations of adult children with their parents. In E. Shanas & G. Streib (Eds.), *Social structure and the family: Generational relations* (pp. 62–92). Englewood Cliffs, NJ: Prentice-Hall.

Sussman, M. B. (1976). The family life of old people. In R. H. Binstock & E. Shanas (Eds.), *Handbook of aging and the social sciences* (1st ed., pp. 218–244). New York: Van Nostrand Rheinhold Co.

Sussman, M. B., & Burchinall, L. (1962). Parental aid to married children: Implications for family functioning. *Marriage and Family Living, 24,* 320–332.

Taeuber, C. M. (1989). *The issues facing the White House Conference on Aging.* Oakland, NJ: Scott, Foresman.

Taeuber, C. M. (1990). Diversity: The dramatic reality. In S. Bass, E. A. Kutz, & F. M. Torres-Gil (Eds.), *Diversity in aging.* Glenview, IL: Scott, Foresman.

Taeuber, C. M., & Smith, D. (1988). *Minority elderly: An overview of demographic characteristics and 1990 census plans.* Paper presented at the National Council on Aging Symposium, Washington, D.C.

Taylor, R. J., & Chatters, L. M. (1991). Extended family networks of older Black adults. *Journals of Gerontology: Social Sciences, 46,* S210–S217.

Tolsdorf, C. C. (1976). Social networks, support and coping: An exploratory study. *Family Process,* 15, 407–417.

Torres-Gil, F. (1990). Aging in Hispanic America. In *Aging and old age in diverse populations: Research papers presented at Minority Affairs Initiative Empowerment Conferences.* Washington, DC: American Association of Retired Persons.

Towsend, P. (1963). *The family life of old people: An inquiry in East London.* London: Penguin.

Towsend, P. (1968). The structure of the family. In E. Shanas, P. Towsend, D. Widderburn, H. Friis, P. Milhoj, & J. Stehouver (Eds.), *Old people in three industrial societies* (pp. 132–176). New York: Atherton Press.

Troll, L. E. (1987). Mother-daughter relationships through the life span. In S. Oskamp (Ed.), *Family processes and problems* (pp. 284–303). Newbury Park, CA: Sage.

Troll, L. E. (1971). The family at later life: A decade review. *Journal of Marriage and Family, 33,* 263–290.

Troll, L. E. (1989). New thoughts on old families. *The Gerontologist, 28,* 586–591.

Troll, L. E., Miller, S. J., & Atchley, R. C. (1979). *Families in later life.* Belmont, CA: Wadsworth Publishing Co.

Uhlenberg, P., & Myers, M. P. (1986). Divorce and the elderly. In L. E. Troll (Ed.), *Family issues in current gerontology.* New York: Springer.

U. S. Census Bureau. (1985). *Projections of the populations of the United States by age, sex, and race: 1988–2080.* Series P-25, No. 1018. Washington, DC: U.S. Government Printing Office.

U. S. Census Bureau. (1990). *Census of Population and Housing.* Washington, DC: U. S. Department of Commerce

U. S. Census Bureau. (1992). *The Asian and Pacific Islander population in the United States: March 1991 and 1990.* Current Population Reports. Washington, DC: U. S. Government Printing Office.

U. S. Census Bureau. (1995). *Sixty-five Plus in the United States.* Washington, DC: U. S. Department of Commerce

U. S. Comptroller General. (1977). *The well-being of older people in Cleveland, Ohio.* Washington, DC: General Accounting Office, HCD. 70–77.

U. S. Department of Health and Human Services. *1982 National Long Term Care Survey.* 1982 National Technical Information Service Accession Nos. P.B.-86-161775 and P. B. 86-16173.

U. S. General Accounting Office. (1977). *Home health and the need for a national policy to provide for the elderly.* Report no. HRD-78-19. Washington, DC: Author.

Valle, R., & Mendoza, L. (1987). *The elderly Latino.* San Diego, CA: The Companille Press, San Diego State University.

Verbrugge, L. M. (1984). Longer life but worsening health? Trends in health and mortality of middle-age and older persons. *The Milbank Quarterly, 62,* 475–519.

Verbrugge, L. M. (1989). The dynamics of population aging and health. In S. J. Lewis (Ed.), *Aging and health: Linking research and public policy.* Chelsea, MI: Lewis Publishers.

Wallace, S. P., Campbell, K., & Lew-Ting, C. (1994). Structural barriers to the use of formal in-home services by elderly Latinos. *Journal of Gerontology: Social Sciences, 49,* S253–S263.

Watkins, S. C., Menken, J. A., & Bongaarts, J. (1987). Demographic foundations of family change. *American Sociological Review, 52,* 346–358.

Watkins, S. C., Menken, J. A., & Bongaarts, J. (1989). Demographic foundations of family change. *American Sociological Review, 52,* 346–358.

Wiener, J. M., & Stevenson, D. G. (1997). *Long-term care for the elderly and state health policy, Series A, No. A-17.* Washington, DC: The Urban Institute.

Zborowski, M., & Herzog, E. (1952). *Life is with people: The culture of the Shtel.* New York: Schocken.

Appendix A

Study Methodologies of The Elderly in the Inner City of New York (1970) and Growing Older in New York City in the 1990s

THE ELDERLY IN THE INNER CITY OF NEW YORK [1970]

The sample frame was designed to provide population parameters of the 60-years-old and older population living in the 26 designated poverty neighborhoods in the five boroughs of New York City (Manhattan, the Bronx, Queens, Brooklyn, and Staten Island). Poverty areas consisted of multiple census tracts, and two frames were constructed consisting of an inner frame of the most distressed ghetto neighborhoods (which tended to have large proportions of Black and Latino residents) as well as outer frames with high proportions of poverty households (having greater proportions of White residents). Using this frame, a stratified probability sample of 1552 individuals was drawn using a single-stage procedure. Individuals in the outer poverty areas as well as those residing in public and public-assisted housing units were oversampled to obtain adequate numbers for subgroup analysis; the total sample was then weighted to adjust for this oversampling.

Sample frames were constructed using maps, U. S. Bureau of the Census poverty area definitions, and contiguous areas of census tracts constituting poverty areas according to New York City Human Resource Administration definitions. Stratification was conducted by outer versus inner poverty areas, New York City borough within-frames, poverty areas within boroughs, and new public housing starts.

- Each frame and subframe was divided into 18 thin zones or equal segments, consisting of 46,510 housing units for the inner frame and 19,666 in the outer frame. For the public housing subframe, one thin zone was created for each sample frame.
- Five sampling points were randomly selected within each thin zone, resulting in a total of 190 clusters, which in fact constituted five matched samples of 38 clusters. One hundred eighteen clusters were included in the final sample.
- Location was determined according to census tract and block with the randomly selected household number within each cluster. This key address was used to form contiguous block area clusters of approximately 400 households. These were then divided into four segments of 100 households.
- One segment was randomly selected from each cluster, and households were contacted to screen for eligible respondents. Seventy-two percent of those contacted provided age information, for a total of 2180 eligible respondents. (If more than one respondent was identified in a household, one was randomly selected.)
- Up to six call-backs were used to complete 1552 in-person interviews, resulting in a response rate of 71%.

GROWING OLDER IN NEW YORK CITY IN THE 1990S

A probability sample of all noninstitutionalized persons aged 65 years and older in New York City served as the sample frame. The sample frame was constructed using a list of Medicare enrollees supplied through the cooperation of the Health Care Financing Administration (HCFA) and was comprised of 5% of Medicare beneficiaries in New York City. Because of the desire to include a sufficient number of persons aged 75 years or more and ethnic minorities (i.e., Latinos and Blacks), these groups were oversampled to insure sufficient numbers for subgroup analysis. Potential Latino respondents were identified using a list of 12,500 Spanish surnames obtained from the U.S. Bureau of the Census and compared by computer with the sample frame list. Final determination of ethnicity and age was made during the in-person interview.

A two-stage clustering procedure was used to obtain the final study sample. In the first phase, 150 names were selected from the sample frame as primary sampling units (PSUs). Systematic selection was used within PSUs using a random number. Fourteen additional names were chosen based on geographic proximity to each PSU, ties were decided on the numerically closest address. These additional names were chosen to account for inability to contact potential respondents as well as refusals. Seventy-five additional PSUs in predominantly Black and Latino communities were also selected to provide sufficient numbers in the frame to oversample these groups. The goal was to complete one-third or five interviews among households identified in the PSUs. The first sampling stage resulted in 1114 completed interviews.

While the first sampling stage obtained adequate numbers of older Whites, insufficient numbers of elderly Latinos and Blacks were interviewed. Therefore, the second sampling stage required identifying the primarily Black and Latino PSUs and selecting an additional 15 names from that location using the same technique as the first stage. Elderly Whites identified at this second stage were also included. An additional 456 interviews were completed , for a total of 1570.

Two invitational letters were sent to each potential respondent, the first was an introduction from HCFA endorsing the study and the second was from the field team. Potential respondents were then either contacted by telephone, in-person, or through a drop-off letter if they did not have a phone and were not home during the attempt to contact them. If after four attempts no contact was made, the name was moved to a nonresponse list and an additional name was selected for the PSU using procedures outlined above. Persons who refused to participate or terminated the interview were contacted by a different individual to see if a completed interview could be obtained. If this second attempt was unsuccessful an additional name was selected for that PSU.

Fifty-two interviewers from Louis Harris and Associates conducted the in-person interviews after having received extensive training. Interviews were conducted in either English or Spanish and lasted approximately 1.5 hours. The response rate was calculated by Louis Harris and Associates at 62%. Because minority and older elderly individuals were oversampled, the total sample of 1570 was weighted by age and ethnicity based on 1989 U.S. Bureau of the Census Data to make it representative of the population 65 years and older residing in New York City. This weighted sample consisted of 1577 individlluals.

Index

Page numbers followed by t indicate table.

Access issues. *See also* Pathways
  future recommendations, 299–300
  Latino elderly, 186–192
  future implications, 198–200
Acculturation. *See also* Nativity
  Latino elderly study, 140–141
Acculturation, Latino elderly study,
  142t, 173–176
Activities of daily living (ADLs). *See
  also* Instrumental support
  in care continuum, 260
  future implications of social care,
    264–265
  unmet formal need
    African American elderly study,
      248, 249t
    Jewish elderly study, 124t
    Latino elderly study, 184–185,
      184t
Additive model, 34
ADLs. *See* Activities of daily living
  (ADLs)
Adult children. *See* Children
Advice
  from child
    African American families, 230
    Jewish families, 96–97
    Latino families, 162
  from elderly parent
    African American families,
      228–229
    Jewish families, 94–95
Advocacy

  future implications for African
    American elderly, 253
  importance of in future, 298–299
  support preference, 51t, 52–53
    effect of race on, 56t
  unmet formal need
    African American elderly study,
      248, 249t
    Jewish elderly study, 124t
    Latino elderly study, 184t
Affective support, 44
African American children
  contact with parent, 223–225
  degree of closeness, 225
  intergenerational assistance, 219,
    225–231
  profile of, 222–223
    age, 222
    gender, 222
    geographic location, 222–223
African American elderly
  income, emergence of moderate-
    income elderly, 202,
    204–205
  preference on "critical incidents,"
    53–54, 55t–56t, 57–58
African American elderly study,
  201–253, 207, 209
  demographics of respondents,
    204–211, 208t
  formal support, 241–245, 244t,
    246t
  future implications, 240, 248–253

African American elderly study
    (continued)
  informal support, 218–240, 221t
    children, 220–231, 221t
    friends, 221t, 232–234
    grandchildren, 225–227
    neighbors, 221t, 234–235
    relatives, other, 221t, 232
    siblings, 221t, 231
    spouse, 220–221t
  living arrangements, 211–212
  socioeconomic status of respon-
    dents, 212–217
African Americans, demographics,
    United States, 201
Age
  African American elderly study
    of children, 222
    of friends, 233
    of respondent, 207, 208t
  Jewish elderly study
    of children, 89
    of friends, 103–104
    of respondent, 75, 76t
  Latino elderly study
    of children, 153–154
    of friends, 169
    of respondent, 140, 142t
Age composition, future of social
    care, Jewish elderly study,
    132–134
Alternative resource theory, for
    under utilization, 179–180
American Jewry, 66–67
Angel, J. L. & Hogan, D. P., 263
Antonucci, T., 27–30
Assistance
  child to parent
    African American elderly study,
      229–230
    Jewish families, 93–9595–97
    Latino elderly study, 161–163
  and functional impairment,
    20–23, 22t

high need elderly, Jewish elderly
    study, 125–128, 126t
Jewish ability to accept, 74
parent to child
  African American families, 219,
    227–229
  Jewish families, 93–95
  Latino families, 158–161
support preference
  1970 to 1990, 48–53, 50t–51t
  effect of race on, 53–58, 55t–56t
Asymmetrical model, 34

Barrier theory, for underutilization,
    180
Barriers
  future implications for formal
    support, 298
  to utilization, formal, Latino
    elderly study, 186–192
Bengtson, v, 38
Binstock, R., 291–292, 295
Birth rate, declining, and increased
    elderly
  population, 261–262
Black elderly. See African American
    elderly

Cantor, M.
  future of social care, 303
  Hierarchical-Compensatory
    model, 33, 36–37. See also
    Hierarchical-Compensatory
    model
  macro-level social care model,
    17–24, 18f, 22t, 30–31, 32t
  spouses as caregivers, 275–276
Cantor social care model, 17–24, 18t
  model comparison, 30–31, 32t
Chatters, L., et al., 40
Child care, caring for elderly and,
    277–282
Children. See also African American
    children; Jewish children;

Latino children
as informal support
African American elderly study,
220–231, 221t
Jewish elderly study, 88–98
Latino elderly study, 151–164,
152t
as primary caregiver, 276–282
future trends, 282–284
Choice. *See also* Preferences
gerontological research on, 38–43
Civil rights movement, implications
for African American
elderly, 204
Community based care. *See also*
Formal support
role of, 3–4
Community services
in Jewish community, 73–74
in Latino community, 197–200
Confidants. *See also* Friends
African American elderly study,
221t, 232–234
defined, 101
Jewish elderly study, 101–104
Latino elderly study, 152t, 167–170
Connidas, I. et al, 43
Contact
face-to-face. *See* Visitation patterns
telephone
African American elderly study,
with children, 224–225
Jewish elderly study
with children, 91–92
with friends, 103
Latino elderly study
with children, 156
with friends, 169–170
with siblings, 165–166
Continuum of care, functional ability and, 259–260
Convoy model of social care, 27–30
model comparison, 30–31, 32t
Counseling, unmet formal need for

African American elderly
study, 249t
Jewish elderly study, 124t
Latino elderly study, 184t, 185
Crisis intervention, by children
African American families, 230
Jewish families, 96
"Critical incidents," support
preference, 48–53, 50t–51t
effect of race on, 53–58, 55t–56t
Cuban-Americans, as Latino
population component,
137–138
Cultural barriers
future implications for Latino
elderly, 198
hierarchical regression model,
187–192, 189t–190t
Cultural diversity. *See* Diversity
Cultural pluralism, gerontology
and, 62
Cultural themes of, Jewish
community, 69–74
Culture, and assistance patterns,
African American elderly, 205

Daughters, as primary caregiver,
276–277
Dependency, value conflicts
regarding, 15–16
Disability
among minority elderly, 265–267
and future of social care, 264–267
reason for decline in, 265
Distributive justice, 25
Diversity
amongst African American
elderly, 202
future implications, 249–251
amongst Latino elderly, 136–138
future implications, 192–193
future of, 11
in gerontological research, 6
in United States, 61–62

Dominicans, as Latino population
  component, 137
Doty, P. et al, 279–281
Dowd, J., 25–27

Economic security, future implications for Latino elderly, 197
Economic well-being, perceptions of
  African American elderly study,
  216–217
  Jewish elderly study, 80t, 83
Education level, of respondent
  African American elderly study,
  208t, 209–210
  Jewish elderly study, 76t, 78
  Latino elderly study, 143, 145t
Elderly. *See also* African American
  elderly; Jewish elderly;
  Latino elderly
  minority
  disability amongst, 265–267
  future, demographics, 262–264
  moderately frail, current formal
  support, 286–288
  young, current formal support,
  285–286
Elderly in the Inner City of New
  York, The, landmark study.
  See 1970 study
Elderly New Yorkers. *See* New York
  City elderly
Elderly of future. *See also* Future
  trends
  characteristics, future implications,
  300–301
  trends, 260–680
Elderly population, demographics,
  future, 261
Emergency room, formal support
  utilization
  African American elderly study,
  244t
  Jewish elderly study, 115t, 117–118
Emotional support

perceptions of
  African American elderly study,
  237–239
  Jewish elderly, 110–111
  Latino elderly study, 177–178
  preference for, 51t, 52–53
  effect of race on, 56t
Employers, eldercare and, 282
Employment, caring for elderly and,
  277–282
Entitlements
  formal support utilization, 288
  African American elderly study,
  243, 244t
  Jewish elderly study, 115t
  Latino elderly study, 181, 182t
Equity theory, social care model. *See*
  Exchange theory
Ethnic diversity. *See* Diversity
Exchange theory
  model comparison, 30–31, 32t
  social care model, 25–27

Family. *See also* Kin
  attitudes about role in social care,
  283–284
  future implications, 268–284
  for African American elderly,
  252–253
  changing structure of, 268–272
  for Jewish elderly, 132
  for Latino elderly, 193–194,
  195–196
  importance of, African American
  elderly study, 203–204,
  218–219
  Jewish community and, 70–72
  as primary caregiver, 272–273
  in United States, 14–15
  history of, 270
Financial assistance
  from children
  African American families, 229
  Jewish families, 96

Latino families, 162
from parent, African American
 families, 229
Financing issues
for formal support, 292–297
options for long-term care,
 293–297
Formal support. *See also* Utilization
of formal support
African American elderly study,
 241–249
unmet needs, 247–248, 249t
utilization of, 241–245, 244t,
 246t
current status of, 285–288
financing issues, 292–297
future of, 285–304
macro level policy, 297
micro level policy, 297–301
history of, 289–291
Jewish elderly study, 111–125
need for, 112–113
unmet needs, 122–128, 124t
utilization of, 114–122, 115t
Latino elderly study, 179–192
unmet needs, 183–186, 184t
utilization of, 180–183, 182t
linkage with informal, 3–4,
 111–112, 179, 259–260,
 303–304
predictors for use of, African
 American elderly study,
 245, 246t
Frail elderly, assistance received, 21,
 22t, 23
Friends. *See also* Informal support
as informal support
African American elderly study,
 221t, 232–234
Jewish elderly study, 101–104
Latino elderly study, 152t,
 167–170
role in social care, 4
Task-Specific model and, 35

Fries, J., 266–267
Functional ability
continuum of care, 259–260
future implications of social care,
 264–265
of high need elderly, Jewish
 elderly study, 126–127, 126t
Functional element, 33
Functional impairment, and
assistance received, 20–23,
 22t
Functional support, Hierarchical-
Compensatory model, 37
Functionality, of child-parent
relationship, Jewish elderly
study, 90, 126t, 128
Future
of elderly, 260–680
of family, 268–284
of formal social care, 285–304
of informal social care, 257–284
Future implications
African American elderly study,
 240, 248–253
Jewish elderly study, 131–133
Latino elderly study, 192–200
Future trends
decline of disability, 264–267
higher proportion of elderly,
 261–264
social factors, 267–268

Gender
African American elderly study,
 207, 208t
children, 222
of elderly, implications for future,
 267–268
Jewish elderly study, 75–77, 76t
children, 89
Latino elderly study, 140, 142t
children, 153–154
Generational interdependence. *See
 also* Reciprocity

Generational interdependence
    (continued)
    African American families, 219,
        225–231
    Cantor social care model, 20
    effect on support preference, 1970
        to 1990, 53
    Jewish families, 71–72, 93–98
    Latino families, 159–164
Geographic location
    of children
        African American elderly study,
            222–223
        Jewish elderly study, 89–90
        Latino elderly study, 154
    of family, future implications for
        social care, 270–271
    of friends
        African American elderly study,
            233
        Jewish elderly study, 102–103
        Latino elderly study, 169
Gerontological research
    on elderly choice of support,
        38–43
    on social care, 5–6
Glicksman, A & Koropecky-Cox, T.,
    72
Graebner, W., 290
Grandchildren, informal support and
    African American elderly study,
        225–227
    Jewish elderly study, 98
    Latino elderly study, 157–159
Great Depression, history of formal
    support and, 285
Group identity, Jewish community,
    69–70
Growing Old in New York City in
    the 1990s, landmark study.
    See 1990 study

Hareven, T., 268, 270
Health
    perceived

African American elderly study,
    208t, 210
Jewish elderly study, 76t, 78
Latino elderly study, 141, 142t,
    143
relationship to socioeconomic
    status, 266
Health care
    formal support utilization
        African American elderly study,
            244t
        Jewish elderly study, 115t
        Latino elderly study, 182t
    future implications for Latino
        elderly, 196–197
    unmet formal need
        African American elderly study,
            248, 249t
        Jewish elderly study, 124t
        Latino elderly study, 184t, 185
Hierarchical-Compensatory model,
    36–38
    conceptual framework, 39
    model comparison, 43–46
Hierarchical regression model,
    Latino elderly study and,
        187–192, 189t–190t
    future implications, 198
Hierarchy of choice
    1970 to 1990 study results, 53
    Hierarchical-Compensatory
        model, 36
High assistance need, Jewish elderly
    study, 125–128, 126t
Hollingshead's (1957) Index of
    Social Position (ISP)
    African American elderly study,
        213
    Jewish elderly study, 79, 80t
    Latino elderly study, 143–144, 145t
Horowitz, B., 67–69
Hudson, R., 290–291

IADLs. *See* Instrumental activities of
    daily living (IADLs)

Immigration
  age at, Latino elderly, 138–139
  patterns
    Jewish population, 66–67
    Latino population, 136–138
Impairment level, assistance
    received and, 20–23, 22t
In-home services
  formal support utilization
    African American elderly study,
      243, 244t
    Jewish elderly study, 115t,
      118–120
    Latino elderly study, 181, 182t
  future importance of, 286–287
Income
  effect on assistance needed, 248,
    249t
  effect on primary caregiver, 281
  effect on support utilization,
    African American elderly
    study, 243–245, 244t
  future implications for African
    American elderly, 250–252
  level of
    African American elderly study,
      205, 206–207, 213–214
    Jewish elderly study, 80t, 81
    Latino elderly study, 144, 145t,
      146
  source of
    African American elderly study,
      215–216
    Jewish elderly study, 80t, 82–83
    Latino elderly study, 145t,
      146–147
Independence
  ability to maintain, 4–5
  support preference and, 48–49
  United States notion of, 13
Informal Caregivers Survey, 273
Informal social care, future of,
    257–284
Informal support. *See also* Family;
    Kin

African American elderly study,
    218–240, 221t
  children, 220–231, 221t
  friends, 221t, 232–234
  grandchildren, 225–227
  neighbors, 221t, 234–235
  relatives, other, 221t, 232
  siblings, 221t, 231
  spouse, 220–221t
Cantor social care model, 19–20
future of, 257–284
hierarchical regression model,
    187–192, 189t–190t
Jewish elderly study, 85–111
  child, 88–98
  friends, 101–104
  grandchild, 98
  neighbors, 104–107
  relatives, other, 99–101
  siblings, 99–100
  spouse, 86–87
Latino elderly study, 149–179
  children, 151–164, 152t
  friends, 152t, 167–170
  grandchildren, 157–159
  neighbors, 152t, 170–171
  relatives, other, 152t, 166–167
  siblings, 152t, 164–166
  spouse, 151, 152t
  unmet needs, 172
linkage with formal, 3–4, 111–112,
    179, 259–260, 303–304
perceptions of
  African American elderly study,
    236–239
  Jewish elderly study, 107–111
  Latino elderly study, 176–178
Information assistance. *See*
    Advocacy
Instrumental activities of daily
    living (IADLs). *See also*
    Instrumental support
  in care continuum, 260
  future implications of social care,
    264–265

Instrumental support, 44
  from child
    African American families, 230
    Jewish families, 96–97
    Latino families, 162
  from elderly parent
    African American families, 228
    Jewish families, 94
    Latino families, 160–161
  perceptions of
    African American elderly study,
      236–237
    Jewish elderly, 108–109
    Latino elderly study, 176–177
  preference for, 49, 50t–51t, 52
    effect of race on, 55t–56t
Intergenerational assistance
  African American families, 219,
    225–231
  Cantor social care model, 20
  Jewish families, 93–98
  Latino families, 159–164
"Intimacy at a distance," 268

Jewish children
  closeness, degree of, 92–93
  contact with parent, 90–92
  functionality of, 90
  implications for social care,
    129–131
  intergenerational assistance,
    93–98
  profile of, 88–93
    age, 89
    gender, 89
    geographic location, 89–90
Jewish community
  cultural themes of, 69–74
  future of social care, 133
  importance of community
    services, 73–74
  importance of family, 70–72
Jewish continuity, 84–85
Jewish elderly study, 65–134, 80t

demographics of respondents,
    74–79, 76t
  formal support, 111–125
  future implications, 131–133
  informal support, 85–111
    child, 88–98
    friends, 101–104
    grandchild, 98
    neighbors, 104–107
    relatives, other, 99–101
    siblings, 99–100
    spouse, 86–87
  living arrangements, 78–79
  non-Jewish white elderly *vs.*,
    86–107, 87t
  socioeconomic status of
    respondents, 79–84
Jewish families, 86–101
  implications for social care,
    129–131
Jewish population
  demographics
    New York City, 67–69
    United States, 65–67
  immigration patterns, 66–67
Jewish theology
  family importance, 70–71
  sense of community, 73–74
Johnson, C., 41

Kahana, E. et al, 72
Kahn, R. et al, 27–30
Kendig, H., 25–26
Kendig , H. et al, 42
Kin. *See also* Family; Informal
    support
  Cantor social care model, 19–20
  Convoy model, 27–30
  Hierarchical-Compensatory
    model, 36–37
  importance of support from, 15
  reciprocity and, 25–27
  role in social care, 4
  as support preference, 40–42

in "critical incidents," 53–54,
55t–56t, 57–58
Task-Specific model and, 35
Kinship roles, in caring for elderly,
270–271

Language limitations, access issue
for Latino elderly, 198–199
Language spoken at home
African American elderly study,
210–211
Jewish elderly study, 76t, 77
Latino elderly study, 140–141,
142t
Latino children
contact with parent, 154–157
degree of closeness, 157
as informal support, 151–164, 152t
intergenerational assistance,
159–164
living arrangements, 148
profile of, 153–157
age, 153–154
gender, 153–154
geographic location, 154
Latino elderly
demographics, New York City,
135–138
preference on "critical incidents,"
53–54, 55t–56t, 57–58
Latino elderly study, 135–200, 142t,
145t
demographics of respondents,
139–143, 142t
formal support, 179–192
unmet needs, 183–186, 184t
utilization, 180–183, 182t
future implications from, 192–200
informal support, 149–179
children, 151–164, 152t
friends, 152t, 167–170
grandchildren, 157–159
neighbors, 152t, 170–171
relatives, other, 152t, 166–167

siblings, 152t, 164–166
spouse, 151, 152t
living arrangements, 147–149
socioeconomic status of respondents, 143–147
Latino families, as informal support,
151–167, 152t
Latino population
demographics, United States,
135–136
future implications for Latino
elderly, 197
immigration patterns, 136–138
Life course perspective, social care
model, 27–30
Life-cyle perspective, independence
and, 14
Life expectancy, and increased
elderly population, 261
Litwak, E. *See also* Task-Specific
model
Task-Specific model, 33, 34–36
Living arrangements
African American elderly study,
211–212
future implications, 249–250
effect on primary caregiver, 281
future implications for social care,
269–270
Jewish elderly study, 76t, 78–79,
126t, 127
Latino elderly study, 147–149
future implications, 194–195
Long-term care. *See also* Formal
support
defined, 292
future of, 291–304
for Latino elderly, 195–196
Long-term care insurance, as long-
term care financing option,
294–295
Longitudinal Study on Aging, 1984,
265

Macro level policy, future of formal
support, 297
Macro level social care model,
Cantor, 17–24, 18f, 22t
Marital status
African American elderly study,
207, 208t, 209
caregiving and, 274–275
implications for future, 267–268
Jewish elderly study, 76t, 77, 87
Latino elderly study, 140, 142t
Medicare, as long-term care
financing option, 296–297
Methodology
1970 study, 6–7, 321–322
1990 study, 8–9, 322–323
Micro level policy, future of formal
support, 297–301
Micro level social care model
Convoy model, 27–30
exchange theory, 25–27
Minority elderly
demographics, future, 262–264
disability amongst, 265–267
Models of social care, 17–31, 32t
comparison, 30–31, 32t
macro-level, 17–24, 18f, 22t
micro-level, 25–30
Moderately frail elderly, current
formal support, 286–288
Multicultural. *See* Diversity

National Alliance for Caregiving,
273, 278, 279, 280
National Long-Term Care
Demonstration Project, 274
National Long-Term Care Survey,
1982, 274
National Long-Term Care Survey,
1984, 274
National Long-Term Care Survey,
1989, 273
National Long-Term Care Survey,
1982-84, 265

National Long-Term Channeling
Demonstration project, 276
Nativity. *See also* Acculturation
African American elderly study,
210–211
Jewish elderly study, 76t, 77
Latino elderly study, 140–144,
142t
Nature of task. *See also*
Specialization
choice of support and, 42–43
Need. *See also* Unmet need
for formal support
African American elderly study,
245, 246t, 247–248
Jewish elderly study, 112–113,
122–128, 124t
Latino elderly study, 183–186,
184t, 189t–190t
Needs-based entitlements, use of,
Jewish elderly study, 80t, 82
Neighborhood, importance of in
future, 298
Neighbors. *See also* Informal
support
as informal support
African American elderly study,
221t, 234–235
Jewish elderly study, 104–107
Latino elderly study, 152t,
170–171
role in social care, 4
Task-Specific model and, 35
New York City, demographics
African Americans, 201
Jewish population, 67–69
Latino elderly, 135–138
New York City elderly. *See also*
African American elderly
study; Jewish elderly study;
Latino elderly study
1970 study, 6–7, 321–322
1990 study, 8–9, 322–323
study comparison, 10–12

New York Jewish population study,
1991, 67–69
1970 study
methodology, 6–7, 321–322
sample, 7
vs. 1990 study
sample, 10–12
support preference, 48–53,
50t–51t
1990 study
methodology, 8–9, 322–323
sample, 9
vs. 1970
sample, 10–12
support preference, 48–53,
50t–51t
Nursing homes, long-term care
financing and, 292

Older Americans Act, history of
formal support and,
285–286
Oldest-old elderly
future demographics, 263
implications for future, 262

Pathways. *See also* Access issues
formal support use, African
American elderly study,
245, 246t, 253
Perceptions
of economic well-being
African American elderly study,
216–217
Jewish elderly study, 80t, 83
of economic well-being, perceptions of
Jewish elderly study, 80t
of emotional support
African American elderly study,
237–239
Jewish elderly study, 110–111
Latino elderly study, 177–178
of health

African American elderly study,
208t, 210
Jewish elderly study, 76t, 78
Latino elderly study, 141, 142t,
143
of informal support
African American elderly study,
236–239
Jewish elderly study, 107–111
Latino elderly study, 176–178
of instrumental support
African American elderly study,
236–237
Jewish elderly study, 108–109
Latino elderly study, 176–177
Peters, G. et al, 41–42
Political institutions, social care role,
17–19, 18f
Poverty level
African American elderly study,
214–215, 218–219
future implications for formal
support, 297–298
Jewish elderly study, 80t, 82, 126t,
128
Latino elderly study, 145t, 146,
197
Preference(s)
for assistance
1970 to 1990, 48–53, 50t–51t
effect of race on, 53–58, 55t–56t
gerontological research on, 38–43
Hierarchical-Compensatory
model, 36–38
provider selection and, 31–46
Task-Specific model, 34–36
Primary caregiver
children as, 276–284
family as, 272–284
spouse as, 274–275, 282–284
Private sector financing, for formal
support, 294–296
Public sector financing, for formal
support, 296–297

Puerto Ricans, as Latino population
     component, 137

Quality of life
     components of, 4–5
     as research theme, 5–6

Racial diversity. *See* Diversity
Racism, African American popula-
     tion and, 201–202, 218–219
Reciprocity
     African American families, 219,
          225–231
     effect on support preference, 1970
          to 1990, 53
     in exchange theory, 25–27
     Jewish families, 71, 93–98
     Latino families, 159–164
Relatives, other, as informal support
     African American elderly study,
          221t, 232
     Jewish elderly study, 99–101
     Latino elderly study, 152t,
          166–167
Religion, importance of, Jewish
     elderly study, 84–85
Residency, length of, Latino elderly
     study, 140–141, 142t
Resources, alternative
     future implications for Latino
          elderly, 198
     hierarchical regression model,
          187–192, 189t–190t
Rivlin, A. et al, 294–295
Rook, K. S., 39, 44
Rosen, E. J. & Weltman, S. F., 91
Rowe, J. W. & Kahn, R. L., 264, 265
Rubenstein, R. L., 69, 70

Sample
     1970 to 1990 study comparison,
          10–12
     African American elderly study,
          204–217

Jewish elderly study, 74–83
Latino elderly study, 139–147
New York elderly 1970, 7
New York elderly 1990, 9
Sandwich generation
     caring for elderly and, 277–282
     for Latino children, 196
Secondary caregiver
     role of, 273
     sons as, 276–277
Senior centers
     formal support utilization
          African American elderly study,
               244t
          Jewish elderly study, 115t,
               120–122
          Latino elderly study, 181, 182t
     role in formal support, 285–286
Service organizations, social care
     role, 18f, 19
Shanas, E., 40–41
Siblings, as informal support
     African American elderly study,
          221t, 231
     Jewish elderly study, 99–100
     Latino elderly study, 152t, 164–166
Single entry point
     access issue for Latino elderly,
          199–200
     future implications for formal
          support, 299–300
          African American elderly, 253
Social care. *See also* Formal support;
     Informal support
     concept of, 258
     defined, 16–17
     gerontological research on, 5–6
Social care system, components, 5
Social class, assistance patterns and,
          African American elderly,
          205
Social class diversity. *See* Diversity
Social insurance program, for for-
     mal support financing,

296–297
Socialization
  Jewish neighbors, 106
  unmet need for
    African American elderly study,
      248, 249t
    Jewish elderly study, 124t
    Latino elderly study, 184t, 185
Social network. *See also* Informal
  support
  size of
    African American elderly study,
      235–236
    Latino elderly study, 172–176,
      175t, 185–192, 189t–190t
Social Networks in Adult Life,
  national survey, 29–30
Social Security Act of 1935, history
  of formal support and, 285
Socioeconomic status
  African American elderly study,
    212–213
  Jewish elderly study, 79, 80t, 126t,
    127–128
  Latino elderly study, 143–144, 145t
  relationship to health, 266
Specialization, task
  choice of support and, 42–43
  degree of, 33–34
  provider selection and, 31–46
  Task-Specific model and, 34–35
Spouse
  Hierarchical-Compensatory
    model and, 36
  as informal support
    African American elderly study,
      220, 221t
    Jewish elderly study, 86–87
    Latino elderly study, 151, 152t
  as primary caregiver, 274–275
  future trends, 282–284
  role as support, 45
  Task-Specific model and, 35
"Squaring of morbidity curve,"

266–267
Stoller, E. et al, 42
Substitution
  gerontological research on, 38–43
  Hierarchical-Compensatory
    model, 37
  provider selection and, 31–46
  Task-Specific model and, 35–36
"Successful aging," components of,
  258–259
Support. *See* Assistance
Sussman, M., 25–27
Synagogue attendance, Jewish
  elderly study, 84–85

Task specialization
  choice of support and, 42–43
  degree of, 33–34
  provider selection and, 31–46
  Task-Specific model and, 34–35
Task-Specific model, 34–36
  choice of helper, 42–43
  conceptual framework, 39–40
  model comparison, 43–46
Theoretical formulations, of social
  care. *See* Models of social
  care

United States
  demographics
    African Americans, 201
    Jewish population, 65–67
    Latino population, 135–136
    diversity in, 61–62
Unmet need
  for formal support
    African American elderly study,
      247–248, 249t
    Jewish elderly study, 122–128,
      124t
    Latino elderly study, 183–186,
      184t
  for informal support, Latino
    elderly study, 172

Utilization of formal support
  African American elderly study,
    241–245, 244t, 246t
    number of services used, 242,
      246t
    by type, 242–245, 244t
  Jewish elderly study, 114–122, 115t
    by type, 114–116
  Latino elderly study, 180–183,
    182t
    barriers to, 186–192
    future implications, 197–200
    by type, 182t

Value conflicts, regarding
    dependency, 15–16
Visitation patterns
  African American elderly study,
    children, 222–223

Jewish elderly study
  children, 90–91
  friends, 103
Latino elderly study
  children, 154–156
  friends, 169–170
  siblings, 165–166
Vulnerability, African American
    elderly, 202–203
  future implications, 251–252

Well-elderly, assistance received, 21,
    22t
White elderly, preference on
    "critical incidents," 53–54,
    55t–56t, 57–58

Young elderly, current formal
    support, 285–286

SP *Springer Publishing Company*

Serving Minority Elders in the 21st Century

May L. Wykle, PhD, RN, FAAN and

Amasa B. Ford, MD, Editors

Minority elders, including African Americans, Hispanics, Native Americans, and Asian Americans, carry special burdens on their physical and mental health into their later years. The numbers of minority elders in care will increase rapidly in the new century: experts writing from a range of disciplines promote the need for awareness of the unique ethical, physical and cultural issues in each ethnic group. The authors propose directions for research and policy development that will ensure a continuum of appropriate care for aging minority populations.

Contents: A Tribute to Eliza Simmons Bryant • Section One: Physical and Functional Health • Public Policies and Minority Elders • Serving Minority Elders: Preventing Chronic Illness and Disability in the African American Elderly • Preventing Chronic Illness and Disability: Asian Americans • Preventing Chronic Illness and Disability among Native American Elders • The Health of Mexican American Elderly: Selected Findings from the Hispanic EPESE • Osteoporosis Overview: Should Minorities Be Concerned? • Coronary Heart Disease in Women • Section Two: Mental Health • Mental Health and the Future of Elders • Status on Mental Health Needs of Asian Elderly • Mental Health, Aging, and Americans of African Descent • Culture, Aging, and Mental Health • Barriers to Mental Health Care Access Faced by Hispanic Elderly • Section Three: Community • Bridging the Gap: Community Solutions for Black Elder Healthcare in the 21st Century • Culturally Competent Care • Culturally Competent Care Teams • Perceptions of Community Services by African American and White Older Persons • Evaluating a Model of Successful Aging for Urban African American and White Elderly • Epilogue • Directions for Future Research

1999 360pp. 0-8261-1255-2 www.springerpub.com

536 Broadway, New York, NY 10012-3955 • (212) 431-4370 • Fax (212) 941-7842

⑤ *Springer Publishing Company*

Ethnogerocounseling
Counseling Ethnic Elders
and Their Families
Virginia S. Burlingame, MSW, PhD

Foreword by **Gwen Yeo**, PhD, Director, Stanford Geriatric Education Center

"Dr. Burlingame has done an excellent job in synthesizing social, psychological, and physical aging with specific aspects of various cultural groups...she has provided conceptual perspectives and knowledge that will enable gerocounselors to work more effectively with older clients and their families in ways that are sensitive to the...needs of all involved."
            -**William Powell**, PhD, CICSW ,Associate Professor of Social Work,
                                        University of Wisconsin-Whitewater

Here is a true multicultural counseling model to meet the reality of an increasingly varied population of elders. Dr. Burlingame presents effective gerocounseling techniques for four major ethnic groups in North America: Hispanic, Native American, Asian American/Pacific Islander, and African American. Each section explores the psychological, spiritual, and social implications of each group's culture, and how those factors inform late life issues, from family support responsibilities to end of life decisions. Each detailed section contains descriptive cases, ethnogerocounseling strategies and discussion questions.

Contents: Foreword • Prologue • Section I: Ethnogeroncounseling • The Ethnic Lens • The Gero Chi Model • The Gero Counseling Model • References • Section II. American Indian/Alaskan Native (AI/AN) Elders • The AI/AN Ethnic Lens • The AI/AN Gero Chi • AI/ANs and Gerocounseling • Section III. Hispanic-Latino (H-L) Elders • The H-L Ethnic Lens • The H-L Gero Chi • H-Ls and Gerocounseling• Section IV. African American (AA) Elders • The AA Ethnic Lens • The AA Gero Chi • AAs and Gerocounseling • Section V. Asian/Pacific Island (A/PI) Elders • The A/PI Ethnic Lens • The A/PI Gero Chi • A/PIs and Gerocounseling • Epilogue

1998   296pp   0-8261-1217-X   www.springerpub.com

536 Broadway, New York, NY 10012-3955 • (212) 431-4370 • Fax (212) 941-7842

S *Springer Publishing Company*

The Aging Network
Programs and Services, Fifth Edition
Donald E. Gelfand, PhD

"For nearly twenty years Donald Gelfand's work has been the definitive voice on aging programs and services in the United States. The fifth edition continues the tradition of providing a comprehensive overview of the complex array of services and programs. It remains the authoritative book the subject."

> -**Scott Bass**, PhD, Dean of the Graduate School and Vice Provost for
> Research,University of Maryland, Baltimore County

This thoroughly revised and updated fifth edition of the standard reference to services for the elderly places special emphasis on new programs, especially those mandated by the Older Americans Act. Professionals will find a comprehensive listing of federal, state, and local programs that can locate transportation, legal assistance, employment, income maintenance, and volunteer programs in every region of the country. It describes the key components of hundreds of programs, and addresses issues that confront providers of services for the aged.

Contents: Preface • Introduction • Part I. The American Elderly and Programs • The Older American • Legislative Bases for Programs and Services • Part II. Income Maintenance Programs • Age, Employment, and Income Maintenance • Illness, Medical Care, and Income Maintenance • Part III. Programs for the Aged • Information and Assistance • Health and Mental Health • Transportation • Crime and Legal Assistance Programs • Employment, Volunteer, and Educational Programs • Nutrition Programs • Part IV. Service for the Aged • Multipurpose Senior Centers • Housing • In-Home Services • Adult Daycare • Long-Term Care Residences • The Future of Aging Programs and Services • Appendixes: A National Nonprofit Resource Groups in Aging • Index

1998   264pp   0-8261-3057-7   www.springerpub.com

536 Broadway, New York, NY 10012-3955 • (212) 431-4370 • Fax (212) 941-7842